Lecture Notes in Computer Science   11551

Commenced Publication in 1973
Founding and Former Series Editors:
Gerhard Goos, Juris Hartmanis, and Jan van Leeuwen

More information about this series at http://www.springer.com/series/7409

Svetlana S. Bodrunova ·
Olessia Koltsova · Asbjørn Følstad ·
Harry Halpin · Polina Kolozaridi ·
Leonid Yuldashev · Anna Smoliarova ·
Heiko Niedermayer (Eds.)

Internet Science

INSCI 2018 International Workshops
St. Petersburg, Russia, October 24–26, 2018
Revised Selected Papers

 Springer

Editors
Svetlana S. Bodrunova (iD)
St. Petersburg State University
St. Petersburg, Russia

Asbjørn Følstad (iD)
SINTEF
Trondheim, Norway

Polina Kolozaridi
National Research University
Higher School of Economics
Moscow, Russia

Anna Smoliarova
St. Petersburg State University
St. Petersburg, Russia

Olessia Koltsova (iD)
National Research University
Higher School of Economics
St. Petersburg, Russia

Harry Halpin
Inria
Le Chesnay, France

Leonid Yuldashev
National Research University
Higher School of Economics
Moscow, Russia

Heiko Niedermayer
TU München
Munich, Germany

ISSN 0302-9743   ISSN 1611-3349   (electronic)
Lecture Notes in Computer Science
ISBN 978-3-030-17704-1   ISBN 978-3-030-17705-8   (eBook)
https://doi.org/10.1007/978-3-030-17705-8

LNCS Sublibrary: SL3 – Information Systems and Applications, incl. Internet/Web, and HCI

This Springer imprint is published by the registered company Springer Nature Switzerland AG
The registered company address is: Gewerbestrasse 11, 6330 Cham, Switzerland

Preface

The 5th international conference 'Internet Science' (INSCI 2018) took place during October 24–26, 2018 in St. Petersburg, Russia, and was organized by the School of Journalism and Mass Communications and the Faculty of Applied Mathematics and Control Processes, St. Petersburg State University. This conference built on the success of the First and Second International Conferences on Internet Science that took place in Brussels, Belgium, that were organized by the FP7 European Network of Excellence in Internet Science (EINS) project, with the support of the European Commission. In its third year, the conference moved to Florence, Italy, with support from the Collective Awareness Platforms for Sustainability and Social Innovation (CAPS) initiative. In 2017, the conference was organized by CERTH Information Technology Institute in Thessaloniki, Greece.

Workshops have been an integral part of INSCI, as they have always supported the scope of the conference, which is to foster the development of the Internet as both a socially responsible and a socially responsive phenomenon. The workshops have been a truly international and intense part of the conference bringing together scholars from a variety of disciplines in computer science, social sciences, and humanities.

The workshops of 2018 followed suit; they were all oriented toward linking social interaction and communication to rapidly developing zones in user-oriented Internet industries and/or human behavior online and methods for its detection. The overall topicality of the workshops and the width of international representation of the participants mirrored the general INSCI 2018 theme, "User Empowerment in World Regions."

Workshop 1, Detecting Social Problems in Online Content, was chaired by Olessia Koltsova (National Research University – Higher School of Economics, Russia) and Svetlana Bodrunova (St.Petersburg State University). This workshop has united Russian scholars who work on Russian-language datasets. They put their effort into, first, detecting harmful content (e.g., hate speech or call for actions against social groups); second, refining methods of working with the datasets themselves (e.g., developing text clusterization methods for the Russian language); third, detecting potential social unease (e.g., protest spillovers to the streets or emotional outbursts in online discussions) via online content. The papers of this workshop addressed the vagueness of the social science concepts that lay behind the computational efforts, as well as the nascent state of mixed methodologies in this research area.

Workshop 2, CONVERSATIONS 2018: An International Workshop on Chatbot Research and Design, was organized by scholars from Norway (mostly SINTEF), Greece, and the UK, was supported by the Research Council of Norway, and was a clear example of a research community that regularly discusses the novel issues in their research and production area. Chatbots as a new type of interaction interface have induced a growing body of research, but this research zone still lacks conceptualization beyond particular challenges in chatbot design and implementation. The workshop has become an important contribution to chatbot studies, as not only were case studies, but also the literature was critically reviewed, chatbot typology suggested, and new challenges in chatbot research identified.

While Workshops 1 and 2 were more method-oriented, Workshops 3 and 4 focused on discussing policy and discourses around decentralized and distributed technologies for governance, as well as around the Internet itself. This parity between science and policy goals in the constellation of workshops corresponds clearly to the INSCI initial intention to link research and policing on one academic platform.

Workshop 3, The Future of Decentralized Governance: A Workshop on Encryption, Blockchains, and Personal Data, was assembled by Harry Halpin (Inria, France). At this workshop, scholars and industry representatives from France, The Netherlands, the UK, and Russia discussed distributed governance technologies based on blockchain and other privacy-protecting technologies. As in other INSCI workshops, the authors went beyond discussing individual cases of technological success in distributed technologies; they saw these technologies as a chance to bring back the idea of a decentralized Internet where monopolies of platforms are challenged by collective decision-making and data distribution and storage. The Workshop 3 outcomes will be presented in the form of policy recommendations to the European Commission within the NEXTLEAP project (nextleap.eu).

Workshop 4, Internet as an Issue: An International Workshop on Government and Media Narratives, was organized by Polina Kolozaridi and Leonid Yuldashev with the support by scholars gathered from Russia and supported by the Club of Internet and Society Enthusiasts in Moscow. This workshop took a rare approach and regarded the Internet as a focus for public discussion. Two papers that assessed the Internet historically both tried to show the national boundaries of either national Internet segments or the approaches to its assessment. Three other papers were united by looking at the Internet as a shared sociotechnical imaginary structure of critical importance and an object of extensive regulation on behalf of the state as a unitary actor.

The workshops have once again proved that the Internet in its social dimensions is an inspiring and intriguing research object, as well as the future that unites countries and peoples, both in development and problematization.

The Local Organizing Committee is grateful to the Steering Committee, the conference TCP chairs, Anna Smoliarova (Russia) and Heiko Niedermayer (Germany), the workshop chairs, discussants, and participants, all the Program Committee members and external reviewers and sub-reviewers, and all the volunteers, as well as the Department of Public Events at the administration of St.Petersburg State University, for making an important conference happen and move successfully to 2019.

November 2018   Svetlana S. Bodrunova

Organization

Program Committee

Theo Araujo	University of Amsterdam, The Netherlands
Moritz Bartl	Center for the Cultivation of Technology, Germany
Ruslan Bekurov	St. Petersburg State University, Russia
Natalia Belyakova	ITMO University, Russia
Oliver Bendel	School of Business FHNW, Switzerland
Ivan Blekanov	St. Petersburg State University, Russia
Svetlana Bodrunova	St. Petersburg State University, Russia
Petter Bae Brandtzaeg	SINTEF, Norway
Ilia Bykov	St. Petersburg State University, Russia
Despoina Chatzakou	Aristotle University of Thessaloniki, Greece
Yulia Danilova	St. Petersburg State University, Russia
Massimiliano Dibitonto	Link Campus University, Italy
Frank Dignum	Utrecht University, The Netherlands
Simon Enni	SINTEF, Norway
Ahmed Fadhil	University of Trento, Fondazione Bruno Kessler (FBK), Italy
Andrew Feenberg	Simon Fraser University, USA
Anastasia Folts	Lomonosov Moscow State University, Russia
Asbjørn Følstad	SINTEF, Norway
Anna Gladkova	Lomonosov Moscow State University, Russia
Harry Halpin	Inria, France
Z. Isadora Hellegren	Internet Foundation in Sweden, Sweden
Dmitry Ilvovsky	National Research University Higher School of Economics, Russia
Marios Issakides	University College London, UK
Rricha Jalota	Data Science Group, Paderborn University, Germany
Suhas Govind Joshi	University of Oslo, Norway
Yury Kabanov	National Research University Higher School of Economics, Russia
Lorenz Cuno Klopfenstein	University of Urbino Carlo Bo, Italy
Polina Kolozaridi	National Research University Higher School of Economics, Russia
Olessia Koltsova	National Research University Higher School of Economics, Russia
David Kuboň	Charles University, Prague, Czech Republic
Bogdan Kulynych	EPFL, Switzerland
Yanina Ledovaya	St. Petersburg State University, Russia

Contents

Part III The Future of Decentralized Governance: An International Workshop

Part IV Internet as an Issue: An International Workshop on Government and Media Narratives

Part I
Detecting Social Problems in Online Content: An International Workshop

Detecting Social Problems in Online Content: A Preface to the International Workshop

Olessia Koltsova[1] and Svetlana Bodrunova[2]

[1] National Research University Higher School of Economics,
16 Soyuza Pechatnkov, 190005, St. Petersburg, Russia
[2] St. Petersburg State University,
Universitetskaya nab. 7/9, 199034 St. Petersburg, Russia
ekoltsova@hse.ru

Abstract. This workshop was dedicated to discussing the latest development in detecting a broad range of social issues in online content, from inequalities expressed in texts (hate speech, prejudice, divisive/uncivil messages, political bias and racism etc.), to social polarization based on user views and sentiment. With proliferation of social media, such content is increasingly impactful, while its detection at scale presents a huge methodological challenge. The workshop participants shared their research experience by reflecting both on advantages and limitations of new automated and mixed research methods of text analysis they had used for processing and analysing such content. The workshop was held for the first time at INSCI'2018.

Keywords: Problematic content • Online data • Machine learning • Text clustering • Big social data • Limitations

1 Major Challenges of Harmful Content Detection

As social media are becoming an integral part of our daily lives, so do different types of hateful, uncivil, and problematic content, since content production is no longer constrained by editorial policies of professional media. Detecting such content is important – both for reducing its destructive impact and for using it as an indicator of emerging social problems. But, at large, methods to do so are in their cradle. They are being developed mostly within computer science and mathematical communities and often for the goals different from those of social science (e.g. for marketing purposes). Thus, it is crucial to link social scientists, psychologists, and media scholars to computer linguists, mathematicians, and software developers, as many research tasks stemming from user-generated texts demand interdisciplinary reflection.

The major goal of this workshop was to formulate and discuss the challenges discovered by the participants in doing interdisciplinary research in the area of detection and categorization of problematic content on social media and to share their methodological findings or doubts.

On a more detailed level, we can identify the following key challenges in today's interdisciplinary analysis of problematic online content.

First, social science concepts, such as hate speech, prejudice, divisive and uncivil messages, political slant and bias, racism and ethnocentrism, problematized framing, and social stigmas are all difficult to define in a way suitable for further application of machine learning. Second, all procedures involving human participation, such as text mark-up for classification or labeling unsupervised machine learning results, are often taken for granted in computer science.

Third, the choice of relevant algorithms and their parameters that serve best the final research goals is an important issue for discussion. Oftentimes, social scientists expect algorithms to demonstrate features they inherently lack or to provide final solutions without any methodological input on the part of a social scientist. Computer scientists, on their side, leave algorithm-related choices to end users without providing any criteria for such choices. Therefore, academic community needs investigation of limitations of the algorithms by the end users, since it is them who are able to formulate requirements for those algorithms and assess how far the algorithms are from meeting the research aims.

Fourth, it is user-generated texts themselves that pose particular methodological challenges for today's researchers. Thus, the nature of the texts is oral-written, which implies that such texts are much less coherent in lexicon and grammar. Many of them are extremely short (e.g. tweets) and have other platform-induced limitations. In aggregate, user texts are much less rational and bear higher emotional load than media/document collections. In general, this means that most online data in natural language are not only noisy, but poorly suited for 'understanding' by a machine: they are ambiguous, referential, context-sensitive, polysemous or homonymic. As current algorithms lack the entirety of human experience necessary to make sense of such texts, specific techniques of disambiguation or meaning enrichment are needed.

Fifth, there is a huge disparity that has already formed in interdisciplinary computational text analysis – namely, the Anglo-American orientation of most of the research done so far. Expanding the extant methodological approaches to other world regions and languages often runs into severe limitations due to varying features of languages as well as to the lack of expertise in countries beyond Euro-Atlantics and China. Thus, it is necessary to de-westernize research on non-hieroglyphic texts, especially for the countries that use Cyrillic. The new approaches elaborated in this region can also contribute to the studies done in the Western countries.

2   Main Workshop Contributions

The contributions by the workshop participants to the field are diverse and mutually complimentary. Olessia Koltsova [1] gives a broad overview of problems faced by detection of hate speech and other types of attitudes in the sphere of ethnicity – from concept definition to text processing to algorithm choice and performance. She compares supervised and unsupervised machine learning approaches and presents partial solutions implemented in an online WebTopicMiner system for Russian language. Oleg Nagornyy [2] builds upon this overview and reflects on the necessity to differentiate between social media user attitudes expressed towards their ethnic in-groups and out-groups. He shows that attitudes towards in-groups are significantly more positive than those towards out-groups and that some gender variation is also present.

Kamilla Nigmatullina and Svetlana Bodrunova [3] bring the discussion on the research of ethnicity-related attitudes beyond revealing opinions in the negative-positive positive continuum. They explore different types of emotions expressed in relation to an ethnic conflict and evaluate their prevalence. They find that messages clearly fall into two groups: non-emotional and those that express a mixture of different types of emotions, and detect patterns of emotion expression (e.g. 'emotional loops'). Anna Smoliarova and colleagues [4] go even further and raise the question of the link between online ethnicity-related discussions and offline street violence. They show that standard tests are often unable to capture such link and opt for a mixture of automated exploratory text analysis and qualitative matching of its results with offline events. They show that, with such a mixed methodology that includes topic modeling, some important links can be traced; their research, thus, demonstrates the need for more fine-grained and context-sensitive approaches to big online data research.

Finally, two remaining papers focus on hard-core methodological aspects of text processing and analysis. Metsker et al. [5] offer an approach to enrich highly ambiguous open online text data with knowledge databases that can help find similar meanings and categories expressed with different wordings and thus help improve further text classification and other types of text analysis. Andrey Orekhov [6] raises an old and important problem of finding the optimal number of clusters in text clutering – a problem that significantly limits application of unsupervised machine learning by social scientists. Applying a specific stopping criterion to an agglomerative hierarchical clustering algorithm, he proposes to stop agglomeration when the function of mean inter-cluster distance makes a sharp leap.

Thus, the papers presented at the workshop cover a broad range of questions addressing the problem of problematic online content detection and analysis addressed from a wide number of angles.

References

1. Koltsova, O.: Methodological challenges for detecting interethnic hostility on social media. In: Bodrunova, S., et al. (eds.) Proceedings of 5th International Conference on Internet Science (INSCI'2018), (Workshops), vol. 2, pp. 5–17 (2019)
2. Nagornyy, O.: User ethnicity and gender as predictors of attitudes to ethnic groups in social media texts. In: Bodrunova, S., et al. (eds.) Proceedings of 5th International Conference on Internet Science (INSCI'2018), (Workshops), vol. 2, pp. 32–40 (2019)
3. Nigmatullina, K., Bodrunova, S.: Patterns of emotional argumentation in Twitter discussions. In: Bodrunova, S., et al. (eds.) Proceedings of 5th International Conference on Internet Science (INSCI'2018), (Workshops), vol. 2, pp. 71–77 (2019)
4. Smoliarova, A., Yakunin, A., Bodrunova, S., Blekanov, I., Maksimov, A.: Detecting pivotal points in social conflicts via topic modeling of twitter content. In: Bodrunova, S., et al. (eds.) Proceedings of 5th International Conference on Internet Science (INSCI'2018), (Workshops), vol. 2, pp. 60–70 (2019)

5. Metsker, O., et al.: Holistic monitoring and analysis of healthcare processes through public internet data collection. In: Bodrunova, S., et al. (eds.) Proceedings of 5th International Conference on Internet Science (INSCI'2018), (Workshops), vol. 2, pp. 41–49 (2019)
6. Orekhov, A.V.: Agglomerative method for texts clustering. In: Bodrunova, S., et al. (eds.) Proceedings of 5th International Conference on Internet Science (INSCI'2018), (Workshops), vol. 2, pp. 18–31 (2019)

Methodological Challenges for Detecting Interethnic Hostility on Social Media

Olessia Koltsova[✉]

Laboratory for Internet Studies, National Research University Higher
School of Economics, Room 117, 55/2 Sedova Street, Saint-Petersburg, Russia
ekoltsova@hse.ru

Abstract. Detection of ethnic hate speech and other types of ethnicity representation is user texts is an important goal both for social and computer science, as well as for public policy making. To date, quite a few algorithms have been trained to detect hate speech, however, what policy makers and social scientists need are complete pipelines, from definition of ethnicity to a user-friendly monitoring system able to aggregate results of large-scale social media analysis. In this essay, the author summarizes the experience of development of such a system in a series of projects under the author's leadership. All steps of the offered methodology are described and critically reviewed, and a special attention is paid to the strengths and the limitations of different approaches that were and can be applied along the developed pipeline. All conclusions are based on prior experiments with several large datasets from Russian language social media, including 15 000 marked up texts extracted from a representative one-year collection of 2.7 million user messages containing ethnonyms.

Keywords: Ethnic representations · Machine learning · Social media

1 Introduction

Studies of interethnic relations and related issues have a long tradition and well-developed methodologies based on approaches of social science. They allow using the results for practical purposes, including ethnic conflict forecasting and prevention, monitoring ethnic fractionalization and inter-ethnic hostility, development of ethnic tolerance, among others. Nevertheless, in the last two decades two new factors have emerged allowing a new research optics being applied to monitoring of interethnic relations. First, rapid development of the Internet has made it a repository of attitudes of the growing "online population" and a space where socially important discussions and conflicts evolve. Even now user generated content can be regarded as an important source of public opinion, or at least its reasonable proxy, which can supplement and sometimes substitute opinion polls. Second, development of data mining, especially related to large text collections, enables researchers to automatically detect trends in such collections, e.g. to reveal topical structure of discussions, topic salience, sentiment prevailing in texts and topics, etc. This has been shown in many works, including those by our research group [1, 2].

S. S. Bodrunova et al. (Eds.): INSCI 2018 Workshops, LNCS 11551, pp. 7–18, 2019.
https://doi.org/10.1007/978-3-030-17705-8_1

Thus, the analysis of internet data with such methods can be used for monitoring of interethnic hostility, its strength, context, geolocation and a range of other parameters. However, until recently data mining research was developing mainly within mathematics and/or computer science and was aimed at development of algorithms and mathematical models rather than at social modeling based on such tools. This methodological gap has been shown by our research group. Thus, one of the main algorithms for studying large text collections – topic modeling [3–5] – is widely used in scientometrics, but only in the last few years the first attempts have been made to apply it for the analysis of social problems based on texts of internet users [6, 7]. Supervised machine learning has been more widely used for a wide range of goals [8–10] including hate speech [11, 12], still its application to the ethnicity-related issues is in its cradle [13, 14].

The first attempts to apply machine learning to user content for social science goals, including those of detecting ethnicity related opinions have revealed a whole range of methodological problems. The nature of these problems is absolutely new for social scientists. These problems are related not only for technical obstacles and lack of mathematical expertise among social scientists, but mainly to the absence of verified approaches to connecting new mathematical models and technical solutions with social science tasks. An incomplete list of such problems includes: formulation of tasks for data driven research that are nevertheless relevant to important social science problems, operationalization of concepts in a way applicable for machine learning, making meaningful samples from big text collections, procedures for interpretation of machine learning results, hypothesis testing on big data where standard statistics does not work, and more. In this paper we address some of those problems focusing on a task of detecting human opinions about ethnicity expressed in social media.

The rest of this methodological essay is structured as follows. In the next section the author describes the data that were used in methodological experiments in different projects lead by the author. These experiments serve the bases for methodological conclusions made in the subsequent sections. Section 3 addresses approaches to defining ethnicity as the object to be detected in user texts. Section 4 reviews advantages and limitations of different methods to detecting representations of ethnicity that were tested in the mentioned above experiments. Finally, Sect. 5 describes solutions implemented in the online system developed under supervision of the author. It shows how some of the mentioned problems may be solved in practice.

2 Data

Methodological reflections presented in this paper are based on the following data.

1. A range of samples created from the LiveJournal data collected for different projects. These samples include all posts by top 2000 Russian speaking bloggers for the periods: (1) 12 months from mid-2013 to mid-2014 – 1.58 million messages; (2) for one month of 2013 – 103,000; (3) for 3.5 months 2013 – 364,000; (4) for 4 months 2013 – 235,000. These different collections were created for different experiments.

2. Collections of random VKotakte users that include all their posts and comments to them, for two years 2013 and 2014. VKontakte users were selected randomly from each of 87 Russian regions; approximately 800 users from each region. This produced a collection of 74,000 users, approximately 9 million posts and 1 million comments to them. From this collection, a smaller sample was made that included only three regions (Tatarstan, Buryat republic and Tver oblast) and 222,545 messages.

3. A collection of messages from all Russian-language social networking sites monitored by IQBuzz commercial aggregator. This collection contains all messages containing at least one of the words or bigrams from a specially constructed vocabulary of Post-Soviet ethnonyms for two years – 2013 and 2014. After cleaning from duplicates the collection comprise around 2.7 million messages of which 80% are produced by VKontakte. Of them, 60% come from group pages and 40% - from individual accounts.

4. A marked-up collection of 15,000 messages selected randomly from collections 2 and 3 so as to represent each of 115 Post-Soviet ethnic groups. Each text of this collection contains from 10 to 90 words and has been hand coded by at least three assessors answering a long list of questions.

Collections 2–4 were collected specifically for the study of ethnic relations online. Numerous experiments performed on them are described in the respective papers [1, 2, 15, 16]. Here, we do not give all details of these experiments focusing on reflecting on our methodological experience instead.

3 Defining Ethnicity and Texts on Ethnicity

The concept of ethnicity has been much theorized about, while public opinions about ethnicity have been a constant object of empirical research. However, this stream of literature turns to be irrelevant when it comes to automatic detection of opinions about ethnicity online.

The concept of ethnicity has been most often discussed together with the related concepts of nation and nationality [17, 18]. One typical opposition in this context is described with primordial vs constructivist approach opposition [19: pp. 39–46, 17: pp. 20–45]. Primordialist approach claims that ethnicity is determined by ancestry, that the ethnic status is ascribed at birth and that the ethnic boundaries are fixed. Constructionist approach claims that ethnicity is nothing more than self-perception and perception of an individual by others, i.e. it claims that ethnic status and ethnic boundaries are collectively constructed, negotiated and challenged. That makes ethnicity a purely social category as opposed to "biological". Within constructionism one can discern culture-centered approaches and polity-centered approaches, the latter making ethnicity close to the concept of nation. However, defining ethnicity according to any of these approaches gives no cues for mining attitudes to ethnicity in lay texts, because lay persons do not usually have knowledge of theoretical concepts, neither they follow them in everyday talk even if they do know social theory. Ethnicity in user texts is thus the usage of ethnic markers by text authors.

A researcher's task at this point may seem to be reduced to compiling a list of ethnic status markers (names of ethnic groups, or ethnonyms) and retrieving texts containing these words. However, as shown in our experiments, this approach works only partially. First, there is no formal criterion to discern between ethnonyms and nation names: formally, we can distinguish stateless ethnic groups (Roma, Kurds), non-ethnic nations (Egyptians, Indians) and those that coincide or nearly coincide (French, Norwegians). By including French and excluding Indians one makes an overall vol-untaristic choice. When all ethnic groups and nations are included, many texts that are yielded with such keyword search in fact deal with what obviously looks like inter-national relations and war. Plural form of ethnonyms may be used to denote govern-ments or generally states and countries. On the other hand, texts with ethnonyms denoting individuals may deal with issues other than ethnicity, while ethnicity is in fact used as one of identifiers along with gender, age, profession, personal name and other markers that may be used in non-discriminative and non-problematic manner. Such texts include those that present results of international contests, including sports and culture, in case they do not politicize or "ethnicize" those issues. Finally, ethnicity may be discussed without mentioning any ethnonyms if more general concepts are applied or if a text is referential (e.g. a reply to a post where ethnonyms are mentioned).

This ambiguity is explained with the fact that lay text authors use ethnonyms for different purposes and do not have a goal of differentiating between ethnically related and ethnically irrelevant texts. Drawing the boundary between such texts thus turns to be the task of a researcher. Returning to the start of this section we can see that for studying opinions about ethnicity in lay texts researcher's role shifts from defining ethnicity per se, as an abstract concept, to defining what a text about ethnicity is. In our works we suggest the following solution [2]. Texts about ethnicity are defined as texts:

1. where the major actors are private persons of a given ethnicity or ethnic groups, and not states or their official representatives (e.g. "Turks have broken a recent inter-national agreement" is not about ethnicity, while "Chinese are not good at European languages" is);
2. where ethnicity is important for the outcomes or is used as an explanation (e.g. "The singer was a real Yakut, so we've heard an authentic throat singing" is about ethnicity; "We've just returned from an exhibition of a French photographer, and it's too late to go anywhere else" is not).

This is not the only possible solution. In fact, solutions should depend on research goals, but this example shows that, furthermore, sampling relevant texts turns into a separate machine learning problem. It can be broken into two parts: first, building an approach and an instrument for automatic differentiating between relevant and irrele-vant texts, and second, finding such texts among millions of other texts without sub-stantial losses in precision, recall (completeness), time, memory and computational resources. Although these two tasks seem unrelated, our experiments show that dif-ferentiating between relevant and irrelevant texts in a small high-relevant collection and in a collection of millions of noisy texts are two very different tasks. Therefore, a single algorithm is needed that can simultaneously look for texts based on preliminary criteria and then classify them in real time.

To the best of our knowledge, no research deals with this problem. Studies on ethnic hate speech detection and related topics usually focus on text classification once the texts are already available, and the proportion of the target class is high [11, 20, 21]. To our knowledge, only the newest research in China tackles this problem of "finding a needle in a haystack", although mostly in relation to monitoring crises and broader risky events [22]. Research on algorithms of real-time classification of streaming online data does exist, but it somehow attempts to develop domain-independent or at least ethnicity unrelated classification methods [23, 24]. Our system introduced in the last section so far gives only a partial solution for this problem.

4 Strengths and Weaknesses of Different Approaches to the Detection of Ethnic Representations in User Texts

Different methods of automatic text analysis possess different advantages and limitations, and the social science community is just beginning to get acquainted with those. Comprehensive overviews of automated approaches to text analysis for social scientists are provided in [25] who focus on political science tasks and [26] interested in journalism and media studies tasks. The former authors illustrate an explanation of different methods with a variety of research goals, such as classification of political texts into topical categories, known or unknown beforehand, extraction of political slants from texts and placement of text characters in political spectra. Broadly speaking, it is possible to extract unknown categories with unsupervised machine learning (UML) techniques, akin to cluster analysis, while those that are known beforehand are better to be searched for with supervised machine learning approaches (SML) that demand algorithm tuning and validation on a collection of texts whose categories are already marked up.

Many of our experiments with ethnic texts have been based on topic modeling, a group of UML algorithms that allow to co-cluster both texts and words into topics returning lists of most probable words and texts for each cluster. In our experiments, it is represented by three main algorithms: variational LDA [5], LDA with Gibbs sampling [4] and BigARTM [27]. This approach is very useful when topics – or in our case contexts in which different ethnic groups are discussed – are unknown beforehand. It is also good when topics are changing and any mark-up gets outdated fast. Finally, it is good when mark-up is too costly. However, our experience has revealed a number of severe limitations of this approach that has made it hardly usable for our goals.

First, it turned out that topic modeling is unable to extract relevant topics from large collections when the proportion of texts devoted to the topics of interest is very low (well below 1%). This is the case of ethnicity discussion online: a vast majority of user texts is everyday talk; only a small minority is related to social or political issues, and of them ethnicity is again a minority. It is important to note that for some reason TM is sensitive to the proportion, not the absolute number of relevant texts: when a few thousands of relevant texts are extracted from millions with alternative methods, and then mixed with a few thousand of irrelevant texts, TM works well. However, for such enrichment some mark-up is usually needed which partially makes UML senseless.

Second, although it is known that TM works poorly on short texts, our experience shows that it does not work at all if the texts, apart from being short, also represent everyday talk. Around 90% of topics yielded from random VKontakte collections turn to be uninterpretable, independently of the collection size or the number of topics. We have also observed that when a collection of short texts contains some proportion of longer ones TM interpretability improves a lot. Thus, mean length of texts in our IQBuzz sample is 332 words against 16.5 in random VKontakte collection; although both have power-law distribution, the first has yielded much more interpretable results than the second. Third, most topics that were yielded on non-enriched collections were rather about international relations than ethnicity. The effect when smaller topics get overshadowed by related larger topics has been also observed on other tasks. Likewise, less frequently mentioned ethnic groups get overshadowed by more frequently mentioned that tend to form larger and more interpretable topics. Among Post-Soviet ethnic groups, the most frequent are Ukrainians, Jews and Chechens. However, all of them, in turn, get overshadowed by nations of the global influence, first of all Americans and Germans. Finally, our experiments on news data [7, 28] show that TM results produced on them are way better than those obtained on collections of social media texts. This makes us think that topic modeling, at least in its current form, is not really suitable for short user texts. It is thus difficult to apply it for studying user opinions, even most broadly understood.

Supervised machine learning has been more widely applied to opinion detection. The most relevant literature in the field is mostly aimed at automatic detecting of hate speech in user-generated content [29] not always specific to the ethnicity issue, while the "positive" side of ethnic representations online misses researchers' attention at all. Hate speech is broadly understood as hostility based on features attributed to a group as a whole, e.g. based on race, ethnicity, religion, gender and similar features.

This research is very different in breadth and scope: some studies seek to perform race- or ethnicity-specific tasks, for instance aim to detect hate speech against Blacks only [30]. Others attempt to capture broader types of hate speech, e.g. related to race, ethnicity/nationality and religion simultaneously [13, 21], or even generalized hate speech [12] and abusive language [31]. Most studies acknowledge that hate speech is domain specific although some features may be shared by all types of hate speech, therefore some try to catalogue common targets of hate speech online [32].

In such works, a large variety of techniques is being offered and developed, including lexicon-based approaches [21], classical classification algorithms [20] and a large number of extensions for quality improvement, such as learning distributed lowdimensional representations of texts [33], using extra-linguistic features of texts [11] and others. Some draw attention to the role of human annotators and the procedure of annotations for classification results [34, 35].

This latter topic leads to the problem of definition of hate speech needed to help annotators understand their job. Computer science papers seldom or never address this problem relying on human judgment as the ultimate truth, and when they do address it, they mostly focus on making annotators capture the existing definitions of hate speech, not on critically assessing them or developing new ones. Meanwhile, most existing definitions we know are ethically non-neutral which makes them a difficult object for automatic detection. From the overviews we learn that hate speech, or harmful speech is usually defined via such attributes as "bias-motivated", "hostile" "malicious", dangerous" [36] "unwanted", "intimidating", "frightening" [37] which can be summarized as actually, bad. The related concepts of prejudice are somewhat more precisely defined. As it has been noted by Quillian [38] that most of them rely on early Allport's definition which views prejudice as "an antipathy based on faulty and inflexible generalization" [39] while the positive counterpart of prejudice is usually referred to as positive stereotype.

All the mentioned definitions mark the concepts they seek to define as ethically unacceptable. If so, to correctly detect them, human annotators have to share common values with the researchers, otherwise they would not be able to recognize hate speech in texts. Since not every derogation, disapproval or condemnation is ethically unacceptable (e.g. condemnation of genocide is considered absolutely desirable), language features of disapproval or derogation per se do not necessarily point at what the Western liberal discourse usually means by hate speech, and this makes it especially elusive when applied beyond the Western world.

We tend to think that for opinion detection on political sensitive issues it is important to elaborate concrete questions for human coders that would allow them to annotate texts independently of their political views or cultural values. In our research, we employed a range of questions that include both text-level and instance level aspects of opinions. Text-level aspects are: (1) general problematization of the topic in the text (does the text contain negative/positive sentiment); (2) conflict presence (does the text mention inter-ethnic conflict or positive inter-ethnic interaction?); (3) text topics (a choice from among 14 social and political topics, including ethnicity and "other"). Instance-level aspects are: (4) general attitude (What is the general attitude of the text author to a given ethnic group? Negative/positive/neutral); (5) perception of ethnic hierarchy (Does the author treat a given ethnic group as superior/inferior?); (6) danger perception (Does the author perceive a given ethnic group as dangerous?); (7) blame attribution (In case of conflict, does the author present a given ethnic group as a victim/an aggressor?); (8) call for violence (Does the author call for violence against a given ethnic group?). This is, again, not the only way to approach ethnicity-related opinion detection, however, it has produced reasonably good quality in prediction of some of the aspects.

We specially instructed coders that they are not expected to make moral judgements of text authors for the opinions they express. All coders were also trained to recognize attitudes in texts. Still we find a lot of divergence among coders. At meetings, they posed many questions and expressed difficulties in classifying different types of texts. Their overall judgement was that most categories were vague and prone to subjectivity. We must point at this as one of the major limitations of classification of social issues in texts. A machine cannot be expected to classify texts better than humans, and while humans widely diverge, the machine learning result will stay low. Even if some group of coders can be trained to think unanimously, their judgement will reflect the result of training and not the way in which a broader society thinks. A promising way to overcome this problem is not in seeking for consensus among a narrow group of trained humans, but accommodating for the lack of consensus within the procedure of machine learning through fuzzy logic. Texts should be assigned to classes with weights corresponding to the level of inter-coder agreement which will yield sets of core and periphery texts for each class. An algorithm then might be trained to guess the level of consensus and to differentiate between the most typical and less typical texts in each class.

Another problem we have encountered is a trade-off between working with text-level and instance-level items. We find that around a half of ethnicity-relevant texts contain more than one ethnic group; of them 15% contain a combination of neutral and emotional attitudes to different ethnic groups, and 6% are opposite attitudes. In such situation, while predicting instance-level items, that is aspects of attitudes to specific ethnic groups, with the entire set of text features sometimes leads to prediction of different opinions with the same data. This misleads the algorithm and decreases its quality. This situation does not occur with the text-level items, but they are less informative in sociological sense.

One of the potential solutions for this problem is to try to detect attitudes to specific ethnic groups at the sentence level. So far, it has been seldom done. Most studies use only unigrams or bigrams as features, as we have already done [8, 11–14, 22, 31, 40–42]. Syntactic features have been used in [13, 14, 21, 31]. The problem with user texts is that their syntax is often flawed. However, sentences, according to our experience, are relatively well delimited either with dots or emoticons. Thus one could apply an approach based on windows of fixed length and additionally limited by end-of-sentence markers, without stricter syntactic parsing. Another problem is, however, that with such ambiguous issues as ethnicity opinion is most often expressed indirectly and dispersed across multiple sentences while co-reference resolution is difficult due to flawed syntactic structure. This problem to our knowledge has no solution so far. Below, we describe the solutions to some of the listed above problems implemented in our system.

5   Solutions Implemented in TopicMiner

Our system is devised to monitor ethnic relations on the Post-Soviet space. Its main goal is to trace, in a semi-automatic way, distribution of discussions about ethnicity in the Russian-language social media over time and space. The primary task of this tracing is early prevention of emerging inter-ethnic conflicts through a sequence of methodological steps. Those steps been translated into a system of concrete methods and algorithms, and they in turn have been implemented in a user-friendly software available online.

Online system is available at: https://topicminer.hse.ru/. It contains the following functionality and components.

First, the methodology takes into account that a user may have access only to noisy, unfiltered data with a low proportion of texts about ethnicity (e.g. raw dumps of social media messages). Our system does not collect data, but it contains a number of instruments for text preprocessing, whose core is a methodology that filters texts non-relevant to the topic of ethnicity. As mentioned above, our experiments have shown that detection of any ethnicity-related trends in large collections of texts is impossible without pre-filtering. Therefore, the methodology consists of two components: text selection based on a lexicon of ethnonyms containing 3680 individual words and 12670 bigrams (precision up to 74%) and a machine learning based selection (precision and recall around 74%). We recommend to combine these two approaches to increase recall.

Second, based on such collection enrichment, our system allows to extract topics, or contexts in which ethnical issues are discussed and which are not known to researchers beforehand. For this, we offer a number of improvements for topic modeling algorithms whose quality has been tested both manually and with a specially developed quality metric – tf-idf coherence. Our experiments have shown that a basic pLSA algorithm with our lexicon of ethnonyms yields the best results among all BigARTM algorithms. It is best suited for revealing the entire range of ethnicity related topics existing in a given collection, for comparison of those topics by their volume, and for detection of topics devoted simultaneously to several ethnic groups. To extract contexts related to a single pre-defined ethnic group, a better option is our other algorithm with a more aggressive partial supervision – ISLDA which also exceeds basic LDA both by the proportion of ethnically relevant topics and by their tf-idf coherence.

Introduced algorithms were tested on different collections listed above. Good results were achieved with collections containing a certain proportion of relevant and long texts. The main contribution into quality of the tested models came from our lexicon of ethnonyms. The overall conclusion from the experiments is that although topic modeling cannot be used for extraction of relevant texts from collections with a low proportion of such texts (and this task was solved via supervised classification), topic modeling nevertheless works well for detection of contexts in which ethnicity is discussed. All listed above algorithms are implemented in our system which also has functionality of tipping on ethnically relevant topics based on comparison of topics' top words with our lexicon of ethnonyms.

Third, the system is able to yield distributions of ethnically relevant topics over time and space and visualize them on a time scale or on the map of Russia, respectively. Besides simply summing the probabilities of a given topic over all texts of a given region or time period, our methodology includes specially tuned multimodal algorithms of topic modeling where timestamps and geolocation tags are made a separate modality. Our experiments have shown that this approach works better than simple summing for revealing topics concentrated in time, although it penalizes topics evenly distributed over time. For obtaining a more precise distribution by the Russian regions we have also calculated a set of correction coefficients accounting for uneven penetration of social networks across Russian subjects of Federation.

Fourth, our methodology allows revealing the listed above aspects of attitudes to the problems of ethnicity. This part of methodology is based on algorithms trained with a marked-up collection containing 15,000 messages about 115 postSoviet ethnic groups. For such aspects as danger and call for violence, there was no sufficient data to train a classifier. Other instance-level aspects have produced mixed results, of them the best quality was obtained for classes "superior" and "aggressor". At the text level, negative aspects – conflict presence and negative sentiment – are predicted better than positive ones; algorithms trained to predict these two aspects have been integrated into our online system. Besides this, the system was equipped with a function of sentiment analysis of topics based on comparison of topics' topwords with our sentiment lexicon.

Our experiments have also shown that doubling the size of the marked-up collection, although it improves quality of classification, does not solve the problem radically; furthermore, the quality seems to be unrelated to the level of inter-coder agreement. This suggests that ways of further improvement of classification of attitudes to ethnic issues should be searched for via extracting specific grammatical constructions.

It should be noted that as direct calls for violence against any ethnic groups occur in less than 1% of ethnically relevant texts, negative attitudes are mostly expressed more indirectly or vague. Beyond LiveJournal positive aspects of attitude prevail over negative ones, although this may be explained with over-representation of small nationalities in the marked-up sample. Simultaneously, these marked-up texts are more characterized by generalized vision of ethnic groups, negative sentiment and conflict mentioning than by positive sentiment, mentioning of positive inter-ethnic interaction and of concrete persons of a given ethnicity. In other words, users problematize the topic of ethnicity in general more often than they express a direct negative attitude to certain ethnic groups or persons.

6 Conclusion

This methodological essay, based on a whole series of our projects, did not aim at presenting ready solutions that we report elsewhere. Instead, we have tried to attract the attention of the research community to important methodological problems that are seldom discussed in published academic papers because the latter tend to focus on successful results, not on the difficulties a researcher encounters on the way to them. We have shown that the existing methods to automatically detect ethnic hostility online, as well as other social categories, are still under development and should not be used as black boxes. At the same time, it makes little sense to wait until they ripen because efficient development of methods may occur only in collaboration of those who develop methods (computer scientists) and those who set the goals for them (social scientists).

Acknowledgements. This paper is mainly based on the experience from the research project "Development of concept and methodology for multi-level monitoring of the state of interethnic relations with the data from social media" RSF grant No 15-18-00091, 2015–2017, as well as the ongoing research implemented in the Laboratory for Internet Studies in the framework of the Basic Research Program of National Research University Higher School of Economics. The author is thankful to all project participants: Sergei Koltcov, Konstantin Vorontsov, Sergey Nikolenko, Svetlana Bodrunova, Murat Apishev, Svetlana Alexeeva, and Oleg Nagornyy.

References

1. Koltsova, O., Alexeeva, S., Nikolenko, S., Koltsov, M.: Measuring prejudice and ethnic tensions in user-generated content. Ann. Rev. CyberTherapy Telemed. (2017)
2. Koltsova, O., Nikolenko, S., Alexeeva, S., Nagornyy, O., Koltcov, S.: Detecting interethnic relations with the data from social media. In: Alexandrov, D.A., Boukhanovsky, A.V., Chugunov, A.V., Kabanov, Y., Koltsova, O. (eds.) DTGS 2017. CCIS, vol. 745, pp. 16–30. Springer, Cham (2017). https://doi.org/10.1007/978-3-319-69784-0_2

3. Hofmann, T.: Unsupervised learning by probabilistic latent semantic analysis. Mach. Learn. **42**(1), 177–196 (2011)
4. Griffiths, T., Steyvers, M.: Finding scientific topics. Proc. Natl. Acad. Sci. **101**, 5228–5235 (2004)
5. Blei, D.M.: Probabilistic topic models. Commun. ACM **55**(4), 77–84 (2012)
6. Flaounas, I., et al.: Research methods in the age of the digital journalism: massive-scale automated analysis of news content. Digit. Journal. **1**(1), 102–116 (2013)
7. Nagornyy, O., Koltsova, O.: Mining media topics perceived as social problems by online audiences: use of a data mining approach in sociology. NRU Higher School of Economics, (WP BRP 74/SOC/2017)
8. Chen, Y., Zhou, Y., Zhu, S., Xu, H.: Detecting offensive language in social media to protect adolescent online safety. In: Privacy, Security, Risk and Trust (PASSAT), International Conference on Social Computing (SocialCom), Amsterdam, Netherlands, pp. 71–80 (2012)
9. Scharkow, M.: Thematic content analysis using supervised machine learning: an empirical evaluation using German online news. Qual. Quant. **47**(2), 761–773 (2013)
10. Burscher, B., Odijk, D., Vliegenthart, R., de Rijke, M., de Vreese, C.H.: Teaching the computer to code frames in news: comparing two supervised machine learning approaches to frame analysis. Commun. Methods Meas. **8**(3), 190–206 (2014)
11. Waseem, Z., Hovy, D.: Hateful symbols or hateful people? Predictive features for hate speech detection on Twitter. In: SRW@ HLT-NAACL, pp. 88–93 (2016)
12. Warner, W., Hirschberg, J.: Detecting hate speech on the world wide web. In: Proceedings of the Second Workshop on Language in Social Media, Stroudsburg, PA, USA, pp. 19–26. Association for Computational Linguistics (2012)
13. Burnap, P., Williams, M.: Cyber hate speech on Twitter: an application of machine classification and statistical modeling for policy and decision making. Policy Internet **7**(2), 223–242 (2015)
14. Burnap, P., Williams, M.: Us and them: identifying cyber hate on Twitter across multiple protected characteristics. EPJ Data Sci. **5**(1), 1–15 (2016)
15. Apishev, M., Koltsov, S., Koltsova, O., Nikolenko, S., Vorontsov, K.: Mining ethnic content online with additively regularized topic models. Computacion y Sistemas **20**(3), 387–403 (2016)
16. Nikolenko, S., Koltcov, S., Koltsova, O.: Topic modelling for qualitative studies. J. Inf. Sci. **1**, 1–15 (2017)
17. May, S.: Ethnicity, Nationalism and the Politics of Language. Taylor & Francis, Abingdon (2012)
18. Song, S.: The subject of multiculturalism: culture, religion, language, ethnicity, nationality, and race? In: Bruin, B., et al. (eds.) New Waves in Political Philosophy. Palgrave McMillan, London (2009). https://doi.org/10.1057/9780230234994_10
19. Yang, P.Q.: Ethnic Studies: Issues and Approaches. State University of New York Press, New York (2000)
20. Tulkens, S., Hilte, L., Lodewyckx, E., Verhoeven, D., Daelemans, W.A: Dictionary-based approach to racism detection in Dutch social media. In: First Workshop on Text Analytics for Cybersecurity and Online Safety (TA-COS2016), pp. 11–16 (2016)
21. Gitari, N.D., Zuping, Z., Hanyurwimfura, D., Long, J.: A lexicon-based approach for hate speech detection. Int. J. Multimed. Ubiquit. Eng. **10**(4), 215–230 (2015)
22. Xu, Z., Liu, Y., Mei, L., Luo, X., Wei, X., Hu, C.: Crowdsourcing based description of urban emergency events using social media big data. IEEE Trans. Cloud Comput. **99** (2016)
23. Zubiaga, A., Spina, D., Martínez, R., Fresno, V.: Real-time classification of Twitter trends. J. Assoc. Inf. Sci. Technol. **66**(3), 462–473 (2015)

24. Yar, E., Delibalta, I., Baruh, L., Kozat, S.S.: Online text classification for real life tweet analysis. In: 24th Signal Processing and Communication Application Conference (2016)
25. Grimmer, J., Stewart, B.M.: Text as data: the promise and pitfalls of automatic content analysis methods for political texts. Polit. Anal. **21**(3), 267–297 (2013)
26. Günther, E., Quandt, T.: Word counts and topic models: automated text analysis methods for digital journalism research. Digit. Journal. **4**(1), 75–88 (2016)
27. Vorontsov, K., Frei, O., Apishev, M., Romov, P., Dudarenko, M.: BigARTM: open source library for regularized multimodal topic modeling of large collections. In: Khachay, M.Y., Konstantinova, N., Panchenko, A., Ignatov, D.I., Labunets, V.G. (eds.) AIST 2015. CCIS, vol. 542, pp. 370–381. Springer, Cham (2015). https://doi.org/10.1007/978-3-319-26123-2_36
28. Koltsova O., Pashakhin S.: Agenda divergence in a developing conflict: a quantitative evidence from a Ukrainian and a Russian TV newsfeeds. Sociology, WP BRP 79/SOC/2017
29. Bartlett, J., Reffin, J., Rumball, N., Williamson, S.: Anti-social media. Demos, 1–51 (2014)
30. Kwok, I., Wang, Y.: Locate the hate: detecting tweets against blacks. In: des Jardins, M., Littman, M.L. (eds.) AAAI, Bellevue, Washington, USA, pp. 1621–1622. AAAI Press (2013)
31. Nobata, C., Tetreault, J., Thomas, A., Mehdad, Y., Chang, Y.: Abusive language detection in online user content. In: Proceedings of the 25th International Conference on World Wide Web, pp. 145–153. International World Wide Web Conferences Steering Committee (2016)
32. Silva, L., Mondal, M., Correa, D., Benevenuto, F., Weber, I.: Analyzing the targets of hate in online social media. In: Proceedings of the 10th International Conference on Web and Social Media, ICWSM 2016, pp. 687–690 (2016)
33. Djuric, N., Zhou, J., Morris, R., Grbovic, M., Radosavljevic, V., Bhamidipati, N.: Hate speech detection with comment embeddings. In: Proceedings of the 24th International Conference on World Wide Web, pp. 29–30. ACM (2015)
34. Attenberg, J., Ipeirotis, P.G., Provost, F.J.: Beat the machine: challenging workers to find the unknown unknowns. In: Proceedings of 11th AAAI Conference on Human Computation, pp. 2–7 (2011)
35. Waseem Z.: Are you a racist or am i seeing things? Annotator influence on hate speech detection on Twitter. In: Proceedings of 2016 EMNLP Workshop on Natural Language Processing and Computational Social Science, pp. 138–142. ACL, Austin (2016)
36. Gagliardone, I., Patel, A., Pohjonen, M.: Mapping and Analysing Hate Speech Online: Opportunities and Challenges for Ethiopia. University of Oxford, Oxford (2014)
37. Faris, R., Ashar, A., Gasser, U., Joo, D.: Understanding Harmful Speech Online. Berkman Klein Center Research Publication No. 2016-21 (2016)
38. Quillian, L.: New approaches to understanding prejudice and discrimination. Ann. Rev. Sociol. **32**, 299–338 (2009)
39. Allport, G.W.: The Nature of Prejudice. Addison, New York (1954)
40. Sood, S.O., Churchill, E.F., Antin, J.: Automatic identification of personal insults on social news sites. J. Am. Soc. Inf. Sci. Technol. **63**(2), 270–285 (2012)
41. Van Hee C., et al.: Detection and fine-grained classification of cyberbullying events. In: Proceedings of Recent Advances in Natural Language Processing, Proceedings, Hissar, Bulgaria, pp. 672–680 (2015)
42. Hosseinmardi, H., Mattson, S.A., Rafiq R.I., Han, R., Lv, Q., Mishra, S.: Detection of cyberbullying incidents on the Instagram social network. CoRR, abs/1503.03909 (2015)

Agglomerative Method for Texts Clustering

Andrey V. Orekhov$^{(\boxtimes)}$ (iD)

St. Petersburg State University, 7/9, Universitetskaya embankment,
St. Petersburg 199034, Russian Federation
`a_v_orehov@mail.ru`

Abstract. Usually, text documents are represented as a vector of n-dimensional Euclidean space. One of the main it the problem of the typology of texts using cluster analysis is to determine the number of clusters. In this article was researched the agglomerative clustering algorithm in Euclidean space. A statistical criterion for completing the clustering process was deriving as the Markov moment. Was considered the problem of cluster stability. As an example, it was considered retrieval of the harmful content.

Keywords: Cluster analysis · Clustering method ·
Least squares method · Euclidean space · Markov moment ·
Harmful content

1 Introduction

Information retrieval consists of four steps: the formulation of an information request, the definition of information sources, the extraction of information from identified information arrays, the analysis, and evaluation of search results.

One of the private, but essential tasks of information retrieval on the Internet is the clustering of documents. The purpose of the clustering is to automatically typify texts by identifying groups of semantically similar documents from a certain set.

The fundamental difference between clustering and classification is that groups of documents are formed only by the proximity of texts. In this case, unlike the classification, neither the significant characteristics of these groups of documents nor the number of clusters is known.

To typify text documents, usually used their vector representation (Vector Space Model) [1]. Therefore, clustering algorithms in Euclidean space will be considered here.

An arbitrary clustering algorithm is a map

$$\mathcal{A}: \begin{cases} X \longrightarrow \mathbf{N} \\ \overline{x}_i \longmapsto k \end{cases}$$

Supported by St. Petersburg State University.

© Springer Nature Switzerland AG 2019
S. S. Bodrunova et al. (Eds.): INSCI 2018 Workshops, LNCS 11551, pp. 19–32, 2019.
https://doi.org/10.1007/978-3-030-17705-8_2

which maps any element $\bar{x}_i$ from the set X to the only natural number k that is the cluster number to which $\bar{x}_i$ belongs. Thus, the clustering process splits the X on set disjoint subsets X_h, called clusters:

$$X = \bigcup_{h=1}^{m} X_h,$$

where for $\forall\ h, l\ |\ 1 \leq h, l \leq m\ :\ X_h \cap X_l = \varnothing$.

Consequently, clustering defines an equivalence relation on X. As independent representatives of these classes are elected centroids. In the n-dimensional Euclidean space E^n, the coordinates of the centroids are equal to the arithmetic mean of the corresponding coordinates of all the vectors entering the cluster. If we identify each vector from E^n as a material point of unit mass, then centroids can be considered as centers of mass.

An essential problem of cluster analysis is the determination of the preferable number of clusters. With the solution of this question, the determination of the moment of completion of the clustering process is connected. This relationship assumes that the criteria for determining the number of clusters and the criteria for completing the clustering algorithm depend on each other. As a rule, the decision on the number of clusters is taken either during the process itself or even before its beginning (for example, using the k-means method) and in both cases is subjective. The determination of the number of clusters during the clustering process itself is based on the visual analysis of dendrograms, by which the preferred number of clusters [2–4] can be determined. However, this approach is heuristic, and the essence of heuristic methods is that the solution of the problem is based on some plausible assumptions, rather than on rigorous mathematical conclusions.

The problem of determining the true number of clusters has not been solved. In the book on multidimensional statistical methods in archeology, Baxter writes that the most common approach for determining the number of clusters will be the use of informal and subjective criteria based on the expert estimate [5]. Everitt writes that the lack of consensus on this issue makes Baxter's comment the most accurate [2]. Nevertheless, especially when clustering large arrays of empirical data or large-scale data (which is typical for texts typology), the role of cluster analysis cannot be overemphasized. So this makes it necessary to obtain objective (formal) criteria for determining the number of clusters (the completion of the clustering process) for various algorithms that implement this process. It is possible that for precisely this reason, now, the papers devoted to determining the number of clusters consider not the general, but various particular cases of the realization of the clustering process.

It should be noted the article Zugar and James, which considers an algorithm based on the search and estimation of jumps of the so-called index functions [6]. The main drawback of this method is its greater computational complexity. Granichin and joint authors suggested using randomized algorithms [7,8] to solve this problem. Another approach to the automatic determination of the number of clusters is based on an estimate of the distribution density of the elements of a set, for example [9, 10]. In the article [10] devoted to the k-means method, much attention is paid not only to determining the number of clusters but also to the robustness of the clustering process. Similar problems are studied in [11, 12].

2 "Single Linkage" Method

The most popular of the modern methods of numerical data clustering is the "k-means method", was invented in the middle of the 20-th century by Steinhaus and Lloyd [13, 14]. This algorithm seeks to minimize the total quadratic deviation of elements of equivalence classes from their centers of mass. The action of the k-means algorithm starts with the fact that the set X is divided into a predetermined number of clusters with randomly selected centroids. The main idea of this method is that at each iteration the center of mass is recalculated for each cluster obtained in the previous step. Then the elements are divided into new equivalence classes, relatively of their proximity to new centroids. The algorithm is completed when at the next iteration, there is no change in the total quadratic deviation of the elements from the centers of mass. The k-means method is realized for a finite number of iterations since the number of possible partitions of the finite set X is finite, and at each step, the total quadratic deviation decreases, so the algorithm converges [2, 15, 16].

The k-means method has three significant drawbacks. First, this method does not guarantee the achievement of a global minimum of the total quadratic deviation, but only one of the local minimum. Secondly, the result of clustering depends on the choice of initial centroids, and their optimal choice is unknown. Third, and most importantly, the number of clusters must be specified in advance. Which means that can specify a "training sample" and practically clusterization becomes a classification. As an alternative to the k-means method, for a truly automatic clustering in E^n, we can suggest a hierarchical algorithm of the "single linkage" [2, 16].

Formally, this method can be described as follows.

Let $X = \{\overline{x}_1, \overline{x}_2, \ldots, \overline{x}_m\}$ is the set in which any $\overline{x}_i$ of X belongs to the n-dimensional Euclidean space $\mathbf{E}^n$, i.e. $\forall \overline{x}_i = (x_i^1, x_i^2, \ldots, x_i^n)$ and for $\forall i, j$ such that $1 \leq i \leq m$, $1 \leq j \leq n : x_i^j \in \mathbf{R}$.

In the space $\mathbf{E}^n$, used the standard Euclidean metric $\rho \mid \forall \overline{x}, \overline{y} \in \mathbf{E}^n$:

$$\rho(\overline{x}, \overline{y}) = \sqrt{\sum_{j=1}^{n}(x_j - y_j)^2}.$$

If the set X contains m vectors, then initially it is assumed that X is split into m clusters containing one element: $X_1 = \overline{x}_1, X_2 = \overline{x}_2, \ldots, X_m = \overline{x}_m$.

$$X = \bigcup_{h=1}^{m} X_h.$$

In this case, the centroids of the clusters coincide with them: $X_h = \widehat{X}_h$ for $\forall h \mid 1 \leq h \leq m$. The iterations of the algorithm $\mathcal{A}$ realizing the "single linkage" method can be described as follows. The first step of the first iteration of $\mathcal{A}_1$, for algorithm $\mathcal{A}$, is the construction of the diagonal distance matrix between the clusters X_h.

$$
\begin{pmatrix}
0 & \rho(X_1, X_2) & \rho(X_1, X_3) & \cdots & \rho(X_1, X_m) \\
 & 0 & \rho(X_2, X_3) & \cdots & \rho(X_2, X_m) \\
 & & \ddots & & \\
 & & & 0 & \rho(X_{m-1}, X_m) \\
 & & & & 0
\end{pmatrix}
$$

Then calculate minimal element this matrix

$$
F_1 = \min(\rho(X_h, X_l)),
$$

where $1 \leq h, l \leq m$, F_1 is the minimum distance between clusters for $\mathcal{A}_1$.

Then the clusters X_h and X_l for which the distance ρ is minimal unite into one cluster. We denote this cluster as X_1, and its centroid is $\widehat{X}_1$. The clusters X_h and X_l are replaced by the centroid $\widehat{X}_1$. Thus, after $\mathcal{A}_1$, the set X contains $m - 1$ clusters.

Without loss of generality, we assume that at the beginning of the g-th iteration of $\mathcal{A}_g$, for agglomerative clustering algorithm $\mathcal{A}$, the set X is divided into p clusters. The first step $\mathcal{A}_g$ is the construction of a diagonal matrix of distances between clusters. Then, the minimal element of this matrix is determined:

$$
F_g = \min(\rho(X_h, X_l)).
$$

Where $1 \leq h, l \leq p$, F_g is the minimum distance between clusters for $\mathcal{A}_g$.

Clusters X_h and X_l, for which the distance was minimal, are combined into the cluster, which we denote as X_g. Its centroid $\widehat{X}_g$ has coordinates equal to the arithmetic mean of the corresponding coordinates of all vectors from X_h or X_l combined into X_g. At the end of $\mathcal{A}_g$, the clusters X_h and X_l are replaced by the centroid $\widehat{X}_g$. Thus, after the iteration of $\mathcal{A}_g$ is completed, the set X is split into a $p - 1$ clusters.

The main advantage of the "single linkage" method is its mathematical properties: the results obtained using this method are invariant to monotonic transformations of the similarity matrix. The availability of same data does not hinder the use of this method. Therefore, it is especially effective in Euclidean spaces. This method, in comparison with other clustering algorithms, is highly resistant [16].

If there is no criterion for the completion of the clustering process, then after the $m - 1$ iteration of this method, the set X will be merged into one cluster, which is an absurd result. Consider the set of minimum distances obtained after $m - 1$ iterations of the algorithm described above. This set has the form $\{F_1, F_2, \ldots, F_{m-1}\}$, and is linearly ordered to the numerical values of its elements: $0 \leq F_1 \leq F_2 \leq \ldots \leq F_{m-1}$.

We use this set to derive a statistical criterion of the completion of an agglomerative clustering that implements the "single linkage" method in the Euclidean space $\mathbf{E}^n$.

3   Approximation-Evaluation Test

Consider the set X consisting of 30 ordered pairs: $X = \{(0, 0), (1, 1), (3, 1), (2, 0), (3, 3), (3, 4), (2, 4), (8, 4), (8, 9), (9, 10), (11, 10), (12, 10), (9, 11), (11, 12), (12, 12), (13, 12), (12, 13), (13, 13), (13, 15), (21, 20), (21, 22), (22, 19), (22, 22), (23, 2), (23, 17), (23, 19), (23, 20), (23, 21), (23, 22), (1, 23)\}$, which can be identified with points from a bounded region on a plane.

In this simplest case, the number of clusters and their location can be determined visually; three clusters and two isolated points (see Fig. 1). The elements of the set of minimum distances take the following values: $F_1 = 1, F_2 = 1, F_3 = 1, F_4 = 1, F_5 = 1, F_6 = 1, F_7 = 1, F_8 = 1, F_9 = 1.12, F_{10} = 1.12, F_{11} = 1.34, F_{12} = 1.41, F_{13} = 1.41, F_{14} = 1.5, F_{15} = 1.58, F_{16} = 1.77, F_{17} = 1.8, F_{18} = 2, F_{19} = 2.24, F_{20} = 2.5, F_{21} = 3.36, F_{22} = 3.44, F_{23} = 3.7, F_{24} = 4.06, F_{25} = 6.37, F_{26} = 12.64, F_{27} = 16.35, F_{28} = 17.36, F_{29} = 18.77.$

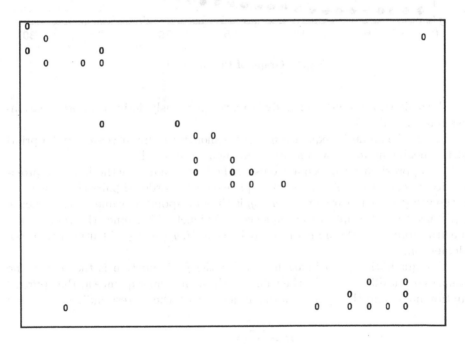

Fig. 1. The set X (point (0,0) is located at the top left).

When clusters merge or when one of the isolated points joins any of them, a sharp change in the numerical value of the function of minimum distance. According to common sense, this moment coincides with the moment of completion of the clustering process. The graph of the values of F_i clearly shows that the function in the node F_{25} is best approximated not by a straight line, but by a parabola (see Fig. 2).

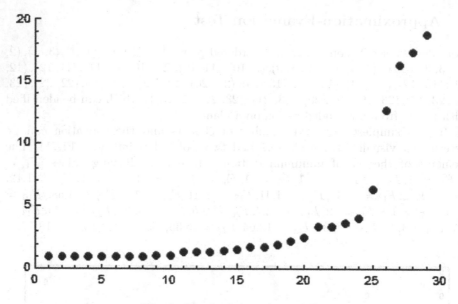

Fig. 2. Graph of the values of F_i.

We define this moment formally using the previously derived "approximation-evaluation test" [17].

Let us the numeric sequence y_n always monotonically increases, and a priori at the beginning y_n grows linearly, and then parabolically.

We approximate this sequence using the least squares method. The approximation nodes for the y_n numerical sequence are the ordered pairs (i, y_i), where i is the value of the natural argument, y_i is the corresponding value of the sequence y_n. Since the subscript of the sequence y_n uniquely determines the value of the natural argument, the node of approximation (i, y_i) will be identified with the element y_i.

The quadratic approximation error for the $f(x)$ function is the sum of the squares of the differences for the values of the numerical sequence at the approximation nodes and the approximating function with the corresponding argument:

$$\delta_f^2 = \sum_{i=0}^{k-1}(f(i) - y_i)^2.$$

We will distinguish the linear approximation in the class of functions of the form $l(x) = ax + b$ and the incomplete parabolic approximation (without linear term) in the class of functions $q(x) = cx^2 + d$.

Quadratic errors on k nodes for linear and incomplete parabolic approximation will be respectively equal to:

$$\delta_l^2(k) = \sum_{i=0}^{k-1}(a \cdot i + b - y_i)^2; \quad \delta_q^2(k) = \sum_{i=0}^{k-1}(c \cdot i^2 + d - y_i)^2. \tag{1}$$

If in our reasoning the number of approximation nodes obvious from the context, then the corresponding quadratic errors will simply be denoted δ_l^2 and δ_q^2. When comparing δ_l^2 and δ_q^2, three cases are possible: $\delta_q^2 < \delta_l^2; \quad \delta_q^2 > \delta_l^2; \quad \delta_q^2 = \delta_l^2$.

We say that the sequence y_n has a linear increase if y_n is monotone and quadratic errors of linear and incomplete parabolic approximation are related by the inequality: $\delta_q^2 > \delta_l^2$. If the inequality holds true: $\delta_q^2 < \delta_l^2$, then we say that the sequence y_n has a parabolic increase. The node y_{k-1} is called critical if for the set of approximation nodes: $y_0, y_1, \ldots, y_{k-1}$, equality is fulfilled $\delta_q^2 = \delta_l^2$.

We calculate the coefficients a, b for the linear function $ax + b$ which approximating the nodes $y_0, y_1, \ldots, y_{k-1}$.

$$a = \frac{6}{k(k^2 - 1)} \sum_{i=0}^{k-1}(2i + 1 - k)y_i; \qquad b = \frac{2}{k(k + 1)} \sum_{i=0}^{k-1}(2k - 1 - 3i)y_i. \qquad (2)$$

Now, we calculate the coefficients c, d for the incomplete quadratic function $cx^2 + d$ which approximating the nodes $y_0, y_1, \ldots, y_{k-1}$.

$$c = \frac{30}{k(k - 1)(2k - 1)(8k^2 - 3k - 11)} \sum_{i=0}^{k-1}(6i^2 - (k - 1)(2k - 1))y_i; \qquad (3)$$

$$d = \frac{6}{k(8k^2 - 3k - 11)} \sum_{i=0}^{k-1}(3k(k - 1) - 1 - 5i^2)y_i. \qquad (4)$$

In order to determine the moment when the character of increasing of a monotone sequence y_n changes from linear to parabolic, we construct an "approximation-evaluation test" δ^2.

We assume by definition that for the nodes approximation: $y_0, y_1, \ldots, y_{k-1}$ criterion $\delta^2 = \delta^2(k_0) = \delta_l^2(k_0) - \delta_q^2(k_0)$. In this case, we assume that $y_0 = 0$ is always. It is easy to achieve this condition at any approximation step using the transformation:

$$y_0 = y_j - y_j, \ y_1 = y_{j+1} - y_j, \ \ldots, \ y_{k-1} = y_{j+k-1} - y_j. \qquad (5)$$

We calculate, using the formulas (1), (2), (3) and (4), the quadratic errors of the linear and incomplete parabolic approximations over four points y_0, y_1, y_2, y_3.

$$ax + b = \frac{1}{10}(-y_1 + y_2 + 3y_3)x + \frac{1}{10}(4y_1 + y_2 - 2y_3);$$

$$cx^2 + d = \frac{1}{98}((-5y_1 + y_2 + 11y_3)x^2 + \frac{1}{98}(42y_1 + 21y_2 - 14y_3).$$

Then

$$\delta_l^2(4_0) = \sum_{k=0}^{3} \left[\frac{1}{10}(k(-y_1 + y_2 + 3y_3) + (4y_1 + y_2 - 2y_3)) - y_k \right]^2$$

$$= \frac{1}{10}(7y_1^2 + 7y_2^2 + 3y_3^2 - 4y_1y_2 - 2y_1y_3 - 8y_2y_3),$$

$$\delta_q^2(4_0) = \sum_{k=0}^{3} \left[\frac{1}{98}(k^2(-5y_1 + y_2 + 11y_3) + (42y_1 + 21y_2 - 14y_3)) - y_k \right]^2$$

$$= \frac{1}{98}(61y_1^2 + 73y_2^2 + 13y_3^2 - 44y_1y_2 + 6y_1y_3 - 60y_2y_3).$$

$$\delta^2(4_0) = \frac{1}{245}(19y_1^2 - 11y_2^2 + 41y_3^2 + 12y_1y_2 - 64y_1y_3 - 46y_2y_3). \qquad (6)$$

It can be said that near the element y_k the character of increasing the sequence y_n changed from linear to parabolic, if for nodes $y_0, y_1, \ldots, y_{k-1}$ linear approximation is not worse than incomplete parabolic, that is $\delta^2 = \delta_l^2 - \delta_q^2 \leq 0$, and for a set of points, $y_1, y_2, \ldots, y_k$, shifted by one step of discreteness, the inequality holds $\delta^2 = \delta_l^2 - \delta_q^2 > 0$.

4   Clustering Process Stability Problem

Now we to consider "clustering stability problem" and to formulate the condition for the completion of the agglomerative method of "single linkage".

At first, we solve the "reverse problem". Let the sequence values y_n in the nodes: y_0, y_1, y_2 be known. It is necessary to determine at what numerical value of y_3 this point will become critical. Equating the quadratic form (6) to zero and replacing y_3 with x we solve the quadratic equation:

$$41x^2 - (64y_1 + 46y_2)\,x + \left(19y_1^2 + 12y_2y_1 - 11y_2^2\right) = 0$$

for which

$$x_{1,2} = \frac{32y_1 + 23y_2 \pm 7\sqrt{5}\,(y_1 + 2y_2)}{41}.$$

Taking into account that $0 \leq y_1 \leq y_2 \leq y_3$, we finally get:

$$y_3 = \frac{32y_1 + 23y_2 + 7\sqrt{5}\,(y_1 + 2y_2)}{41}. \qquad (7)$$

Recall the transformation introduced above (5), if $y_j = y_{j+1} = y_{j+2}$, then not only $y_0 = 0$ but and $y_1 = y_2 = 0$. According to (6), for any $y_{j+3} > y_{j+2}$, even if $y_3 = y_{j+3} - y_j > 0$ is arbitrarily small, the quadratic form $\delta^2 > 0$.

For example, for the above set of minimum distances $\{F_1, F_2, \ldots, F_{29}\}$, the criterion $\delta^2(4_0)$ will take the following values:

$$\delta_4^2 = 0, \quad \delta_5^2 = 0, \quad \delta_6^2 = 0, \quad \delta_7^2 = 0, \quad \delta_8^2 = 0, \quad \delta_9^2 = 0.002,$$

the symbol δ_4^2 denotes the criterion value by nodes: F_1, F_2, F_3, F_4, the symbol δ_5^2 denotes the criterion value by nodes: F_2, F_3, F_4, F_5, etc.

According to the conventions adopted above, the agglomerative clustering algorithm for the set X should terminate after iterating $\mathcal{A}_9$. However, in this case, the set X will be divided into 8 clusters and 13 isolated points, which can hardly be considered a satisfactory result (see Fig. 3).

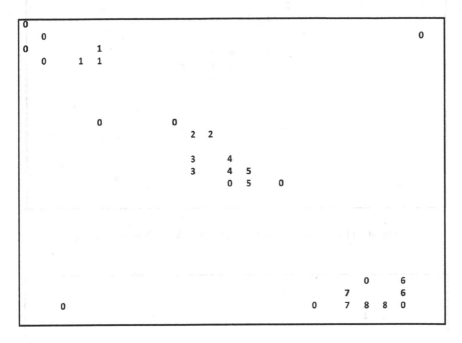

Fig. 3. The results of clustering the set X with $q \in [0,\ 0.1]$.

If we introduce the transformation $y_i = F_i + q \cdot i$, then we get the set $\{y_1, y_2, \ldots, y_k\}$, which we call "trend set", and q which we call "trend coefficient". When applying the criterion δ^2, not to the set $\{F_1, F_2, \ldots, F_{29}\}$, but to the set $\{y_1, y_2, \ldots, y_{29}\}$, the result of clustering changes qualitatively.

For $q = 0.2$, the set X is divided into 4 clusters and 5 isolated points. The same clustering result is obtained when $q = 0.3, q = 0.4, q = 0.5$ (see Fig. 4). If q varies from 0.6 to 2.2, then the set X is divided into 3 clusters and 2 isolated points (see Fig. 5). When q ranging from 2.3 to 6.1, the set X is divided into 2 clusters and 2 isolated points (see Fig. 6). With trend coefficient $q \geq 6.2$, the set X is represented as one cluster consisting of 30 points.

In this regard, the following should be noted.

The clustering process is completed using an approximation-evaluation test. This test evaluates the jumps of a monotonically increasing sequence of minimum distances. The magnitude of a significant jump sufficient to stop the clustering process depends on the sensitivity of the stop criterion, which is specified using

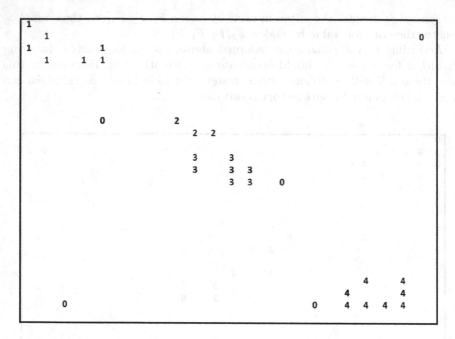

Fig. 4. The results of clustering the set X with $q \in [0.2, 0.5]$.

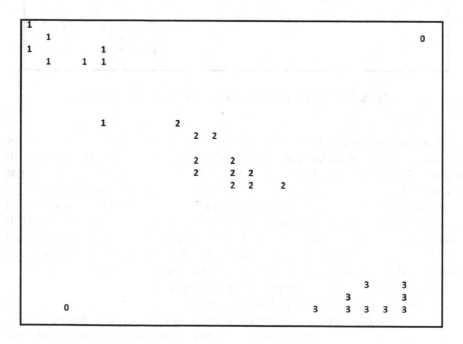

Fig. 5. The results of clustering the set X with $q \in [0.6, 2.2]$.

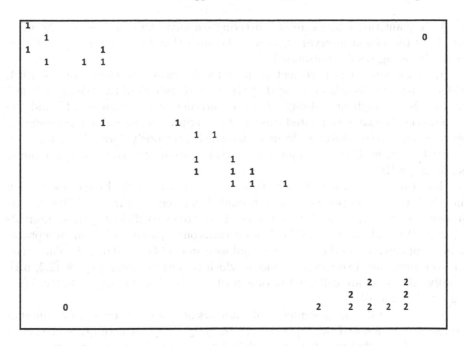

Fig. 6. The results of clustering the set X with $q \in [2.3, 6.1]$.

a non-negative coefficient q. The larger the value of q, the lower the sensitivity of the criterion for stopping the clustering process. The stopping criterion has the highest sensitivity at $q = 0$. In this case, as a result of clustering, the most significant number of clusters will be obtained. Increasing q can reduce the sensitivity of the stopping criterion so that the process will continue until all m vectors are combined into one cluster. Indeed, if the nodes y_0, y_1, y_2 change as an arithmetic progression with a difference z, then the formula (7) takes the form

$$y_3 = \frac{1}{41} \left(78 + 35\sqrt{5}\right) z \simeq 3.811z.$$

That is, the approximation nodes, in this case, take the values 0, z, $2z$, $3.811z$. This means that with an increase in the q the sensitivity of the criterion decreases. It to achieve the critical value a more change is necessary the numerical value of the minimum distance.

Cluster analysis, in a certain sense, has a high degree of subjectivity. Therefore, the interpretation of its results depends mainly on the researcher himself. For example, in the paper [7] does not give a strict definition of "sustainable clustering", but introduces its intuitive notion, namely, the stability of clustering shows how different the resulting groupings are obtained after repeatedly applying of the clustering for the same data. A small discrepancy between the results is interpreted as high stability.

As a quantitative measure of clustering stability, we can consider the magnitude of the closed interval $Q_i = [\alpha_i, \beta_i]$, such that for every $q \in [\alpha_i, \beta_i]$ the same clustering result is obtained.

In this regard, it is pertinent to note the following; In their work of 1984, Aldenderfer and Blashfield argue that the main drawback of the "single linkage" method is the high probability of the occurrence of a "chain effect" and the formation of the large elongated cluster. As we approach the end of the clustering process, one large cluster is formed, to which previously formed clusters and isolated points join. The authors confirm their statement with the corresponding dendrogram [16].

Here can see an illustration of this process in a numerical experiment with the clustering of 30 points from a bounded flat region. First, subclusters (as proper subsets) are formed with values of the trend coefficient q from intervals $Q_1 = [0, 0.1]$ and $Q_2 = [0.2, 0.5]$. Then it turns out a partition into an acceptable number of clusters (in the sense of visual assessment) $Q_3 = [0.6, 2.2]$. Then they are combined into two clusters (one of which is "large oblong") $Q_4 = [2.3, 6.1]$. Finally, all points are collected in one cluster of 30 elements $Q_5 = [6.2, \infty)$ (see Figs. 3, 4, 5 and 6).

In the general case, a sequence of intervals of stable clustering, for different values of q, is denoted by: $Q_1, Q_2, \ldots, Q_{e-2}, Q_{e-1}, Q_e$, where Q_e is the set of values of the coefficient q for which all points are combined into one cluster.

Based on the analysis of the above numerical experiment and general considerations, we can formulate the following hypothesis: "An acceptable number of clusters is formed when $q \in Q_{e-2}$".

McCaffrey published in MSDN Magazine an article devoted to the software implementation of one of the modifications of the k-means method [18]. In this article, the author clusterizes points on a Euclidean plane, and a partition is given a priori into three clusters. By the method described in the article, the same result, without an a priori assumption, was obtained with $q \in Q_{e-2} = [0.3, 0.9]$, with $q \in Q_{e-1} = [1, 2.7]$ the data was divided into two clusters, and for $q > 2.7$ all points united into one cluster.

5   Retrieval of the Harmful Content

As an example of the automatic separation of text into different types, consider the problem of finding harmful content on the Internet. With the development of electronic communication, an avalanche-like growth of information occurs, among which there is a huge amount of harmful content. Even if only computer networks are considered, the number of negative messages is so large that it is impossible to manage without their automatic recognition. One approach to solving this problem may be a preliminary typology of text messages using cluster analysis. Here we will not discuss the methods of the vector representation of texts, assuming possible any of the generally accepted algorithms for mapping text into Euclidean space is adequate.

The main types of harmful content on the Internet include: information promoting war, terrorism, national and religious hatred, justifying extremist activity, promoting violence and cruelty, deviant behavior, as well as life-threatening actions and human health, information on methods and means of committing crimes, sexually explicit content and other obscene information, foul language, frightening content, including an image or description of violence, cruelty, catastrophe or accident, defamatory information, advertising of goods and services that can harm human life and health, etc [19].

The above implies not only an understanding of the fact that the list of various types of harmful content is enormous but also the understanding that this list is continuously updated due to new negative subjects. Therefore, for example, finding ourselves in "the Procrustean bed" of the k-means method we cannot solve the problem of the formation of new types of negative content, since an apriori, we set the number of content types (clusters). This information (about the number of types) should be obtained a posteriori.

To solve this problem, can use the agglomerative clustering method described in this article. The basic idea is that by obtaining automatic splitting of texts into clusters, we can compare texts closest to the centroids with actual samples of harmful content or evaluate such texts with the help of experts. The main thing here is that if the display of texts in a vector form is adequate, then all informational messages from a fixed cluster have the same meaning, the same emotional coloring, etc. This means that the texts can be identified.

6   Conclusion

The statistical criterion for stopping the agglomerative clustering process based on the "single linkage" method in the $\mathbf{E}^n$ Euclidean space can be formulated as follows. Let $\{F_1, F_2, \ldots, F_k\}$ be a linearly ordered set of minimum distances, and let the set $\{y_1, y_2, \ldots, y_k\}$ is "trend set", obtained using the transformation $y_i = F_i + q \cdot i$, where q is "trend coefficient", i is the iteration number of the $\mathcal{A}$ of the agglomerative clustering algorithm.

The clustering process is considered complete at the k, iteration, for the nodes $y_{k-4}, y_{k-3}, y_{k-2}, y_{k-1}$, if inequality $\delta^2 \leq 0$ is true and for the set of nodes $y_{k-3}, y_{k-2}, y_{k-1}, y_k$, the inequality $\delta^2 > 0$ where

$$\delta^2 = \frac{1}{245}(19y_1^2 - 11y_2^2 + 41y_3^2 + 12y_1y_2 - 64y_1y_3 - 46y_2y_3).$$

In other words, the Markov moment for the clustering algorithm $\mathcal{A}$ is equal to statistics

$$\tau(F_1, F_2, \ldots, F_k) = \min\{k \mid \delta^2 > 0\}.$$

To determine the preferred number of clusters, can cluster the X sample for different values of the q parameter, increasing it from zero to the value at which all points of the X set will gather into one cluster. The final solution to this issue is subjective, but the most interesting is the division into clusters with $q \in Q_{e-2}$.

References

1. Clark S.: Vector space models of lexical meaning. In: Handbook of Contemporary Semantics, 2nd edn. Blackwell, Oxford (2014)
2. Everitt, B.S.: Cluster Analysis, 5th edn. Wiley, Chichester (2011)
3. Duda, R.O., Hart, P.E., Stork, D.G.: Pattern Classification, 2nd edn. Wiley, New York (2001)
4. Calirnski, T., Harabasz, J.: A dendrite method for cluster analysis. Commun. Stat. **3**, 1–27 (1974)
5. Baxter, M.J.: Exploratory Multivariate Analysis in Archaeology. Edinburgh (1994)
6. Sugar, C.A., James, G.M.: Finding the number of clusters in a dataset. J. Am. Stat. Assoc. **98**(463), 750–763 (2003)
7. Granichin, O.N., Shalymov, D.S., Avros, R., Volkovich, Z.: A randomized algorithm for estimating the number of clusters. Autom. Remote Control **72**(4), 754–765 (2011)
8. Avros, R., Granichin, O., Shalymov, D., Volkovich, Z., Weber, G.-W.: Randomized algorithm of finding the true number of clusters based on Chebychev polynomial approximation. Intell. Syst. Ref. Libr. **23**, 131–155 (2012)
9. Zhang, G., Zhang, C., Zhang, H.: Improved K-means algorithm based on density Canopy. Knowl.-Based Syst. **145**, 1–14 (2018)
10. Jiali, W., Yue, Z., Xv, L.: Automatic cluster number selection by finding density peaks. In: 2nd IEEE International Conference on Computer and Communications, ICCC 2016 – Proceedings, pp. 13–18 (2017). https://doi.org/10.1109/CompComm.2016.7924655
11. de Amorim, R.C., Hennig, C.: Recovering the number of clusters in data sets with noise features using feature rescaling factors. Information Sciences. **324**, 126–145 (2015)
12. Lozkins, A., Bure, V.M.: Single hub location-allocation problem under robustness clustering concept. Vestnik Sankt-Peterburgskogo Universiteta, Prikladnaya Matematika, Informatika, Protsessy Upravleniya **13**(4), 398–406 (2017)
13. Steinhaus, H.: Sur la division des corps materiels en parties. Bull. Acad. Polon. Sci. **IV**, 801–804 (1956)
14. Lloyd S.: Least square quantization in PCM's. Bell Telephone Laboratories Paper (1957)
15. Hartigan, J.A.: Clustering Algorithms. Wiley, New York (1975)
16. Aldenderfer, M.S., Blashfield, R.K.: Cluster Analysis. Sage Publications, Beverly Hills (1984)
17. Orekhov, A.V.: Criterion for estimation of stress-deformed state of SD-materials. In: AIP Conference Proceedings, vol. 1959, p. 070028 (2018). https://doi.org/10.1063/1.5034703
18. McCaffrey, J.: Test run – k-means++ data clustering. MSDN Mag. **30**(8), 62–68 (2015)
19. Bryant, J., Thompson, S.: Fundamentals of Media Effects. McGraw-Hill, New York (2002)

User Ethnicity and Gender as Predictors of Attitudes to Ethnic Groups in Social Media Texts

Oleg Nagornyy$^{(\boxtimes)}$ (iD)

National Research University Higher School of Economics,
Saint Petersburg, Russia
onagorny@hse.ru

Abstract. Out-group bias in the context of race and ethnicity has been widely studied. However, little research has been done to study this phenomenon online. In this paper we explore how ethnicity and gender of Russian social media users affects their attitude toward other ethnic groups. Out results show that ethnicity of social media users plays a significant role in their attitude towards ethnic groups. On the average social media users tend to experience more positive attitude to the ethnic groups they belong to, but there are some exceptions—Russians and Tatars. Gender also influence the attitude insofar as men expressed stronger negative emotions toward foreign peoples.

Keywords: Ethnicity · Social media · Russia · Out-group bias · Stereotypes

1 Introduction

Both Russian and international researchers spend a lot of efforts studying ethnicity. Being an extremely debatable topic, this phenomenon was influenced by the revolutionary development of mass media, the key one being the Internet, which gave a new impetus to ethnic researches. The transformations that initiated the development of information technologies and the emergence of a worldwide network made it possible for every active user of this network to participate in the production of ethnic discourse and they also provide an opportunity for studying big data. The Internet, and especially social media, is an important public arena for discussions about various ethnic groups and a place where "new ethnicities" are emerging [13].

Thus, data from the Internet, although they do not fully replace ethno-demographic data from the public opinion polls, are nevertheless a valuable source of information about the actual ethnocultural and ethno-political processes, including ethnic stereotypes. The results of a study conducted in the United States has shown that these processes have real-world consequences [7]. Researchers have found a positive correlation between Internet access and the number of crimes motivated by racial hatred, and this correlation is stronger in areas with higher levels of racism.

Given all the above, it seems to us that data from the Internet can be used to analyze ethnic processes. Moreover, as a data source, the Internet has an advantage over traditional offline media because it blurs the boundaries between the consumer and the

© Springer Nature Switzerland AG 2019
S. S. Bodrunova et al. (Eds.): INSCI 2018 Workshops, LNCS 11551, pp. 33–41, 2019.
https://doi.org/10.1007/978-3-030-17705-8_3

creator of the content. Now any user can register on social media sites and write a blog post, thereby gaining his own voice in the process of global content production. This feature of online content production makes it possible to measure public opinion on a wide-range of important social issues, which was hardly possible to analyze using traditional media.

Another feature of the Internet that makes data from this source especially useful for analyzis of ethnic processes is the high degree of authors' anonymity. Anonymity reduces the power of social control [19], which is especially important in communication on such sensitive topics as ethnicity.

There are a lot of sociopsychological studies on racial ingroup and outgroup bias [6, 8, 12, etc.], but very few of them touches upon this issue in relation to the Internet and social media in particular. This is an important issue, since among all of the mass media that the global network has given life to, social media provide the most favorable environment for the development of discussions, including on ethnic topics [10].

In this study we are trying to investigate whether there is a connection between ethnicity and gender of Russian social media users and their attitudes toward various ethnic groups they live with as it expressed in the posts they write in social media. Russian social media provide an unique opportunity for this kind of research for three reasons: (1) Russia is a multi-national state with over 194 ethnic groups according to the latest census [16], (2) most of the population speaks Russian language regardless of their ethnicity [17], (3) Russia has quite high level of Internet penetration (73.09% in 2016 which is not much less than, for example, in USA for the same period of time—76.18%) [18].

2   Hypothesis

The key issue of this study is to determine how the author's ethnic identity in social media affects his/her attitude to different ethnic groups.

Hypothesis 1: author's attitude towards ethnic group mentioned in the text will be significantly more positive if the author belongs to the mentioned ethnic group. The causes of this phenomenon are explained by a fundamental psychological inclination of humans to divide people into two classes—in-group and out-group [3].

Hypothesis 2: the size of the effect expressed in Hypothesis 1 will significantly vary across ethnic groups. This hypothesis is based on the assumption that some cultures are more open to out-groups than others, and this is usually related to the extent to which a group feels its identity or interests to be endangered from the outside [9].

Hypothesis 3: males will express significantly more negative attitudes to the ethnic groups they mention, as compared to females.

3   Data

At the first stage we compile a comprehensive list of ethnonyms used to search for the texts related to ethnic discursions. This list included most common forms of post-Soviet ethnonyms. To ensure representativeness we collect all texts related to ethnic discussions from the period of time from January 2014 to December 2015. The text is considered as relevant to ethnic discussions in case it contained at least one word or bigram from the generated list. The texts were gathered using the social media monitoring service IQBuzz which monitor pages from thousands of websites looking for predefined words.

To reveal the presence of ethnic stereotypes, we created a subsample of 15,000 texts for manual coding. Each ethnonym in this subsample was represented by 75 texts (with the exception of those that were found in fewer texts) and each text was evaluated independently by three people. Coders were asked to answer the questions listed in the Table 1.

Then we removed the texts that cause difficulties in understanding, removed ethnic groups with <100 labels and average the labels. Thus, we got 10364 unique text with 22763 labels on the level of ethnonyms.

4 Inter-coder Agreement

As mentioned earlier, we showed each text to three persons. To evaluate intercoder reliability we used the Krippendorff's alpha coefficient [11], which is widely used for these purposes and showed good results [1]. We also considered that this coefficient depends on the level in which the respondent's response was measured.

Krippendorff's coefficients for our questions are presented in the Table 1. By convention the Krippendorff's alpha less than 0.67 indicates insufficient agreement of the coders on the given question to draw reliable conclusions [11]. Our results show that for the most questions Krippendorff's alpha does not reach the necessary threshold, so they were to be excluded from the analysis.

Table 1. Inter-coder agreement on different questions

Variable's title	Krippendorff's α	Measurement level
What is the overall author's attitude to this group/person? (negative/neutral/positive)	0,89	Ethnicity
Is the ethnic group or person portrayed as a victim or an aggressor in interethnic relations? (yes/no/unclear/irrelevant)	0,87	Ethnicity
Is the ethnic group or person portrayed as superior or inferior compared to others? (former/latter/unclear/irrelevant)	0,86	Ethnicity
How strongly a general negative sentiment is expressed in the text? (no/weak/strong)	0,82	Text
Does the text contain one, several or no ethnonyms?	0,73	Text
Does the author belong to the ethnic group s/he is writing about? (yes/no/not mentioned)	0,72	Ethnicity
How strongly a general positive sentiment is expressed in the text? (no/weak/strong)	0,70	Text

(continued)

Table 1. (*continued*)

Variable's title	Krippendorff's α	Measurement level
Does the author refer to a concrete representative of an ethnic group or to the group as a whole? (former/latter/unclear)	0,57	Ethnicity
Does the text contain the topic of religion?	0,55	Text
Does the text contain the topic of history?	0,51	Text
Does the text contain the topic of politics?	0,49	Text
Is the text? (yes/no/other language)	0,45	Text
Does the author call for offline violence against the mentioned ethnic group/person? (no/openly/latently)	0,42	Ethnicity
Does the text mention interethnic conflict? (yes/no/unclear)	0,42	Text
Does the text contain the topic of culture?	0,39	Text
Does the text contain the topic of economics?	0,38	Text
Does the text mention positive interethnic interaction? (yes/no/unclear)	0,38	Text
Is the ethnic group or person portrayed as dangerous? (yes/no/unclear)	0,33	Ethnicity
Does the text contain the topic of migration?	0,28	Text
Does the text contain understandable the topic of humor?	0,27	Text
Does the text contain the topic of ethnicity?	0,19	Text
Does the text contain any other topic?	0,17	Text
Does the text contain the topic of daily routine?	0,17	Text

Looking at such deplorable results one may ask why it is so. It should be said that we are not the first who encountered this problem. According to a recent study devoted to measuring the reliability of coding texts for the presence of hate speech in them, the convergence of the encoder responses, measured with the help of Krippendorff's alpha, varies from 0.18 to 0.29 [15]. And the consent of the coders did not depend on whether they were shown the definition of the language of hostility or they were guided only by their own criteria. The authors suggested that the problem lies in the fact that the concept of "hate speech" is a complex concept that has no unambiguous definition (similar conclusions were expressed in other works [4, 5]), and therefore it is necessary to approach its definition more carefully and divide complex concepts into simpler ones. These conclusions can also be applied to our work, since the definition of the language of hostility is closely related to our. Therefore, following the advice of the authors, we divided this concept into several simpler ones. Without it we could expect even lower results of convergence.

5 Methods and Results

In order to measure attitudes towards ethnicities we used a set of mixed regression models which allowed us to control the factors that can influence the dependent variable. Text ID was specified as random variable, and others which are ethnic group mentioned in the text, gender and ethnicity of the author as fixed. We also tested whether it is necessary to use region of author's residence as a random variable, but ICC was <0.01 so less than 1% of the variance in the variables is due to the regions.

To check the Hypothesis No. 1 we built mixed regression Model 1 with dependent variable "What is the overall author's attitude to this group/person?". Kernel density estimation plot showed that the distribution of this variable is close to normal, so we used linear regression model. As for independent variables we specified one fixed variable which is "Does the author belong to the ethnic group s/he is writing about?" and two random variables—text ID (random intercept), ethnicity (random intercept). Thus, our model assumes that the average attitude towards different ethnic groups mentioned in different documents may vary.

To test Hypothesis 2, we added to Model 1 the assumption that the relationship between the author's belonging to an ethnic group and his attitude may differ depending on the ethnic group. In other words, we assume the existence of ethnic groups whose members are less positive toward group they represent compared to others. Figure 1 shows random effects for every ethnonym in the model. The first column shows average attitude towards ethnic group, the second—the strength of author's preference to his/her own ethnic group.

Finally, we created Model 3 with additive and multiplicative interaction between variables "Gender" and "Does the author belong to the ethnic group s/he is writing about?" to test if the author's gender influences his attitude to the ethnic groups. All results are shown in the Table 2 (Fig. 2).

Table 2. Results of regression models with dependent variable "What is the overall author's attitude to this group/person?"

Variable	Model 1	Model 2	Model 3
Fixed effects			
Does the author belong to the ethnic group s/he is writing about? (Yes)	0.42 $p < 0.001$	0.43 $p < 0.001$	0.35 $p < 0.001$
Gender (Males)	–	–	−0.07 $p < 0.001$
Interaction between Gender (Males) and Author's ethnicity (Yes)	–	–	0.09 $p < 0.001$
Random effects			
Ethnic Group ICC (random intercept)	ICC = 0.05	ICC = 0.05	ICC = 0.05
Text ID (random intercept)	ICC = 0.40	ICC = 0.40	ICC = 0.39
Does the author belong to the ethnic group s/he is writing about? (random slope)	–	–	See Fig. 1
Marginal/conditional R^2	0.092/0.501	0.095/0.503	0.098/0.497

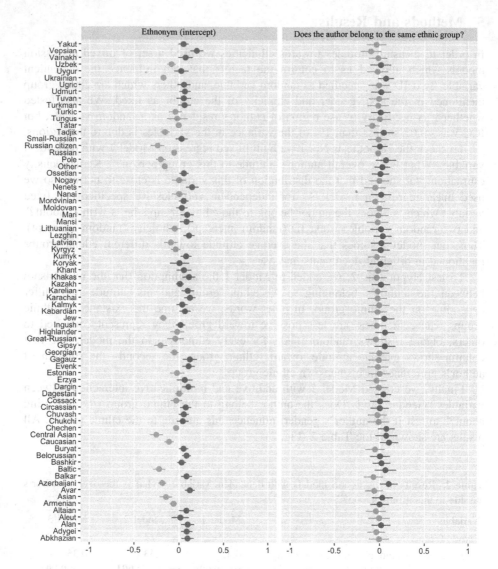

Fig. 1. Model 2: random effects.

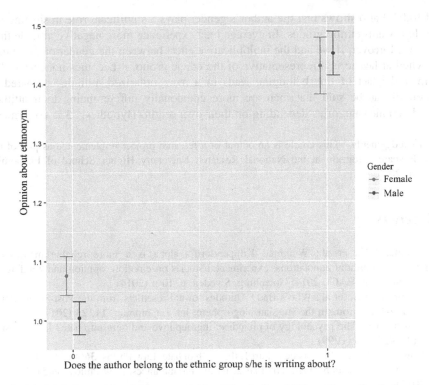

Fig. 2. Model 3: interaction between variables "Gender" and "Does the author belong to the ethnic group s/he is writing about?"

6 Conclusion

In this paper, we confirmed the hypothesis that the ethnicity of social media users has a significant effect on their attitude towards ethnic groups. This single factor accounts for 9.2% of the variance of the dependent variable in a multilevel regression model, thus Hypothesis 1 is confirmed.

At the same time, if we consider each ethnic group separately, the factor of the author's ethnicity rarely plays a significant role. Tatars, Russians, Caucasians, and Azeibajans are the few groups for which it is significant (Fig. 1). Representatives of Tatars and Russians tend to rate themselves more negatively, and representatives of Caucasians and Azeris more positively. Hereby Hypothesis 2 is partly confirmed.

The last two ethnic groups are part of the peoples of the Caucasus, regarding which in Russia is a widespread stereotype about their great national pride [14], which may explain the observed effect. Interestingly, these two ethnic groups are also characterized by a significantly more negative attitude on average, which is also confirmed by empirical researches [2].

It is more difficult to explain the lower self-esteem of the Tatars and Russians. In the case of Russians, we can refer to a study that revealed negative Russian autostereotypes, such as laziness, laxity and drunkenness [20].

Model 3 also shows that the author's gender plays a significant role in shaping the attitude towards ethnic groups. In average men experience more negative attitude than women. Moreover, if we add the multiplicative effect between the gender of the author and whether he/she is a representative of the ethnic group, it becomes noticeable that for men the fact of this belonging leads to a more polarized attitude compared to women. It can be said that men are more emotionally differentiating their attitude towards ethnic categories depending on their own origin. Hypothesis 3 is confirmed.

Acknowledgements. This article is an output of a research project implemented as part of the Basic Research Program at the National Research University Higher School of Economics (HSE) in 2018.

References

1. Antoine, J.-Y., et al.: Weighted Krippendorff's alpha is a more reliable metrics for multicoders ordinal annotations: experimental studies on emotion, opinion and coreference annotation. In: EACL 2014, Gotenborg, Sweden, p. 10 p (2014)
2. Bodrunova, S.S., et al.: Who's Bad? Attitudes toward resettlers from the Post-Soviet South versus other nations in the Russian blogosphere. Int. J. Commun. **11**, 23 (2017)
3. Brewer, M.B.: The psychology of prejudice: ingroup love and outgroup hate? J. Soc. Issues **55**(3), 429–444 (1999)
4. Brown, A.: What is hate speech? Part 1: the myth of hate. Law Philos. **36**(4), 419–468 (2017)
5. Brown, A.: What is hate speech? Part 2: family resemblances. Law Philos. **36**(5), 561–613 (2017)
6. Cassidy, K.D., et al.: The influence of ingroup/outgroup categorization on same- and other-race face processing: the moderating role of inter-versus intra-racial context. J. Exp. Soc. Psychol. **47**(4), 811–817 (2011)
7. Chan, J., et al.: The internet and racial hate crime: offline spillovers from online access. MIS Q. Manag. Inf. Syst. **40**(2), 381–403 (2016)
8. Dickter, C.L., Bartholow, B.D.: Racial ingroup and outgroup attention biases revealed by event-related brain potentials. Soc. Cogn. Affect. Neurosci. **2**(3), 189–198 (2007)
9. Fischer, R., Derham, C.: Is in-group bias culture-dependent? A meta-analysis across 18 societies. SpringerPlus **5**, 70 (2016)
10. Kietzmann, J.H., et al.: Social media? Get serious! Understanding the functional building blocks of social media. Bus. Horiz. **54**(3), 241–251 (2011)
11. Krippendorff, K.H.: Content Analysis: An Introduction to Its Methodology. Sage Publications Inc., Thousand Oaks (2003)
12. Levin, S., Sidanius, J.: Social dominance and social identity in the United States and Israel: ingroup favoritism or outgroup derogation? Polit. Psychol. **20**(1), 99–126 (1999)
13. Parker, D., Song, M.: New ethnicities and the internet. Cult. Stud. **23**(4), 583–604 (2009)
14. Rakacheva, Y.: "Caucasians" in the Russian region: formation of stereotype image and overcoming of prejudice. Soc. Sociol. Psychol. Pedagogy **2** (2012). (in Russian)
15. Ross, B., et al.: Measuring the reliability of hate speech annotations: the case of the European Refugee Crisis. arXiv:170108118 Cs (2017)
16. The Russian Census of 2010: National composition of the population. http://www.gks.ru/free_doc/new_site/perepis2010/croc/Documents/Vol4/pub-04-01.pdf
17. The Russian Census of 2010: Population by ethnicity and ability to speak Russian. http://www.gks.ru/free_doc/new_site/perepis2010/croc/Documents/Vol4/pub-04-03.pdf

18. The Telecommunication Development Sector: Percentage of individuals using the internet. https://www.itu.int/en/ITU-D/Statistics/Documents/statistics/2018/Individuals_Internet_2000-2017.xls
19. Widyanto, L., Griffiths, M.: An empirical study of problematic internet use and self-esteem. Int. J. Cyber Behav. Psychol. Learn. IJCBPL **1**(1), 13–24 (2011)
20. Kryaklina, T.F.: EHtnicheskie stereotipy kak predmet ehtnopolitologicheskogo ana-liza. Nauchno-Metodicheskij EHlektronnyj ZHurnal «Koncept» **20**, 1716–1720 (2014). (in Russian)

Holistic Monitoring and Analysis of Healthcare Processes Through Public Internet Data Collection

Oleg G. Metsker[1], Sergey A. Sikorskiy[1], Anna A. Semakova[1],
Alexey V. Krikunov[1], Marina A. Balakhontceva[1,2],
Natalia B. Melnikova[1], and Sergey V. Kovalchuk[1,2(✉)]

[1] ITMO University, Saint Petersburg, Russia
{olegmetsker, aasemakova, avkrikunov, mbalakhontceva,
kovalchuk}@corp.ifmo.ru, sikorskiy.s@hotmail.com,
naunat@mail.ru
[2] Almazov National Medical Research Centre, Saint Petersburg, Russia

Abstract. Currently, the Internet provides access to the large amount of public data describing various aspects of the healthcare system. Still, the available data has high diversity in its availability, quality, format, etc. The issues regarding collection, processing and integration of such diverse data can be overcome through the holistic semantic-based analysis of the data with data-driven predictive modeling supporting systematic checking and improving the quality of the data. This paper presents an ongoing work aimed to develop a flexible approach for holistic healthcare process analysis through integration of both private and public data of various types to support enhanced applications development: personalized health trackers, clinical decision support systems, solution for policy optimization, etc. The proposed approach is demonstrated on several experimental studies for collection and integration of data publicly available on the Internet within the context of data-driven predictive modeling in the healthcare.

Keywords: Data crawling · Public Internet data · Personalized medicine · Healthcare data

1 Introduction and Related Works

Today, the healthcare process is characterized by high complexity, a multitude of aspects and stakeholders. In order to understand and describe the healthcare system and processes, multiple aspects of a patient's life and the care system have to be collected, processed and integrated to provide the holistic view to the situation. On the other hand, there are many data sources currently available on the Internet, which describe various aspects of the healthcare from the point of view both of a patient and the healthcare system (hospitals, policymakers, etc.). One of the most fruitful sources of information is social media [1]. Nevertheless, many more sources may be considered in relation to the health: description of the healthcare system's parts (public reports, official statistics, etc.), external conditions (weather, city environment, etc.), personal

© Springer Nature Switzerland AG 2019
S. S. Bodrunova et al. (Eds.): INSCI 2018 Workshops, LNCS 11551, pp. 42–50, 2019.
https://doi.org/10.1007/978-3-030-17705-8_4

online activity (customer reports, professional online activity, etc.). These data may be collected from various websites [2, 3] and vary significantly in accessibility, quality, trustworthiness, etc. Another feature of the medicine and public health as subject areas is the weak structuredness of generated data. The data model may not be specified explicitly or absent altogether. It means that using various data sources and formats leads to development of specialized technologies for data integration. The ontology-based approach can be proposed to solve the problem of heterogeneity from the semantic aspect. For ontology description, one can use standardized models in RDF Format [4] and developed in RDF Schema [5] and OWL [6] languages. The SPARQL query language [7] is used for manipulating RDF-based data. There are some medical ontologies, which specify medical terms: SNOMED CT [8], ICD [9], UMLS [10]. According to [11], there are two strategies of ontology integration: replacement of different ontologies with a new one, which covers them all, and sharing common knowledge resources between ontologies. Regardless of the type of integration, the problem of obtaining general or common knowledge arises. Big data technologies are often used to solve the problems of collecting and integrating healthcare data [12]. To provide more convenient access to data and its unification, researchers offer a patient-centric cyber-physical system for healthcare applications and services based on cloud technologies and big data [13].

Nevertheless, partial information from different sources may support reconstruction of the healthcare system and process, mutual verification of sources and reliable description of the system and prediction of its state. Within the presented study, we consider the approach to holistic data collection and processing using diverse classes of data sources for description of the healthcare system. The results may be used to improve and extend existing data-driven predictive modeling [14], medical decision-making [15], policy elaboration [16], and other model-based solutions.

2 Public Data Sources for Complex Healthcare Process Description

Public data sources, available on the Internet, describe different aspects of the healthcare process. Below are few examples of data currently available online: personalized activity tracks in social media; feedback on healthcare services; prices in healthcare and pharmacy; description of various types of drugs; healthcare services in city environment; weather and ecology conditions (influencing health), etc.

Aiming towards the support of personalized healthcare, all the sources may be organized around the individual patient health. Within our approach, we arranged data sources into three main groups (see Fig. 1):

- information about the environment, including city environment, natural environment, available services (including healthcare as a service);
- information about personal statements and activities of a patient, including social, professional, financial activities and health conditions;
- information about the healthcare system, including the structure and operations of healthcare organizations, professional activities of doctors, etc.

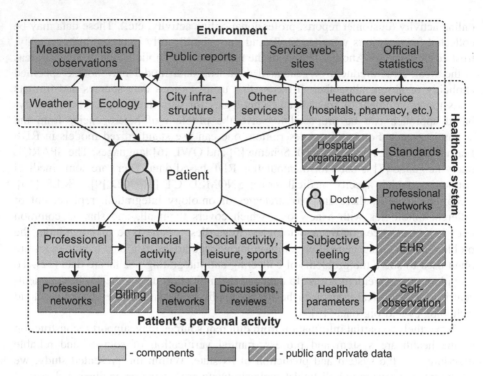

Fig. 1. Data sources for complex healthcare process description

We consider two types of physical persons, involved in the data generation, namely, the patient and the doctor (or a healthcare professional in general). Adding the doctor as a source of information is caused by two reasons: (a) subjective, personalized professional activity of the doctor may be reflected in the profile of organization or professional social networks (see, e.g. professional social network "Doctor at work", popular among Russian physicians[1]); (b) assessment of particular doctors (especially those of high expertise) by the patients published in the organization website or in independent resources.

Along with public data sources, we consider private data, which may be available within the context of the particular task and under the limited conditions. E.g., self-observation data or personal billing data may be used within the personalized recommending system. Electronic health records and data on hospital organization may be used in a context of clinical decision-making. Private data sources may play a crucial role in the integration process within a particular application. Therefore, we consider them along with data publicly available on the Internet.

The available data sources may have a different format, accessing procedures, and level of formalization. For example, the following entities may be considered as data sources within the considered context:

---

[1] https://www.doktornarabote.ru/.

- websites as a collection of web-pages with internal and external web links;
- documents published online in a form of web-pages or explicit documents (e.g., pdf-files);
- datasets, available for downloading;
- streaming data.

Finally, the data may have different purpose, interpretation and description target. For example:

- descriptive data provides information about existing objects, processes, conditions (weather conditions, health parameters, drug lists, etc.);
- regulatory documents (standards, laws, rules, policies, etc.) provide prescriptive information about particular processes;
- estimations of various states (diagnosis, subjective feeling, quality assessment, etc.);
- opinions and discussions in a free form published in a forum, blogs, discussion groups, etc.;
- aggregated reports with various kind of statistical analysis of the healthcare system and processes.

The mentioned diversity in characteristics of data sources leads to the following requirements for technological solutions for data collection, processing and integration:

- technology for data collection (e.g., based on crawling engines [17]) should be flexible and adaptable for various data sources and structures;
- considering the multitude of aspects in the healthcare process, semantic data structures should be used for unification and integration of data from various sources;
- while many data sources are per se imperfect (subjective, uncertain, imprecise, etc.), the quality of integrated data should be carefully controlled;
- data integration should be supported with holistic descriptive and predictive modeling [14] to control uncertainty and support target application development.

3   Experimental Study

We conducted two experimental studies for applying the proposed approach. The first one was about the collection and structuring of medical information from public Internet data sources. As a result, therapy data with 6,000 drug names were retrieved. The second experimental study was the cost estimate of treatment based on consumer basket data and data on pharmacy costs from open sources.

3.1   Collection and Structuring of Medical Information from Public Internet Data

Monitoring of open source medical data, as we have mentioned earlier, is a complex task. The solution for this problem includes not only trivial data crawling, but also the development of methods for integrating and unifying data from heterogeneous sources.

To ensure semantic interoperability of heterogeneous data and knowledge sources in case of public Internet data for the healthcare, it is necessary to use several ontological specifications from different fields of knowledge. For practical use of heterogeneous data and knowledge at the semantic level in decision-making, it is necessary to produce compliance of ontological models. As part of an experimental study, a conceptual scheme was proposed (see Fig. 2). This scheme reflects the main stages and entities of monitoring data to improve their quality within the collection and structuring processes. The main feature of this scheme is orientation to text mining and predictive data-based models.

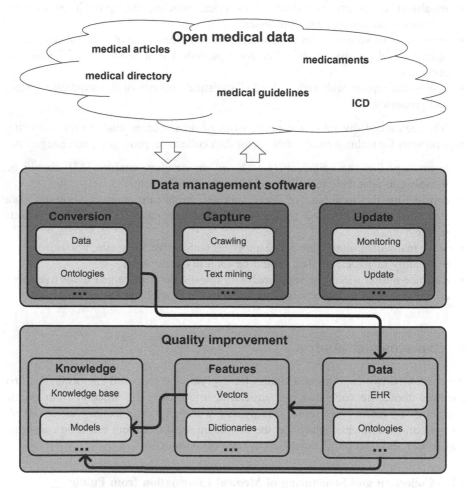

Fig. 2. Scheme for collection and structuring of open source medical data.

The results of the experiment on collection and structuring of medical information from open source medical data are described below. During the experiment, it was possible to collect and structure medical data on various types of drugs and diseases.

Electronic healthcare records (EHR) have significant variability. The same treatment can be provided with different drugs and recorded in the medical information system (MIS) in different terms. Doctors can describe the same disease using different synonyms. This makes a direct analysis of EHR much more difficult. Medical open source data which include e.g. a reference guide, medical guidelines, ICD, medical directory, medical articles contains significantly structured information, which, with the right approach, can improve the quality of knowledge extraction from EHR. This, in turn, can improve the quality of prognostic models based on this knowledge, which in consequence can improve the quality of clinical decisions and healthcare quality. It was possible to collect and structure the following data: a drug with an active ingredient, international name and code of the drug, interaction with other types of drugs, diseases, in case of which the drug is used, synonyms of diseases and ICD codes.

Use of such knowledge in pre-processing of MIS data allows reducing features dimension describing the treatment process. Reduced data complexity improves the quality of predictive models and improves performance. For example, in the impact analysis of the treatment process by therapy, it is essential to know an active ingredient; in some cases, only its pharmacological group, and not a drug name. As a result, the collection of therapy data with 6,000 drug names has been retrieved. The active ingredient of these drugs constitutes just 1,800 variants in 1,000 pharmacological groups, which reduces the features therapy vector by 3 or 6 times. Thus, it becomes possible to conduct flexible analysis and modeling of treatment processes regarding therapy factors at different scales, depending on the task.

3.2   Cost Estimate of Treatment Based on Public Internet Data

As part of this experiment, the cost of treating patients with a diagnosis of arterial hypertension was evaluated. Appointment of pharmacotherapy after confirmation of hypertension does not always depend on the formal recommendations only. It is necessary to take into account not only the health condition of the patient, but also his financial well-being. The physician that prescribes the therapy cannot always get relevant information on the financial component of the treatment process. The relationship between the dynamics of the average receipt index based on data on the consumer basket and the dynamics of the average receipt in the pharmacy is considered. The consumer basket reflects the information on purchases that come in online mode from 35,000 customers in cities with a population of 10,000 people [18]. The average receipt in a pharmacy is calculated as the weighted average cost of treating one patient during a month as a part of monotherapy with recommended antihypertensive drugs [19]. The dynamics of the average receipt in a pharmacy is estimated separately for each recommended antihypertensive drug, expressed in the most common active ingredients: Metoprolol (beta-blocker), Perindopril (ACE inhibitor), Losartan (sartan), Amlodipine (calcium antagonist), Indapamide (diuretic). Figure 3 shows the results for the three drugs. The results show (a) downtrend for Amlodipine; (b) side trend for Indapamide; (c) uptrend for Metoprolol.

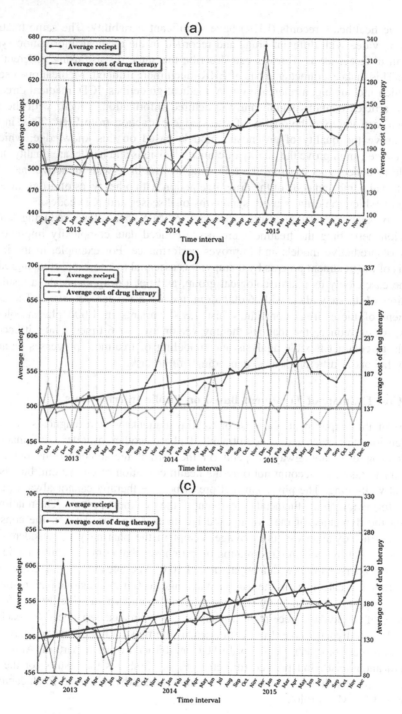

Fig. 3. The dynamics of the average receipt for the consumer basket and the average receipt for (a) Amlodipine; (b) Indapamide; (c) Metoprolol

4   Conclusion and Future Works

The proposed approach is aimed to develop a holistic technology for collection, processing and integration of both private and public data. It includes crawling technology to collect public data on the Internet, semantic technology to integrate data and predictive modeling elements to improve the quality and consistency of data. The presented work is currently ongoing. Main directions for further development include (a) formal description of basic concepts for the holistic healthcare process description which are needed for automation of data collection and processing; (b) development of the semantic data integration technology based on existing and original ontologies for healthcare domain; (c) extension of experimentally collected data from various public sources within a context of the holistic healthcare process description; (d) use of obtained integrated data for predictive modeling of healthcare processes both on public and personal level.

Acknowledgements. This research is financially supported by The Russian Scientific Foundation, Agreement #17-15-01177.

References

1. More, S., Joshi, P.P.: Novel approach for data mining of social media to improve health care using network-based modeling. Int. J. Emerg. Trends Technol. **4**, 8189–8192 (2017)
2. Lutes, J., Park, M., Luo, B., Chen, X.: Healthcare information networks: discovery and evaluation. In: 2011 IEEE First International Conference on Healthcare Informatics, Imaging and Systems Biology, pp. 190–197. IEEE (2011)
3. Berland, G.K., et al.: Health information on the internet. Access. Qual. Readability Engl. Span. JAMA **285**, 2612–2621 (2001)
4. RDF - Semantic Web Standards. https://www.w3.org/RDF/
5. RDF Schema 1.1. https://www.w3.org/TR/rdf-schema/
6. OWL 2 Web Ontology Language Document Overview, 2nd edn. https://www.w3.org/TR/owl2-overview/
7. Aliprand, J.: Unicode Consortium.: The Unicode Standard. Addison-Wesley, Boston (2003)
8. SNOMED International. https://www.snomed.org/snomed-ct
9. WHO: International Classification of Diseases, 11th Revision (ICD-11). WHO (2018)
10. Unified Medical Language System (UMLS). https://www.nlm.nih.gov/research/umls/
11. Riaño, D., et al.: An ontology-based personalization of health-care knowledge to support clinical decisions for chronically ill patients. J. Biomed. Inform. **45**, 429–446 (2012)
12. Wang, Y., Kung, L., Byrd, T.A.: Big data analytics: understanding its capabilities and potential benefits for healthcare organizations. Technol. Forecast. Soc. Change **126**, 3–13 (2018)
13. Zhang, Y., Qiu, M., Tsai, C.-W., Hassan, M.M., Alamri, A.: Health-CPS: healthcare cyber-physical system assisted by cloud and big data. IEEE Syst. J. **11**, 88–95 (2017)
14. Krikunov, A.V., Bolgova, E.V., Krotov, E., Abuhay, T.M., Yakovlev, A.N., Kovalchuk, S.V.: Complex data-driven predictive modeling in personalized clinical decision support for acute coronary syndrome episodes. Procedia Comput. Sci. **80**, 518–529 (2016)

15. Kovalchuk, S.V., Krotov, E., Smirnov, P.A., Nasonov, D.A., Yakovlev, A.N.: Distributed data-driven platform for urgent decision making in cardiological ambulance control. Future Gener. Comput. Syst. **79**, 144–154 (2018)
16. Kovalchuk, S.V., Moskalenko, M.A., Yakovlev, A.N.: Towards model-based policy elaboration on city scale using game theory: application to ambulance dispatching. In: Shi, Y., et al. (eds.) ICCS 2018. LNCS, vol. 10860, pp. 404–417. Springer, Cham (2018). https://doi.org/10.1007/978-3-319-93698-7_31
17. Butakov, N., Petrov, M., Mukhina, K., Nasonov, D., Kovalchuk, S.: Unified domain-specific language for collecting and processing data of social media. J. Intell. Inf. Syst. **51**, 389–414 (2018)
18. Romir Scan Panel. http://romir.ru/consumer_scan_panel
19. Drug ordering service. https://apteka.ru/

"All these …": Negative Opinion About People and "Pejorative Plural" in Russian

Olga Blinova(✉)

Saint Petersburg State University,
7/9 Universitetskaya nab., St. Petersburg 199034, Russia
o.blinova@spbu.ru

Abstract. The paper discusses plural forms of Russian nouns (in particular, of the surnames) like *vsjakie tam Ivanovy* ('various Ivanovs', 'all sorts of Ivanovs'), expressing negative opinion about the referents. The co-occurrence patterns of the Pl.Pej forms by Web-corpus data is revealed. Pl.Pej forms foremost fit together with universal quantifiers including 'all', 'all of these' etc., and can be easily integrate in quantificational expressions, e.g., combinations with numerals, collective nouns, and expressions that include number words like *mnogo* ('many'). These elements are able to convey and support the meaning of multiplicity, non-uniqueness of the objects, denoted by forms of Pl.Pej.

Among the usages of Pl.Pej the names of "oligarchs" and "right-wing, liberal politicians" predominate. The form mainly appears in heavily politicized texts. The studied form and co-occurrence patterns are a legacy of the Soviet socio-political discourse and originate from the language of Soviet newspapers.

The Pl.Pej form is still a part of an aggressive leftist discourse, directed against a "group of the rich". The addressant of such discourse is a representative of a "group of the poor, oppressed, socially humiliated".

Keywords: Russian · Internet · Web-corpus · Hate speech ·
Secondary meanings of plural · Proper noun · Pejorative plural ·
Humbling names · Co-occurrence

1 One Secondary Meaning of Grammatical Number in Russian

Linguists distinguish a range of secondary meanings of grammatical number in Russian. One of them is so called "pejorative plural" form of a noun.

According to [1], there is, inter alia, "hyperbolic plural" of the type *Ty chto eto klumby*-Pl *topchesh*? ('Why are you trampling on the flower beds-Pl?', the context concerns only one object), and "plural of pejorative alienation", or "negative plural" of the type *Ja verchus' kak prokljataja, a ty po teatram*-Pl *hodish* 'I'm like a damned squirrel on a treadmill, and you are visiting the theaters-Pl'. A separate submeaning is so called "pejorative plural" like *Tam vystupajut vsjakie pugachevy*-Pl *i kirkorovy*-Pl 'Various pugachevas and kirkorovs sing there' [1].

S. S. Bodrunova et al. (Eds.): INSCI 2018 Workshops, LNCS 11551, pp. 51–60, 2019.
https://doi.org/10.1007/978-3-030-17705-8_5

The forms of the type *pugachevy-Pl*, *kirkorovy-Pl*, denoting persons, derived from proper nouns, with an "observable negative shade of meaning of the referents of word forms in plural" [1] will be studied in this paper.

The forms of Pl from the names of persons have an "intermediate" nature: such forms are "in between" the proper and common nouns [2]. Semantic peculiarities of pejorative plural forms (Pl.Pej), which arise, according to N. Pertsov, as a result of the connotation "limited quantity ~ large quantity" should influence compatibility, making it possible, in particular, to create combinations with quantifiers.

This paper aims at study of composition of noun phrases with Pl.Pej forms. Such study will allow to pick out the stable features, supporting the connotation "limited quantity ~ large quantity" and the meaning of non-uniqueness of referents of plural forms in question.

This study is based on materials taken from the Internet and collected in large web corpus. These are texts from thousands of various sites of the domain ***.ru.

2   The Usages of Pejorative Plural in the Web Corpus

The co-occurrence patterns of pejorative plural (Pl.Pej) forms is studied on the basis of the searching results in the RuTenTen corpus [3]. The first searching was performed by morphological tags using Corpus Query Language. The parameters, proposed in "MULTEXTEast Morphosyntactic Specifications" [4] were used. The searching results for the query [tt_tag = "Npcpny"] specifying "common" gender and the case, are more consistent with the aims of analyzing the forms Pl.Pej. This search was repeated for all case forms (see the Fig. 1 below).

The frequency lists for searching output were analyzed, and the lists of lowercase spellings were created. It became clear, that with lowercase letters mostly well-known surnames are written. First and foremost, these are the surnames of very wealthy businessmen ("oligarchs"), politicians and officials, scientists, terrorists.

After the searching by word forms it emerged that usages of plural from the scientists' surnames like *ejnshtejny* 'einsteins' do not have any negative connotations, cf.: *budushhie ejnshtejny sjehalis' v Novosibirsk na Vserossijskuju olimpiadu po fizike* 'Future einsteins came to Novosibirsk to the All-Russia olympiad in physics'.

Conversely, the output of searching by the surnames of businessmen, politicians, pop singers contains the usages of Pl.Pej forms. This is correlated with the I.I. Revzin's observations on the neutralization of opposition singular/plural and "journalistic expedients" of Soviet-era newspapers with humbling names of the type *zoshchenki*, *jungmany*, beginning with a lowercase letter [5].

As a result of the searching by word forms using POS tag and retaining case type like [word = "sidorovy" & tag = "N.*"] 4,105 sentences were fetched, 3,730 sentences contained forms we were searching for. The top-10 entries are listed in the Table 1.

Table 1. Search results (data for 3,730 sentences)

Freq	Word form
1185	*abramovichej*
1052	*chubajsov*
767	*chubajsy*
447	*gajdary*
222	*el'ciny*
219	*deripasok*
204	*gajdarov*
145	*berezovskih*
139	*abramovicham*
134	*chubajsam*

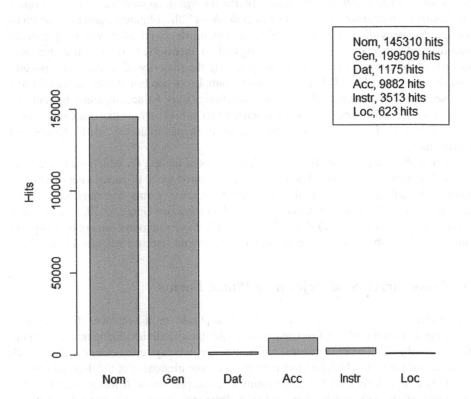

Nom, 145310 hits
Gen, 199509 hits
Dat, 1175 hits
Acc, 9882 hits
Instr, 3513 hits
Loc, 623 hits

Fig. 1. Search results, obtained by queries of the type [tt_tag = "Npcpny"]

Among the usages of Pl.Pej the names of "oligarchs" and "right-wing, liberal politicians" predominate. So, by the surnames of the "oligarchs" 72% of all relevant sentences were found.

The uses of Pl.Pej forms are found primarily in heavily politicized texts, many of which could be called agitational or propagandist.

As a result of assessing the frequency of certain surnames in the Pl.Pej form, a kind of "unpopularity rating" could be formed. The second position after "oligarchs" will be taken by the politicians. Then follow celebrities and artists, terrorists, and foreign businessmen (*billy gejtsy* 'bill-Pl gates-Pl' and some other).

Verbally attacked group can be described by an explicit common name, cf: *oligarhi* 'oligarchs', *liberasty* 'liberasts' (the derogatory name, associated with the noun *liberal* 'liberal' and the noun *pederast* 'gay'), *pravye* 'right-wing politicians', *pravye liberasty* 'right-wing liberasts', *reformatory* 'reformers', *liberal-reformatory* 'liberal reformers', *ugnetateli trudjashhejsja Rossii* 'oppressors of working Russia', *vragi naroda* 'public enemies', *izmenniki* 'traitors', *demokratizatory* 'democratizers' etc. The following example is fairly typical: *oligarhi potaniny, abramovichi, chernomyrdiny i prochie chubajsy, lishiv v odnochas'e ves' sovetskij narod vseh prirodnyh i drugih bogatstv, ne tol'ko prisvoili sebe jeti bogatstva, no i razrushili vsjo narodnoe hozjaj-stvo, vvergnuv bol'shinstvo truzhenikov v nishhetu i bezyshodnost'* 'the oligarchs, potanins, abramo-vichs, chernomyrdins and other chubaises, having deprived all Soviet people of all natural and other riches, not only arrogated to themselves these riches, but also destroyed the entire national economy, plunging the majority of workers into poverty and despair'. Anti-liberal rhetoric in some examples is combined with nationalist and anti-semitic. The criticism of artists and celebrities may be accompanied by anti-gay attacks, cf. the following example: *sodomity i razvratniki vseh mastej, moiseevy, verki, tatu i izhe s nimi* 'catamites and libertines of all stripes moiseevy, verki, tattoos and others like them'.

The authors seek to forcibly create plural forms of names, for which the plural form coincides with the singular. The Pl forms are formed even in cases where such for-mation is difficult. As a result, the output contains forms like *kirienki*-Nom.pl, *shumejki*-Nom.Pl, *kirienkov*-Gen(Acc).Pl, *aleksashenkov*-Gen(Acc).Pl, *svanidz*-Gen (Acc).Pl, *orbakajt*-Gen(Acc).Pl etc. If the plural form of a surname cannot be formed in any way, the authors add to the last name a first name like in *vladimiry*-Pl *mau*-Pl.

3   Co-occurrence of Pejorative Plural Forms

According to [6], proper noun is "a word, a phrase or a sentence, that serves to distinguish a named object from series of similar ones, individualizing and identifying the given object". The Pl.Pej forms, apparently, are to be systematically combined with elements of context, which indicate multiplicity, nonuniqueness of the denoted objects.

This article deals with the components of noun phrases with forms of Pl.Pej. The elements of the left context are analyzed. Primarily these are universal quantifiers (attributive pronouns such as *vse, vsjakie* 'all') counting nouns *desjatki sidorovyh* 'tens of sidorovs', and adverbs and adverbial expressions as part of quantificational phrases like *mnogo sidorovyh* 'many sidorovs', nouns denoting "group of people" as in the example *kuchka sidorovyh* 'group of sidorovs' etc.

The real surnames in the cited examples with the of *ivanovs, petrovs, sidorovs* are replaced. Forms of Pl.Pej in the output routinely belong to long compound noun phrases of the type *vse eti ivanovy, petrovy, sidorovy, kuznecovy, smirnovy i drugie vasil'evy* 'all these ivanovs, petrovs, kuznetsovs and other vassilievs' or comitative-compound noun phrases of the type *kakie-nibud' ivanovy s petrovymi i prochie sidorovy* 'whatever ivanovs with petrovs and other sidorovs'. The number of the forms of pejorative plural in examples is saved (to showcase the bulkiness of noun phrases). It is necessary to determine certain contextual components, which can support the connotation "limited quantity ~ large quantity".

3.1 Components of Noun Phrases of the Type *raznye* -A *sidorovy*-N 'Various Sidorovs'

In noun phrases of the type AN (there N is a form of pejorative plural in any case, A is an prepositional attribute) the following components are used:

- universal pronoun *vse*-Pl 'all',
- pronouns and adjectives, "pointing to an arbitrary object of the set" [7] *vsjakie, vsjakie tam, vsjacheskie* 'different, all sorts of, every',
- adjectives *raznye, raznoobraznye, razlichnye, vsevozmozhnye* 'various, diverse, any' and 'all',
- demonstrative pronouns *eti* 'these', *te zhe* 'those' (about the possibility of pejorative use of demonstrative pronouns in Russian, see, e.g., [8], cf. Table 2.

Table 2. The most frequent components of noun phrases of the type AN

vsjakie 'all kinds' (#114)	*te zhe* 'the same' (#8)
vse, vse eti 'all these' (#43), (#174)	*drugie* 'other' (#5)
eti 'these' (#37)	*raznoobraznye* 'various' (#4)
svoi 'one's own' (#33)	*kakie-nibud'* 'some' (#3)
raznye 'different, various' (#30)	*razlichnye* 'various' (#3)
vsjakie tam 'all sorts of' (#22)	*ocherednye* 'yet other' (#3)
vsevozmozhnye 'all possible' (#16)	*vsjacheskie* 'various' (#2)
nikakie 'none of' (#11)	*beschislennye* 'countless' (#2)

The specified elements are able to form chains of two, three or more components, cf.: *vse eti* 'all these' (#174), *vse vashi, vsjakie eti, vsjakie raznye, vsjakie prochie, prochie raznye, eti samye, te zhe samye, eti gadkie, svoi primitivnye, vsevozmozhnye beskonechnye, vsjo novye i novye, vse i vsjacheskie, vse eti vashi, vse eti rjazhenye* etc.

A set of adjectives, defining forms of Pl.Pej, is much wider, than the list, presented in Table 2. This table is listing predominantly the adjectives, which are close in meaning to pronouns (*raznye, raznoobraznye, vsevozmozhnye*), adjectives with a semantic component 'many', 'large number' (*beschislennye, mnogochislennye, beskonechnye*). Such adjectives do not express any explicit evaluation, as well as other most common adjectives used with the forms of Pl.Pej: *novye* 'new-Pl' (#26), *mestnye* 'local-Pl' (#15), *nyneshnie* 'current-Pl' (#15), *togdashnie* 'of that time' (#14), *budushhie* 'future-Pl' (#7), *otechestvennye* 'homegrown-Pl' (#6).

At the same time, evaluative adjectives occur in the output, but do not prevail, cf. Table 3.

Table 3. Adjectives of negative evaluation

Adjective	Count	Adjective	Count
presytivshiesja	4	dremuchie	1
***dskie	2	zhirejushhie	1
gadkie	2	zhirinovistye	1
zhirnye	2	zaokeanskie	1
zhirujushhie	2	nabedokurivshie	1
zabugornye	2	nabitye	1
kartavye	2	naglye	1
melkie	2	nedobitye	1
merzkie	2	nedruzheskie	1
nenavistnye	2	neradivye	1
nerusskie	2	operetochnye	1
neschastnye	2	podlye	1
novojavlennye	2	primitivnye	1
obogashhajushhiesja	2	proamerikanskie	1
odurevshie	2	prodazhnye	1
sytye	2	samodovol'nye	1
shustrye	2	soplivye	1
bol'nye	1	tolstye	1
vorovatye	1	uzhasnye	1
demonicheskie	1	ushlye	1
domoroshhennye	1	hor'kovatye	1

3.2   Components of Quantificational Expressions with Pl.Pej

In the noun phrases of the type NumN, NquantN.GEN, NgroupN.GEN, AdvN.GEN, there N is a case form like *sidorovyh*-Gen, Acc, *sidorovym*-Dat, *sidorovymi*-Instr, N. GEN – is a case form of genitive *sidorovyh*-Gen, Num – is a quantitative or collective numeral, Nquant – is a quantitative noun like *sotnja* 'hundred', *pjatok* 'quint', *para* 'pair', Ngroup – is a collective noun like *banda* 'gang', *armija* 'army', *klika* 'cabal', Adv – is a adverb or adverbial expression like *mnogo* 'many', *t'ma t'mushhaja* 'jillion', primarily the components, indicated in Table 4, are used.

In combinations of the type NgroupN.GEN also other collective nouns are used, cf.: *vataga* 'band, horde', *klika* 'cabal, clique', *vorovskaja klika* 'thievery clique', *klan* 'clan', *kogorta* 'cohort', *komanda* 'command', *uzkaja gruppa* 'narrow group', *shobla* 'motley crew, rabble', *gruppirovka* 'grouping', *konglamerat* 'conglomerate', *krug* 'scope', *kucha* 'trickle', *nebol'shaja kogorta* 'little cohort', *nebol'shaja oligarhicheskaja gruppirovka* 'little oligarchic grouping', *neprikasaemaja kasta* 'untouchable caste', *nyneshnjaja koloda* 'current deck', *tolpa* 'crowd' etc.

Table 4. Components of noun phrases of the type NumN

kuchka 'trickle' (#11)
svora 'doggery' (#5)
mnogo 'many' (#4)
desjatok 'ten' (#4)
sonm 'swarm, array' (#4)
para 'pair' (#2)
s desjatok 'ten, appr.' (#2)
skol'ko 'how much' (#2)

A few nouns (*svora* 'doggery', *klika* 'cabal, clique', *shobla* 'motley crew, rabble' etc.) have extreme negative connotations. Some lexemes were actively used in Soviet-era social and political discourse, cf. the collocations like *kapitalisticheskaja klika* 'capitalist clique', *burzhuaznaja svora* 'bourgeois gang'. The other came from criminal jargon and typically used in informal registers, cf. *shobla* 'motley crew, rabble'.

3.3 Some Constructions with Forms of Pejorative Plural

Alternative means for expressing the "multiplicity" and "nonuniqueness" are the constructions. The most common are:

- elective construction with preposition *iz* 'of', 'of',
- constructions, that mean belonging to a certain class of objects with *tipa* 'of the type',
- expressions like *raznogo roda*, *vsjakogo roda* 'all sorts'.

Firstly, it is an elective construction with preposition *iz* of the type *mnogie iz* N. GEN 'many of N.GEN', *odin iz* N.GEN 'one of N.GEN', *koe-kto iz* N.GEN 'someone of N.GEN', *nekotorye iz* N.GEN 'some of N.GEN', *nikto iz* N.GEN 'none of N.GEN', cf.: *koe-kogo iz ivanovyh i petrovyh ne povesili* 'some of ivanovs and petrovs were not hanged'; *sovremennoj dejatel'nosti koe-kogo iz sidorovyh i kuznecovyh* 'current activities of some of the sidorovs and kuznetsovs'; *hot' odin iz nashih "petrovyh"* 'at least one of our "petrovs"'; *mnogie iz "sidorovyh"* 'many of sidorovs'.

It is also worth mentioning the construction with preposition *sredi* 'among', cf. *ne nabljudaju sredi ivanovyh, petrovyh i sidorovyh hotja by odnogo professora Preobrazhenskogo* 'I don't observe at least one professor Preobrazhensky among ivanovs, petrovs and sidrovs'.

Secondly, it there is a construction, that means belonging to a certain class of objects with *tipa* N.GEN 'of the type', *vrode* N.GEN 'kind of', see the following examples: *"velikie gosudarstvennichki" tipa ivanovyh, petrovyh, sidorovyh, kuznecovyh, smirnovyh, vasil'evyh* 'great statesmans such as ivanovs, petrovs, sidorovs, kuznetsovs, smyrnovs, vassilievs'; *soblazniteli – sovratiteli tipa nyneshnih sidorovyh* 'seducers such as the current sidorovs'; *vplot' do nedoumkov tipa ivanovyh* 'up to idiots like ivanovs'; *pijavki, tipa ivanovyh i petrovyh* 'leeches, such as ivanovs and petrovs'; *pijavok na tele obshhestva vrode raznyh kuznecovyh i smirnovyh* 'leeches on the body of society like different kuznetsovs and smirnovs', cf. constructions with collective substantive *izbavitsja ot shushery tipa sidorovyh* 'get rid of rag-tags like sidorovs'.

Finally, one should also mention expressions like *raznogo roda, vsjakogo roda* 'all sorts', *vseh mastej* 'of all stripes', such as: *vsjakogo roda ivanovyh, petrovyh, sidorovyh i prochih ugnetatelej trudjashhihsja Rossii* 'all sorts of ivanovs, petrovs, sidorovs and other oppressors of working people'; *simvoly jasny vsjakogo roda sidorovym, kuznecovym, smirnovym i prochim provodnikam i storonnikam kapitalizma* 'the symbols are clear to all sorts of sidorovs, kuznetsovs, smirnovs and other adherers and supporters of capitalism'. These expressions are close in meaning to the pronouns and adjectives *vsjakie, raznye, raznoobraznye, razlichnye, vsjacheskie*.

4 Conclusion

This paper shows some elements of the context used together with forms of Pl.Pej. These elements are very different in their syntactic behavior, but are able to convey and support the meaning of multiplicity, non-uniqueness of the objects, denoted by forms of Pl.Pej. The forms of pejorative plural foremost fit together with

1. quantifiers:

   - attributive and other pronouns,
   - adjectives like *vsevozmozhnye* 'of all sorts';

2. words that convey the meaning of the quantity:

   - numerals,
   - collective substantives,
   - collective nouns (names of groups of the type *banda* 'gang', *svora* 'doggery'),
   - adverbs like *mnogo* 'many'.

In addition, they are embedded in elective constructions and constructions with *tipa* and *vrode* (*shushera tipa sidorovyh* 'rag-tags like sidorovs'). And finally, the forms in question are used with the expressions *raznogo roda, vsjakogo roda, vseh mastej*.

The elements of left context are considered, while in the right context there are various components of bulky noun groups, which make them even longer. This are expressions like *<sidorovy> i prochie ivanovy, i drugie petrovy, i tomu podobnye kuznecovy, i prochee zhul'jo, i vsjacheskaja inaja drjan', a takzhe i pr., i t.d., i t.p., etc., i Ko, i prochaja, i kompanija, sotovarishhi*. Such expressions serve to convey the same meanings of multiplicity and non-uniqueness, cf. Table 5 below.

Table 5. 4-word clusters for the term "*abramovichi*"

Rank	Cluster
1	*abramovichi i t.d*
2	*abramovichi, fridmany, urinsony i*
3	*abramovichi i izhe s*
4	*abramovichi i ostal'nye gajdary*
5	*abramovichi i prochie gajdary*
6	*abramovichi i prochie grefy*
7	*abramovichi i chubajsy po*
8	*abramovichi, deripaski, gusinskie, hodorkovskie*
9	*abramovichi, fridmany i deripaski*
10	*abramovichi, chernomyrdiny i prochie*
11	*abramovichi, chubajsy tiho tyrjat*
12	*abramovichi, chubajsy, gusinskie i*
13	*abramovichi, chubajsy, fridmany, fel'dmany*
14	*abramovichi afrikanskomu narodu prosveshhenie*
15	*abramovichi bolee, chto ona*
16	*abramovichi zhe samoe, chto*
17	*abramovichi i veksel'bergi nadejutsja*
18	*abramovichi i vsjakaja merzost'*
19	*abramovichi i deripaski, pu*
20	*abramovichi i im podobnye*

Hence, in the article on a sample of sentences with forms of pejorative plural, derived from proper nouns (family names), denoting persons, the context elements accompanying these forms are defined. It can be assumed, that these elements will be able to diagnose the presence of various nouns denoting people with a negative evaluation of the referents.

The form of pejorative plural appears in heavily politicized texts. It is formed primarily from the family names of rich businessmen (so called "oligarchs") and some politicians. It seems that the studied form and co-occurrence patterns are a legacy of the Soviet socio-political discourse and originate from the language of Soviet newspapers.

The Pl.Pej form is still a part of an aggressive leftist discourse, directed against a "group of the rich". The addressant of such discourse is a representative of a "group of the poor, oppressed, socially humiliated", cf. the following examples: *my soglasilis' byt' rabami i rabotat' na nih – karaganovyh, abramovichej, chubajsov i prochih kapitalistov* 'we agreed to be slaves and work for them – for karaganovs, abramovichs, chubaises and other capitalists', *a za kogo voevat' to nado, za chubajsa abramovichej i vseh aligarhov* <sic>, *a my s hleba na vodu perebivaemsja* 'and for whom it is necessary to fight for, for chubais abramovichs and all aligarchs, and we are living from hand to mouth'.

In the considered examples one can observe how the name of a person turns into the name of a group possessing significant properties of the name's owner. The form of Pl.Pej denote negative evaluation of the referents. However, this negative evaluation is not so often marked additionally (for example, with the help of evaluative adjectives).

References

1. Pertsov, N.V.: Invariants in the Russian Inflection [Invarianty v russkom slovoizmenenii]. Iazyki russkoi kul'tury Publ., Moscow (2001). (in Russian)
2. Penkovsky, A.B.: Essays on Russian Semantics [Ocherki po russkoj semantike]. Iazyki russkoi kul'tury Publ., Moscow (2004). (in Russian)
3. Russian Web 2011 (ruTenTen11). Corpus description. https://www.sketchengine.co.uk/rutenten-corpus/. Accessed 01 June 2018
4. MULTEXT-East Morphosyntactic Specifications, Version 4. 3.10.3. Russian Noun. https://www.sketchengine.co.uk/russian-tagset/. Accessed 01 June 2018
5. Revzin, I.I.: The so called "non-marked plural" in Russian [Tak nazyvaemoe "nemarkirovannoe mnozhestvennoe chislo" v sovremennom russkom jazyke]. In: Issues in Linguistics, vol. 3, pp. 102–110 (1969). (in Russian)
6. Yartseva, V.N. (ed.): Linguistic Encylopaedic Dictionary [Lingvisticheskij enciklopedicheskij slovar']. The Great Russian Encyclopedia Publ., Moscow (2002). (in Russian)
7. Levin, Ju.I.: On semantics of pronouns [O semantike mestoimenij]. In: Some problems of grammatical modeling [Problemy grammaticheskogo modelirovanija]. Nauka, Moscow (1973). (in Russian)
8. Krasavina, O.N.: Demonstrative group usage in Russian narrative discourse [Upotreblenie ukazatel'noj gruppy v russkom povestvovatel'nom diskurse]. In: Issues in Linguistics, no. 3, pp. 51–68 (2004). (in Russian)

Detecting Pivotal Points in Social Conflicts via Topic Modeling of Twitter Content

Anna S. Smoliarova[⊠] ⓘ, Svetlana S. Bodrunova ⓘ,
Alexandr V. Yakunin ⓘ, Ivan Blekanov ⓘ, and Alexey Maksimov ⓘ

St. Petersburg State University,
Universitetskaya nab. 7/9, 199034 St. Petersburg, Russia
a.smolyarova@spbu.ru

Abstract. The linkages between intensity and topicality of online discussions, on one hand, and those of offline on-street political activity, on the other hand, have recently become a subject of studies around the world. But the results of quantitative assessment of causal relations between onsite and online activities of citizens are contradictory. In our research, we use conflicts with violent triggers and the subsequent lines of events that include street rallies, political manifestations, and/or peaceful mourning, as well as public political talk, to trace the pivotal points in the conflict via measuring Twitter content. We show that in some cases Granger test does not work well, like in the case of Cologne mass harassment, for detecting the causality between online and onsite activities. In order to suggest a way to qualitatively assess the linkages between online and offline activities of users, we deploy topic modeling and further qualitative assessment of the changes in the topicality to link the topic saliency to the time of offline events. We detect several periods with varying topicality and link them to what was going on in the offline conflict.

Keywords: Twitter · Social conflicts · Topic modeling · Granger test · Spillover

1 Theoretical Framework

Twitter is believed to be actively used in protest activities for mobilization [1, 2]. Researchers tried to study as many factors as possible to understand why the street protests start in one case and do not start others; why their dynamic may be different (see review in [3]). Majority of researchers agree upon the fact that social media platforms, including Twitter, are actively used during social unrests or street actions as a main source of information [4, 5]. Social media help activists organize street actions and mobilize potential supporters [6, 7]. But within all the corpus of the existing studies, our knowledge on the relations between street mobilization during social conflicts and digital technologies remains contradictory, as studies of causal relation between mobilization results and *ad hoc* discussions on Twitter did not reach agreement [8].

For instance, authors [9] have studied the role of Twitter and Facebook in mobilization of protest movements and have shown the causality between communication in social networks and protest activities. Their results are based on the Granger causality

© Springer Nature Switzerland AG 2019
S. S. Bodrunova et al. (Eds.): INSCI 2018 Workshops, LNCS 11551, pp. 61–71, 2019.
https://doi.org/10.1007/978-3-030-17705-8_6

tests for three cases (the Indignados in Spain, the Occupy, and the Vinegar protests in Brazil) and prove that protest-related social media activity on Twitter and Facebook enables forecasting protest-related onsite activity. But the opposite results have been proven by another group of authors [1]. They have shown a low level of interrelation between offline political activity and Twitter discussions for the same events.

We aim at suggesting a qualitative way to look at the linkages between discussion topicality and intensity, on one hand, and people's street actions, on the other hand, for the cases where causality tests are either impossible to perform due to scarcity of data or provide mixed results. For this, we first show that the Granger causality test does not provide evidence for the online-offline linkages and then employ topic modeling, time series reconstructions of online and offline activities, and qualitative assessment of topics to formalize the pattern of online-offline linkages in time.

The paper is organized as follows. In Sect. 2, we describe the case under scrutiny and data collection. Section 3 shows the result of the Granger causality test as the premise for further research. Section 4 describes our method of topic modeling and the results of topic assessment against the timing of major political events within the case. Section 5 discusses and generalizes the results.

2   Case Description

New Year's Eve sexual assaults in Germany were chosen for the case study due to several reasons. The event was reported massively on Twitter but did not reach the key quality news media in Germany. This fact triggered a significant discussion about accountability of German quality news media. Although local newspapers published the news already on January 1, national media have not paid attention to the event until January 5. Press service of Cologne police has published the official statement on the 2nd of January and this one-day delay has also provoked accusations of concealment against the elites. The absence of coverage of the event on the public service broadcasting and in quality newspapers was explained by the editorial houses first in terms of lack of human resources during the last days of the Christmas holidays; involvement of the rest of journalists into coverage of Munich terrorist attack; banality of criminal activities on the New Year's Eve. The major German news agency DPA evaluated the importance of the event as very low and this decision could also influence the level of attention given by weekend editors to the event. While quality news media were blamed in a significant failure in detecting an important social problem, it remains understudied whether the causality between online and onsite protest activity can be detected in this case.

The data from Twitter was gathered during the period from 1.01.2016 to 31.01.2016 via a set of hashtags. The sample includes more than 99000 users (the core consists of 12000 users) and more than 64000 tweets. The specially developed web-crawler was used to download the data. We have described our data collection method extensively in our previous works [10, 11], and here we will not stop on this.

Table 1. Street actions and official statements of German authorities during January 2016.

Date	Political activity (estimated number of partaking people – in brackets)
02.01.2016	Press service of Cologne police has published the official statement mentioning sexual assaults
04.01.2016	Demonstrations of PEGIDA supporters in Dresden (400) and Leipzig (370) No clashes with police, nobody has been arrested The Head of Cologne's police Wolfgang Albers, North Rhine-Westphalia's Interior Minister Ralf Jäger name the suspects as North African refugees
05.01.2016	Demonstration of women in Cologne (400) No clashes with police, nobody has been arrested The mayor of Cologne Genriette Recker promises to provide more resources for the police in the future but states that she still doesn't have evidences about refugees involved into the assaults
06.01.2016	A public statement made by the press secretary of Angela Merkel about the negotiations between the chancellor and the mayor of Cologne Genriette Recker. Merkel expressed her 'outrage' with the violence and demanded a 'harsh response from the state'
07.01.2016	Major quality newspapers – *FAZ, Sueddeutsche Zeitung, Tagesspiegel, Die Welt* – publish official responses about the reasons of silence of their outlets in first days of January
08.01.2016	North Rhine-Westphalia's Interior Minister Ralf Jäger dismissed the Head of Cologne's police Wolfgang Albers
09.01.2016	Protests in Cologne: demonstration of women (1000), PEGIDA supporters (1700), counter-protest demonstration 'Cologne against the right-wing' (1300). Clashes with police; seizures of participants
11.01.2016	Demonstrations in Leipzig: Anti-LEGIDA – 2500, LEGIDA supporters – 3000. Nobody was arrested North Rhine-Westphalia's Interior Minister Ralf Jäger presents a report to an extraordinary committee of the Internal Affairs Committee of North Rhine-Westphalia's state parliament and confirms that majority of suspects are people with migrant background Right extremists attack group of refugees. Minister of Justice Heiko Maas condemned the attack
12.01.2016	Demonstration in Cologne: PEGIDA supporters (2000) No clashes with police, nobody was arrested
13.01.2016	Demonstration in Erfurt: PEGIDA supporters (2200) No clashes with police, nobody was arrested
14.01.2016	Minister President of North Rhine-Westphalia Hannelore Kraft presents the package of actions to be taken for improving security and integration
18.01.2016	Demonstrations in Dresden: PEGIDA supporters (4000), NOPEGIDA (500) No clashes with police, nobody was arrested
20.01.2016	Demonstrations in Dresden: PEGIDA supporters (700), NOPEGIDA (900) No clashes with police, nobody was arrested
23.01.2016	Demonstration in Stolberg PEGIDA supporters (1600) No clashes with police, nobody has been arrested
25.01.2016	Demonstration of PEGIDA supporters in Dresden and in Cologne (4000) No clashes with police, nobody was arrested

3   Granger Test

The data about political activities in Germany during January 2016 was collected from the media reports and publications [12]. The level of the protest mobilization was estimated accordingly to the number of participants of a political activity (see Table 1): not only anti-migrant activists were calculated, instead the feminist human rights movement activists and counter-PEGIDA unions were also included into the estimation, as suggested by [9] and [13]. In case of contradictory data from mass media, the average between the data in media publications was calculated [9].

3.1   Casual Relations Between Online and Offline Activities in the Case Study

To test whether Twitter discussion on the New Year's Eve's sexual assaults in Germany is causally related with political activities in Germany during January 2016, we applied the Granger causality test to measure if the time lags of level of the protest mobilization (number of participants in the days of street actions in the dataset) relates to the distribution of the level of Twitter activity (number of tweets for each day of the studied period) over time. The data about daily users' activity in Twitter and street protests is visualized as the time series graph (Fig. 1).

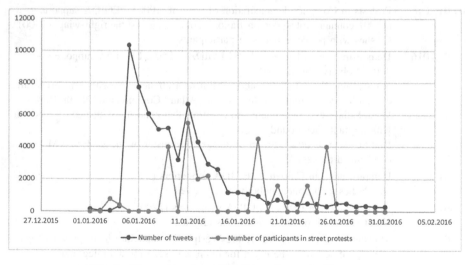

Fig. 1. Time series for online discussion and offline events

Granger causality test can statistically determine when one variable precedes and predictively explains another variable [14] in case when the influence of one 1-dimensional time series parameters (xt) on another time series parameters (yt). The Granger causality analysis are carried out by evaluating of two types of regression:

$$yt = \alpha0 + \alpha1yt - 1 + \ldots + \alpha p \; yt - p + \beta1xt{-}1 + \ldots + \beta1xt - p + \varepsilon t$$

and

$$xt = \alpha0 + \alpha1xt - 1 + \ldots + \alpha p \; xt - p + \beta1yt{-}1 + \ldots + \beta1yt - p + ut$$

to prove the null hypothesis $\beta1 = \ldots = \beta p = 0$.

The regressions were carried out in a special program for statistical calculation EViews (Quantitative Micro Software, Version 10). The time lag is set at 2, the level of significance, α, is set at 5%, We compared two time series – data with number of participants and data about number of tweets. The null hypothesis about the absence of influence of online activities on the offline activities has been confirmed (Probability = 0,4696), as well as null hypothesis about absence of the opposite causal relation (Probability = 0,8315).

Hence, the idea of causal relationship between street demonstrations and Twitter communication about the event is rejected. Political activities in German cities triggered by New Year's Eve's sexual assaults in January 2016 and discussion about them on Twitter demonstrated an asynchronous character and do not depend on each other in the time dynamic.

4 Detecting Pivotal Points via Topic Modeling

4.1 The Method

On the second step of our work with the case, we have tried an alternative methodology to detect patterns of interaction between online and offline activities. Our idea was to trace the change of topicality during the immediate aftermath of the conflict and to see whether the patterns repeat across several cases. In this paper, we look at just one case but we already see a particular pattern in interaction of topicality and protest activity.

To define the pattern, topic modeling was performed on the tweets to model the topic distribution for each day from the period of the study. The algorithm Biterm Topic Model has been chosen due to time restrictions and computational capabilities. BTM has been developed for short texts: this is an efficient algorithm that allows getting coherence topics for short text collections [15].

The BTM algorithm assigns the topics to each document; then, the grouping of the messages and the corresponding topic distribution is performed, whereas the time of publication is used as a criterion for the grouping procedure. After several pre-tests with the number of topics from 20 to 200, 50 topics were chosen to perform the modeling procedure. The list of the topics with distribution coefficients p(z) for each day of the period has been visualized in a form of a heat map (see Fig. 2).

To analyze the semantic structure of the discussion, we formed the list of the most salient topics. If the weight of a topic (p) on a particular date exceeded 0,047 (more than 50% in the daily topic distribution), it indicated that the actuality of this topic has increased sharply. 26 topics that were at particular points more salient than 0,047 are unevenly distributed in the course of January 2016, with most salient topics visible in the first three days of the conflict (five topics on January 1 and 2, six at January 3). In the discussion below, the topics are listed 1 to 50 (instead of 0 to 49 on the heat map).

5   Results

As visualized on Fig. 3, four topics were salient on more than five days during the period of study. Their semantic structure is listed in the Table 2. Every topic includes nominations of place, actors, and hashtags employed by the users to frame the issue.

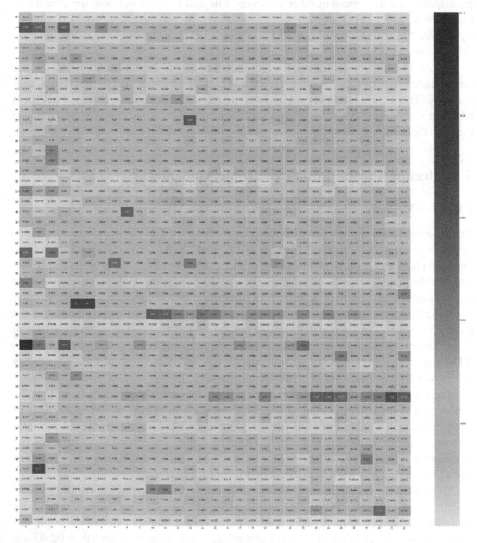

Fig. 2. Distribution of topics during January 2016 (axis x) according to their coefficients p(z) (axis y)

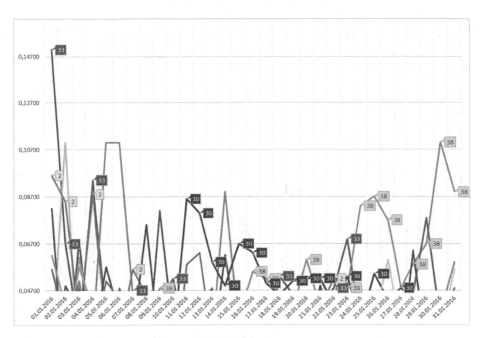

Fig. 3. The most salient topics in the Twitter discussion about New Year's Eve's sexual assaults (axis y = weight of a topic)

Table 2. Semantic structure of the regularly salient topics.

Topic N	Top words	Dates of saliency
2	Ausnahmslos, gewalt, koelnhbf, rassismus, sexualisierte, frauen, sexismus, immer, sexuelle, aufschrei	January 1, 2, 4, 7, 22
33	Koelnhbf, ausnahmslos, koeln, muslime, rapefugees, versuch, neue	January 1, 2, 4, 7, 18, 22, 23
30	Koelnhbf, koeln, polizei, medien, silvesternacht, amp, mueller	January 11 to 17
38	Koelnhbf, ausnahmslos, merkel, amp, pegida, schon, mal, abmerkeln, brief	January 19, 20, 21, 23, 25, 27

Juxtaposition of the most salient topics clearly shows that there are four periods on the time-series graph when different topics dominated with a varying degree of saliency: January 1 to 7; January 8 to 15; January 16 to 23; January 24 to 31 (see Fig. 4).

In the first period (January 1 to 7, 2016), nominations among the top words define direct participants (topics N2 and N33): women ('frauen') against Muslims and 'rapefugees'. Hashtags #ausnahmslos and #aufshrei indicate a feminist voice in the Twitter discussion: the hashtag #aufschrei was introduced first in 2013 by feminism activist Anne Wizorek. This period was the most 'buzzy', according to the number of salient topics.

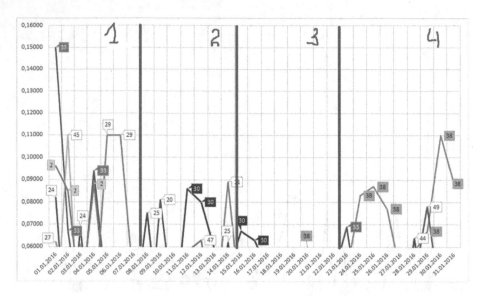

Fig. 4. Periods in topic distribution

In the second period (January 8 to 15, 2016), topic N30 is the most salient. It demonstrates the public debate on the role of police and German media during the conflict: both actors were heavily criticized on Twitter. The second most salient topic during one day was the topic N20 that discusses more extensively political authorities who participated in the debate: Minister President of North Rhine-Westphalia Hannelore Kraft, North Rhine-Westphalia's Interior Minister Ralf Jäger, and North Rhine-Westphalia's parliamentarian from FDP Christian Lindner.

The third period (January 16 to 21, 2016), as the heat map shows, is a 'gap' period between topic N30 that is becoming less salient from its maximum on January 11, and topic N38 that increases in salience tremendously since 24th of January. According to our time series analysis (see Table 1), both PEGIDA and NOPEGIDA demonstrations have taken place but the number of tweets reduced significantly from more than 2500 on January 14 to less than 500 on January 23.

Topic N38 dominates the discussion in the last period (January 22 to 31, 2016). It reflects the activity of the PEGIDA movement and its supporters who use the hashtags #abmerkeln and #merkelmussweg – both urge Angel Merkel to leave her Chancellor post.

We tried to trace manually whether the topics relate to the events. Concerning street actions, PEGIDA movement was mentioned only in 3 topics of 50 in our model (N21, N28, N38). Topic N21 goes beyond the saliency threshold only once, on January 2, while the first street action of PEGIDA supporters happened on January 4. Topic N28 passes the salience threshold only once, on January 31, after a wave of street actions. Topic N38 has been most salient before the street protests on January 18 as well as on the days when street actions took place (January 9, 20, 23, and 25). It reaches the highest level of salience (weight of a topic (p) exceeds 0,08) on January 24 and 25 in comparison to p = 0,048 on January 23. In both cases, on January 18 and 25, the biggest number of participants took part in PEGIDA street actions (4000, as estimated by German media reports).

On January 14, Minister President of North Rhine-Westphalia Hannelore Kraft presented the package of actions to be taken for improving security and integration. Salient topics do not mention Kraft and do not relate directly neither to N11 (most salient, p = 0,089, mentions the Head of Cologne's police Albers fired on January 4 and North Rhine-Westphalia's Interior Minister Ralf Jäger) nor to N25 (mentions political parties CDU/CSU, AFD, SPD and FDP), nor to N30 (mentions feminist hashtags #aufschrei and #ausnahmlos as well as popular hashtag related to the mayor Reker #einearmlaenge). On the next day, the only topic N30 exceeded the level of p > 0,047. In this case, we do not observe any connection between a political act of authorities and Twitter debate.

6 Conclusions

Scholars have tested a wide range of factors influencing political mobilization and, in particular, mass participation in a street action. Internet penetration, online user behavior and participation in online discussions were studied among other parameters. We argue that online behavior cannot be seen is a sole, dominant predictor for spill-overs of protest to the street, as scholars that focused on interrelation between online and offline political activities have revealed controversial evidences on the causal relations between them.

In this paper, we presented the pilot study of relations between online and offline political activities triggered by New Year's Eve's sexual assaults in Germany 2016. The Granger causality test conducted in a way suggested by authors [9], has failed, partly because the case study is characterized with the lack of parameters and data to compare the level of commitment among Internet users and street actions participants. In such cases, alternative ways to assess the relations between online and offline activities might be needed.

To prove the inter-relation between online discussion and offline political activities, new criteria and parameters are needed to be operationalized. To reveal these parameters for further research, we analyzed the data with the help of topic modelling that has visualized how the topics develop through the online debate.

Based on the results of the topic modeling, we juxtaposed the development of the most salient topics and the timing of the offline political activities in January 2016. Four periods were revealed, including the 'gap' period where topic saliency was the lowest. While in two first periods authorities and their (dis)activities were the main focus of the discussion, the fourth period is dominated by the topic that reflects far-right discourse (N38).

Several topics have gone beyond the saliency threshold (weight of a topic (p) exceeding 0,047) before, on, and after the days of street actions; the most visible topics have also reached the highest level of saliency (weight of a topic (p) exceeding 0,08) before the offline events. These intersections should be studied in a more nuanced way, *i.a.* hour by hour. Hence, topic modeling has provided evidence that visibility of political activists precedes the street actions they organize. Moreover, the rapid change of the level of saliency that we observed for the topic N38 took place before the day the biggest number of participants took part in PEGIDA street actions in two cities simultaneously on January 25. If the peak of the topic in an online discussion precedes the mass participation in an offline street action, one might argue that the platform participated actively in forming of protest consensus. Rapid appearance of a peak within a topic, just like we observed for topic N38, might be a predictor for the forthcoming successful mobilization.

We assume that the Granger causality test might provide more accurate results in cases like New Year's Eve's sexual assaults in Germany 2016 if the level of street activity is examined against the level of salience of the dominant topics. Significant changes in the level of salience (rapid appearance of a peak with the topic distribution, as observed for topic N38) might be a predictor for the forthcoming successful mobilization. For more conclusions, we will in future compare several case studies of the same nature, to see whether the patterns that we have discovered for Cologne repeats for other countries and cases within Germany.

Acknowledgements. This research has been supported in full by Russian Science Foundation, grant 16-18-10125.

References

1. Theocharis, Y., Lowe, W., Van Deth, J.W., García-Albacete, G.: Using Twitter to mobilize protest action: online mobilization patterns and action repertoires in the occupy Wall Street, Indignados, and Aganaktismenoi movements. Inf. Commun. Soc. **18**(2), 202–220 (2015)
2. Caren, N., Gaby, S.: Occupy online: Facebook and the spread of occupy wall street. Soc. Sci. Res. Netw. (2011). https://doi.org/10.2139/ssrn.1943168
3. Koltsova, O., Selivanova, G.: Explaining offline participation in a social movement with online data: the case of observers for fair elections (2015)
4. Anduiza, E., Gallego, A., Cantijoch, M.: Online political participation in Spain: the impact of traditional and internet resources. J. Inf. Technol. Polit. **7**(4), 356–368 (2010)
5. Tufekci, Z., Wilson, C.: Social media and the decision to participate in political protest: observations from Tahrir Square. J. Commun. **62**(2), 363–379 (2012)
6. Earl, J., Kimport, K.: Digitally Enabled Social Change: Activism in the Internet Age. MIT Press, Cambridge (2011)
7. Flesher-Fominaya, C.: Debunking spontaneity: Spain's 15-M/Indignados as autonomous movement. Soc. Mov. Stud. **14**(2), 142–163 (2015)
8. Mercea, D.: Digital prefigurative participation: the entwinement of online communication and offline participation in protest events. New Media Soc. **14**(1), 153–169 (2011)
9. Bastos, M.T., Mercea, D., Charpentier, A.: Tents, tweets, and events: the interplay between ongoing protests and social media. J. Commun. **65**(2), 320–350 (2015)
10. Bodrunova, S.S., Blekanov, I.S., Maksimov, A.: Measuring influencers in Twitter ad-hoc discussions: active users vs. internal networks in the discourse on Biryuliovo bashings in 2013. In: Proceedings of the AINL FRUCT 2016 Conference, #7891853 (2017)
11. Bodrunova, S.S., Litvinenko, A.A., Blekanov, I.S.: Please follow us: media roles in Twitter discussions in the United States, Germany, France, and Russia. J. Pract. **12**(2), 177–203 (2018)

12. Koopmans, R., Rucht, D.: Protest event analysis. Methods Soc. Mov. Res. **16**, 231–259 (2002)
13. Castells, M.: Networks of Outrage and Hope. Polity Press, Cambridge (2012)
14. Groshek, J., Clough Groshek, M.: Agenda trending: reciprocity and the predictive capacity of social network sites in intermedia agenda setting across issues over time. Media Commun. **1**(1), 15–27 (2013)
15. Cheng, X., Yan, X., Lan, Y., Guo, J.: BTM: topic modeling over short texts. IEEE Trans. Knowl. Data Eng. **1**, 1 (2014)

Patterns of Emotional Argumentation in Twitter Discussions

Kamilla Nigmatullina(✉) [ID] and Svetlana S. Bodrunova [ID]

St. Petersburg State University, Universitetskaya nab. 7/9,
199034 St. Petersburg, Russia
k.nigmatulina@spbu.ru

Abstract. The paper presents the results of an ongoing research of Twitter discussions on inter-ethnic conflicts. The case of Biryulevo bashings is already thoroughly analyzed by the research group; in this paper, we develop a qualitative method for finding patterns of emotional (irrational) argumentation, the patterns that would link emotion and argumentation. Our pilot empirical study is based on 306 tweets of 7 top non-media users; the tweets are analyzed qualitatively for the spectrum of emotions for conflict cases – sadness/sorrow, surprise/fear, anger/indignation, as well as for irony and call to action for complete reconstruction of the chains of emotions. We find that there are two patterns in tweeting strategies – broadcasting the development of the conflict and 'broadcasting' emotions of individuals that reflect collective ones. The total number of expressed emotions was counted, followed by reconstructing chains of emotions chronologically. There are three groups of patterns: starting and ending with neutral informing; starting and ending with one certain emotion, no clear pattern with different emotions in the start and in the end. Despite we find only a few sustainable patterns, we argue that further computational research can be done to connect the type of a top user and his/her emotional patterns.

Keywords: Twitter discussions · Collective emotions · Argumentation · Inter-ethnic conflicts

1 Introduction

Argumentation patterns in online discussions constitute a new research issue in media and communication studies which involves qualitative and quantitative analysis of messages and comments in social media. While a lot of computational research is done to detect patterns of information spreading (cascades, viral information, discussion growth patterns etc.), very few works are dedicated to tracing argumentation strategies; especially few deal with the emotional side of the argumentation patterns. On the other side, a large amount of works on, e.g., hate speech do not look at how hate speech is used in argumentation.

But, in many cases, it is the emotion that becomes a 'social contagion' [1, 2], and in order to understand how the emotions (including hate and aggression) are spread, one needs to understand how they form in the online speech. Describing this may then help

© Springer Nature Switzerland AG 2019
S. S. Bodrunova et al. (Eds.): INSCI 2018 Workshops, LNCS 11551, pp. 72–79, 2019.
https://doi.org/10.1007/978-3-030-17705-8_7

detecting the particular moments when a constructed emotion becomes 'contagious' and starts to spread in the surrounding speech.

Yet the topic is heavily understudied, and there is not much evidence upon consistent speech patterns based on emotional and rational arguments. It is clear that social networks uncover emotional and affective nature of human personal interaction. However, the 'quality' of emotional arguments may differ in certain communicative situations. We suggest that discussions which include hate speech and speculations about migration issues are especially sensitive and reveal a wide spectrum of emotions, not simply sentiments in general. Such discussions help in reconstructing user argumentative strategies based on emotions and affect. Our goal is, first, to discover the patterns of emotion-based argumentation and, second, to assess the chances for automatization of their retrieval.

2 Literature Review

Argumentation and Its Analysis. Recent research may be divided into two groups – argumentation in natural language detected via computational methods and argumentation in human interaction analyzed with the help of argumentation theories and discourse analysis. The first stream of literature uses quantitative methodologies, while, in most cases, the theoretical background relates to social science, as authors deploy abstract categories from argumentation theories. E.g. the authors [3] define an argument as 'an entity that represents some grounds to believe in a certain statement and that can be in conflict with arguments establishing contradictory claims' [3]; here, the definition focuses on conflictual nature of argumentation. Another helpful definition states that argumentation is a type of discourse where speakers try to persuade their audience about the reasonableness of a claim by displaying supportive arguments [4]. Thus, the notion of discourse has also to be employed when analyzing Twitter discussions, as they exist not in vacuum but in the context and are limited not only by the tweeters' statuses and capacities but also by the platform affordances. Argument can also be defined as 'a set of assumptions that, together with a conclusion, is obtained by a reasoning process. Argumentation as an exchange of pieces of information and reasoning about them involves groups of actors, human or artificial' [5]. It is important that, in automated analysis, the arguments 'are compared, evaluated in some respect and judged in order to establish whether any of them are warranted' [5].

Computational analysis of argumentation in texts is often based on Dung's social abstract argumentation framework which 'incorporates social voting by adding votes for and against arguments, where votes are assumed to be extracted from an online debating system and represent the arguments' strength' [6]. We would add that 'the voting system' in interhuman discussions is very difficult to extract because the way Twitter users express emotions linguistically might often be interpreted as both supportive and oppositional, due to irony and sarcasm. Despite this, there are attempts to link (or, de-facto, to equalize) argumentation and the resulting user opinions; in such works, tweets themselves become arguments with attached argument values that describe relative social relevance of the tweets [7]; thus, valued abstract argumentation allows to see how users' opinions diverge due to varying argument values, whatever these values might be. This leads us away of understanding arguments as discursive constructs that permeate texts but provides us with an idea of a measurement system for emotional load and rationality of tweets. Our idea is to replace 'argument values' that assess social relevance with emotional values of tweets, having in mind the wide spectrum of different expressions of attitudes and sentiments.

Described this way, the method seems to be suitable for automatization; but we also need to take into account the other stream of literature which insists that argumentation is structurally complicated, and analyzing individual bits (arguments) may not be enough. This branch of argumentation theory has developed the notion of argumentation schemes [8]; it formalizes arguments in a different way that, too, allows to structure user opinions and, thus, the online discussions altogether [9]. In the aforementioned works, argumentation schemes are described as stereotyped patterns of human reasoning that can improve users' understanding of discussions and provide a means to evaluate what users have stated and why. But we argue that it is rather complicated to find stereotyped patterns by automated search if discussions involve emotions; however, it may possible with the help of qualitative textual analysis.

The authors [8] develop a typology of argumentation schemes which is quite hard to operationalize for automated text assessment. Thus, in their typology, there are arguments 'from' expert opinion, sign, example, commitment, position to know, lack of knowledge, cause to effect, goal to action, and analogy, as well as *ad hominem*, 'sunk costs', and 'slippery slope' arguments. Historically, these schemes descend from Aristotle's works [9]. Despite the classic background, and while the very idea of argumentation schemes remains interesting, the typology obviously contaminates several dissimilar classification grounds, which makes it doubtful and highly resource-demanding in terms of automatization, as it would demand employing machine learning with large labeled text collections for training and evaluation. The classification system originally proposed and revised by D. Walton consisted of three main categories: reasoning arguments, source-based arguments, and arguments applying rules to cases [10] and was easier to operationalize, but we are unaware of any successful attempts to use it for automated analysis of argumentation strategies.

Emotions in Argumentation and Reasoning. The research area that closely links argumentation and emotions is the research on the nature of reasoning. For example, the authors [10] describe a tri-dimensional reasoning process that involves cognitive, social, and emotional phenomena into the basic processes of education. The study is built on the modern understanding of the role of emotions in argumentation; here, employing emotions for reasoning is not fallacious as it used to be considered for several centuries. Relying on current philosophical research [11–15], the authors claim that emotions play complex functions in argumentation. We find this approach useful to explain discussion patterns in Twitter and follow the author [12] who distinguishes four types of emotion semiotization in argumentation: (1) 'argued emotions', thematized and explicitly supported by justifications; (2) 'said emotions', explicitly mentioned using emotional lexicon; (3) 'shown emotions', inferred from 'downstream' signals of emotion symptom (e.g. a red face standing for anger or shame); and (4) 'scaffolded emotions', inferred from 'upstream' signals (for example, a burial is associated to sadness). So, the normative 'deviance' of emotions turned to be 'inseparability of reason and emotion' in today's research that describes 'arguability' of emotions and their argumentative potential.

We will build upon all the three major ideas that we have discussed above, namely the argument values, the argument schemes, and the idea of 'argued emotions', to uncover the patterns of emotional argumentation on Twitter, including negative argumentation. Our methodology during the pre-test will be qualitative, as we first need to see whether the argumentation patterns that we expect to find are to be found there.

We do not pose any particular hypotheses towards the tweets under scrutiny; our study is exploratory, and we want to single out the possible argumentative schemes/patterns/rules by which emotion participates in argumentation, with a goal for future to automatize this process. Since this methodological task is satisfactorily accomplished, we will be able to pose substantial hypotheses towards the studied datasets.

3   Sample and Method

Our study is based on the dataset collected from Twitter after the infamous anti-immigrant bashings in the Moscow district of Biryulevo in 2013. This case has been already described in several papers that the research group has published in 2016 [16] and 2017 [17, 18]. The tweets were gathered with the help of a specialized Twitter crawler developed by the research group as early as in 2012; the crawler collects the data based on the input of a word collection.

The sample for this particular study included tweets of the top users of the dataset. To define the top users, we have reconstructed the web graph of the discussion and, according to these data, have created user ratings by 9 parameters, namely the number of tweets, likes, retweets, and comments, as well as the graph centralities: in-degree, out-degree, degree, betweenness, pagerank. For this pilot study, only the top1 users were taken; media were excluded, since, as our previous research shows [18], their discourse differs substantially from that of 'ordinary people'. Altogether, we assessed 306 tweets of 7 accounts (as some of the accounts were on top by different metrics).

There are several approaches to classifying emotions in texts. Author [19] showed six of them – happiness, sadness, fear, anger, disgust, and surprise – plus non-emotional expressions. Almost the same was said in 'Collective emotions' [20] – anger, disgust, fear, joy, sadness and surprise (referring to an earlier work [21]).

For English, there are lexicons for affect, as well as for the user tone (sentiment) – see our review in [22]; for Russian, there are no such lexicons available yet for computational analysis. While working upon this task in general, for this paper, we suggest the heuristic approach based on social networks' emoticons that represent like/love, joy/laugh, sadness/sorrow, anger/indignation and surprise/fear.

We will especially focus on the three last emotional categories, as we consider them to be manifesting the conflict. It is obvious that these emotions may be expressed by various linguistic means; thus, computational sentiment analysis might not reflect the full spectrum of these emotions in user texts. That is why we decided to apply to tweets qualitative textual analysis combining it with the context of the conflict. Also, an important parameter for studying Russian texts is presence of irony and sarcasm in expressing emotions.

Thus, we have selected 306 tweets from 7 top non-media accounts and have manually marked rational and emotional arguments. We used the following marking scheme:

INFO (for simple informing, not arguing); plus emotions for informing of a certain mood; plus IRONY as a connotation for informing;

RATIONAL ARGUMENT (for non-emotional arguments);

EMOTIONAL – divided into sadness/sorrow, anger/indignation and surprise/fear.

We also used CALL TO ACTION marks to find any correlation between emotions, arguments, and mobilization, but more studies should be done on this particular question. What we have reached so far is reconstructing patterns of sequences of emotions. We believe these patterns may be used in future detection of information spread and emotional turns in the discussions.

4 Results

The first result was that we have found almost no rational argumentation in discussions about the inter-ethnic conflict. Emotions were expressed during both informing and arguing upon a position, with quite expressive language. For their distribution, see Table 1. For ethical reasons, we do not publish the account names of top users; we just mark the users by their respective metric.

Table 1. Extracted emotions, top 7 Twitter users, the Biryulovo bashings case

User's metric	Total tweets	Non-emo	Sorrow	Anger	Indignation	Surprise	Fear	Irony
Top tweets	101	90	7	1	1	18	11	6
Top likes and top comments	17	15	1	0	1	2	0	9
Top retweets	6	5	0	1	0	1	0	2
Top in-degree and top degree	17	9	2	1	5	1	0	3
Top out-degree	103	84	6	7	10	3	0	10
Top betweenness	51	9	0	37	3	1	0	1
Top pagerank	11	5	2	0	1	1	0	2

Second, there are two patterns in tweeting strategies while dealing with the conflict, namely 'broadcasting' the development of the conflict and 'broadcasting' emotions while reflecting upon collective imaginaries.

Third, it was important not to simply count arguments and emotions, but to trace their development over time depending on the type of a top account. The top accounts were reporting every moment of the Biryulevo bashings, the use of arguments was minimal and escalation and fading of emotions referring to facts was the following:

INFO – RATIONAL ARGUMENT – FEAR – INDIGNATION – SORROW – multiple
SURPRISE – IRONY – SURPRISE – RATIONAL ARGUMENT – INFO

Top-likes and top-comments accounts had much fewer tweets, less information and almost no arguments, half of information was in pictures, and expressed emotions were not varied:

INFO – IRONY – SORROW – INDIGNATION – SURPRISE – multiple IRONY – INFO

We see that ironic informing with no arguing provokes audience commenting and liking while expressing various emotions does not allow people to contribute a lot to authors' sentiments.

Top degree and in-degree user (who is a famous oppositional politician) was not simply emotional but mainly expressed indignation and anger, which might be called righteous anger, because contextually it is based on the conflict between personal political values of the author and government 'non-human' reaction to bashings. Again, we see that each Twitter 'broadcast' starts and ends with neutral informing, but then the first reaction provokes different chains of emotions:

INFO – INDIGNATION – IRONY – SURPRISE – multiple INDIGNATION – SORROW -
INFO

Top retweets user tweeted scarcely and made no arguing. His tweets contained call to action and ironical informing, as well as obscene language:

INFO – CALL TO ACTION – IRONY – ANGER

So, a call to action with fewer emotions and arguments tended to provoke retweets.

Top out-degree user expressed mainly indignation and anger; he also tweeted and retweeted a lot, involving different authors in his chain of emotions. It should be noted that these emotions did not refer to classical hate speech, although there was an obvious object of anger, namely government and police. The clearest pattern here is a need in new portion of information before next emotions in chain:

INFO – INDIGNATION – CALL TO ACTION – SORROW – INFO – ANGER – INFO –
INDIGNATION – SORROW – CALL TO ACTION – ANGER – INFO

Top betweenness user expressed mostly hate speech, and did it mainly through obscene language. There was no clear pattern or chain in his expressed emotions, but we can see that the starting point and the end are obviously based on expressing anger:

Multiple ANGER – SURPRISE – INFO – multiple ANGER – INDIGNATION – INFO –
ANGER

Finally, top pagerank user expressed few emotions, his informational messages were mainly links to other sources of information. Here we cannot trace exact chain of emotions, the dominating context is sorrow and surprise:

IRONY – INFO – SORROW – SURPRISE

Discovered patterns differ a lot, but we tried to find some similarities.

There are three groups of patterns: (1) starting and ending with neutral informing, (2) starting and ending with one certain emotion, (3) no clear pattern, usually different emotions in the start and in the end.

5 Discussion

Studying emotional sequences in argumentation in Twitter discussions has a big potential beyond simple sentiment analysis and automated detection of positive and negative clusters in the discussions.

At this stage of research, we may suggest that Twitter discussions use mainly emotional argumentation as an interesting, non-rational way of arguing one's position. There is evidence that emotions are expressed according to particular patterns in time. To detect such patterns in such emotional sequences, discourse analysis methods are needed; there needs to be a scholarly debate on how to automate this exploration.

Also, prevalence of certain types of emotions and 'legal' use of emotional arguments should be explored. Analysis of inter-relations between top user types and emotional sequences should be automated. Correlation between personal and collective emotions should be traced.

Acknowledgements. This research has been supported in full by Russian Science Foundation, grant 16-18-10125.

References

1. Iyengar, R., Van den Bulte, C., Valente, T.W.: Opinion leadership and social contagion in new product diffusion. Mark. Sci. **30**(2), 195–212 (2011)
2. Aral, S., Walker, D.: Creating social contagion through viral product design: a randomized trial of peer influence in networks. Manag. Sci. **57**(9), 1623–1639 (2011)
3. Alsinet, T., et al.: A distributed argumentation algorithm for mining consistent opinions in weighted Twitter discussions. Soft Comput., 1–20 (2018). https://doi.org/10.1007/s00500-018-3380-x
4. Hidey, C., et al.: Analyzing the semantic types of claims and premises in an online persuasive forum. Logos, pathos and ethos, claims and premises. In: Proceedings of the 4th Workshop on Argument Mining, pp. 11–21. Association for Computational Linguistics (2017)
5. Villata, S., et al.: Emotions and personality traits in argumentation: an empirical evaluation 1. Argum. Comput. **8**(1), 61–87 (2017)
6. Alsinet, T., et al.: An argumentative approach for discovering relevant opinions in Twitter with probabilistic valued relationships. Pattern Recogn. Lett. **105**, 191–199 (2018)
7. Alsinet, T., et al.: Weighted argumentation for analysis of discussions in Twitter. Int. J. Approx. Reason. **85**, 21–35 (2017)
8. Walton, D.: Using argumentation schemes for argument extraction: a bottom-up method. Int. J. Cogn. Inform. Nat. Intell. Arch. **6**(3), 33–61 (2012)
9. Heras, S., Atkinson, K., Botti, V., Grasso, F., Julián, V., McBurney, P.: Research opportunities for argumentation in social networks. Artif. Intell. Rev. **39**(1), 39–62 (2013)

10. Walton, D.: The Place of Emotion in Argument. Penn State Press, University Park (2010)
11. Polo, C., Plantin, C., Lund, K., Niccolai, G.: Group emotions in collective reasoning: a model. Argumentation **31**(2), 301–329 (2017)
12. Hekmat, I., Micheli, R., Rabatel, A. (eds).: Modes des émiotisation et fonctions argumentatives des émotions. Semen, 35 (2013)
13. Micheli, R.: Emotions as objects of argumentative constructions. Argumentation **24**, 1–17 (2010). https://doi.org/10.1007/s10503-008-9120-0
14. Plantin, C.: Les bonnes raisons des émotions: Principes et méthode pour l'étude du discours « émotionné». Peter Lang, London (2011)
15. Plantin, C.: Emotion and affect. In: Tracy, K., Ilie, C., Sandel, T. (eds.) The International Encyclopedia of Language and Social Interaction, pp. 514–523. Wiley, Boston (2015)
16. Bodrunova, S.S., Litvinenko, A.A., Blekanov, I.S.: Influencers on the Russian Twitter: institutions vs. people in the discussion on migrants. In: Proceedings of the International Conference on Electronic Governance and Open Society: Challenges in Eurasia, pp. 212–222. ACM (2016)
17. Bodrunova, S.S., Blekanov, I.S., Maksimov, A.: Measuring influencers in Twitter *ad hoc* discussions: active users vs. internal networks in the discourse on Biryuliovo bashings in 2013. In: Proceedings of Artificial Intelligence and Natural Language Conference (AINL), pp. 1–10. IEEE (2016)
18. Bodrunova, S.S., Litvinenko, A.A., Blekanov, I.S.: Please follow us: media roles in Twitter discussions in the United States, Germany, France, and Russia. J. Pract. **12**(2), 177–203 (2018)
19. Ghazi, D., Inkpen, D., Szpakowicz, S.: Hierarchical versus flat classification of emotions in text. In: Proceedings of the NAACL HLT 2010 Workshop on Computational Approaches to Analysis and Generation of Emotion in Text, pp. 140–146. Association for Computational Linguistics (2010)
20. Von Scheve, C., Salmela, M.: Collective Emotions: Perspectives from Psychology, Philosophy, and Sociology. Oxford University Press, Oxford (2014)
21. Strapparava, C., Mihalcea, R.: Learning to identify emotions in text. In: Proceedings of the 2008 ACM Symposium on Applied Computing, pp. 1556–1560. ACM (2008)
22. Bodrunova, S.S., Blekanov, I.S., Kukarkin, M., Zhuravleva, N.: Negative a/effect: sentiment of French-speaking users and its impact upon affective hashtags on *Charlie Hebdo*. In: Bodrunova, S.S. (ed.) INSCI 2018. LNCS, vol. 11193, pp. 226–241. Springer, Cham (2018). https://doi.org/10.1007/978-3-030-01437-7_18

Part II
CONVERSATIONS 2018:
2nd International Workshop
on Chatbot Research and Design

Preface for CONVERSATIONS 2018 - 2nd International Workshop on Chatbot Research

Asbjørn Følstad[1], Symeon Papadopoulos[2], Ole-Christoffer Granmo[3],
Effie L.-C. Law[4], Ewa Luger[5], Petter Bae Brandtzaeg[1]

[1] SINTEF, Oslo, Norway
asf@sintef.no

[2] Information Technologies Institute, Centre for Research
and Technology Hellas, Thessaloniki, Greece

[3] Centre for Artificial Intelligence Research (CAIR),
University of Agder, Grimstad, Norway

[4] University of Leicester, Leicester, UK

[5] University of Edinburgh, Edinburgh, UK

Abstract. Chatbots are emerging as a promising user interface to data and services. However, a number of research challenges need to be resolved in order to realize the potential in chatbots. In this workshop on chatbot research and design a cross-disciplinary attendance of researchers shared theoretical and empirical work. The eight full papers presented at the workshop are included in the proceedings.

Keywords: Chatbots · Natural language user interfaces · Conversational user interfaces

1 Introduction

Chatbots enable users to interact with digital services in natural language, through text or voice dialogue. Customer service [1] and virtual assistants [2] are applications areas where chatbots already have substantial impact. Also in other application areas, such as health [3] and education [4], a similar impact is foreseen.

However, chatbot technology is still in its emergence, and a number of important challenges remain [5]. As summarized in the previous edition of the workshop, four key challenges concern the democratization of chatbots to reduce digital divides, chatbot user experience, context awareness in chatbots, and natural language capabilities [6].

Motivated by this set of cross-disciplinary challenges, researchers with an interest in chatbots met for a full day workshop at the 5th International Conference on Internet Science, October 26, 2018. The workshop included the presentation of peer-reviewed papers, as well as group and plenary sessions for collaboration.

2   Paper Invitation and Review Process

Researchers were invited to submit papers on theoretical and empirical research concerning chatbots. The call for papers was distributed in relevant networks, mailing lists, and as personal invitations to selected researchers with a track record in chatbot research.

Twelve papers were submitted to the workshop; all reviewed by three members of the program committee holding relevant expertise. The reviewers provided thorough and constructive textual feedback and scored the papers as *accept, minor revision, major revision, or reject*. Reviews were summarized by a meta-reviewer. In the case of low scores, or large divergence in scores, the reviewers were invited to an online discussion to make the final recommendation. For submissions authored by one or more of the workshop organizers, the entire review and decision making process was conducted by the other organizers without the authoring organizer being involved or given insight.

The final decision on the papers were made by the workshop organizers. Eight of the twelve papers were accepted as full papers, provided the authors revised these in line with the reviewers' recommendations. The remaining four were rejected as full papers; one of these reworked as a position paper following the reviewers recommendations.

All accepted papers were revised and resubmitted prior to the workshop. Resubmissions were checked by one of the workshop organizers. Also, the authors of accepted papers were recommended to make a final revision following workshop feedback.

3   Workshop Outcomes

The workshop papers and presentations addressed relevant and interesting topics in chatbot research. Cameron et al., Skjuve and Brandtzaeg, and Lunde and Volden targeted different aspects of chatbot usability and user experience. Klopfenstein et al. and Huang and Zaïane presented and discussed novel chatbot technologies. Piccolo et al. contributed a critical review of the chatbot literature, Følstad et al. presented a typology of chatbots, and Havik et al. presented how chatbots may be used as an alternative to questionnaire-based screening instruments.

The presented papers provide a valuable contribution to the growing body of chatbot research. The workshop also included a collaborative process to identify possible approaches to address key chatbot research challenges.

Motivated by the positive experiences from this workshop, as well as that of 2017, we aim to arrange an edition of the CONVERSATIONS workshop also in 2019.

4   Workshop Organization

The workshop organizing team consisted of: Asbjørn Følstad, SINTEF, Norway. Symeon Papadopoulos, Centre for Research and Technology Hellas, Greece. Ole-Christoffer Granmo, University of Agder, Norway. Effie L.-C. Law, University of Leicester, UK. Ewa Luger, University of Edinburgh, UK. Petter Bae Brandtzaeg, SINTEF, Norway.

We are grateful for the thorough and helpful work done by the 23 workshop program committee members. These were: Adam Tsakalidis, University of Warwick, UK. Ahmed Fadhil, University of Trento, Fondazione Bruno Kessler (FBK), Italy. Brahim Zarouali, University of Antwerp, Belgium. Christian Löw, University of Vienna, Austria. David Kuboň, Charles University, Prague, Czech Republic. Despoina Chatzakou, Aristotle University of Thessaloniki, Greece. Dmitry Ilvovsky, National Research University Higher School of Economics, Russia. Eleni Metheniti, Saarland University, Germany. Federica Tazzi, Link Campus University, Italy. Frank Dignum, Utrecht University, the Netherlands. Jordi Vallverdú, Universitat Autònoma de Barcelona, Spain. Juanan Pereira, Universidad del País Vasco/Euskal Herriko Unibertsitatea, Spain. Lorenz Cuno Klopfenstein, University of Urbino "Carlo Bo", Italy. Marita Skjuve, SINTEF, Norway. Massimiliano Dibitonto, Link Campus University, Italy. Massimo Mecella, Sapienza Università di Roma, Italy. Oliver Bendel, School of Business FHNW, Switzerland. Ricardo Usbeck, Data Science Group, Paderborn University, Germany. Rricha Jalota, Data Science Group, Paderborn University, Germany. Simon Enni, SINTEF, Norway. Stefanos Vrochidis, Centre for Research and Technology Hellas, Greece. Suhas Govind Joshi, University of Oslo, Norway. Theo Araujo, University of Amsterdam, the Netherlands.

Acknowledgements. The workshop was arranged with support from the project grant Human-Chatbot Interaction Design, Research Council of Norway.

References

1. Xu, A., Liu, Z., Guo, Y., Sinha, V., Akkiraju, R.: A new chatbot for customer service on social media. In: Proceedings of the 2017 CHI Conference on Human Factors in Computing Systems, pp. 3506–3510. ACM, New York (2017). https://doi.org/10.1145/3025453.3025496
2. Porcheron, M., Fischer, J.E., Reeves, S., Sharples, S.: Voice interfaces in everyday life. In: Proceedings of the 2018 CHI Conference on Human Factors in Computing Systems, pp. 640–651. ACM, New York (2018). https://doi.org/10.1145/3173574.3174214
3. Fitzpatrick, K.K., Darcy, A., Vierhile, M.: Delivering cognitive behavior therapy to young adults with symptoms of depression and anxiety using a fully automated conversational agent (Woebot): a randomized controlled trial. JMIR Ment. Health 4(2) (2017). https://doi.org/10.2196/mental.7785

4. Fryer, L.K., Carpenter, R.: Bots as language learning tools. Lang. Learn. Technol. **10**(3), 8–14 (2006). https://doi.org/10125/44068
5. Brandtzaeg, P.B., Følstad, A.: Chatbots: changing user needs and motivations. Interactions **25** (5), 38–43 (2018). https://doi.org/10.1145/3236669
6. Diplaris, S., Satsiou, A., Følstad, A., Vafopoulos, M., Vilarinho, T.: Internet Science. LNCS, vol. 10750. Springer, Cham (2018). https://doi.org/10.1007/978-3-319-77547-0

Adapting a Conversational Text Generator for Online Chatbot Messaging

Lorenz Cuno Klopfenstein$^{(\boxtimes)}$, Saverio Delpriori, and Alessio Ricci

DiSPeA, University of Urbino, Urbino, Italy
cuno.klopfenstein@uniurb.it

Abstract. Conversational interfaces and chatbots have a long history, but have only recently been hyped as a disruptive technology ready to replace mobile apps and Web sites. Many online messaging platforms have introduced support to third-party chatbots, which can be procedurally programmed, but usually rely on a retrieval-based specification language (such as AIML), natural language processing to detect the user's intent, or on machine learning. In this work we present a work-in-progress integration of a widely-used system for story generation, the *Tracery* grammar, a conversational agent design tool, the *Bottery* system, and online messaging platforms. The proposed system provides a complete and easy-to-use system that allows the creation of chatbots with a graph-based dialogue structure, a contextual memory, pattern-based text matching, and advanced text generation capabilities, that aims for being well-suited for experts and technically unskilled authors alike. Features of the system and future additions are discussed and compared to existing solutions.

Keywords: Conversational interfaces · Chatbots · Story generation · Generative text

1 Introduction

Software applications that engage with users through text-based conversations using natural languages, usually called "chatbots", have been making headlines recently and have captured the interest of major tech companies [17].

Chatbots have a long history, which includes attempts at emulating human language patterns as seen in the conversational mechanisms of ELIZA [25]. These early experiments arguably fueled many of the later tries at playing Turing's "Imitation Game" and to make natural language conversation with a computer possible. ALICE is one of the noteworthy systems developed with this aim: a chatbot based on the AIML language and capable of responding based on pattern matching, which allowed it to achieve the Loebner prize multiple times [24].

While exchanging messages through a teletype console could appear as an interesting contraption in 1966, almost fifty years later the majority of the human

© Springer Nature Switzerland AG 2019
S. S. Bodrunova et al. (Eds.): INSCI 2018 Workshops, LNCS 11551, pp. 87–99, 2019.
https://doi.org/10.1007/978-3-030-17705-8_8

population is accustomed to daily sending and receiving SMS or using online messaging. Top messaging apps nowadays reach a vast audience, rivalling that of the most popular social networks [22]. These highly popular messaging platforms have shown to be the ideal ground for chatbots: over the course of the last years, starting in 2014, many of these platforms have added support to chatbots, in the form of third-party software that can conduct text conversations with their users. Thanks to their quickly rising prominence, chatbots have been announced as the new platform aimed at replacing mobile apps and Web sites [10]. Most messaging platforms also allow chatbots to access features that go beyond simple text exchanges: bots can now exchange messages with pictures, sounds, or geographical positions. Some platforms also include advanced UI elements that can enhance the look or the functionality of chatbot messages, using buttons, quick replies, or special representations for common online transactions [12].

Users show a growing interest in chatbots, not only for small talk, but also as aids for productivity tasks, entertainment, and communication [4]. Successful chatbot applications in real-world usage include customer assistance, conversational commerce, ELIZA-like "chatterbot" conversations [14], virtual assistants, which may exploit contextual information or known personal preferences [1], multiplayer games [13], or emphatic learning companions for kids [26].

Major tech companies have also started focusing heavily on conversational interfaces. Many chatbot middleware systems open to third-party developers are now on offer, including a multi-platform connector with procedural dialogues and NLP capabilities[1], machine learning systems for virtual assistants[2], intent-detection text processors[3], hosting platforms for AIML-based chatbots[4], and solutions with graphical dialogue building and NLP support[5].

Conversational interfaces in literature often rely on pattern matching systems (such as the AIML syntax originally used by ALICE) or different natural language processing (NLP) techniques, which attempt to extract the user's intent from text. Some recent attempts make use of deep learning techniques [11]. Chatbot systems can be categorized into retrieval-based or generative-based (whether they pick predefined responses or generate new ones) and into their application to an open or closed domain [20]. Many chatbots can make use of external linguistic resources or knowledge ontologies, they can extract answers from knowledge bases using information retrieval techniques, or they can be integrated with existing systems in order to provide access to services [21].

However, conversational interfaces often fall short of their user's expectations. Current systems generally have poor social skills, with limited capabilities for the reuse of previous knowledge and context [2]. While most chatbots and virtual assistant promise a natural and human-like interaction, they often fail at clearly revealing their effective capabilities and in correctly processing the full context of a

---

[1] Microsoft Bot Connector, https://dev.botframework.com.
[2] Dialogflow, backed by Google, https://dialogflow.com.
[3] Wit.ai, https://wit.ai.
[4] Pandorabots, https://pandorabots.com.
[5] IBM Watson Assistant, https://www.ibm.com/watson/services/conversation/.

conversation [16]. A very careful design and user interaction (UX) effort must be made to ensure success, suggesting conversational UX design to be a distinctive and emerging discipline focused on replicating human conversation [19].

1.1 Contribution

Most common messaging platforms provide programming interfaces and software development kits for easy chatbot development. Many middleware solutions allow development of chatbots for a multitude of messaging platforms. However, development platforms either require advanced programming skills or they provide generic chatbot templates that offer limited customization—especially for unskilled users. In this work, this issue is tackled by proposing a flexible and easy-to-use system for creating modern chatbots based on *Bottery*, a prototyping system for generative contextual conversations modelled as finite state machines, which is specifically designed for non-technical users.

In the next section, an operative overview of *Bottery* is provided. A thorough presentation of its design and syntax helps in filling the lack of an adequate documentation of the system in previous literature. A novel system for creating chatbots is proposed, illustrating how it combines the flexibility of *Bottery*-based conversational agents and the UX features of modern messaging platforms. In the last section, advantages and shortcomings of the proposed system are discussed, along with possible future developments and extension to the existing *Bottery* syntax.

2   Conversational Agents with Bottery

Bottery is a conversational agent prototyping platform [7]. Originally released in 2017, it takes inspiration from *Tracery* and provides a syntax, an editor, and an integrated simulator that allows for interactive testing of an agent. To the best of our knowledge, this paper provides *Bottery*'s first documentation in literature.

In the following sections, we will introduce the two systems mentioned above and describe the process of adapting them to be used as an online messaging chatbot. The design choices in transforming conversational agent interactions into a message-based conversation are outlined, together with a proposed software architecture.

2.1 Tracery and Generative Text

Tracery is an easy-to-use and lightweight grammar system that enables users to generate any kind of texts or stories [9]. Syntax and authoring tools were published in 2014 [5]. An online editor is available and allows users to create and test *Tracery* grammars interactively [8].

The system is based on a standard context-free grammar, defined by a set of *rewrite rules* that operate on the input text. Symbols within the text, which are enclosed in '#' hashtags, are replaced with a string. Replacement strings can, in turn, be terminals (strings on which no further rewrite rules can be applied) or they can be composed by more symbols. When multiple replacement strings apply to a symbol, the system picks one at random. Other rewrite rules can perform simple but desirable text transformations, such as word capitalization or switching between "a" and "an" depending on how a symbol is expanded.

Context-free grammars exhibit strong limitations and have been shown to be inadequate to generate complex stories, since they generally lack the ability to maintain contextual history and formal causality [3], even though *Tracery* includes the ability to keep a limited form of context while processing rewrite rules [5]. These limitations notwithstanding, the system has been successfully adopted in games and more elaborate story generation tools [6,15,23].

A *Tracery* grammar is expressed in JSON format as a simple list of rewrite rules that associate symbols with one or more expanded strings.

```
{
  "alienName": [ "Jaglan Beta", "Santraginus V", "Kakrafoon", "Traal" ],
  "action": [
    "wrap it around you for warmth as you bound across #alienName#",
    "lie on it on the brilliant marble-sanded beaches of #alienName#",
    "sleep under it beneath the stars which shine so redly on #alienName#",
    "use it to sail a raft down the slow heavy river #alienName#"
  ],
  "origin": [ "The towel has great practical value, you can #action#; #action
        #; and of course #action#." ]
}
```

This grammar can, for instance, generate the following text:

```
The towel has great practical value, you can sleep under it beneath the stars which shine so
  redly on Santraginus V; use it to sail a mini raft down the slow heavy river Traal; and of
               course lie on it on the brilliant marble-sanded beaches of Kakrafoon.
```

2.2   Bottery Agent Syntax

The *Bottery* syntax allows authors to create an agent by specifying 4 components:

(a) A set of **states** in which the agent can be, with information that describes the conditions in which the agent moves from one state to another;
(b) A **memory** that can be read and manipulated freely, giving a "blackboard"-style representation of the agent's state for dialogue and text generation [18];
(c) An optional set of global **transitions**, that allow the agent to switch to a given state in response to certain conditions;
(d) An optional *Tracery*-based **grammar**. Text produced by the agent is used as an input string for text generation through the grammar. The expanded text is used as the agent's final output for the user.

Agent States. States describe the agent's position within the dialogue, as defined by the script. Each state is uniquely identified by an identifier. A state contains instructions about the agent's behavior (its output) and its reactions to user input.

In particular, states of the agent are composed of the following:

(a) An alphanumeric **ID**, unique within the same chatbot script (the initial state must have the ID "origin" by convention);
(b) A list of **actions** that are executed when the state is entered by the bot;
(c) A list of **exits** that describe transitions to another state and the conditions they require;
(d) A set of **suggestion chips**: suggested text inputs that are provided by the agent.

Actions. On entering a state, the agent will perform a set of actions. These can be expressed in a variety of ways. For instance, "onEnter" actions are always performed when the state is entered. On the contrary, "onEnterDoOne" actions are prefixed by conditions: the agent will only perform the first action whose condition is satisfied, if any. Actions expressed as "onEnterSay" provide simple text strings that are always output by the agent. Additionally, agents may also play audio files through "onEnterPlay" actions or execute arbitrary Javascript functions through "onEnterFxn".

Actions executed by "onEnter" and "onEnterDoOne" are expressed using *action syntax*: a space-delimited sequence of expressions that are executed in order. Expressions can rely on a very limited set of operations using a Javascript-inspired syntax, that allows to operate on variables in the agent's *blackboard* (e.g., "counter++" increments a variable). String expressions or constants are evaluated using the *Tracery* grammar and output by the agent.

Conditions for "onEnterDoOne" actions can also be written using a limited syntax, which includes basic arithmetic and logical operators, that accesses variables in the *blackboard* (e.g., "counter>4"). Simple strings are directly matched against the last user input. The asterisk character '*' matches any user input. When no condition is given, the condition is always verified.

Exits. All states have one or more exits that describe possible transitions of the agent to other states. Exists are expressed following this syntax:

"[condition ...] -> target [action ...]"

Conditions and actions are expressed using the same syntax as above. The target state is referenced by its ID. The '@' character can be used to reference the agent's current state (i.e., the agent re-enters the same state).

Executing an Agent. An agent based on this system acts like a finite state machine (FSM). It can be displayed as a graph, with states connected by arcs, each of which marked with a condition that must be satisfied to transition the agent from one state to another.

On entering a state, the agent will: (1) execute all available *actions*; (2) display *suggestion chips* to the user, if any; (3) wait for user input; (4) evaluate *exits* and pick the first that satisfies its condition; (5) execute *actions* associated with the picked *exit*; (6) move to the target state; repeat.

2.3 Adapting Bottery to Online Messaging Platforms

The basic mechanism animating the FSM-based execution flow of a *Bottery* agent can be adapted to the reactive nature of online messaging: (1) receive new user input; (2) evaluate *exits* on the current state (including global *exits*) and pick the first whose conditions are satisfied; (3) execute all *actions* associated with the *exit*; (4) move agent to the target state; (5) execute all *actions* of the new state; (6) display *suggestions chips*, if any.

The direct interface between the target messaging platform and the conversational agent simulation is limited to sending and receiving text messages. When receiving a text message, the conversational agent will handle the input by performing a state change, executing actions, and/or outputting any number of text responses, before returning to a waiting state.

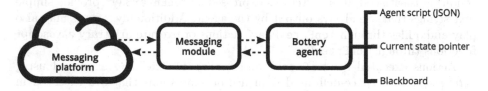

Fig. 1. Software architecture of the proposed system.

The proposed system's architecture is shown in Fig. 1: a messaging module (a specialized software module that interacts with an online messaging platform) receives messages from users and forwards them to the *Bottery* engine. Any output generated by the agent is returned back to the user in the form of text messages.

While the system in development only includes a messaging module for the Telegram platform (chosen for ease of development), any number of messaging modules can be added, making the system multi-platform.

The *Bottery* agent is composed by: an agent script (specified in JSON using the syntax described in Sect. 2.2), a pointer to the agent's current state, a *blackboard* memory (as a map of variable names and values).

In order to keep the system's state for multiple concurrent users, the system will store the current state pointer and the blackboard for each conversation (e.g., in a database system, identifying each conversation with a unique chat ID), while the agent's scripts can be stored once in static JSON files. On receiving a new message the system will load the agent's script and restore the conversation context, by moving the agent to the last state and loading its blackboard into memory.

Figure 2 describes a simple chatbot providing access to weather information. The chatbot offers a guided conversation allowing users to pick a city and a date for which the forecast must be fetched. The conversation is structured over a set of 7 states, depicted as a graph on the right. The forecast generation makes use of *Tracery* to generate random weather information and of an array to keep a

```
{
  "grammar": {
    "forecast": ["fair", "a little cloudy", "cloudy", "rain", "storm"]
  },
  "states": {
    "origin": {
      "onEnterSay": "Welcome to WeatherBot",
      "exits": "->choose_city"
    },
    "choose_city": {
      "onEnterSay": "Enter the city for which you want to know the weather",
      "exits": "'*' ->choose_day city=INPUT"
    },
    "choose_day": {
      "onEnterSay": "Choose the day for which you want to know the weather",
      "chips": ["today", "tomorrow", "day after tomorrow", "change city"],
      "exits": [
        "'today' ->search_forecast day=INPUT",
        "'tomorrow' ->search_forecast day=INPUT",
        "'day after tomorrow' ->search_forecast day=INPUT",
        "'change city' ->choose_city",
        "'*' ->error_choose"
      ]
    },
    "error_choose": {
      "onEnterSay": "Sorry, I don't understand",
      "exits": "->choose_day"
    },
    "search_forecast": {
      "exits": ["(list_city[city][day]!=undefined) ->send_forecast",
                "->ask_forecast"]
    },
    "ask_forecast": {
      "onEnter": "list_city[city][day]='#forecast#'",
      "exits": "->send_forecast"
    },
    "send_forecast": {
      "onEnter": "weather=list_city[city][day]",
      "onEnterSay": ["#/day# in #/city# the weather will be #/weather#"],
      "exits": "->choose_day"
    }
  }
}
```

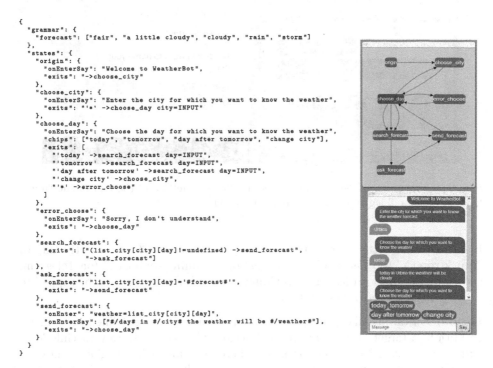

Fig. 2. Simple weather chatbot implemented using *Bottery* (left), states graph (top right) and example conversation (bottom right).

memory of past queries. An actual implementation of the chatbot could of course retrieve real weather information within the ask_forecast state by calling an arbitrarily complex Javascript function.

2.4   Advanced Messaging Features

Most current online messaging platforms are not limited to the exchange of simple text messages, but also allow users and bots to exchange pictures, audio messages, and locations. Chatbots in particular have the ability to use advanced UI elements, such as buttons, commands, and structures messages on some platforms (e.g., Telegram and Facebook Messenger) [12]. The basic *Bottery*-based system described previously provides some extension points that would allow chatbot authors to make use of these features.

Audio Output: actions marked as "onEnterPlay" instruct the chatbot to play a given audio file. On supported platforms (such as Telegram) the audio file can be sent and received by the user as a voice note.

Suggestion Chips: one of the optional components of a *Bottery* state. They take the form of one or more strings that are shown to users as suggestions while waiting for the next input. When a suggestion chip is clicked, the chatbot

Fig. 3. Comparison of "suggestion chips" in *Bottery* (left) and the equivalent "inline keyboard" in a Telegram bot conversation (right).

behaves just as if the user sent its content as a message. Chips perfectly map to "quick replies" (on Facebook Messenger) or an "inline keyboard" (on Telegram, shown in Fig. 3), both features providing a list of buttons that can be tapped to provide a preset reply to the chatbot.

Global Exits: just like normal *exits* from a state, they are defined providing a condition, a target state, and optional actions to execute. However, while local exits are evaluated only on the state where they are defined, global ones are evaluated every time the chatbot receives input. This provides a straightforward opportunity to provide support for top-level always-on interface elements, such as "commands" in Telegram (messages that start with '/' and are shown in the bot's UI) or "persistent menus" in Facebook Messenger.

3   Discussion

Bottery is a complete conversational agent system that provides a full-featured editing and simulation environment. In its adaptation for online messaging, it is well suited to implement chatbots with a structured conversation flow—given its internal representation as an FSM—while retaining the capability to generate rich and varied responses, thanks to a grammar-based text generator, and the ability to keep track of the conversation's context.

3.1   Future Work

The proposed system is currently in development and is available under an open source license on GitHub[6]. While the development version of the system supports Telegram as a messaging platform, integration with additional platforms is highly desirable. These additions would also provide additional opportunities for making use of advanced messaging platform features, outlined in Sect. 2.4.

---

[6] Official repository: https://github.com/ComputerScienceUniUrb/messaging-bottery.

```
{
  "grammar": {
    "forecast": ["fair", "a little cloudy", "cloudy", "rain", "storm"],
    "ask_preamble": ["what's the", "how's the"],
    "ask_weather": ["weather in", "weather like in"],
    "ask": ["#ask_preamble# #ask_weather#", "#ask_weather#"],
    "conjunction": ["and", ""]
  },
  "states": {
    "origin": {
      "onEnterSay": "Welcome to WeatherBot"
    },
    "forecast_today": {
      "onEnterSay": "Today in #/city# the weather will be #forecast#"
    },
    "forecast_tomorrow": {
      "onEnterSay": "Tomorrow in #/city# the weather will be #forecast#"
    }
  },
  "exits": [
    "'#ask# *?' ->forecast_today city=STAR",
    "'#ask# * today?' ->forecast_today city=STAR",
    "'#ask# * tomorrow?' ->forecast_tomorrow city=STAR",
    "'#conjunction# today?' ->forecast_tomorrow",
    "'#conjunction# tomorrow?' ->forecast_tomorrow",
  ],
  "initialBlackboard": {
    "city": "Urbino"
  }
}
```

Fig. 4. Proposed weather chatbot implementation using extensions to *Bottery* for enhanced pattern matching.

The *Bottery* grammar could also be extended in order to introduce support for pictures, locations, and other data types that are not contemplated by the original syntax.

Pattern matching capabilities provided by *Bottery* are very limited, being constrained to using the '*' character to match the whole user input. Future versions of the system will introduce AIML-like pattern matching, where the asterisk can match a sequence of any length. The matched sequence will be available to the agent as a variable for further processing.

Similarly, pattern matching will be further extended to exploit the agent's generative text capabilities: user input will positively match if it can be generated by any symbol expansion in the pattern, according to a given *Tracery* grammar. The ability of using *Tracery* to easily express variations of the same concept (including typos) would allow even unskilled chatbot authors to flexibly match user inputs.

Both these enhancements to pattern matching are shown in Fig. 4, describing a possible weather chatbot implementation similar to the one in Fig. 2. In this example user input is processed using global exits, using both partial '*' and *Tracery* expansions matching, thus providing a very concise implementation and a more natural conversation for users.

The introduction of a more capable pattern matching mechanism would make the system potentially equivalent to AIML-based interpreters. Efforts will be made to formally map the capabilities of the proposed system to AIML constructs, with the purpose of providing a way of automatically transforming an AIML-based bot into a *Bottery* agent.

Finally, while the transactions between states provided by *Bottery* allow the agent to freely jump from one branch of dialogue to another, keeping track of the switch is left to the script author. The system can be extended to allow "context digressions" that maintain a stack-based context of the conversation, in a fashion similar to function calls in a programming language. This would make it easier for authors to keep track of dialogue state and to structure conversations into bite-sized sections, for instance providing procedures that handle specific sub-questions or general conversations for when the chatbot needs to ask for clarification [1].

3.2 Conclusions

Online messaging chatbots based on the proposed system have several significant capabilities. They can: (a) easily define a structured dialogue tree, using states connected by exits; (b) perform question-answer dialogues using a pattern matching system based on categories (correspondence between user input and a string), in particular if extended with capabilities described in Sect. 3.1; (c) rely on a general-purpose memory that can be used to guide conversation, provide context, or drive more advanced "business" logic; (d) make use of a *Tracery* grammar for text generation, either to make chatbot output more variegated or for more advanced story generation; (e) make use of logical and arithmetic conditions; (f) call any procedural function, using the power of a Turing complete language like Javascript with access to the chatbot's memory.

Tracery's text generation features can be used in this context to provide distinctive and various output with minimal programming expertise. The system's elementary text generation capabilities gain much higher potential thanks to the interaction with *Bottery*'s states graph and the adoption of a general-purpose memory. Both measures allow the agent to maintain a detailed knowledge of the state of the conversation, which can easily be used to model more complex agent behavior and more appropriate text generation.

While the proposed system places itself firmly among other retrieval-based closed-domain chatbot systems, such as those based on AIML, there are some noteworthy improvements that *Bottery* provides. According to the categories established by Augello et al., the use of tree-structured dialogues provides facilities to support context management at practice level: independent branches of conversation can be assigned to a specific situation and can be split up into scenes, thus granting a much more powerful alternative to AIML "topics". At a functional level, while AIML and ChatScript offer the "that" tag or "rejoinder" rules to manage small one-level conversation trees, the same functionality can be replicated using a dialogue branch [2]. Structured memory, that can be accessed by the chatbot's logic, offer a powerful alternative to the "get" and "set" tags in AIML. On the other hand, while AIML offers the ability to add new rules (through the "learn" tag), the proposed system offers no such option to dynamically extend the chatbot's intelligence.

The overall syntax used to define a chatbot is mostly declarative and can be expressed in simple, structured JSON. The option to make use of imperative Javascript code provides a powerful extension point, which can be also exploited to provide service integration or access to external knowledge bases [21]. However, it weakens the declarative nature of the chatbot's JSON-only script.

A graph-based chatbot script provides several options for visualization, which allow users to more easily explore and edit the flow of a conversation. The system's ease of use—especially if compared with editing complex XML files with pattern matching strings or unfathomable NLP rules—harks back to *Tracery*'s long history of making advanced text generation tools available to technically unskilled users [5].

References

1. Angara, P., et al.: Foodie fooderson a conversational agent for the smart kitchen. In: Proceedings of the 27th Annual International Conference on Computer Science and Software Engineering, pp. 247–253 (2017). http://dl.acm.org/citation. cfm?id=3172795.3172825
2. Augello, A., Gentile, M., Dignum, F.: An overview of open-source chatbots social skills. In: Diplaris, S., Satsiou, A., Følstad, A., Vafopoulos, M., Vilarinho, T. (eds.) INSCI 2017. LNCS, vol. 10750, pp. 236–248. Springer, Cham (2018). https://doi. org/10.1007/978-3-319-77547-0_18
3. Black, J.B., Wilensky, R.: An evaluation of story grammars. Cogn. Sci. **3**(3), 213–229 (1979). https://doi.org/10.1016/S0364-0213(79)80007-5
4. Brandtzaeg, P.B., Følstad, A.: Why people use chatbots. In: Kompatsiaris, I., et al. (eds.) INSCI 2017. LNCS, vol. 10673, pp. 377–392. Springer, Cham (2017). https:// doi.org/10.1007/978-3-319-70284-1_30
5. Compton, K., Filstrup, B., Mateas, M.: Tracery: approachable story grammar authoring for casual users. In: Proceedings of the AIIDE Workshop, Intelligent Narrative Technologies 2014, pp. 64–67 (2014). https://www.aaai.org/ocs/index. php/INT/INT7/paper/view/9266
6. Compton, K., Kybartas, B., Mateas, M.: Tracery: an author-focused generative text tool. In: Schoenau-Fog, H., Bruni, L.E., Louchart, S., Baceviciute, S. (eds.) ICIDS 2015. LNCS, vol. 9445, pp. 154–161. Springer, Cham (2015). https://doi. org/10.1007/978-3-319-27036-4_14
7. Compton, K., Leigh, N., et al.: "Bottery" official source code repository. https:// github.com/google/bottery. Accessed 23 Aug 2018
8. Compton, K., et al.: Online Tracery editor. http://brightspiral.com/tracery/. Accessed 23 Aug 2018
9. Compton, K., et al.: "Tracery" official source code repository. https://github.com/ galaxykate/tracery. Accessed 13 Sept 2018
10. Dale, R.: The return of the chatbots. Nat. Lang. Eng. **22**(5), 811–817 (2016). https://doi.org/10.1017/S1351324916000243
11. Kamphaug, Å., Granmo, O.-C., Goodwin, M., Zadorozhny, V.I.: Towards open domain chatbots—a GRU architecture for data driven conversations. In: Diplaris, S., Satsiou, A., Følstad, A., Vafopoulos, M., Vilarinho, T. (eds.) INSCI 2017. LNCS, vol. 10750, pp. 213–222. Springer, Cham (2018). https://doi.org/10.1007/978-3-319-77547-0_16
12. Klopfenstein, L.C., Delpriori, S., Malatini, S., Bogliolo, A.: The rise of bots: a survey of conversational interfaces, patterns, and paradigms. In: Proceedings of the 2017 ACM Conference on Designing Interactive Systems, DIS, pp. 555–565 (2017). https://doi.org/10.1145/3064663.3064672

13. Klopfenstein, L.C., Delpriori, S., Paolini, B.D., Bogliolo, A.: Code hunting games: a mixed reality multiplayer treasure hunt through a conversational interface. In: Diplaris, S., Satsiou, A., Følstad, A., Vafopoulos, M., Vilarinho, T. (eds.) INSCI 2017. LNCS, vol. 10750, pp. 189–200. Springer, Cham (2018). https://doi.org/10.1007/978-3-319-77547-0_14

14. Kuboň, D., Metheniti, E., Hladká, B.: Politician – an imitation game. In: Diplaris, S., Satsiou, A., Følstad, A., Vafopoulos, M., Vilarinho, T. (eds.) INSCI 2017. LNCS, vol. 10750, pp. 201–212. Springer, Cham (2018). https://doi.org/10.1007/978-3-319-77547-0_15

15. Kybartas, B., Verbrugge, C., Lessard, J.: Subject and subjectivity: a conversational game using possible worlds. In: Nunes, N., Oakley, I., Nisi, V. (eds.) ICIDS 2017. LNCS, vol. 10690, pp. 332–335. Springer, Cham (2017). https://doi.org/10.1007/978-3-319-71027-3_37

16. Luger, E., Sellen, A.: "Like having a really bad PA": the gulf between user expectation and experience of conversational agents. In: Proceedings of the 2016 CHI Conference on Human Factors in Computing Systems, CHI 2016, pp. 5286–5297 (2016). https://doi.org/10.1145/2858036.2858288

17. McTear, M.F.: The rise of the conversational interface: a new kid on the block? In: Quesada, J.F., Martín Mateos, F.J., López-Soto, T. (eds.) FETLT 2016. LNCS (LNAI), vol. 10341, pp. 38–49. Springer, Cham (2017). https://doi.org/10.1007/978-3-319-69365-1_3

18. Montfort, N., Pérez y Pérez, R., Harrell, D.F., Campana, A.: Slant: a blackboard system to generate plot, figuration, and narrative discourse aspects of stories. In: Proceedings of the Fourth International Conference on Computational Creativity, ICCC 2013, p. 168 (2013). http://www.computationalcreativity.net/iccc2013/download/iccc2013-montfort-et-al.pdf

19. Moore, R.J., Arar, R., Ren, G.J., Szymanski, M.H.: Conversational UX design. In: Proceedings of the 2017 CHI Conference Extended Abstracts on Human Factors in Computing Systems, CHI EA 2017, pp. 492–497 (2017). https://doi.org/10.1145/3027063.3027077

20. Ramesh, K., Ravishankaran, S., Joshi, A., Chandrasekaran, K.: A survey of design techniques for conversational agents. In: Kaushik, S., Gupta, D., Kharb, L., Chahal, D. (eds.) ICICCT 2017. CCIS, vol. 750, pp. 336–350. Springer, Singapore (2017). https://doi.org/10.1007/978-981-10-6544-6_31

21. Satu, M.S., Parvez, M.H., Shamim-Al-Mamun: Review of integrated applications with AIML based chatbot. In: 1st International Conference on Computer and Information Engineering, ICCIE 2015, pp. 87–90 (2016). https://doi.org/10.1109/CCIE.2015.7399324

22. Smith, J.: The messaging apps report. Technical report (2018). https://www.businessinsider.com/messaging-apps-report-2018-4

23. Veale, T.: Appointment in samarra: pre-destination and bi-camerality in lightweight story-telling systems. In: Proceedings of the Ninth International Conference on Computational Creativity, ICCC 2018, pp. 128–135 (2018). http://computationalcreativity.net/iccc2018/sites/default/files/papers/ICCC_2018_paper_35.pdf

24. Wallace, R.S.: The anatomy of A.L.I.C.E. In: Epstein, R. (ed.) Parsing the Turing Test: Philosophical and Methodological Issues in the Quest for the Thinking Computer, pp. 181–210. Springer, Netherlands (2009). https://doi.org/10.1007/978-1-4020-6710-5_13

25. Weizenbaum, J.: ELIZA—a computer program for the study of natural language communication between man and machine. Commun. ACM **9**(1), 36–45 (1966). https://doi.org/10.5100/jje.2.3_1
26. Wiggins, J., Mott, B., Pezzullo, L., Wiebe, E., Boyer, K., Lester, J.: Conversational UX design for kids: toward learning companions. In: Proceedings of the Conversational UX Design CHI 2017 Workshop (2017). http://researcher.watson.ibm.com/researcher/files/us-rjmoore/Wiggins.pdf

Generating Responses Expressing Emotion in an Open-Domain Dialogue System

Chenyang Huang(iD) and Osmar R. Zaïane(✉)(iD)

Department of Computing Science, University of Alberta, Edmonton, Canada
{chuang8,zaiane}@ualberta.ca

Abstract. Neural network-based Open-ended conversational agents automatically generate responses based on predictive models learned from a large number of pairs of utterances. The generated responses are typically acceptable as a sentence but are often dull, generic, and certainly devoid of any emotion. In this paper we present neural models that learn to express a given emotion in the generated response. We propose four models and evaluate them against 3 baselines. An encoder-decoder framework-based model with multiple attention layers provides the best overall performance in terms of expressing the required emotion. While it does not outperform other models on all emotions, it presents promising results in most cases.

Keywords: Open-domain dialogue generation · Emotion · Seq2seq · Attention mechanism

1 Introduction

Open-domain conversational systems [2,3,21] tackle the problem of generating relevant responses given an utterance as input. Compared to the non-open-domain scenario, also known as task-oriented dialogue generation, where it is possible for agents to rely on knowledge for a narrowed domain and detect intent then use specific templates to generate responses, such as a travel booking system [30].

Open-domain dialogue systems have seen a growing interest in recent years thanks to neural dialogue generation systems, based on deep learning models. These systems do not encode dialog structure and are entirely data-driven. They learn to predict the maximum-likelihood estimation (MLE) based on a large training corpus. The machine learning-based system basically learns to predict the words and the sentence to respond based on the previous utterances. However, while such a system can generate grammatically correct and human-like answers, the responses are often generic and non-committal instead of being specific and emotionally intelligent.

However, an absolute "automatic" system may find itself in situations where any inattentive response, even if correct and to the topic, may be improper or

© Springer Nature Switzerland AG 2019
S. S. Bodrunova et al. (Eds.): INSCI 2018 Workshops, LNCS 11551, pp. 100–112, 2019.
https://doi.org/10.1007/978-3-030-17705-8_9

even negligent or offending. For example, if a person is expressing loneliness, or the death of a friend, the response should better be expressing empathy and support rather than a generic and careless possible response. In this work, we are tackling the problem of how to control the emotions expressed in generated responses. As shown in Fig. 1, the proposes methods take as input a source sentence as well as an emotion to be expressed. It will not only respond with an relative sentence, but also express the given emotion in the response.

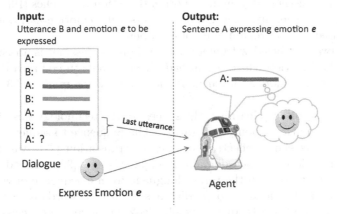

Fig. 1. The task of generating response given emotions

To this end, a sufficiently large dialogue corpus labeled with emotions is required to train such a system which is both open-domain and emotionally intelligent. We follow the pipelines described in [7]:

1. Train a classifier for emotion mining from text [31].
2. Label the Opensubtitles dataset [15] with emotions using the classifier.
3. Design and train models using the labeled dialogue corpus.
4. Evaluate the models.

In addition, we proposed 4 models: *Dec-start, Enc-att, Dec-proj* and *Dec-trans*. Experiment results show that all the proposed models are capable of the task and *Enc-att* outperforms the baseline models in [7] without adding too many parameters to the neural models.

2   Related Work

Emotion category classification serves as one of the basics of this work. The task of emotion mining from text is mainly composed of the following 3 aspects.

– Identify the categories.
– Obtain a large, high quality labeled dataset.
– Train a good classifier for emotions from text.

Ekman, one of the earliest emotion theorists, suggested 6 basic emotions in 1972 [4]: *anger, disgust, fear, joy, sadness* and *surprise*. The following work by Shaver [25] and Parrott [20] suggest removing *disgust* and adding *love*. Shahraki [24,31] combine the aforementioned emotion models by involving two additional emotions (*guilt* and *thankfulness*) but keeping *disgust*.

Human annotation is one straightforward approach to obtain labeled datasets but it is costly. Only very small amount of manually labeled categorical dataset is available at the time of writing this paper. As an alternative, distant supervision [18] has been investigated in many emotion detection researches [19] and proven to be efficient. Generally, they harvest tweets with emotion-carrying hashtags which are used as a surrogate of emotion labels.

Having tweets labeled with emotions, training a classifier is a task of supervised text classification which has already been a well-studied area [14,26]. The recent state-of-art models are usually neural network models [33] with pre-trained.

With the rise of deep learning, the success of the technology was also demonstrated in automatic response generation. The Sequence-to-sequence (Seq2seq) model which was shown effective in machine translation [27], was adopted in response generation for open domain dialogue systems [29]. Instead of predicting a sequence of words in the target language from a sequence of words in the source language, the idea is to predict a sequence of words as a response of another sequence of words. In a nutshell, Seq2seq models are a class of models that learn to generate a sequence of words given another sequence of words as input. Many works based on this framework have been conducted to improve the response quality from different points of view. Reinforcement learning has also been adopted to force the model to have longer discussions [12]. [23] proposed a hierarchical framework to process context more naturally. Moreover, there are also attempts to avoid generating dull, short responses [11,13].

The work in [10] is able to generate personalized responses given a specific speaker, which can be considered as one of the first attempts that control the generations of seq2seq models. In terms of controlling emotions, [32] tackles this problem with a sophisticated memory mechanism while [7] uses three concise but efficient models to achieve equally good performance.

3   Seq2seq with Attention

Seq2Seq is a conditional language model which takes as input source-target pairs (X, Y), where $X = x_1, x_2, \cdots, x_m$ and $Y = y_1, y_2, \cdots, y_n$ are sentences consisting of sequences of words. By maximizing the probability of $P(Y|X)$, these models can generate estimated sentences $\hat{Y}$ given any input X.

Despite the variants of Seq2seq models, they usually consist of two major components: encoder and decoder. Such models can be referred as an encoder-decoder framework. The encoder will embed a source message into a dense vector representation s which is then fed into the decoder. The encoder and decoder are usually randomly initialized and jointly trained afterwards.

The decoder will generate $\hat{Y} = \hat{y}_1, \hat{y}_2, \cdots$ in an autoregressive fashion. This procedure can be described as $s = \text{Encoder}(X)$, $\hat{Y} = \text{Decoder}(Y, s)$.

The choice of our encoder is an LSTM [6] and it can be formulated as the following:

$$h_t^{En}, c_t^{En} = \text{LSTM}^{En}(M(x_i), [h_{t-1}^{En}; c_{t-1}^{En}])$$
$$h_0^{En} = c_0^{En} = \mathbf{0} \tag{1}$$

Where h_t^{En} and c_t^{En} are encoder's hidden state and cell state at time t. $M(x)$ is the vector representation of word x [17]. In our experiments, we apply the state-of-the-art *FastText* [8] pre-trained model.

Adapting attention mechanism in sequence generation has shown promising improvement [1,16]. In our case, we use the global attention with general score function [16] under the assumption that generated words can be aligned to any of the words in the previous dialogue utterance. We use another LSTM to decode the information. The decoder with attention can be described as:

$$\mathbf{h}^{En} = [h_1^{En}, h_2^{En}, \cdots, h_m^{En}] \tag{2}$$
$$\alpha_t = \text{softmax}(h_t^{De}\text{Tanh}(W_a\mathbf{h}^{En})) \tag{3}$$
$$\hat{h}_t = \alpha_t \cdot \mathbf{h}^{En} \tag{4}$$
$$h_t^{De}, c_t^{De} = \text{LSTM}^{De}\left(M(y_i), [\hat{h}_{t-1}; c_{t-1}^{De}]\right) \tag{5}$$
$$y_i = \text{argmax}\left(\text{softmax}(Proj(h_i^{De}))\right)$$
$$\hat{h}_0 = h_m^{En}, \quad c_0^{De} = c_m^{En} \tag{6}$$

Where h_t^{De} and c_t^{De} are hidden state and cell state. α_t is the attention weights over all hidden states of encoder. W_a is a trainable matrix which is initialized randomly.

The seq2seq with attention mechanism is shown in Fig. 2, where $\mathbf{E}$ and $\mathbf{D}$ represent two LSTM models for encoder and decoder respectively. α_t in Eq. 3 is known as attention scores. According to Eqs. (3),(4) and (5), the attention score has to be calculated at every decoding step repeatedly. In Fig. 2, the illustration of the attention layer is only for $h_1^{De} \rightarrow h_2^{De}$. $Proj(h_i^{De})$ is a linear layer that projects the hidden state of time step i to the one dimensional space of vocabulary. After normalization, e.g. softmax, the output of $Proj(h_i^{De})$ is the probability of the next token. The most possible one is considered as $\hat{y}_i$. During the training, the loss is calculated by comparing the difference between Y and $\hat{Y}$. The resulting cross entropy loss can be calculated by Eq. 7,

$$H(Y, \hat{Y}) = \sum_{i=1}^{n} \left[y_i \log \hat{y}_i + (1 - y_i) \log(1 - \hat{y}_i) \right] \tag{7}$$

4 Emotion Injection

As mentioned above in Sect. 3, general seq2seq models are learning the probability of $P(Y|X)$. While in the task of controlling responses by an instructed emotion, each (X, Y) pair is assigned with an additional desired response emotion e. The goal is therefore to estimate the target sequence Y given the joint probability of $X \cap e$, which can be written as $P(Y|X \cap e)$.

4.1 Baseline Models

We propose three models (*Enc-bef*, *Enc-aft* and *Dec*) in [7]. *Enc-bef* and *Enc-aft* are models that inject an emotion e in the encoder by putting special tokens before or after the input sequence X. The *Dec* model, on the other hand, puts e at each decoding step, which is similar to the method in [10]. *Dec* changes (5) to the following:

$$h_t^{De}, c_t^{De} = \text{LSTM}^{De}\left(M(y_i), [\hat{h}_{t-1}; c_{t-1}^{De}; v_e]\right) \tag{8}$$

In Eq. (8) v_e is randomly initialized and trainable vector for each of the emotions. To be more precise, we will refer to the *Dec* model as *Dec-rep* in the follow text.

4.2 Proposed Models

The Encoder-Decoder framework provides us with a flexible foundation which makes joining additional modules into it straightforward and intuitive. In this work, inspired by [7] and [32], four models are proposed.

Dec-start. In [7] *Enc-bef* and *Enc-aft* models have been shown to be successful and effective. By creating a special token T_e for every emotion, these two methods are essentially modifying X to $[T_e; X]$ or $[X; T_e]$ in both training and evaluating. As shown in Fig. 2, to start decoding, a special token $<s>$ is fed into the decoder. h_1^{De} is obtained by calculating $LSTM^{De}(M(<s>), [h_m^{En}, c_m^{En}])$.

In this Dec-start model, we simply substitute the start token $<s>$ with an emotion token T_e as shown in Eq. (9).

$$h_1^{De}, c_1^{De} = LSTM^{De}\left(M(T_e), [h_m^{En}, c_m^{En}]\right) \tag{9}$$

Dec-trans. As an alternative, we multiply the h_t^{De} with another matrix to transform the hidden state of time t with respect to the emotion to be expressed. Denote the transforming matrix as $Trans_e$, Eq. 6 is changed as following:

$$y_i = \text{argmax}\left(\text{softmax}\left(Proj\left(Trans_e(h_i^{De})\right)\right)\right) \tag{10}$$

Dec-proj. [32] also proposed an external memory which maps the hidden state h_t^{De} into a slightly different vocabulary space for each of the emotions. By taking a step forward, we propose a *Dec-proj* model which will make h_t^{De} to totally independent vocabulary spaces. This is done by making unique projection layer $Proj_e$ for each of the emotion. Equation 6 is thus changed to the following:

$$y_i = \operatorname{argmax}\Big(\operatorname{softmax}\big(Proj_e(h_i^{De})\big)\Big) \tag{11}$$

Enc-att. The attention mechanism has been proven to be very powerful in many sequence to sequence tasks. [28] even outperformed many tasks by using an attention only encoder-decoder model. [16] proposed three methods to calculate the attention score. The one we chose in Eq. 3 is referred to as *general* score in their paper. It is a parameterized method compared to *dot* score. Since the general attention has individual parameters, making different attention layer for different emotion is possible as well. The *Enc-att* model changes Eq. 3 to the following:

$$\alpha_t = \operatorname{softmax}(h_t^{De}\operatorname{Tanh}(W_e \boldsymbol{h}^{En})) \tag{12}$$

Compared to the original equation, the universe matrix for calculating attention score W_a is replace with W_e for each of the given emotion e. Figure 2 shows where the emotion is injected into standard seq2seq with attention model.

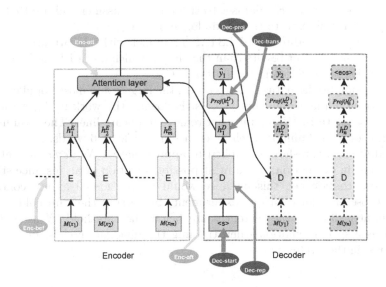

Fig. 2. Comparison among the four proposed models and three baseline models

5   Dataset

As mentioned in Sect. 1, there is no dataset that contains pairs of dialogue exchanges and corresponding emotions. But there are categorical datasets for emotion classification in text. For example, *Cleaned Balanced Emotional Tweets (CBET)* dataset [24,31], *Twitter Emotion Corpus (TEC)* [19] and the *International Survey on Emotion Antecedents and Reactions (ISEAR)* [22]. There are some other dimensional datasets but they can not directly fit into this task. Table 1 shows more details about the aforementioned datasets.

Table 1. Details of three categorical datasets for emotion classification

Dataset	# of categories	# instances	Emotions
CBET	9	81,163	anger, surprise, joy, love, sadness, fear, disgust, guilt, thankfulness
TEC	6	21,051	anger, disgust, fear, joy, sadness, surprise
ISEAR	7	7,666	joy, fear, anger, sadness, disgust, shame, guilt

Considering the size of the datasets and also for consistency with the work in [7], we choose the CBET dataset to train a text classifier and use that to tag the corpus which is used to train a dialogue model.

By applying a bidirectional LSTM [5] model with self-attention [14] We achieve a slightly better results than that in [7], which has a F1-score of 54.33% with precision of 66.20% and recall of 51.29%.

The OpenSubtitles dataset [15] is one of the largest and most popular dataset to train open domain dialogue systems. Following the work in [7], we use the pre-processed data by [10] and further remove duplicate lines. The total number of utterances is 11.3 million, each utterance has at least 6 words.

In addition, a threshold is applied to approximate a *Non-emotion* category. This means, in evaluation, if the most possible emotion of an instance still has a very low 'confidence', this instance would be considered as not containing any of those emotions. In our experiment, by setting the threshold to 0.35, approximately 35% of the sentences are below the threshold. *Non-emotion* is treated as a special emotion when training the dialogue models, but it is not considered in the evaluation.

6   Experiments

6.1   Parameters Setup

For the purpose of comparison, the parameters of the proposed models are set to as close to the baseline models as possible. The dimension for both encoder

LSTM and decoder LSTM is 600. The dropout ratio is 0.75. The choice of opti-
mizer is Adam [9] with learning rate set to 0.0001. The number of the vocabulary
is set to 25,000. *FastText* [8] pre-trained word embedding model is used and set
to trainable. The size of held-out test set is 50k samples. The training and development split ratio is 0.95 to 0.05. The padding length is 30.

6.2   Evaluation Metric

The main goal of this research is to check the ability of generating responses
while given a specific emotion. That being said, the quality and relevance of
generated responses are not the focus of this research. Hence, our interest lies
in checking if the generated sentences contains the instructed emotions or not.
The size of the test set is 50k and 7 models are evaluated: 3 baselines and our
4 proposed models. Further more, every instance in the test set is assigned to
9 emotions for the model. Thus, a total of 3,150k ($50k \times 7 \times 9$) responses are
generated for evaluation.

Fortunately, unlike the work by [10], expensive human evaluation is not
needed. Instead, we evaluate the output using the emotion mining classifier
again. Since every source sentence we generate 9 responses (i.e. one for each
emotion), for each emotion category, we check the proportion of the responses
where the corresponding emotions are indeed expressed. Such proportion is considered as the *estimated accuracy*. Therefore, for each model, we can obtain 9
estimated accuracy scores for the 9 emotions.

7   Results and Discussion

7.1   Result Analysis

The *estimated accuracy* scores of the 7 models are shown in Table 2. Moreover,
we draw the confusion matrices of the 4 proposed models to show the misclassifi-
cation errors (Fig. 2). For the confusion matrices of the 3 baseline models, please
refer to [7].

From the table, we can see that despite the fact that the *Enc-att* model only
achieves 38.71% accuracy for the emotion *joy*, it still outperforms the others
on most of the emotions. From Fig. 2, one can observe a significant mismatch
between *joy* and *thankfulness*. Instead of expressing *joy*, *Enc-att* conveys *thankfulness* which could also be considered reasonable. However, *love* is also confused
with *guilt*. Note that the measured accuracy is also subject to the accuracy of
the emotion tagger used.

It is also noticeable that the performance of model *Dec-start* is close to that of
models *Enc-bef* and *Enc-aft*. This is expected considering the models are simply
injecting the information of emotions by only one special token. The highlighted
numbers in Table 2 show the best accuracy of each emotion. Model *Dec-rep*,
Dec-proj and *Enc-att* have at least 2 best scores whereas the others almost have
none.

Table 2. Per class accuracy of generated response

Emotion	Enc-bef	Enc-aft	Dec-rep	Dec-start	Dec-trans	Dec-proj	Enc-att
anger	60.18%	62.30%	67.95%	66.81%	64.27%	**78.48%**	65.09%
disgust	77.98%	76.79%	79.02%	78.42%	78.33%	**86.43%**	78.29%
fear	**86.40%**	84.17%	83.52%	84.10%	77.15%	73.70%	86.00%
joy	45.69%	41.15%	48.30%	47.42%	49.69%	**59.12%**	38.71%
sadness	94.19%	93.98%	94.21%	94.18%	88.42%	89.83%	**95.09%**
surprise	84.47%	85.09%	87.21%	80.55%	83.61%	80.56%	**92.54%**
love	56.38%	54.69%	58.32%	54.25%	62.82%	**85.14%**	64.56%
thankfulness	87.69%	89.31%	**90.83%**	89.44%	82.03%	61.80%	89.11%
guilt	93.19%	92.17%	91.20%	90.68%	86.64%	50.92%	**94.40%**
Average	76.24%	75.52%	77.84%	76.21%	74.77%	74.00%	**78.20%**

To compare the extended emotion model with Ekman's basic emotions, we highlight the two group of emotions in both Fig. 3 and Table 2. The emotions in red are the six basic emotions, the blue ones are those added by [31].

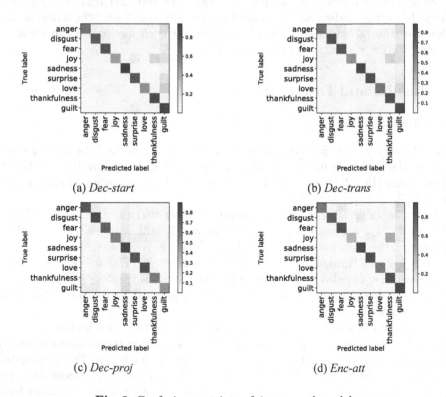

(a) *Dec-start*

(b) *Dec-trans*

(c) *Dec-proj*

(d) *Enc-att*

Fig. 3. Confusion matrices of 4 proposed models

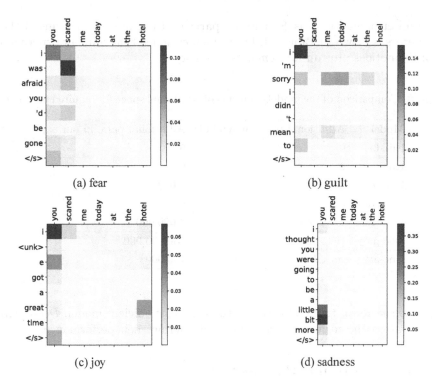

(a) fear

(b) guilt

(c) joy

(d) sadness

Fig. 4. An example of the attention scores of *Enc-att* model

7.2   Enc-att Model Visualization

To show how the *Enc-att* model works, we chose an example utterance and show how the attention scores vary with respect to responses with different emotions. The attention is visualized by heatmaps in Fig. 4. To respond to the utterance *You scared me today at the hotel*, the model focused on *scared* when expressing *fear*. When conveying *guilt*, except for focusing on the pronoun *you*, it focused on *me* and *today* and show a strong preference to using the word *sorry*. When responding with *joy*, it focused on the word *hotel*. Interestingly, to response to the utterance with *sadness*, the model did no pay attention to any words except for the pronoun, but it did try to answer with the phrase *little bit more*.

7.3   Parameter Cost

Apart from the performance of the models, another important comparison of deep learning models is their sizes. Considering that all the 7 models are based on the basic seq2seq with attention model. We only need to compare the additional parameters that are needed. Let's denote the size of vocabulary space as $|V|$, the length of source sentences as m, the dimension of the decoder LSTM as D, and the number of emotions as S. The comparison of the models in terms of these parameters is shown in Table 3. It has to be mentioned that S in our experiments is 10: 9 emotions plus an *non-emotion* category.

Table 3. Comparison of the models in terms of additional space for required parameters

Model	Additional para. in symbols	Additional para. in our exp.
Enc-bef	0	0
Enc-aft	0	0
Dec-rep	$D \times S$	6,000
Dec-start	0	0
Dec-trans	$D \times D \times S$	3,600,000
Dec-proj	$|V| \times D \times S$	150,000,000
Enc-att	$m \times D \times S$	180,000

From the above table, *Dec-proj* is the least cost efficient model. *Dec-rep* and *Enc-att* are both outperforming models considering their performance.

8   Conclusion and Perspectives

In this work, we propose four models that are able to automatically generate a response while conveying a given emotion. We compare our models with the baseline models in [7] in terms of both performance and efficiency. Our *Enc-att* model outperforms the strongest baseline and we show how it works using attention heatmaps. *Dec-rep* and *Enc-att* turn out to be both effective and efficient.

However, in this work, we did not experiment with any combinations of the models. It is shown in [32] that the combination of external and internal memory outperforms each of the single model. We think the combination of *Dec-rep* and *Enc-att* has a potential to give a better result. One major limitation of this work is that we heavily rely on the accuracy of the emotion mining classifier and assume it is of acceptable accuracy. Moreover, the main effort of this research lies on generating responses accurately and efficiently but without focusing on properties like grammar, relevance and diversity.

References

1. Bahdanau, D., Cho, K., Bengio, Y.: Neural machine translation by jointly learning to align and translate. arXiv:1409.0473 (2014)
2. Bessho, F., Harada, T., Kuniyoshi, Y.: Dialog system using real-time crowdsourcing and Twitter large-scale corpus. In: Proceedings of the Annual Meeting of the Special Interest Group on Discourse and Dialogue, pp. 227–231. Association for Computational Linguistics (2012)

3. Bickmore, T.W., Picard, R.W.: Establishing and maintaining long-term human-computer relationships. ACM Trans. Comput.-Hum. Interact. **12**(2), 293–327 (2005). https://doi.org/10.1145/1067860.1067867
4. Ekman, P., Friesen, W.V., Ellsworth, P.: Emotion in the Human Face: Guide-Lines for Research and an Integration of Findings. Pergamon, Oxford (1972)
5. Graves, A., Fernández, S., Schmidhuber, J.: Bidirectional LSTM networks for improved phoneme classification and recognition. In: Duch, W., Kacprzyk, J., Oja, E., Zadrożny, S. (eds.) ICANN 2005. LNCS, vol. 3697, pp. 799–804. Springer, Heidelberg (2005). https://doi.org/10.1007/11550907_126
6. Hochreiter, S., Schmidhuber, J.: Long short-term memory. Neural Comput. **9**(8), 1735–1780 (1997)
7. Huang, C., Zaiane, O., Trabelsi, A., Dziri, N.: Automatic dialogue generation with expressed emotions. In: Proceedings of the Conference of the North American Chapter of the Association for Computational Linguistics, vol. 2, pp. 49–54 (2018). https://doi.org/10.18653/v1/n18-2008
8. Joulin, A., Grave, E., Bojanowski, P., Douze, M., Jégou, H., Mikolov, T.: Fasttext.zip: compressing text classification models. arXiv:1612.03651 (2016)
9. Kingma, D.P., Ba, J.: Adam: a method for stochastic optimization. arXiv:1412.6980 (2014)
10. Li, J., Galley, M., Brockett, C., Spithourakis, G., Gao, J., Dolan, B.: A persona-based neural conversation model. In: Proceedings of the Annual Meeting of the Association for Computational Linguistics, vol. 1, pp. 994–1003 (2016). https://doi.org/10.18653/v1/p16-1094
11. Li, J., Monroe, W., Jurafsky, D.: Data distillation for controlling specificity in dialogue generation. arXiv:1702.06703 (2017)
12. Li, J., Monroe, W., Ritter, A., Galley, M., Gao, J., Jurafsky, D.: Deep reinforcement learning for dialogue generation. arXiv preprint arXiv:1606.01541 (2016). https://doi.org/10.18653/v1/d16-1127
13. Li, J., Monroe, W., Shi, T., Ritter, A., Jurafsky, D.: Adversarial learning for neural dialogue generation. arXiv:1701.06547 (2017). https://doi.org/10.18653/v1/d17-1230
14. Lin, Z., et al.: A structured self-attentive sentence embedding. arXiv:1703.03130 (2017)
15. Lison, P., Tiedemann, J.: OpenSubtitles 2016: extracting large parallel corpora from movie and TV subtitles (2016)
16. Luong, T., Pham, H., Manning, C.D.: Effective approaches to attention-based neural machine translation. In: Proceedings of the 2015 Conference on Empirical Methods in Natural Language Processing, pp. 1412–1421 (2015). https://doi.org/10.18653/v1/d15-1166
17. Mikolov, T., Sutskever, I., Chen, K., Corrado, G.S., Dean, J.: Distributed representations of words and phrases and their compositionality. In: Advances in Neural Information Processing Systems, pp. 3111–3119 (2013)
18. Mintz, M., Bills, S., Snow, R., Jurafsky, D.: Distant supervision for relation extraction without labeled data. In: Proceedings of the Joint Conference of the 47th ACL and the 4th AFNLP, vol. 2, pp. 1003–1011 (2009). https://doi.org/10.3115/1690219.1690287
19. Mohammad, S.M.: # emotional tweets. In: Proceedings of the 1st Joint Conference on Lexical and Computational Semantics, Proceedings of the Main Conference and the Shared Task, Proceedings of the 6th International Workshop on Semantic Evaluation, vols. 1, 2, pp. 246–255 (2012)

20. Parrott, W.G.: Emotions in Social Psychology: Essential Readings. Psychology Press, London (2001)
21. Ritter, A., Cherry, C., Dolan, W.B.: Data-driven response generation in social media. In: Proceedings of the Conference on Empirical Methods in Natural Language Processing, pp. 583–593. Association for Computational Linguistics (2011)
22. Scherer, K.R., Wallbott, H.G.: Evidence for universality and cultural variation of differential emotion response patterning. J. Pers. Soc. Psychol. **66**(2), 310 (1994). https://doi.org/10.1037/0022-3514.67.1.55
23. Serban, I.V., et al.: A hierarchical latent variable encoder-decoder model for generating dialogues. In: AAAI, pp. 3295–3301 (2017). https://doi.org/10.21437/interspeech.2017-628
24. Shahraki, A.G., Zaiane, O.R.: Lexical and learning-based emotion mining from text. In: Proceedings of CICLing (2017)
25. Shaver, P., Schwartz, J., Kirson, D., O'Connor, C.: Emotion knowledge: further exploration of a prototype approach. J. Pers. Soc. Psychol. **52**(6), 1061 (1987). https://doi.org/10.1037/0022-3514.52.6.1061
26. Silva, J., Coheur, L., Mendes, A.C., Wichert, A.: From symbolic to sub-symbolic information in question classification. Artif. Intell. Rev. **35**(2), 137–154 (2011). https://doi.org/10.1007/s10462-010-9188-4
27. Sutskever, I., Vinyals, O., Le, Q.V.: Sequence to sequence learning with neural networks. In: Advances in Neural Information Processing Systems, pp. 3104–3112 (2014)
28. Vaswani, A., et al.: Attention is all you need. In: Advances in Neural Information Processing Systems, pp. 5998–6008 (2017)
29. Vinyals, O., Le, Q.: A neural conversational model. arXiv:1506.05869 (2015)
30. Xu, W., Rudnicky, A.I.: Task-based dialog management using an agenda. In: Proceedings of the 2000 ANLP/NAACL Workshop on Conversational systems, vol. 3, pp. 42–47. Association for Computational Linguistics (2000). https://doi.org/10.3115/1117562.1117571
31. Yadollahi, A., Shahraki, A.G., Zaiane, O.R.: Current state of text sentiment analysis from opinion to emotion mining. ACM Comput. Surv. (CSUR) **50**(2), 25 (2017). https://doi.org/10.1145/3057270
32. Zhou, H., Huang, M., Zhang, T., Zhu, X., Liu, B.: Emotional chatting machine: emotional conversation generation with internal and external memory. In: Proceedings of the AAAI Conference on Artificial Intelligence (2018)
33. Zhou, P., Qi, Z., Zheng, S., Xu, J., Bao, H., Xu, B.: Text classification improved by integrating bidirectional LSTM with two-dimensional max pooling. arXiv:1611.06639 (2016)

Measuring User Experience in Chatbots: An Approach to Interpersonal Communication Competence

Marita Skjuve[1,2(✉)] and Petter Bae Brandzaeg[2]

[1] SINTEF, Oslo, Norway
marita.skjuve@sintef.no
[2] Department of Media and Communications, University of Oslo, Oslo, Norway

Abstract. The increasing usage of chatbots is fundamentally changing the way people interact with new technology. Instead of clicking buttons to functionally navigate on a web page, people can access content and services by the use of natural language in interaction with an artificial agent (e.g., chatbot). This change toward human–chatbot interaction is typically manifested through a social and natural conversational style. This shift of how to interact with data and services has major repercussions for how to explore and measure conversational user experience with chatbots. Hence, in this paper we suggest the importance of measuring the social aspects in human–chatbot interaction through a focus on interpersonal communicational competence (ICC). We build our suggested framework on previous knowledge about communicational competence in successful human–human interaction. Based on this we have developed factors that might be of importance for chatbots' ICC and how these can be measured.

Keywords: Chatbot · Conversational interface · Natural language ·
Human–chatbot interaction · User experience ·
Interpersonal communicational competences

1 Introduction

The ability to demonstrate interpersonal communicational competence (ICC) is critical for functional human–human interaction and relationships. Technology, up to now, has not been required to demonstrate this ability. However, the emergence of conversational interfaces such as chatbots demands new methods in the field of human–computer interaction (HCI) to measure conversational user experiences when interacting with chatbots. Chatbots are understood as machine agents serving as conversational user interfaces to data and services online [1]. The term *"chatbot"* is just one of many names describing this software. Other names include, but are not limited to, conversational interface, conversational agent, and intelligent personal assistant.

Chatbots may utilize artificial intelligence, machine learning, and natural language processing, which makes them capable of communicating with the user the same way humans communicate with each other—through natural language. This results in users no longer having to click their way through a web page. They can simply talk to the chatbot and it will provide them with the information needed.

© Springer Nature Switzerland AG 2019
S. S. Bodrunova et al. (Eds.): INSCI 2018 Workshops, LNCS 11551, pp. 113–120, 2019.
https://doi.org/10.1007/978-3-030-17705-8_10

It is suggested that chatbots will involve a fundamental break with past user interfaces and a change in user motivations and interaction patterns online [2]. This change in future interactions and user interfaces requires a radical rethinking about how to measure the user experiences of chatbots. Chatbots can be regarded as social technologies, and HCIs therefore need to treat them as such rather than just functional technologies. While there has been an awareness of the importance of supporting enjoyable social interaction when designing communication systems [3], this topic is still not fully explored in the user experience literature [4] and certainly not in the context of chatbots.

Chatbots are deemed to be a promising conversational user interface to data and services for several reasons. They are efficient, cost-effective, available, and user-friendly, and are now being "employed" in a variety of different positions. That is, they are working as customer service agents, as health advisors, as therapists, and as teachers. Some can even become your new internet best friend forever (BFF) or significant other. Chatbot developers must therefore be open-minded when thinking about relational development and social trust in human–chatbot interaction.

Chatbots are increasingly stepping into roles that previously belonged to humans. We know from previous research that humans tend to interact with artificial agents much in the same way they interact with humans [5]. This sets the tone for the ability these chatbots need in order to provide the user with a pleasurable interaction and user experience. But how can such user experience be assessed?

User experience is a complex term and is understood and measured in several ways [6], often because it is regarded as a subjective experience [4]. When measuring user experience in the human–chatbot interaction, we cannot rely only on prior usability scales such as a system usability scale (e.g., presented in [7]) simply because the user is not interacting with the technology the same way as they did before. Other types of scales are therefore frequently used, such as variations of the Godspeed questionnaire [8], which measures human likeness, and Social Presence scales, which measure aspects such as how warm or cold, and personal or impersonal a given media is [9].

These scales, presented above, are valuable ways of measuring different user experience aspects of the chatbot and ICC, as presented herein, may affect variables covered in these scales. For example, it is likely that a chatbot that has high ICC is perceived as more humanlike or to have a higher degree of social presence because it communicates in a warmer and more personal way.

New and broader ways of measuring user experience in the human–chatbot interaction are therefore necessary to cover the more conversational nature of chatbots. The aim should be to cover the experience of the communication and exchange process of both information and feelings by means of verbal or non-verbal messages, between the chatbot and the user.

The objective of this paper is therefore to (1) identify factors in previous literature that have been demonstrated to be important for successful communication in human–human interaction, and (2) present an initial scale on how ICC, understood as interpersonal competence, can be measured in chatbots. This work may help us to investigate and measure user experience factors that affect how users perceive human–chatbot interaction in the future.

2   What Is the Recipe for a Successful Conversation?

Spitzberg and Hecht [10] argue that the level of communication competence sets the tone for how an interaction is perceived. According to the authors, communication between two or more individuals needs to be appropriate to the context it is carried out in, and state that "competent communication is a process through which interpersonal impressions are shaped and satisfactory outcomes are derived from an interaction" (p. 576).

Spitzberg and Hecht [10] go on and present the following four important constructs in interpersonal relationships: (1) communication motivation, (2) knowledge, (3) skills, and (4) outcomes. These factors are further argued to be a universal part of creating an impression of having high communicational competence.

Rubin and Martin [11] echo this and state that "interpersonal communication competence (ICC) is an impression or judgment formed about a person's ability to manage interpersonal relationships in communication settings." While Spitzberg and Hecht [10] identify four competences, Rubin and Martin [11] explain that research over the last 20 years has tended to agree upon a total of 10 ICC skills (see Table 1). These competences overlap with the four presented by Spitzberg and Hecht [10], and have been used to test ICC in a variety of settings—ranging from attachment and social support [12] to acceptance of robots [13].

Table 1. Communicational competences important for the user experience.

Competency	Explanation	Relevance
Self-disclosure	The chatbot should be able to share personal thoughts or experiences	Transcripts from human–chatbot interactions indicate that the user asks the chatbot questions about itself [15]. The chatbot should thus be able to share information when appropriate
Empathy	The chatbot should be able to demonstrate that it understands and/or feels with the user when appropriate	Fitzpatrick, Darcy [16] found that the user valued empathic responses in the chatbot, and Kim, Kim [17] showed that teenagers want a chatbot to "empathize with me"
Social relaxation	The chatbot should feel comfortable and secure during the interaction, and not be anxious	Marrinan [18] found that the participants liked that the chatbot seemed calm and relaxed, but also appreciated its "expert" and more professional demeanor
Interaction management	The chatbot should be able to demonstrate turn-taking and discuss and develop different topics	Luger and Sellen [19] found that users often complained about the chatbot's lack of ability to discuss or understand follow-up questions to a topic

(continued)

Table 1. (*continued*)

Competency	Explanation	Relevance
Assertiveness	The chatbot should be able to stand up for itself and its own right, but at the same time be accustomed to, and not violate, the user's right	Curry and Rieser [20] point out that chatbots should be able to use mitigation strategies to avoid facilitating harassment
Altercentrism	The chatbot should make the user feel that it is interested in what he/she has to say, ask appropriate questions, be polite, and display appropriate emotional expressions and content	Kim et al. [17] found that teenagers valued that the chatbot does not get tired of listening to them. They also stated that they want a chatbot that provides appropriate responses
Expressiveness	The chatbot should be able to express its feelings either verbally (e.g., laughter) or non-verbally (emojis)	Fitzpatrick et al. [16] used emojis in their bot to facilitate the chatbot's emotional expressions
Immediacy	The chatbot should be available and open for communication	Fitzpatrick et al. [16] found that users liked that the chatbot automatically checked up on them, and Kim et al. [17] showed how "active listening" capabilities were deemed important
Supportiveness	The chatbot should not judge the user and should make the user feel to be an equal	Kim et al. [17] found that teenagers valued that the chatbot does not judge or get offended
Environmental control	The chatbot should be able to accomplish its goals and objectives	Luger and Sellen [19] argue that chatbots should be clear about explaining what it can and cannot do in order to set the right expectations

While previous research has tended to focus on measuring ICC in human–human interaction, some studies have applied this in user experience tests with artificial agents, such as robots. De Graaf, Ben Allouch [14], for instance, showed that participants who found their robot to lack sociability were more likely to stop using it.

After reviewing the list of competences from Rubin and Martin [11] and the previous chatbot literature, we argue that the following ten competences are important in a human–chatbot interaction (presented in Table 1).

Not all aspects related to the social competences listed in this table may be relevant for all types of chatbots. Different types of chatbots can be identified, based on the way in which they interact with the user, the content, and the context of the application [21]. We should therefore remember that chatbots come in different forms, as well with a variety of social and informational purposes. Some chatbots are in addition used over time, while others are relevant only for one immediate short interaction, such as information about today's weather. Hence, the type of dimension used and measured for different contexts should be related to the various social purposes and general context of the chatbot.

3   How Can We Measure the Chatbot's ICC?

Rubin and Martin [11] present an ICC Scale. We have revised this scale to make it appropriate for measuring the chatbot's ICC. The questions were formulated slightly differently and two items were left out due to a lack of relevance (item 9: "I feel insecure in groups of strangers" and item 26: "I try to look others in the eye when speaking with them") (Table 2).

Table 2. Initial scale measuring each ICC.

Competency	Question
Self-disclosure	The chatbot gave me a sense of who it was The chatbot revealed what it was thinking The chatbot shared its feelings with me
Empathy	The chatbot seemed to know how I was feeling The chatbot seemed to understand me The chatbot put itself in my shoes
Social relaxation	The chatbot seemed to be comfortable talking with me The chatbot seemed relaxed and secure when talking with me
Interaction management	The chatbot took charge of the conversation The chatbot negotiated the topics we were discussing The chatbot seemed to pick up my non-verbal cues such as emojis The chatbot managed to shift smoothly between topics
Assertiveness	The chatbot confronted me when I was rude The chatbot had trouble standing up for itself when I was rude to it
Altercentrism	The chatbot managed to stay focused during the conversation The conversation felt one-sided The chatbot let me know that it understood what I was saying
Expressiveness	The chatbot let me know when it was happy or sad The chatbot didn't have difficulty finding words to express itself The chatbot was able to express itself verbally
Supportiveness	I would describe the chatbot as a "warm" communication partner The chatbot did not judge me The chatbot communicated with me as though we were equals
Immediacy	The chatbot made me feel like it cared about me The chatbot made me feel close to it
Environmental control	The chatbot seemed to accomplish its communication goals The chatbot managed to persuade me to its position The chatbot didn't have trouble convincing me to do what it wanted me to do

Note: Each competence is measured on a Likert scale, ranging thus: 1 = Not true at all, 2 = Mostly not true, 3 = Neither true or not true, 4 = Mostly true, 5 = Very true

4 Conclusion and Future Directions

This paper is an initial attempt to present a new way of measuring user experience in terms of ICC—the interpersonal competence in chatbots. The 10 ICC skills and the ICC scale presented by Rubin and Martin [11] to measure interpersonal competence in human–human interaction were described and tailored to the context of human–chatbot interaction. During the process of tailoring the scale, some observations were made:

First, items measuring "assertiveness" may need to be specified and include references to cases such as harassment. It might be difficult for the user to understand "why the chatbot should stand up for itself." While this may not seem relevant in its current form, we argue that it is relevant in the context of harassment. We have several examples of how users have harassed chatbots in the past [20] and Curry and Rieser [20] argue that it is important that the chatbot mitigate such tendencies to avoid facilitating inappropriate behaviors. Thus, this ICC might be viewed as a necessary competence for regulating the behavior of the user, in cases where that is appropriate.

Second, "social relaxation," as understood by Rubin and Martin [11], might be more about the stress one feels, than the behavior one expresses. The understanding of this factor in a chatbot context may thus need some alteration where the emphasis is more on the ability to express confidence more so than to "feel" relaxed.

Third, the factor "immediacy" is seemingly overlapping with the factor empathy. One suggestion is to focus more on the ability to demonstrate availability though push messages and active listening.

Fourth, because the conversation with the chatbot is computer-mediated, some items addressing this should be added to the scale. This is also in line with Spitzberg [22]. Under "interaction management," for example, items such as (1) the length of the responses was appropriate, (2) the number of responses was appropriate, and (3) the response time was appropriate, would arguably be relevant for the chatbot's ICC.

4.1 Future Directions

We encourage future work to continue to build on this potential framework for measuring a chatbot's ICC. This includes, among other things to:

1. review the suggested measure in this study against other scales and measures (e.g., social presence, or the Godspeed questionnaire) that are increasingly being used to evaluate chatbots in the social robot literature.
2. validate the scale and the factors. Here it will be important to ask whether the scale looks sound, whether it asks about the sorts of thing that we think of as being related to social competence in relation to chatbots (face validity). The scale needs to be tested in terms of: (1) the property of having appropriate relationships with other variables (construct validity) (2) and to what degree the items that compose the scale are related to one another (internal consistency).
3. test the scale among several observers that apply the scale independently, also for a range of various chatbots that need to apply interpersonal competence.
4. Explore other factors and develop guidelines for the contextual importance of each factor. Because the significance of the different factors will vary according to the

context and the role the chatbot performs, not all the dimensions we have suggested in this paper will be relevant for all types of chatbots. Self-disclosure might, for instance, be more important in chatbots that function as a friend, than a customer service chatbot. We also need to investigate how long human–chatbot interaction is necessary in order to judge the chatbot's ICC.

References

1. Dale, R.: The return of the chatbots. Nat. Lang. Eng. **22**(5), 811–817 (2016). https://doi.org/10.1017/S1351324916000243
2. Brandtzaeg, P.B., Følstad, A.: Chatbots: changing user needs and motivations. Interactions **25**(5), 38–43 (2018)
3. Monk, A.: User-centred design. In: Sloane, A., van Rijn, F. (eds.) Home Informatics and Telematics. ITIFIP, vol. 45, pp. 181–190. Springer, Boston (2000). https://doi.org/10.1007/978-0-387-35511-5_14
4. Brandtzæg, P.B., Følstad, A., Heim, J.: Enjoyment: lessons from Karasek. In: Blythe, M.A., Overbeeke, K., Monk, A.F., Wright, P.C. (eds.) Funology. Human-Computer Interaction Series, vol. 3, pp. 331–341. Springer, Dordrecht (2018). https://doi.org/10.1007/1-4020-2967-5_6
5. Nass, C., Steuer, J., Tauber, E.R.: Computers are social actors. In: Proceedings of the SIGCHI Conference on Human Factors in Computing Systems, Boston, Massachusetts, USA, pp. 72–78 (1994). https://doi.org/10.1145/191666.191703
6. Bargas-Avila, J.A., Hornbæk, K.: Old wine in new bottles or novel challenges: a critical analysis of empirical studies of user experience. In: Proceedings of the SIGCHI Conference on Human Factors in Computing Systems, Vancouver, BC, Canada, pp. 2689–2698 (2011). https://doi.org/10.1145/1978942.1979336
7. Brooke, J.: SUS-A quick and dirty usability scale. In: Usability Evaluation in Industry, vol. 189, no. 194, pp. 4–7 (1996)
8. Ho, C.-C., MacDorman, K.F.: Revisiting the uncanny valley theory: developing and validating an alternative to the Godspeed indices. Comput. Hum. Behav. **26**(6), 1508–1518 (2010). https://doi.org/10.1016/j.chb.2010.05.015
9. Biocca, F., Harms, C., Burgoon, J.K.: Toward a more robust theory and measure of social presence: review and suggested criteria. Presence: Teleoper. Virtual Environ. **12**(5), 456–480 (2003). https://doi.org/10.1162/105474603322761270
10. Spitzberg, B.H., Hecht, M.L.: A component model of relational competence. Hum. Commun. Res. **10**(4), 575–599 (1984). https://doi.org/10.1111/j.1468-2958.1984.tb00033.x
11. Rubin, R.B., Martin, M.M.: Development of a measure of interpersonal communication competence. Commun. Res. Rep. **11**(1), 33–44 (1994). https://doi.org/10.1080/08824099409359938
12. Anders, S.L., Tucker, J.S.: Adult attachment style, interpersonal communication competence, and social support. Pers. Relat. **7**(4), 379–389 (2000). https://doi.org/10.1111/j.1475-6811.2000.tb00023.x
13. De Graaf, M.M., Allouch, S.B.: Exploring influencing variables for the acceptance of social robots. Robot. Auton. Syst. **61**(12), 1476–1486 (2013). https://doi.org/10.1016/j.robot.2013.07.007

14. De Graaf, M., Ben Allouch, S., Van Dijk, J.: Why do they refuse to use my robot?: Reasons for non-use derived from a long-term home study. In: Proceedings of the 2017 ACM/IEEE International Conference on Human-Robot Interaction, Vienna, Austria, pp. 224–233 (2017). https://doi.org/10.1145/2909824.3020236

15. Medhi Thies, I., Menon, N., Magapu, S., Subramony, M., O'Neill, J.: How do you want your chatbot? An exploratory Wizard-of-Oz study with young, urban indians. In: Bernhaupt, R., Dalvi, G., Joshi, A., Balkrishan, D.K., O'Neill, J., Winckler, M. (eds.) INTERACT 2017. LNCS, vol. 10513, pp. 441–459. Springer, Cham (2017). https://doi.org/10.1007/978-3-319-67744-6_28

16. Fitzpatrick, K.K., Darcy, A., Vierhile, M.: Delivering cognitive behavior therapy to young adults with symptoms of depression and anxiety using a fully automated conversational agent (Woebot): a randomized controlled trial. JMIR Mental Health 4(2), e19 (2017). https://doi.org/10.2196/mental.7785

17. Kim, J., et al.: Can a machine tend to teenagers' emotional needs?: A study with conversational agents. In: Extended Abstracts of the 2018 CHI Conference on Human Factors in Computing Systems, Montreal QC, Canada, pp. LBW018 (2018). https://doi.org/10.1145/3170427.3188548

18. Marrinan, F.: Qualitative investigations into a virtual CBT therapist: relational features, client experiences and implications for counselling psychology practice. Doctoral thesis, University of Surrey (2018)

19. Luger, E., Sellen, A.: Like having a really bad PA: the gulf between user expectation and experience of conversational agents. In: Proceedings of the 2016 CHI Conference on Human Factors in Computing Systems, San Jose, California, USA, pp. 5286–5297 (2016). https://doi.org/10.1145/2858036.2858288

20. Curry, A.C., Rieser, V.: # MeToo Alexa: how conversational systems respond to sexual harassment. In: Proceedings of the Second ACL Workshop on Ethics in Natural Language Processing, New Orleans, Louisiana, pp. 7–14 (2018)

21. Di Gaetano, S., Diliberto, P.: Chatbots and conversational interfaces: three domains of use. In: Fifth International Workshop on Cultures of Participation in the Digital Age, Castiglione della Pescaia, Italy, vol. 2101, pp. 62–70 (2018)

22. Spitzberg, B.H.: Preliminary development of a model and measure of computer-mediated communication (CMC) competence. J. Comput.-Mediat. Commun. 11(2), 629–666 (2006). https://doi.org/10.1111/j.1083-6101.2006.00030.x

Assessing the Usability of a Chatbot
for Mental Health Care

Gillian Cameron[1,2]($\boxtimes$), David Cameron[1], Gavin Megaw[1], Raymond Bond[2],
Maurice Mulvenna[2], Siobhan O'Neill[3], Cherie Armour[3], and Michael McTear[2]

[1] Inspire Workplaces, 10-20 Lombard Street, Belfast BT1 1RD, UK
{g.cameron,d.cameron,g.megaw}@inspirewellbeing.org
[2] School of Computing, Ulster University, Newtownabbey BT37 0QB, UK
{rb.bond,md.mulvenna,mf.mctear}@ulster.ac.uk
[3] School of Psychology, Ulster University Coleraine Campus,
Coleraine BT52 1SA, UK
{sm.oneil,c.armour1}@ulster.ac.uk

Abstract. The aim of this paper is to assess the usability of a chatbot
for mental health care within a social enterprise. Chatbots are becoming
more prevalent in our daily lives, as we can now use them to book flights,
manage savings, and check the weather. Chatbots are increasingly being
used in mental health care, with the emergence of "virtual therapists".
In this study, the usability of a chatbot named iHelpr has been assessed.
iHelpr has been developed to provide guided self-assessment, and tips
for the following areas: stress, anxiety, depression, sleep, and self esteem.
This study used a questionnaire developed by Chatbottest, and the System Usability Scale to assess the usability of iHelpr. The participants
in this study enjoyed interacting with the chatbot, and found it easy to
use. However, the study highlighted areas that need major improvements,
such as Error Management and Intelligence. A list of recommendations
has been developed to improve the usability of the iHelpr chatbot.

Keywords: Chatbots · Chatbot usability · Mental healthcare ·
User experience · Human Computer Interaction ·
Microsoft Bot Framework · System Usability Scale

1 Introduction

Chatbots have been defined by Shevat [1] as a new kind of user interface, that
can be used for many purposes, such as to book flights [2], purchase goods, and
manage savings [3]. Chatbots are becoming increasingly prevalent in society,
and it has been predicted that users may soon prefer to engage with chatbots,
to complete tasks traditionally done on a web page or mobile application [4].

Voice based chatbots are called upon within mobile devices, computers, and
smart speakers such as Amazon Alexa, and Google Home. Text based chatbots
can be accessed through many channels, such as Messenger, Kik, Slack and

S. S. Bodrunova et al. (Eds.): INSCI 2018 Workshops, LNCS 11551, pp. 121–132, 2019.
https://doi.org/10.1007/978-3-030-17705-8_11

Telegram, or in a web or mobile application. The user can converse with the chatbot using text or quick replies (buttons).

This paper describes a text based chatbot that has been developed, the iHelpr Chatbot. Usability questionnaires are discussed, and adapted to create a usability test to assess the iHelpr chatbot. This paper is a continuation of previous work completed in the area of chatbots for mental health care [5–7].

1.1   Background

The Farmer and Stevenson report sheds light on a significant mental health challenge that the UK faces at work [8]. This report finds that around 300,000 people with a long term mental health problem lose their jobs each year, and around 15% of people that are currently in work have symptoms of a mental health condition. Investors in People produced a report that listed the top five sectors with the most stressed employees, and charities were the third highest [9].

Chatbots are beginning to appear in the area of mental health care. People living in rural communities, or shift workers, may have problems accessing mental health care appointments, and chatbots could be used as a potential solution to this [10]. There is potential to engage students, as Bhakta, Savin-Baden, and Tombs [11] found that students perceived talking to a chatbot as "safe". Chatbots have already been used to support students during periods of exam stress [12]. Woebot [13], a chatbot therapist, has made headlines recently, and receives two million messages per week. A randomised control trial held at Stanford University found students who used Woebot, had significantly reduced symptoms of depression within 2 weeks.

Tess, developed at the company x2-AI by clinical psychologists, delivers support using Cognitive Behaviour Therapy (CBT), Solution-focused Brief Therapy (SFBT), and mindfulness [14].

2   Aims

The aims of this study are:

- to assess the usability of a chatbot for mental health care in a workplace setting.
- to develop recommendations to improve the usability of a chatbot for mental health care.

3   Inspire Support Hub and iHelpr

In previous works [5–7], Inspire Workplaces developed a chatbot, iHelpr, in partnership with Ulster University through a Knowledge Transfer Partnership. Inspire Workplaces provide programmes and wellbeing solutions for private and public sector organisations, and educational institutions across the island of Ireland. Inspire Workplaces is a social enterprise, that sits within a wider charity group, called Inspire. To broaden their service offering, and access to their services, Inspire Workplaces has recently developed a digital intervention to complement their existing face-to-face counselling services. The Inspire Support Hub has been developed, which is a website containing self-help tools and resources. The iHelpr chatbot is embedded within the Hub, to guide the user around the self-help tools and resources and provide tailored self-help recommendations.

3.1   iHelpr

The iHelpr chatbot provides guided self-assessment on the following topics: stress, anxiety, depression, sleep, and self esteem. iHelpr initially allows the user to complete a self-assessment instrument based on the option they have chosen. Figure 1 shows a screenshot of the iHelpr chatbot issuing questions based on the Perceived Stress Scale to assess perceived stress levels. Tailored advice with evidence-based recommendations are then presented to the user, based on the results of the self-assessment survey [15]. The recommendations include links to other support literature available on the Inspire Support Hub website, and recommended e-learning programmes. If there is escalated risk depending on higher scores, the user is given helpline numbers and if necessary, emergency contact information. The iHelpr chatbot was developed using the Microsoft Bot Framework[1], with NodeJS. It is connected to a MySQL database that holds

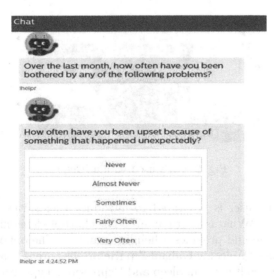

Fig. 1. iHelpr

---

[1] https://dev.botframework.com/.

coping strategies and questionnaire scores. Microsoft's Language Understanding Intelligent Service[2] (LUIS) was incorporated to recognise the utterances made by users and to match them to the correct intent.

Conversation Design. The conversation flow has been designed with a clinical psychologist. Conversation scripts were developed, and refined on numerous iterations with the psychologists to ensure they were fit for purpose. The conversation was then inserted into the prototyping tool Botsociety[3], to visualise the conversation flow in a conversational interface. The user can interact with the chatbot using free text in some areas, but mostly through quick replies. Users cannot send GIFs or Emojis to the chatbot, however GIFS are used within the conversation. Randomised GIFs are shown to the user on greeting, as shown in Fig. 2, and on leaving the conversation.

Fig. 2. GIFs used within iHelpr

Onboarding. The user is prompted to introduce themselves to the chatbot, with the bot asking "What is your name?". The chatbot then onboards the user, explaining the scope and provides a helpline number. The onboarding message the user receives is - "Welcome Gillian! I'm iHelpr! The areas I can help you with are Stress, Anxiety, Self Esteem, Sleep and Depression. Type 'Menu' at any time to view options. If you are in immediate need, please call our helpline on 0800 389 5362. Type Continue to move on with our chat:)".

---

[2] https://www.luis.ai.
[3] https://botsociety.io/.

3.2 Inspire Support Hub

The iHelpr chatbot is embedded within an online self-help portal called the Inspire Support Hub. The features of the Inspire Support Hub include;

- **five ways to wellbeing database:** a searchable database, where users can find resources and groups in their area, based on the Five Ways to Wellbeing which are Be Active, Keep Learning, Take Notice, Give, and Connect with people [16].
- **online self-help library:** reading materials on common mental health conditions including stress, anxiety, depression.
- **e-library of bibliotherapy books:** books on a range of self-help topics.
- **elearning programmes:** on stress, anxiety and depression, sleep, self-esteem and alcohol.
- **thought diary function:** users can track their moods, thoughts and input journal entries.

4   Related Work

4.1   Usability Questionnaires

The term usability is part of a broader term - "user experience". Usability refers to how easy it is to access or use a system. Questionnaires have been observed as the most frequently used tools for usability evaluation. The section below describes three of the most frequently used questionnaires:

The USE Questionnaire developed by Lund, measures Usability, Satisfaction and Ease of use [17]. The questionnaire consists of 30 questions and utilises a seven point Likert rating scale, ranging from −3 totally disagree to +3 totally agree.

Software Usability Measurement Inventory (SUMI) consists of 50 questions, and provides an objective way of assessing user satisfaction with a piece of software [18]. The responses utilise a three point scale - agree, undecided, disagree.

The System Usability Scale (SUS) was developed by Brooke in 1996 [19], and is described as a "quick and dirty" usability scale. It is widely used and allows the researcher to quickly and easily assess the usability of a system. SUS contains 10 questions and participants respond by selecting one of five points that range from strongly disagree to strongly agree. A SUS score ranges between 0–100 and a score above 68 is classed as above average. SUS is very flexible, and can be applied to a wide variety of interfaces, including websites and voice response systems. More recently, it has been adapted to evaluate the usability of chatbot platforms [20].

4.2   Chatbot Usability Testing

Kocaballi, Laranjo and Coiera [21] compared the following questionnaires for measuring user experience in conversational interfaces:

1. AttrakDiff questionnaire; which measures how attractive a product is based on it's hedonic and pragmatic qualities.
2. The Subjective Assessment of Speech System Interfaces (SASSI) questionnaire; which can be used to evaluate speech input quality in speech interfaces.
3. The Speech User Interface Service Quality (SUISQ); which assesses the quality of speech interfaces.
4. MOS-X; which contains 15 items to assess how natural synthetic voices are.
5. The System Usability Scale (SUS); a likert scale questionnaire to assess the ease of use of a system.
6. The Paradigm for Dialogue Evaluation System (PARADISE); which is a framework for assessing user satisfaction.

In their study, it was found that a blend of questionnaires was needed to measure chatbot usability.

Chatbottest has developed a collaborative guide of questions, that fall under 7 different categories to test the specific functionality of chatbots [22]. The 7 categories are: Answering, Error management, Intelligence, Navigation, Onboarding, Personality and Understanding. Chatbottest has built a Chrome extension to test chatbots, that uses the collaborative guide of questions and returns an overall percentage. This percentage is based on how well the chatbot scores on the seven different categories. Furthermore, a report is generated with tips on the areas of your chatbot that need improvement.

5   Methods

5.1   Participants

The participants comprised of 7 employees from a mental health social enterprise. 5 employees were female, 2 were male, 4 were aged between 25 and 34, and 3 between 35 and 44. All employees who participated were in full time employment.

5.2   Procedure

Information sheets about the study were given to the participants, consent forms were signed and any questions from the participants were answered. Demographic information was collected prior to beginning the usability test. Usability studies lasted no longer than 40 min per session. Participants were informed their data would be anonymised. All data was anonymised, with participants given IDs such as participant 1, participant 2. The method used to evaluate usability of the chatbot is the open source questions developed by Chatbottest. Many of the Chatbottest questions start with tasks to perform using the chatbot, followed up by a question. The participants were asked to interact with the chatbot using a PC. In the Chatbottest questionnaire there are 29 questions, and many of the questions have yes/no answers. A screenshot of the start of the Chatbottest questionnaire is shown in Fig. 3.

Does the chatbot have a profile picture?

Yes   No

Is the profile picture a photograph, a cartoon, or a brand?

Photograph   Cartoon   Brand

Start the chatbot. If there's no start button try saying 'Hi'.

Does the chatbot introduce himself?

Yes   No

Does the chatbot explain its scope?

Yes   No

Fig. 3. Chatbottest questions

Once the user completed the Chatbottest questionnaire, they were asked to fill out a SUS questionnaire. As the SUS questions are easily adapted for use with different types of systems, and contains only 10 questions, it was chosen for this study. The SUS questions used in this study are listed below:

1. I think that I would like to use this Chatbot frequently.
2. I found the Chatbot unnecessarily complex.
3. I thought the Chatbot was easy to use.
4. I think that I would need the support of a technical person to be able to use this Chatbot.
5. I found the various functions in this Chatbot were well integrated.
6. I thought there was too much inconsistency in this Chatbot.
7. I would imagine that most people would learn to use this Chatbot very quickly.
8. I found the Chatbot very cumbersome to use.
9. I felt very confident using the Chatbot.
10. I needed to learn a lot of things before I could get going with this Chatbot.

The usability tests were conducted on one-to-one basis, with a researcher observing the participant interact with the chatbot, whilst the participant filled in the questionnaire. Verbal comments throughout the test were recorded. Quantitative data were collected from the two questionnaires, and qualitative data from comments made by the participants while using the chatbot.

6   Results

6.1   SUS Scores

SUS Scores were calculated following the guidelines given by Brooke [19]: For items 1, 3, 5, 7, and 9 subtract 1 from the score given. For items 2, 4, 6, 8, and 10, subtract the score given from 5. Finally, multiply the sum of the scores by 2.5 to get the final score. The average SUS score for the iHelpr Chatbot was 88.2, which is above the average industry score of 68. Two participants gave the iHelpr chatbot 100, and only one participant gave a score that was under the average of 68. Each participant's SUS score is displayed in Fig. 4.

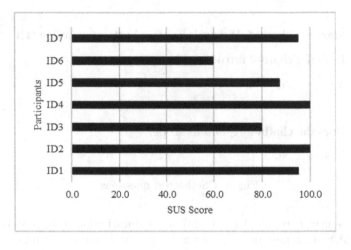

Fig. 4. SUS scores

6.2   Chatbottest Questionnaire

An overall percentage rating is calculated using the Chatbottest chrome extension. Scores out of 100 for each category, Onboarding, Personality, Chatbot Answering, Chatbot Understanding, Navigation, Error Management and Intelligence are also calculated depending on the answers the user gives. The average percentage for the iHelpr Chatbot was 55.6%. The lowest result was 43% and the highest was 74%.

The highest performing categories were Personality, and Onboarding which both scored 100% across all 7 usability tests. Chatbot Answering scored an average of 89% over the 7 tests, however some categories scored very low, with Chatbot Understanding scoring 24% on average, and Error Management scoring 14%. A chart plotting the average scores for each category is shown in Fig. 5. Chatbottest also provide a report detailing tips on how to improve the chatbot based on the participants responses.

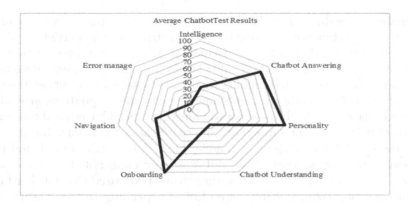

Fig. 5. iHelpr Chatbot performance on Chatbottest

4 out of 7 participants took less than 4 steps to get something valuable out of the chatbot. All participants found that elements such as images, emojis, and Graphic Interchange Format images (GIFs) were not understood by the chatbot, and neither was typing in different languages. 5 out of 7 participants found that the chatbot could maintain a conversation when asked generic questions, such as "How are you" or "Can you tell me a joke?". However, the variability in the chatbot responses was found to be minimal, with 5 out of 7 participants answering "No" to "Say something not really nice to the chatbot. You can start with something like 'idiot' and then go further from there. Does it have answers for your different bad words?". Furthermore, 5 out of 7 participants did not receive a variation of answers when saying "nice" things to the chatbot. All participants found that when they typed a word incorrectly, such as "anious" instead of "anxious" the chatbot did not understand. The participants found there was good use of high quality elements such as GIFs throughout the conversation, as well as rich media elements such as quick reply buttons. The voice and tone of the chatbot were perceived to be consistent, and participants thought the personality of the chatbot was the correct fit for the intended audience.

7   Discussion

The results of this study indicate the chatbot performs well on some areas, such as Onboarding and Personality. The results highlight areas for much needed improvement, in how the iHelpr Chatbot handles errors, and how user requests are understood successfully. The SUS scores are promising, and provide a basis to improve on, and compare with future studies. In Coperich, Cudney and Nembhard's study, SUS was utilised to assess the usability of chatbot development platforms, Watson and Pandorabots [20]. Watson scored an average SUS score of 81.875 and Pandorabot scored 88.75.

During the usability tests, comments were made on the personality of the chatbot, with participant 1 stating iHelpr was "Upbeat" and participant 3 stating the chatbot was "friendly". Participant 1 and 4 both expressed that they "liked" the chatbot. Participant 7 said the chatbot was "amazing". Personality can be a crucial factor in determining whether the user wants to utilise the chatbot again [23]. The chatbottest questionnaire contains a questions around the voice and tone of the chatbot - "Can you identify a specific voice and tone in the chatbot that is consistent throughout the conversation? Do you think the voice and tone fits with the purpose of the chatbot?" Two participants found these questions confusing, as they thought it was more applicable to a voice based chatbot, such as an Amazon Alexa rather than a text based chatbot. For future use, this question could possibly be rephrased depending on the chatbot being evaluated.

When asked the question "Ask the chatbot about common daily stuff. Things like: How are you? - Where are you from? Tell me a joke", participants all asked the chatbot to tell them a joke. The chatbot responded appropriately with randomised jokes, which all participants laughed at. The chatbot sends GIFs to the user at different points in the conversation, and participant 4 stated that these "cheered them up", and participant 7 particularly liked the "animal GIFs". Participants were unable to send emojis or GIFs back to the chatbot, which will need to be addressed to improve the conversational experience. Participant 2 and 4 found the usability test "fun" and liked interacting with the chatbot. When asked to type in another language to the chatbot, participants found this functionality was not supported, and participant 1 stated this would be a very useful feature to implement.

One of the questions in the Chatbottest questionnaire is - "Say something not really nice to the chatbot. Does it have answers for your different bad words?". The chatbot responded with, "That's not very nice - I am only trying to help." Participant 3 stated this could be phrased better, with a response such as "I'm sorry you feel that way". Participant 2 stated that the use of the helpline number in different points of the conversation was beneficial, as it makes users aware they can phone a mental health care professional at any time. Error management in iHelpr requires immediate improvement, as misspelled words are not detected. This could be improved by utilising spell checking APIs, such as Bing Spell Check[4] which can be integrated with LUIS. This allows the mistyped word to be corrected, before being sent to LUIS to predict the intent. Variability in the chatbot responses would ensure the user does not receive the same error message on each occasion.

A limitation of this study is that it was not known if participants were actively experiencing common mental health issues. Many participants stated they would only use the chatbot if they felt like they needed it, therefore a further study with participants who are actively experiencing a mental health issue would need to be undertaken. Another limitation was the small sample size, as hypothesis formed from this study will need further confirmation through future studies, such as monitoring real-world use of the iHelpr chatbot.

---

[4] https://azure.microsoft.com/en-gb/services/cognitive-services/spell-check/.

7.1 Final Recommendations

Drawing on the results and discussion, recommendations to improve the iHelpr chatbot have been derived. The utterances typed during the usability study should be compiled into a dataset to train the chatbot. More variability should be added to the chatbot responses, so that the user does not receive the exact same responses on each interaction. A more robust error management strategy needs to be developed to counteract the errors found during the usability study. A Bing Spell Check API should be integrated with LUIS to correct mistyped words. Functionality to allow the user to interact with the chatbot using Emojis, GIFs, and other elements needs to be developed. Localization should be supported to allow the user to interact with the chatbot in multiple languages. Another usability study should be completed to ensure the issues found are rectified. Furthermore, a usability study with participants who are experiencing a mental health problem should be undertaken.

8 Conclusion

In conclusion, the participants found the iHelpr Chatbot to be enjoyable and easy to use, and stated there is a consistent personality throughout the conversation, and the chatbot performs well at onboarding. Error Management and Intelligence are areas that require urgent attention, as they performed poorly in the questionnaire. Using the chatbottest questionnaire and SUS together was found to be a good combination, as many participants enjoyed completing the usability study. This study was completed with participants in a social enterprise. A further study would need to be undertaken with a larger selection of participants who are experiencing a mental health issue, to assess if the iHelpr Chatbot is useful in this context.

Acknowledgements. This study has been supported by UK Knowledge Transfer Partnership under KTP grant ID 1022267.

References

1. Shevat, A.: Designing Bots: Creating Conversational Experiences. O'Reilly Media Inc., Newton (2017)
2. Kayak. https://www.kayak.com/messenger. Accessed 2 Aug 2018
3. Plum. https://withplum.com/. Accessed 2 Aug 2018
4. Følstad, A., Brandtzæg, P.B.: Chatbots and the new world of HCI. Interactions **24**(4), 39–42 (2017)
5. Cameron, G., et al.: Towards a chatbot for digital counselling. In: Proceedings of the 31st British Computer Society Human Computer Interaction Conference, p. 24. BCS Learning & Development Ltd., Sunderland (2017). http://dx.doi.org/10.14236/ewic/HCI2017.24
6. Cameron, G., et al.: Best practices for designing chatbots in mental healthcare - a case study on iHelpr. In: Proceedings of the 32nd Human Computer Interaction Conference (2018). http://dx.doi.org/10.14236/ewic/HCI2018.129

7. Cameron, G., et al.: Back to the future: lessons from knowledge engineering methodologies for chatbot design and development. In: Proceedings of the 32nd Human Computer Interaction Conference (2018). http://dx.doi.org/10.14236/ewic/HCI2018.153
8. Stevenson, D., Farmer, P.: Thriving at work: the Stevenson/Farmer review of mental health and employers (2017)
9. Investors in People: Managing Mental Health in the Workplace 2018 (2018)
10. Miner, A., et al.: Conversational agents and mental health: theory-informed assessment of language and affect. In: Proceedings of the Fourth International Conference on Human Agent Interaction, pp. 123–130. ACM (2016). https://doi.org/10.1145/2974804.2974820
11. Bhakta, R., Savin-Baden, M., Tombs, G.: Sharing secrets with robots? In: EdMedia: World Conference on Educational Media and Technology, pp. 2295–2301. Association for the Advancement of Computing in Education (AACE) (2014)
12. Kavakli, M., Li, M., Rudra, T.: Towards the development of a virtual counselor to tackle students' exam stress. J. Integr. Des. Process Sci. $16(1)$, 5–26 (2012). https://doi.org/10.3233/jid-2012-0004
13. Fitzpatrick, K.K., Darcy, A., Vierhile, M.: Delivering cognitive behavior therapy to young adults with symptoms of depression and anxiety using a fully automated conversational agent (Woebot): a randomized controlled trial. JMIR Mental Health $4(2)$ (2017). https://doi.org/10.2196/mental.7785
14. X2ai.com. http://x2ai.com/. Accessed 2 Aug 2018
15. Cohen, S., Kamarck, T., Mermelstein, R.: Perceived stress scale. In: Measuring Stress: A Guide for Health and Social Scientists. Oxford University Press, Oxford (1994)
16. New Economics Foundation. https://neweconomics.org/2008/10/five-ways-to-wellbeing-the-evidence/. Accessed 2 Aug 2018
17. Lund, A.M.: Measuring usability with the USE questionnaire. STC Usability SIG Newsl. $8(2)$, 3–6 (2001)
18. Kirakowski, J., Corbett, M.: SUMI: the software usability measurement inventory. Br. J. Educ. Technol. $24(3)$, 210–212 (1993)
19. Brooke, J.: SUS: a "quick and dirty" usability scale. In: Jordan, P.W., Thomas, B., Weerdmeester, B.A., McClelland, I.L. (eds.) Usability Evaluation in Industry, pp. 189–194. Taylor and Francis, London (1996)
20. Coperich, K., Cudney, E., Nembhard, H.: Continuous improvement study of chatbot technologies using a human factors methodology. In: Proceedings of the 2017 Industrial and Systems Engineering Conference (2017)
21. Kocaballi, A.B., Laranjo, L., Coiera, E.: Measuring user experience in conversational interfaces: a comparison of six questionnaires. In: Proceedings of the 32nd Human Computer Interaction Conference (2018). http://dx.doi.org/10.14236/ewic/HCI2018.21
22. Chatbottest. http://chatbottest.com/. Accessed 3 Aug 2018
23. Callejas, Z., López-Cózar, R., Ábalos, N., Griol, D.: Affective conversational agents: the role of personality and emotion in spoken interactions. In: Conversational Agents and Natural Language Interaction: Techniques and Effective Practices, pp. 203–222. IGI Global, Hershey (2011). https://doi.org/10.4018/978-1-60960-617-6.ch009

A Conversational Interface
for Self-screening for ADHD in Adults

Robin Håvik[1], Jo Dugstad Wake[2(✉)], Eivind Flobak[1], Astri Lundervold[1], and Frode Guribye[1]

[1] University of Bergen, Bergen, Norway
{robin.havik,eivind.flobak,astri.lundervold,frode.guribye}@uib.no
[2] NORCE, Bergen, Norway
jo.wake@norceresearch.no

Abstract. Self-screening for mental health problems is commonly used to detect and assess symptoms, as a first step in diagnosing a problem, and to give recommendations for possible treatment. This study explores the potential of conversational interfaces in providing screening services for mental health care. A chatbot was developed to perform a screening for attention deficit/hyperactivity disorder (ADHD) in adults by including the items from the Adult ADHD Self-Report Scale (ASRS). We compared the conversational chatbot interface responses with reports on the standardised paper-based ASRS, and evaluated the user interaction with the chatbot. The results showed a match between the two modalities in the screening results. Based on interviews with participants and chatlogs we discuss the challenges and user experience of doing self-screening in a conversational interface.

Keywords: Conversational interfaces · Chatbots · Mental health · Screening

1 Introduction

Chatbots have received renewed interest as a way of interacting with computers, facilitated partly by the rise of universal chat platforms, advances in machine learning, and the availability of services for natural language processing [6]. Many recent variants directed at the general public have been integrated with major social media and communication platforms [10,17], and have become available in areas such as education, information retrieval, business and customer support [18]. Chatbots have also been explored as a tool to provide assistive tasks for individuals with somatic and mental health problems, for example by context-based tailoring of messages and supporting self-monitoring and behaviour change processes [12]. This paper presents a research through design study [24] aimed at developing a chatbot for the screening for symptoms associated with attention deficit hyperactivity disorder (ADHD). To empirically explore the viability of the idea of using chatbots for mental health screening, and to develop the

S. S. Bodrunova et al. (Eds.): INSCI 2018 Workshops, LNCS 11551, pp. 133–144, 2019.
https://doi.org/10.1007/978-3-030-17705-8_12

prototype further, a small-sample comparative study has been conducted. Concretely, the study has two main goals: (i) to transform a paper-based screening questionnaire – the Adult ADHD Self-Report Scale (ASRS) [13] – to a conversational interface; (ii) to compare the scores when using the chatbot and when using the original paper version. The accuracy of the scores derived from the chatbot conversation is compared to the paper-based answers, which are used as a baseline. Finally, we have interviewed the users to get further insight into their experiences when interacting with the chatbot and their views of its usefulness. This paper thus addresses one of the current research challenges in the study of human-chatbot interaction [5,19]; how chatbots relate to user needs, and to use information from users to develop further versions and studies of chatbots.

1.1   Chatbots and Conversational Interfaces

A chatbot refers to a "machine conversation system that interacts with human users via natural conversation language" [21, p. 489]. There is a growing interest in using chatbots and conversational interfaces as a tool to facilitate interaction between patients and health services. Conversational agents have for example been made for promoting physical activity, providing hospital discharge information, explaining medical documents and family health history-taking [2,3,23]. Bickmore and colleagues [4] designed a conversational interface to search for health information based on the observation that user-supplied keyword-based searches are particularly challenging for specific groups within the general population, such as children and older adults. They found that users with low health literacy were able to search for relevant information using a conversational interface more effectively. Fitzpatrick and colleagues [9] conducted a randomised controlled trial (RCT) with "Woebot", a conversational agent designed to deliver cognitive behaviour therapy (CBT), and found that adults aged 18–28 years experienced reduced symptoms of anxiety and depression by using it [9]. 85% of the participants used Woebot daily or almost daily during the study period. They reported that the Woebot users found the conversational interface to be engaging, and viewed the CBT more favourably than the information-only comparison group [9].

1.2   Screening in Mental Health

Mental disorders are common in the general population [11], but are not always detected and given the optimal treatment. A diagnosis may be dependent on information from family members and others, but this information is not always available. Self-report questionnaires have therefore become a much-used method to assess symptoms of mental health issues [11], and the results are commonly used to decide if an individual needs to be referred to a more in-depth clinical assessment. Saitz et al. [7,20,22] confirmed that brief feedback (i.e. test results or recommendations) is effective in managing several kinds of mental health problems. Digitised, self-administered screening procedures have been developed, and tests that ensure the privacy of the respondents have been seen to increase the reporting of potentially embarrassing or illegal behaviour, including symptoms of mental disorder [14], relevant for self screening for mental health problems. Self screening can also be seen as a starting point in the self-management of mental health problems [16].

Screening for ADHD in Adults. ADHD is a neurodevelopmental disorder which tends to persist into adulthood [1]. The "Adult ADHD Self-Report Scale" (ASRS) [2] is a questionnaire that is commonly used to screen for current symptoms of ADHD in adults [15]. It includes 18 items, covering all symptoms included in the Diagnostic and Statistical Manual of Mental Disorders (DSM-5) for ADHD, and participants are asked to rate their ADHD related behaviour in the past six months on a 5-point scale from 0 ("never") to 4 ("very often"). Kessler and colleagues [15] present strong arguments for using ASRS to detect adults with ADHD in need of treatment.

2   The Chatbot ROB

The chatbot prototype ROB (Fig. 1) presents the ASRS items in a conversational interface. It was built using IBM Watson Assistant's intents and entities structure. Intents are phrases and sentences that describe a category of intent of user input, and typically includes verbs and nouns. Entities provide parameter data that can be input to Watson, and describe the user input.

Fig. 1. ROB user interface.

Interaction with ROB is based on written text, with additional buttons for simple commands (see Fig. 1). Inspired by Fischer and Lam [8], and the notion that a user may not know all relevant symptoms to give a proper result for a symptom check test, the chatbot provides structure to the dialogue with the user.

Intents, entities and dialogue flow was developed to steer the conversation. The following four intents were outlined for this purpose:

– **greeting:** Greets the user when user writes a greeting message.
– **goodbye:** Ends the conversation when the intent is triggered.
– **screening:** Starts the screening sequence if triggered.
– **information:** An intent that is triggered if the user asks about ADHD.

The ASRS questionnaire items guided the dialogue construction. A requirement was that the structure of ASRS should be retained, including the phrases, the order of and possible responses to the questions. The original wordings of the ASRS items were therefore kept.

ROB starts the dialogue with a self-introduction. The user may then start the self-screening sequence by writing a statement that triggers the screening intent, e.g.: *"I want to fill in the ASRS questionnaire"*. Before ROB asks questions, the user is provided with information about the screening. It is communicated that ROB may not understand everything, and that the user should respond to how often he experiences the given symptom from the questions.

User responses that matched the ASRS Likert scale (*never, rarely, sometimes, often, very often*) were automatically accepted by ROB. To improve the flow of dialogue, a set of synonyms, from *thesaurus.com*, were attached to each of the entity types. Using synonyms created new challenges for the design. For example, the synonyms to "often" and "very often", overlap to a certain degree. Also, relevant words that had not been defined as synonyms for ROB, could have been entered by the user. Additionally, a user could be using negations of a word, which could trigger the opposite value of what is intended. These cases are harder to predict and there are challenges to creating an exhausting list of all possible synonyms. Nevertheless, the keywords were all collected under an entity named "@responses".

Additionally, fallback messages were tied to each question, which were triggered if none of the defined keywords were found in the user reply. The fallback message tells the user that ROB did not understand the input, and reminds the user of available answers in the screening dialogue. The following error message was outlined: *"I'm sorry, I didn't get that. Please answer the question in a degree of how often you experience the given symptom."*.

ROB can provide a user with some basic feedback on a result. Answers to ASRS questions are interpreted into numbers based on the defined responses and their synonyms, and computed into a sum which is then averaged and returned to the user as a final report.

3   Methods

The study was carried out as research through design [24] where the construction of the artefact and the challenges encountered in this process are crucial parts of the research process.

11 participants took part in the evaluation of the constructed artefact, and they completed the two different versions of ASRS. To ensure the anonymity of the participants, each participant was assigned a number used for identification throughout the study. Participant names were not recorded or stored. They were also instructed not to divulge identifying information during interaction with ROB, such as their names. They accessed ROB through a web browser on a dedicated PC, and the chat log for each participant was transferred to a word document after each session. ROB did not store user data other than the chat log. The participants provided their signed informed consent according to the ethics board for social science research in Norway.

The participants were divided into two sub-groups, controlling for the order of the presentation of the two versions with a within subjects design. The participants were first introduced to the background of the ASRS. Next, they were introduced to the task and the procedure. Three participants had prior knowledge about the ASRS questionnaire. The users interacted with ROB in a web browser on a PC that was provided, and completed the original paper version of the questionnaire.

A semi-structured interview was conducted to explore the participants' experiences with ROB. Each interview was recorded, coded with the participant number, and transcribed at length. Selected quotes from interviews have been translated to English and care was taken to preserve the participant intentions from the original transcripts.

In the analysis we use the scores from 18 items of the ASRS questionnaire, the time of completion for each screening, the 11 semi-structured interview transcripts about the user experience with the conversational interface, and the chat logs.

4   Findings and Results

This section presents findings from the study. The findings are organised around the themes of modality comparison, conversation and fallback message evaluation, and user experience with ROB.

4.1   Comparing the Two Versions of the ASRS

Table 1 shows the participants' scores on the ASRS and the time for completion, both when using the chatbot and the paper version. Participants 0–5 completed the chatbot screening before the paper version (group A), and 6–10 the other way around (group B). The three who had experience with ASRS before inclusion were part of the latter group.

Table 1. Results across modalities.

Partic.	Time Ch.	Time Pap.	Sum Ch.	Sum Pap.	Deviance
0	05:30	03:00	18	21	−3
1	04:30	02:45	40	38	2
2	06:22	01:56	24	19	5
3	03:12	01:45	35	31	4
4	03:29	01:41	23	14	9
5	10:08	02:10	33	28	5
6	02:20	02:30	6	8	−2
7	09:22	04:10	23	23	0
8	02:37	02:06	22	23	−1
9	05:04	02:26	35	30	5
10	04:15	02:28	20	21	−1

The average completion time of the paper version was 02:39 min faster than in the chatbot version, a difference that was statistically significant according to a paired sample t-test ($t(10) = 3.59$, $p = .005$). This was expected, because the paper version only required that the participant read the question and tick a checkbox to reply. In group A, the participants generally scored higher than in group B, they had a higher deviation from the paper version (average = 4,67) and used longer time to complete the screening. In group B, the deviance score was lower, with an average error score of 1,8. Only one participant in this group obtained a higher score in the conversational interface than in the paper version. Overall, this may indicate that a learning effect from being familiar with the items have influenced the answers in the conversational interface. In this small group, the group difference was, however, not statistically significant.

Early in the analysis we discovered that a few scores from one of the participants had a high deviance from the paper scores. As the chatbot is looking for predetermined words and checks these in the thesaurus, we found that there were some negations of words that had not been registered in ROB's thesaurus. This resulted in participant 1 having a very high error rate between the modalities (7 points). By reviewing the chat log, it was revealed that the participant had written "not very often" two times. This phrase was not explicitly registered in Watson, which led to a misinterpretation in the result calculation. Accordingly, the chat logs were reviewed for intent of the answers. We cleaned the data to reflect intent of the answers given in the conversational modality. This answer had also been registered automatically by the chatbot after adding the relevant negations of words to the thesaurus.

The mean sum scores of the chatbot (23.64(9.39)) was about the same as for the paper version (23.27 (8.32), $t(10) = .27$, $p = 794$). Regarding responses on each of the 18 items for all the participants, there were 197 response pairs in total, as 10 participants answered 18 questions, while one participant answered 17 questions. Figure 2 shows all answers of all participants across the two modalities. We also analysed the difference between the two modalities as response pairs (answers to the same questions by the same participant in the two different modalities). Of the 197 response pairs, 60 of them had discrepancies and the average error rate of those pairs was 1,01 points. In only one of the response pairs there was a discrepancy of two points on the scale. The rest of the 137 response pairs gave the same scores. The large majority of the sample thus gave corresponding answers to the items in both versions of the ASRS.

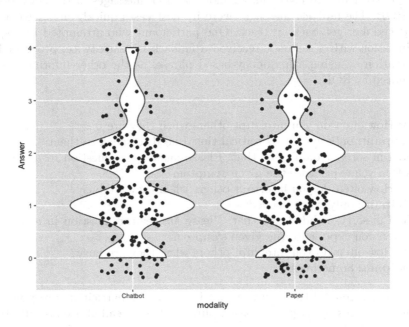

Fig. 2. Scatterplot of answers to all questions across modalities.

4.2   Conversation and Fallback Messages

The conversation logs were analysed to discover response patterns, length of responses, and the number of participants who received fallback messages.

The type of responses ROB received can be divided into three categories. Single phrase responses (1), sentences with the frequency-based phrase (2), and sentences that add extra substance or context to the response (3). The single phrase responses constitute the responses with an alternative from the Likert scale, or one of its synonyms. In the responses from those who responded in sentences there are some responses that may add extra substance to the screening result, but there are also many of them that does not provide additional information. To illustrate the types of answers, some examples for each category that was established are presented here:

Question: *"How often are you distracted by activity or noise around you?"*

- (1) "Not very often."
- (2) "I sometimes get distracted by noise or activity around me."
- (3) "Depends on the noise, but sometimes. Conversations are often focus killers."

Review of the chat logs indicate that the single-phrase responses were generally the most prevalent. Regarding fallback messages, the chat logs reveal that six of the 11 participants received one or more fallback messages in the conversation with ROB. The fallback messages were in most cases quickly understood, and helped the user get back on track. One participant who attempted to respond to a question with a sentence received a fallback message twice, proceeded the conversation by using a frequency-based phrase, as the other information had been noted by ROB:

ROB: How often do you interrupt others when they are busy?
Participant: only when it is critical that I need to speak to them
ROB: I'm sorry, I didn't get that. Please answer the question in a degree of how often you experience the given symptom.
ROB: How often do you interrupt others when they are busy?
Participant: only when needed
ROB: I'm sorry, I didn't get that. Please answer the question in a degree of how often you experience the given symptom.
ROB: How often do you interrupt others when they are busy?
Participant: Sometimes

There is a general trend in the chat logs that the participants responded to fallback messages by frequency-based phrases. The thread above also illustrates that the participant can interpret the question more broadly in the conversational interface than in the paper-based modality, where the Likert scale sets the boundaries of what one could respond to a question.

4.3   Experiences from Use of ROB

Most participants described satisfaction with answering the questions given by ROB. Three participants said that they found it interesting to respond to the questions, because they made them think and reflect on their own behaviour.

The participants were asked to offer opinions about differences between the two versions of ASRS. Several participants responded that writing an answer to a question in their own words made it possible to present reflections that were not possible in the paper version. One participant said *"It did in a way add an extra dimension by writing and having it presented in a known chat interface that you are used to. It felt a bit more personal in a way"*. Some participants also mentioned that they thought they answered the questions in the two versions in a different manner.

The paper-based screening presented all the questions simultaneously. According to some participants, it was easier to read the questions in the conversational interface, due to one question being presented at the time. On the other hand, it was more easy to grasp what to respond when all the response alternatives were available.

Two of the participants mentioned that after answering a few questions they began to see the logic behind ROB: it identified certain keywords or phrases. They both said that this influenced how they responded to the following questions, leading to shorter answers. This was also indicated by all participants in group B who had experience with the screening. The length of the responses was a topic commented on by two of the participants. Participant 10 was a bit uncertain about this aspect and suggested that ROB could send an instructive message giving the user a preferred response length.

The participants were asked about how they felt about answering the questions in an open manner, and if it led to more or less reflection. The participants liked having the opportunity to write more broadly around the questions. A common response was that by having the opportunity to respond openly one can easily add contextualised information to a response, which is not possible in the paper test. Participant 2 argued that this was useful when responding to a question where the context may influence the response. Participant 2 exemplified this by mentioning the question regarding the case of disturbing other people in a work setting, *"this can be necessary sometimes, so I did answer that I do this sometimes. I wrote the reason for this in the prototype. I did not get to explain this in the other test"*.

The conversational interface led to more reflection around the questions. Five participants responded in full sentences, but due to the necessity of having to write the answer instead of checking a box, it lead to more reflection before writing the response, according to the participants.

The design of the conversation was a topic that was brought up by several participants. When a participant successfully responded to a question, ROB asked a new question. Feedback addressing that ROB had received the response to a question was asked for. Participant 2 addressed this topic and said *"I felt like the chatbot was a very cold thing..."*. It was suggested that ROB could provide feedback in the a form of visual cue to the user when a response has successfully been given, or to give textual feedback, for example "I have received your answer", to acknowledge the response.

Ten of the 11 participants reported that they preferred the conversational interface above the paper version. They found that ROB opened for giving more information by making it possible to use own words and sentences, without being strictly bound to the words provided in the questionnaire. The participants also appreciated that they could reflect around a scenario and give more depth to a response.

5   Discussion and Conclusions

This study is concerned with implementing a paper-based, validated, established and standard screening test for symptoms of ADHD as a conversational interface in a chatbot. A central challenge has been the accuracy of the conversational interface in translating natural language to an appropriate Likert scale value. Further, a concern has been the user experience of taking the test in conversation with a chatbot.

The study provides an example of how we can implement one particular self-screening instrument, ASRS, as a chatbot. We have also shown how it can translate answers in natural language to fit into the Likert scale and convert them to the scores obtained by the paper version of ASRS. This includes using a thesaurus to look up synonyms.

The ASRS is, as mentioned, a first screening towards a full clinical evaluation. The result from the screening thus only gives an indication of whether a patient has symptoms of ADHD or not. It is common that a person either completes the screening as a questionnaire or in a conversation with a medical expert. The ASRS can also be used as an interview guide for medical staff. This motivated the present study to explore if a chatbot can simulate such a conversation. Ten of 11 participants reported preference for the chatbot over the paper-based version, regardless of the limitations of the prototype. Additionally, the participants used more time on completing the screening with the chatbot, but the responses from the conversational interface collected more details about the symptom than the paper version. Many of the respondents reported that the chatbot allowed for more reflection around the questions. Some of the users did, however, find the conversation "cold" due to lack of feedback on each of their responses. ROB presents a question without any comments before the next question, reducing the feeling of a conversation. Some of the participants thus experienced uncertainty as to whether ROB had received their response. Small comments and visual effects were suggested to handle this problem. This criticism is relevant, as a goal for making a chatbot can be to simulate human conversation [18].

Based on these results, it seems that a chatbot can be a useful screening utility in the mental health domain, and a useful addition to a paper version when screening for ADHD. That a large majority (137 of 197) of the questions were given the same answer in both versions, indicates the promise of the method of using synonyms in the dialogue design.

A chatbot can easily be deployed to a web page or to a messaging platform and thus be available as an alternative format in which to deliver the screening. This can make screening more accessible for people who may experience symptoms of ADHD, but who have still not been in contact with the health services.

5.1   Limitations and Future Work

While this implementation focused on one particular screening (ASRS), the same approach could include other screening examples of mental health issues. The method of looking up synonyms in a thesaurus should be further investigated. The main limitation of the present study is the small sample size. A study with a larger sample should be conducted, and a longer timespan should be considered. More accurate reports may also be obtained by using buttons with the five possible answers. This may reduce the number of fallbacks in the conversational interface.

Acknowledgements. This research has been carried out through the INTROMAT project, project code 259293/O70, funded by NFR – the Norwegian Research Council. IBM is an industry partner to INTROMAT. The authors would like to express gratitude for the careful reading and suggestions for improvement from the four anonymous reviewers. We also thank the participants that tested ROB.

References

1. American Psychiatric Association: DSM-V, 5th edn. American Psychiatric Association, Washington, DC (2013). https://doi.org/10.1176/appi.books.9780890425596. 744053
2. Bickmore, T.W., Caruso, L., Clough-Gorr, K., Heeren, T.: 'It's just like you talk to a friend' relational agents for older adults. Interact. Comput. **17**(6), 711–735 (2005). https://doi.org/10.1016/j.intcom.2005.09.002
3. Bickmore, T.W., et al.: Usability of conversational agents by patients with inadequate health literacy: evidence from two clinical trials. J. Health Commun. **15**(Suppl. 2), 197–210 (2010). https://doi.org/10.1080/10810730.2010.499991
4. Bickmore, T.W., Utami, D., Matsuyama, R., Paasche-Orlow, M.K.: Improving access to online health information with conversational agents: a randomized controlled experiment. J. Med. Internet Res. **18**(1), e1 (2016). https://doi.org/10.2196/jmir.5239
5. Brandtzæg, P.B., Følstad, A.: Chatbots: changing user needs and motivations. ACM Interact. **25**(5), 38–43 (2018). https://doi.org/10.1145/3236669
6. Braun, D., Hernandez-Mendez, A., Matthes, F., Langen, M.: Evaluating natural language understanding services for conversational question answering systems. In: Proceedings of the 18th Annual SIGdial Meeting on Discourse and Dialogue, pp. 174–185. Association for Computational Linguistics, Saarbrücken (2017). https://doi.org/10.18653/v1/W17-5522
7. Clarke, G., et al.: Overcoming depression on the Internet (ODIN) (2): a randomized trial of a self-help depression skills program with reminders. J. Med. Internet Res. **7**(2), e16 (2005). https://doi.org/10.2196/jmir.7.2.e16
8. Fischer, M., Lam, M.: From books to bots: using medical literature to create a chat bot. In: Proceedings of the First Workshop on IoT-enabled Healthcare and Wellness Technologies and Systems, IoT of Health 2016, pp. 23–28. ACM, New York (2016). https://doi.org/10.1145/2933566.2933573
9. Fitzpatrick, K.K., Darcy, A., Vierhile, M.: Delivering cognitive behavior therapy to young adults with symptoms of depression and anxiety using a fully automated conversational agent (Woebot): a randomized controlled trial. JMIR Mental Health **4**(2), e19 (2017). https://doi.org/10.2196/mental.7785
10. Følstad, A., Brandtzæg, P.B.: Chatbots and the new world of HCI. Interactions **24**(4), 38–42 (2017). https://doi.org/10.1145/3085558

11. Hoeper, E., Kessler, L., Nycz, G., Burke, J., Pierce, W.: The usefulness of screening for mental illness. Lancet **323**(8367), 33–35 (1984). https://doi.org/10.15713/ins. mmj.3
12. Kennedy, C.M., Powell, J., Payne, T.H., Ainsworth, J., Boyd, A., Buchan, I.: Active assistance technology for health-related behavior change: an interdisciplinary review. J. Med. Internet Res. **14**(3), e80 (2012). https://doi.org/10.2196/jmir.1893
13. Kessler, R.C., et al.: The world health organization adult ADHD self-report scale (ASRS). Psychol. Med. **35**(2), 245–256 (2005). https://doi.org/10.1017/S0033291704002892
14. Kessler, R., Barker, P., Colpe, L.: Screening for serious mental illness in the general population. Arch. Gen. Psychiatry **60**(2), 184–189 (2003). https://doi.org/10.1001/archpsyc.60.2.184
15. Kessler, R.C., Adler, L., Barkley, R.: The prevalence and correlates of adult ADHD in the United States: results from the National Comorbidity Survey Replication. Am. J. Psychiatry **163**(4), 716–723 (2006). https://doi.org/10.1176/ajp.2006.163.4.716
16. Kim, E., Coumar, A., Lober, W.B., Kim, Y.: Addressing mental health epidemic among university students via web-based, self-screening, and referral system: a preliminary study. IEEE Trans. Inf. Technol. Biomed. **15**(2), 301–307 (2011). https://doi.org/10.1109/TITB.2011.2107561
17. Luger, E., Sellen, A.: Like having a really bad PA. In: 2016 CHI Conference on Human Factors in Computing Systems - CHI 2016, pp. 5286–5297. ACM Press, New York (2016). https://doi.org/10.1145/2858036.2858288
18. McTear, M., Callejas, Z., Griol, D.: The dawn of the conversational interface. In: McTear, M., Callejas, Z., Griol, D. (eds.) The Conversational Interface, pp. 11–24. Springer, Cham (2016). https://doi.org/10.1007/978-3-319-32967-3_2
19. Piccolo, L., Mensio, M., Alani, H.: Chasing the chatbots. Directions for interaction and design research. In: Proceedings of Internet Science 2018. Lecture Notes in Computer Science. Springer (in press)
20. Saitz, R., Helmuth, E.D., Aromaa, S.E., Guard, A., Belanger, M., Rosenbloom, D.L.: Web-based screening and brief intervention for the spectrum of alcohol problems. Prev. Med. **39**(5), 969–975 (2004). https://doi.org/10.1016/j.ypmed.2004.04.011
21. Shawar, B.A., Atwell, E.S.: Using corpora in machine-learning chatbot systems. Int. J. Corpus Linguist. **10**(4), 489–516 (2005). https://doi.org/10.1075/ijcl.10.4.06sha
22. van Straten, A., Cuijpers, P., Smits, N.: Effectiveness of a web-based self-help intervention for symptoms of depression, anxiety, and stress: randomized controlled trial. J. Med. Internet Res. **10**(1), e7 (2008). https://doi.org/10.2196/jmir.954
23. Wang, C., et al.: Acceptability and feasibility of a virtual counselor (VICKY) to collect family health histories. Genet. Med. **17**, 822 (2015). https://doi.org/10.1038/gim.2014.198
24. Zimmerman, J., Forlizzi, J., Evenson, S.: Research through design as a method for interaction design research in HCI. In: Proceedings of the SIGCHI Conference on Human Factors in Computing Systems, CHI 2007, pp. 493–502. ACM, New York (2007). https://doi.org/10.1145/1240624.1240704

Different Chatbots for Different Purposes: Towards a Typology of Chatbots to Understand Interaction Design

Asbjørn Følstad[1]([⊠]), Marita Skjuve[1], and Petter Bae Brandtzaeg[1,2]

[1] SINTEF, Oslo, Norway
asf@sintef.no
[2] Department of Media and Communication, University of Oslo, Oslo, Norway

Abstract. Chatbots are emerging as interactive systems. However, we lack knowledge on how to classify chatbots and how such classification can be brought to bear in analysis of chatbot interaction design. In this workshop paper, we propose a typology of chatbots to support such classification and analysis. The typology dimensions address key characteristics that differentiate current chatbots: the duration of the user's relation with the chatbot (short-term and long-term), and the locus of control for user's interaction with the chatbot (user-driven and chatbot-driven). To explore the usefulness of the typology, we present four example chatbot purposes for which the typology may support analysis of high-level chatbot interaction design. Furthermore, we analyse a sample of 57 chatbots according to the typology dimensions. The relevance and application of the typology for developers and service providers are discussed.

Keywords: Chatbots · Typology · Interaction design

1 Introduction

There is great variation in how chatbots are implemented. From a user-centred design perspective, the variation in high-level approaches to interaction design is particularly interesting. One source of variation concerns the level of control bestowed on the chatbot. While some chatbots are designed to resemble Victorian servants, only aiming to satisfy their masters' requests, others are designed to persuade its users and lead them towards a particular goal. Another source of variation concerns the duration of the relation with the chatbot. While some chatbots target brief one-off encounters, others aim for establishing and maintaining long-term relations with their users.

Choice of high-level approach to chatbot interaction design is important, as it needs to fit the users' needs and desires in a given use-case and also reflect the strengths and limitations of the underlying technology on which the chatbot depends.

As an illustration of the importance of these choices, consider two well-known chatbots: Woebot (https://woebot.io), a self-help chatbot where users learn to cope with mental health issues, and Google Assistant (https://assistant.google.com), a personal assistant helping users with tasks such as planning, search, and controlling smart home devices. Whereas Woebot takes the user through a long-term program consisting of

S. S. Bodrunova et al. (Eds.): INSCI 2018 Workshops, LNCS 11551, pp. 145–156, 2019.
https://doi.org/10.1007/978-3-030-17705-8_13

brief daily interactions where much of the user input is predefined, Google Assistant awaits the user's requests and seeks to serve these with minimal requirements on the user as to how or what the input should be.

While different chatbot purposes clearly require different overall approaches to interaction design, there is little guidance to be found in the literature on how to classify chatbots and how to analyse interaction design with regard to different chatbot types.

The contribution of this paper is to propose a typology of chatbots, intended as a first step towards a framework that enables chatbot classification and provides better understanding of chatbot interaction design. To exemplify one possible use of the typology to support interaction design, we demonstrate how the proposed typology may be used to guide analysis of high-level interaction design in four common chatbot purposes: customer service, personal assistants, content curation, and coaching. We also apply the typology to classify a set of chatbots of some current prominence.

The paper is structured as follows. First we present a brief overview of relevant background on chatbots, chatbot interaction design, and typologies. We then propose a typology of chatbots, show example uses of the typology to support analysis of high-level interaction design, and present a study where the typology is applied for classifying current chatbots. Finally, we discuss the typology and propose future work.

2 Background

2.1 Chatbots and Chatbot Interaction Design

Chatbots are conversational agents that provide users' with access to data and services through natural language dialogue [7]. While the term *chatbots* typically is applied for text-based interaction, it may also encompass voice-based conversational agents such as Apple's Siri and Amazon's Alexa. Chatbots are used for a range of application areas such as customer support [12], health [6], and education [8], in addition to marketing, entertainment, and general assistance with simple tasks.

While conversational user interfaces have been an object of research and development since the sixties [11], the literature comprehensively treating how to design for chatbots is somewhat limited. However, major tech companies have provided guidelines on conversational interaction design, such as Google's guide to conversation design (https://developers.google.com/actions/design/), IBM's resources on conversational UX design (http://conversational-ux.mybluemix.net/design/conversational-ux/), and Amazon's design guide for Alexa (https://developer.amazon.com/designing-for-voice/). Material on conversational design is also found in developer and designer blogs, and in some practitioner-oriented textbooks on conversational design (e.g. [9]).

2.2 Typologies

Typologies are much used for classification purposes, in particular within the social sciences [1]. Typologies can support analysis and design of information systems as is facilitates learning across instances, for example as transfer of knowledge between instances of the same type [5].

Collier et al. [4] provided a three-step template for typology development. First, the general concept is outlined. Second, key dimensions capturing salient variation in the concept are identified. Third, the dimensions are cross tabulated, and each type within the cross tabulation is described.

Within a typology, the classes of a dimension should be collectively exhaustive and mutually exclusive. That is, the typology should include all possible cases and each case should fit exclusively within only one type.

The current literature provides little support for designers and developers in distinguishing between different chatbots types, and even less on different approaches to analyse chatbot interaction design in correspondence to such types. IBM's research group on conversational UX design suggest to differentiate between four interactional styles in conversational systems: system-centric, content-centric, visual-centric and conversation-centric (https://researcher.watson.ibm.com/researcher/view_group.php?id=8426). Chen et al. [3] distinguished between task-oriented and non-task oriented dialogue systems, but did not detail how this brings to bear on the interaction design of such systems.

3   Research Objective

In response to the lack in support for classifying chatbots, in particular for the purpose of supporting interaction design, three objectives were explicated for the presented work. First, to propose a chatbot typology in compliance with established criteria for typology development [1]. Second, to explore how this typology could be helpful in analyzing different high-level approaches to interaction design. Third, to review a sample of notable chatbots to investigate the potential usefulness of the typology for analysis and classification.

By meeting the research objectives, the presented work should be useful as a starting point for future research on differentiating chatbots and approaches to chatbot interaction design.

4   Research Method

The research method consisted of a four-step process.

Step 1: First, a set of chatbots of some prominence was gathered. We took as starting point the listings of recommendable chatbots from four relevant blogs and news websites (*Chatbot Magazine*, *Wired*, *Forbes*, and the Norwegian *Din Side*), as well as the *Chatbottle Award 2017*. Also, we included chatbots mentioned by two or more participants in a survey on chatbot users [2]. In total, 57 chatbots were included in the set.

Step 2: On the basis of reviewing this initial set of chatbots, dimensions differentiating these were suggested in an explorative manner. Possible dimensions included, for example, application domain (e.g. consumer goods, finance, games and entertainment, health and fitness, media and publishers), purposes (e.g. marketing and ecommerce, news and factual media content, social chatter and connections, customer support, personal assistant), platform (e.g. Facebook Messenger, Slack, Skype, Kik), or user group (e.g. children, youth, professional workers, elderly). However, the dimensions seemingly most promising were more generic, characterizing the intended duration of the relation and the locus of control for the dialogue. The typology was then detailed, following the recommendations of Collier et al. [4].

Step 3: High-level interaction designs for four chatbot purposes were analysed with a starting point in the proposed typology. These purposes were intended to reflect key areas of interest: customer service, personal assistants, content curation, and coaching.

Step 4: The initial set of chatbots were coded in accordance with the typology. The typology was critically discussed based on the four steps of the research method.

5   Chatbot Typology

The initial set of chatbots identified as basis for establishing the typology, belonged to domains such as consumer goods, health, finance, media, food and beverage, travel, social, general utilities. The chatbots served purposes such as social connections and chatter, customer support, marketing and ecommerce, entertainment, news and factual content, and personal assistant.

Within this broad variation, we noted that the chatbot interaction designs could be structured according to two high-level dimensions. We refer to these as: *Locus of Control* and *Duration of Interaction*. These dimensions comply with key requirements for typology classification [4], where the types should be mutually exclusive while covering the area of interest in a comprehensive manner. In the following we briefly describe these two dimensions, before we detail the resulting four chatbot types.

5.1   Dimension 1: Locus of Control

Dialogue between humans typically is characterized by reciprocity, where the dialogue partners are expected to drive the dialogue in relatively equal measures. This in contrast to chatbot dialogue, where different chatbots display markedly different approaches to which of the dialogue partners that are given the role as leaders of the dialogue. In particular, we distinguish between *chatbot-driven dialogue* and *user-driven dialogue*.

Chatbot-Driven Dialogue. Some chatbots provide a highly predefined interaction design; that is, the interaction is to a high degree driven or controlled by the chatbot. This is typically seen in scripted chatbots where the scripts include only limited options for branching or alternative paths. Or chatbots providing their users a small number of choices for standardized content, for examples through the use of menus, tiles, or carousels. Examples of such chatbots include content curating chatbots such as the chatbot of the Wall Street Journal, chatbots serving as coaches or guides, such as Woebot, and chatbots for marketing, such as the chatbot for Kia Motors America.

User-Driven. Some chatbots are set up to enable more flexibility in the possible input users may make, and to be more responsive to variations in user input. This arguably is more challenging, both technologically and in terms of the needed breadth and volume of content. The chatbot will need to identify the users' intent, both on the level of the individual messages and overall for the interaction or parts of the interaction, and also to be able to respond adequately on this intent. In consequence, for some user-driven chatbots, interaction sequences are typically relatively brief. This is for example often the case in customer support chatbots, such as Alibaba's chatbots for first tier response, or personal assistants, such as Google Assistant.

However, chatbots that has social small-talk as their main objective, so called chatterbots, are examples of chatbots that are user-driven and that also may enable longer conversational sequences. Much because social chatter may have an associative character where answers are not easily classified as correct or not, chatbots for small-talk may be set up with the sole purpose of keeping the conversation going. Well-known examples of chatterbots include Mitsuku and Cleverbot.

5.2   Dimension 2: Duration of Relation

Human-chatbot relations may, from the service provider point of view, be intended as either short-term or long-term relations. A short-term relation is characterized by a user engaging with the chatbot once, without user profile information being gathered or stored. A long-term relation is characterized by the chatbot drawing on user profile information for strengthening user experience across visits.

Short-Term Relation. Chatbots for short-term engagement are typically set up to provide users with one-off interactions, without an aim for a sustained relation. Chatbots for short-term interaction may possibly be characteristic of this period in chatbot development still being in early phase. Many companies are still at a level of chatbot maturity at which they are just trying out chatbots without seeing this as a prioritized platform. Hence, the need to generate sustained relations is limited. This does not mean that chatbots for short-term relations are only used once by the same users; users may visit the chatbot several times. However, they are then treated as a newcomer on each visit. Examples of short-term chatbots include content curating chatbots such as those run by CNN and Washington Post and marketing chatbots such as those of Burberry and Kayak.

Long-Term Relation. Chatbots for long-term engagement to a greater degree exploit the potential in user profile information to provide a personalized interaction. Examples of long-term engagements include content curation chatbots that offer recurring updates, chatbots for small-talk that remember what you chatted about in previous interaction sessions, and fitness chatbots that provide your fitness or workout history and schedule. Chatbots situated in messaging platforms such as Facebook Messenger and Kik has a good starting point for establishing long-term relations. The messaging platform provide the chatbot service provider with access to user profile information as well as facilities for easy reengagement.

Some long-term chatbots exploit the duration of the relation to gradually present a rich set of content, such as a complex story or a game, or to gradually build skills and capabilities in the user, such as in educational, fitness or therapy chatbots. Examples of long-term chatbots include content providers with subscription functionality, such as Poncho the weather cat and TechCrunch, educational and coaching chatbots such as Atlas Fitness, Woebot, and St. Panda, and social chatbots such as Replika.

5.3 A Two-Dimensional Typology

With basis in the two typology dimensions, a two-dimensional typology may be established. The typology provides four mutually exclusive categories of chatbots, which arguably overlap well with some of the main chatbot purposes.

Four main chatbot purposes, and their main location in the chatbot typology, is illustrated in Fig. 1. It should however be noted that our placing of the example chatbot purposes in the typology is not definite. That is, customer support chatbots may also be rigged for long-term duration; however, due to current limitations in such chatbots and lack of integration with customer relationship management (CRM) systems such chatbots, as of now, typically are in the upper left-hand corner. Likewise, while content curation chatbots often reside in the upper right-hand corner, some aim at long-term relations with their users, for example in the form of daily updates.

The chatbot typology may be used for the analyses and presentation of chatbot interaction design, as is seen for the examples chatbot purposes below.

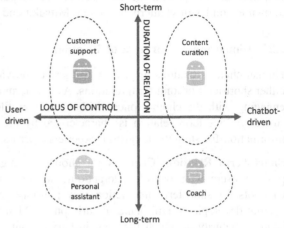

Fig. 1. A typology of chatbots with four example chatbot purposes located within the typology dimensions

6 Analysing Interaction Design on the Basis of the Typology

The proposed typology was used as basis for identifying high-level approaches to interaction design for chatbots reflecting the four chatbot types. We briefly present these for four example chatbot purposes.

6.1 Chatbots for Customer Support

By customer support we mean the provision of help or advice to customers or clients, provided by a company, government body, or non-profit organization. Customer support is typically user-driven, that is, the user engages with customer support with a particular question or concern in mind. The role of the service provider is to identify the customers root problem and provide possible solutions.

Depending on user and service context, interactions may be one-off engagement (e.g. in the case of general enquiries from a prospective customer) or part of a long-term engagement with an existing customer. Hence, chatbots for customer support typically may be classified as having a user-driven Locus of Control. Current chatbots for customer support typically have a short-term Duration of Relation. However, as CRM integrations improve, such chatbots may increasingly be used for building long-term engagement.

The user-driven character of customer support chatbots, typically lead designers to make it easy and efficient for customers to enter their questions or concerns. Often in the form of free-text, which the chatbot uses as basis for identifying topic and intent. The customer then may confirm or critique the response.

For example, in Alibaba's customer support chatbot (Anna), the first customer action is to enter the query. However, the chatbot also provides a short menu of frequently asked question categories.

The main drivers of the dialogue are the user questions, efficient chatbot responses, and an opportunity for the user to provide feedback to query for additional information or provide response of relevance to the quality of the answer (Fig. 2).

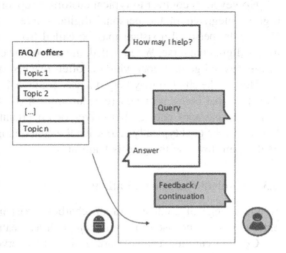

Fig. 2. High-level approach for interaction design in customer service chatbots (user-driven, short-term)

6.2   Personal Assistant Chatbots

Personal assistant chatbots are chatbots designed to serve a user continuously, on the fly, in the users daily tasks. Such as help to look up information, find and present content (typically music or movies), or control the environment through internet of things applications (e.g. turn on/off lights).

Personal assistant chatbots are highly user-driven, that is, the chatbot may respond to a wide range of requests made by the user. The role of the personal assistant is to efficiently and effectively interpret and deliver. The personal assistant is further intended for long-term relations, with high levels of personalization. Personal assistance chatbots may therefore be classified as having a user-driven Locus of Control and long-term Duration of Relation (Fig. 3).

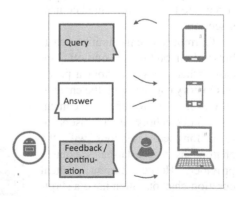

Fig. 3. High-level approach for interaction design in personal assistant chatbots (user-driven, long-term)

In response to the personal assistants' user-driven, interaction design typically aim to make it easy and efficient for customers to enter their questions or concerns. Often in the form of free-text, which the chatbot uses as basis for identifying topic and intent. The customer may then confirm or critique the response. This is much similar to current customer support chatbots as discussed above.

However, in contrast to typical customer support chatbots, the personal assistant is highly integrated in the personal digital universe of the user, often cross-platform. Hence, the personal assistant may be called from a wide range of contexts within the user's digital universe. When called, the aim of the chatbot is to efficiently lead the user to the desired goal, a goal which is often reached outside the chatbot dialogue.

Hence, the chatbot may help the user achieve the goal even without other feedback than the goal being achieved (e.g. turning off the light, or starting to play a desired song.). In cases of choice alternatives or uncertainty, the dialogue may be extended. However, the goal typically is to leave the chat dialogue as soon as the goal is achieved, or the path towards the goal is laid out.

6.3   Content Curation Chatbots

A wide range of content curation chatbots exist in the market, for access to news, entertainment, and useful information such as weather forecasts or flight information.

Content curation chatbots are designed to serve as a point of access to a set of content, either owned by the service provider (e.g. CNN news content) or accessed by the service provider (e.g. weather forecasts). The chatbot hence needs to be set up so as to display and suggest available content to the user. In consequence, content curation chatbots typically have a chatbot-driven Locus of Control where the user initiative is limited to accepting or rejecting content offers, or requesting specific content types, serving to filter the presented content selection.

Current content curation chatbots often address a one-off use-case, where a user without a previous history engages with the chatbot. However, increasingly content curation chatbots invite users to form long-term relations with the chatbot as a regular-basis content provider. Hence, current content curation chatbots often have a short-term Duration of Relation, though this seems to change towards long-term relation as chatbots mature (Fig. 4).

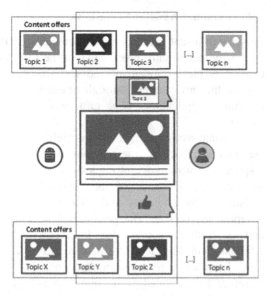

Fig. 4. High-level approach for interaction design in content curation chatbots (chatbot-driven, short-term)

Opposed to the user-driven chatbots seen for customer support and personal assistant chatbots, content curation chatbots actively guides users to recommended content rather than aiming for the user to freely chose and select. This is, in part, due to limitations in the dialogue interface, where browsing and search are less well supported that in regular web-pages or apps. Hence, promoting and recommending relevant and interesting content is critical.

Content typically is promoted through menus or present options, often including visuals to strengthen user experience and engagement.

6.4   Chatbots for Coaching

An increasing number of chatbots appear that aim to serve as coaches or guides for users, to help out with a specific challenge or task over time. For example education, therapy, or exercise.

Such coaching chatbots are designed to establish and maintain a long-term relation with the user. A relation which provides value to the user through, for example, learning new skills or mastering existing challenges. Examples of coaching chatbots are therapy chatbots such as Woebot, or guiding chatbots providing reminders and support to prospective students on their way towards college enrollment [10]. The aim of the chatbot needs to a able to take the user stepwise through a therapeutic or educational program, where the user increasingly gains the means necessary to learn the desired skill or master a specific challenge. Hence, coaching chatbots often have a chatbot-centred Locus of Control and a long-term Duration of Relation.

Coaching chatbots are characterized by taking the user through a predefined program through brief sessions on a recurrent basis, typically involving a few minutes of inter-action every day. Each session typically builds on the next, with the aim of gradually increasing the users knowledge or skill. The interactions within each of the sessions are scripted, where the users may choose between a small number of paths, depending on individual skill level or preference. Likewise, the order of the sessions may to some degree be reorganized to reflect the preferences or needs of the user. Also, some session elements may be recurring. For example, a therapy chatbot may have session elements that may be triggered at different reported states in the user. For example, a user reporting to feel down or depressed may trigger a specific session element addressing this reported state (Fig. 5).

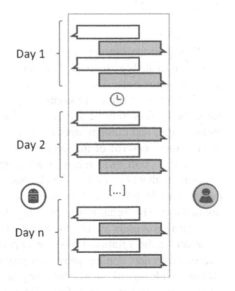

Fig. 5. High-level approach for interaction design in coaching chatbots (chatbot-driven, long-term)

7 Classifying a Larger Set of Chatbots

To explore the usefulness of the proposed typology for analysis and classification purposes, it was applied in an analysis of the 57 chatbots identified in the first step of the presented study.

The basic functionality of each chatbots was explored through interaction by the first author. The chatbots were tried on the platforms of their location, including Facebook Messenger (44), dedicated webpage (7), device (4), Slack (1), and a smartphone app (1). The chatbot was then categorized in terms of Locus of Control (user-driven or chatbot-driven) and Duration of Relation (short-term or long-term).

The chatbots' distribution in terms of the typology is presented in Table 1.

Table 1. Distribution of the 57 chatbots included in the analysis, across the dimensions Duration of Relation (short-term or long-term) and Locus of Control (chatbot-driven or user-driven)

	User-driven interaction	Chatbot-driven interaction	Sum
Short-term relation	8 chatbots Examples: DNB (customer support), Zo (chatter)	24 chatbots Examples: Whole Foods (marketing), CNN (news)	32
Long-term relation	5 chatbots Examples: Google Assistant (assistant), Mitsuku (chatter)	20 chatbots Examples: BBC Politics (news), Atlas Fitness (health)	25
Sum	13	44	57

Note that the sample of chatbots in no way purports to be a representative sample across all available chatbots. The sample is only intended as a set of chatbots that have received some note. The analysis nevertheless provide some interesting insights.

First, chatbot-driven chatbots are prominent among the chatbots that have received some note. This may be seen as a reflection of the relative immaturity in underlying technologies and content, making it challenging for chatbot providers to allow the user to take more control of the interaction.

Second, short-term relations are common. And for quite a few of the long-term relation chatbots (10 of 16), the chatbots merely provided subscriptions to notifications rather than building and extending the relationship with the user. This hints at the opportunities for relationship building through chatbots are not yet fully exploited.

Third, providers within the same market may make different choices in terms of duration of the relation users are expected to have with the chatbot. For example, within news and content provision providers such as CNN and BBC make different choices with regard to whether they want users make a long-term relation with the chatbot, e.g. in terms of subscriptions to daily briefs. This difference may likely be attributed to chatbots for content curation being a relatively new and immature market where different actors use different strategies to try our engagement with chatbots.

8   Discussion

We have in this paper proposed a typology for chatbots, exemplified how the typology can be used as basis for guidance on high-level analysis and guidance on interaction design for chatbot purposes such as content curation, customer support, coaching, and personal assistance.

The chatbot typology has been shown exhaustive (that is, the typology dimensions could be used to categorize all analysed chatbots) and with exclusive types (that is, all analysed chatbots fitted only one type). The dimensions for classification furthermore were found to be sufficiently general and relevant so as to identify meaningful differences between chatbots as seen in the analysis of high-level interaction design for the example chatbot purposes.

The typology dimensions further seems to provide a novel take on chatbot classification as compared to earlier attempts, such as the distinction of four kinds of interactional styles in conversational systems discussed by the IBM's research group on conversational UX design, and the proposed dichotomy of Chen et al. [3] between task oriented and non-task oriented conversational systems. Regarding the former classification, the interaction styles presented may to some degree be seen as a consequence of chatbot type. For example the visual-centric interaction style is frequently seen in chatbots classified as chatbot-driven. Regarding the latter dichotomy, it may be noted that the line between task-oriented and non-task oriented chatbots may be blurry as seen from the availability of chatbots that supports both task support and non-task oriented features, such as marketing chatbots that are intended to engage experientially while at the same time aiming to promote a product or service, or news and factual chatbots supporting both pleasant exploration and task-oriented fact-finding and updates.

The presented work clearly illustrates that chatbots still is an emerging technology which service providers have mainly taken up for exploratory use. This is for example seen in the way different service providers in the same market set up their chatbots differently in terms of Duration of Relation. As chatbot technology, chatbot content, and market uptake of chatbots mature, it may be expected that the distribution of chatbots across the typology dimensions will change. Possibly, towards longer durations of the user relation and more user-driven chatbots. As such, the proposed typology may serve to help service providers set goals for their chatbot developments, for example where service providers could set up goals for more long-term user engagement through chatbots and exploit the assumed potential of chatbots as a relationship-building technology. Such goal-setting will have implications for chatbot interaction design, as well as for requirements regarding the underlying technology and content available through the chatbot.

Chatbots are still emerging as an interactive technology, and their potential uses and purposes are only beginning to be seen. We hope the presented work may serve as a step towards strengthening the usefulness and user experience of chatbots.

Acknowledgement. This work was supported by the Research Council of Norway grant no. 270940.

References

1. Bailey, K.D.: Typologies and Taxonomies: An Introduction to Classification Techniques, vol. 102. Sage, Thousand Oaks (1994)
2. Brandtzaeg, P.B., Følstad, A.: Why people use chatbots. In: Kompatsiaris, I., et al. (eds.) INSCI 2017. LNCS, vol. 10673, pp. 377–392. Springer, Cham (2017). https://doi.org/10.1007/978-3-319-70284-1_30
3. Chen, H., Liu, X., Yin, D., Tang, J.: A survey on dialogue systems: recent advances and new frontiers. ACM SIGKDD Explor. Newslett. **19**(2), 25–35 (2017). https://doi.org/10.1145/3166054.3166058
4. Collier, D., LaPorte, J., Seawright, J.: Putting typologies to work: concept formation, measurement, and analytic rigor. Polit. Res. Q. **65**(1), 217–232 (2012). https://doi.org/10.1177/1065912912437162
5. Eide, A.W., et al.: Human-machine networks: towards a typology and profiling framework. In: Kurosu, M. (ed.) HCI 2016. LNCS, vol. 9731, pp. 11–22. Springer, Cham (2016). https://doi.org/10.1007/978-3-319-39510-4_2
6. Fitzpatrick, K.K., Darcy, A., Vierhile, M.: Delivering cognitive behavior therapy to young adults with symptoms of depression and anxiety using a fully automated conversational agent (Woebot): a randomized controlled trial. JMIR Ment. Health **4**(2), e19 (2017). https://doi.org/10.2196/mental.7785
7. Følstad, A., Brandtzæg, P.B.: Chatbots and the new world of HCI. Interactions **24**(4), 38–42 (2017). https://doi.org/10.1145/3085558
8. Fryer, L.K., Ainley, M., Thompson, A., Gibson, A., Sherlock, Z.: Stimulating and sustaining interest in a language course: an experimental comparison of Chatbot and Human task partners. Comput. Hum. Behav. **75**, 461–468 (2017). https://doi.org/10.1016/j.chb.2017.05.045
9. Hall, E.: Conversational Design. A Book Apart, New York (2018)
10. Page, L, Gehlbach, H.: How an artificially intelligent virtual assistant helps students navigate the road to college. AERA Open **3**(4). https://doi.org/10.1177/2332858417749220
11. Weizenbaum, J.: ELIZA—a computer program for the study of natural language communication between man and machine. Commun. ACM **9**(1), 36–45 (1966). https://doi.org/10.1145/365153.365168
12. Xu, A., Liu, Z., Guo, Y., Sinha, V., Akkiraju, R.: A new chatbot for customer service on social media. In: Proceedings of CHI 2017, pp. 3506–3510. ACM, New York (2017). https://doi.org/10.1145/3025453.3025496

Chasing the Chatbots
Directions for Interaction and Design Research

Lara S. G. Piccolo$^{(\boxtimes)}$ ⓘ, Martino Mensio ⓘ, and Harith Alani ⓘ

Knowledge Media Institute, The Open University, Milton Keynes, UK
{lara.piccolo,martino.mensio,h.alani}@open.ac.uk,
http://www.kmi.open.ac.uk

Abstract. Big tech-players have been successful in pushing the chatbots forward. Investments in the technology are growing fast, as well as the number of users and applications available. Instead of driving investments towards a successful diffusion of the technology, user-centred studies are currently chasing the popularity of chatbots. A literature analysis evidences how recent this research topic is, and the predominance of technical challenges rather than understanding users' perceptions, expectations and contexts of use. Looking for answers to interaction and design questions raised in 2007, when the presence of clever computers in everyday life had been predicted for the year 2020, this paper presents a panorama of the recent literature, revealing gaps and pointing directions for further user-centred research.

Keywords: Chatbots · Interaction design · Conversational interfaces

1 Introduction

More than 10 years ago, in 2007, Human-Computer Interaction (HCI) researchers and practitioners discussed how technology would shape society and how the HCI community should be prepared for that. In the seminal report *Being Human: Human-computer Interaction in the Year 2020* [4], the authors predicted, among other things, a growing presence of *"increasingly clever computers"*, and a more socially-connected world.

Indeed, social and the so-called smart technologies are becoming an important part of daily life activities in general. Also, better connectivity and recent advances in Machine Learning and Natural Language Processing (NLP) are some of the factors favouring the development and dissemination of the clever computers. Additional to that, a number of "user-friendly" toolkits for the design of conversational interfaces (i.e. DialogFlow, Wit.ai, etc.) are recently supporting the dissemination of chatbots as a user interface for services in general [25].

Not only the well-known voice-based services like Amazon Alexa, Siri and Google Home are becoming popular in the domestic environment, but the mainly

This work has received support from the European Union's Horizon 2020 research and innovation programme under grant agreement No. 687847 (COMRADES).

© Springer Nature Switzerland AG 2019
S. S. Bodrunova et al. (Eds.): INSCI 2018 Workshops, LNCS 11551, pp. 157–169, 2019.
https://doi.org/10.1007/978-3-030-17705-8_14

textual chatbot based on the Facebook Messenger platform has also been extensively explored commercially. According to [8], Facebook Messenger, Skype, Slack, etc. together are already hosting more than a million chatbots. Facebook Messenger alone hosts more than 300,000 of them [10]. These numbers are expected to increase in a short time. One indication comes from a recent report on emerging technologies and marketing by Oracle [17]. They found that 80% of consumer brands will be using chatbots for customer interactions by 2020. To date, 36% of the brands have already implemented one. In this context, the chatbots are mostly utility-driven, designed to provide specific and limited services to the user like the pioneer bot to assist with booking flights[1], for choosing a wine[2], or providing e-gov support[3].

Back in 2007, the authors of [4] precisely predicted computers to become more and more present in our lives, more independent and the interaction more like a human-human conversation rather than instruction-based. In that context where we would be living with *"increasingly clever computers"*, these authors raised 3 questions related to interaction and design [4] (p. 40):

1. *What will be an appropriate style of interaction with clever computers?*
2. *What kinds of tasks will be appropriate for computers and when should humans be in charge?*
3. *How can clever computers be designed to be trustworthy, reliable and acting in the interests of their owners?*

We dig into these three questions to analyse the literature on chatbots design and evaluation, evidencing that they are still open issues now, 10 years later, despite the extensive commercial adoption already in place.

As stated in [2], we have recently faced a substantial technology push in chatbot development. But a potential enthusiasm of the users can be led to frustration or disappointment - and rejection - if the technology does not meet the users' expectation, as some reports of failure have recently shown [2,9,19].

Aspiring to a long-life to chatbots, in this paper, we provide an overview of user-centred research discussing pieces of evidences collected in the field [19], as well as some findings and gaps from the literature. We aim at pointing to directions for further research that intend to achieve impact by exploring the potential of chatbots in engaging with the users.

The paper is organised as follows: in Sect. 2, we present a brief analysis of the computing literature looking at how user studies have grown along the years, evidencing how recent is this endeavour. In Sect. 3 we summarise a user study in a humanitarian scenario. In Sect. 4 we analyse the interaction and design research questions. Finally, in Sect. 5 we discuss the findings pointing to research directions. Section 6 concludes the paper.

---

[1] KLM Blue Bot: https://bb.klm.com/.

[2] Lidl Winebot: http://www.facebook.com/lidluk/.

[3] Emma, Virtual Assistant of the US Citizenship and Immigration Service: https://www.uscis.gov/emma.

2   Chatbots Literature Overview

To build a perspective on how the Human-Computer Interaction research domain have coped with this "chatbot wave", we have analysed the ACM Guide to Computing Literature digital library, which contains 2,795,980 records to date on *"all publishers in computing"*[4]. This search includes publications on the topic of 'chatbots' and 'conversational interfaces'. Any publication including at least one of these terms in the title, authors' keywords or abstract has been considered. A total of 330 publications were found between the years of 1975 and 2018.

By filtering the results looking for publications addressing any of these terms (or similar to) 'user(s) study', 'design', 'user evaluation', 'guidelines' in the abstract, a total of 131 entries have been identified and verified. As the chart in Fig. 1 illustrates, research on conversational interfaces is not a recent endeavour, actually, they have been present along most of the computing history, but the peak of interest in the last few years reflect the recent commercial boost. Following that, 46% of the user studies identified in this analysis are concentrated in the years of 2017 and 2018.

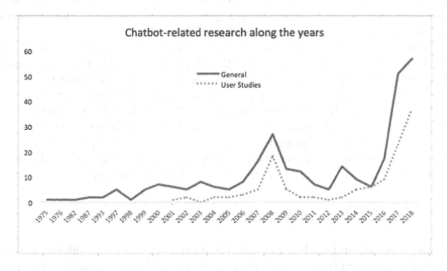

Fig. 1. Number of general publications on chatbots or conversational interfaces on ACM along the years and publications addressing user-related studies

As an indication of the research focus in the Computer Science and HCI literature, the word-cloud in Fig. 2 illustrates the 20 most frequent keywords used by the authors of the 131 papers addressing users' studies in some way. The words 'chatbot(s)', 'conversational interface(s)', 'conversational agent(s)' have been excluded to make the other complementary terms more evident.

---

[4] As informed by ACM at https://dl.acm.org/advsearch.cfm.

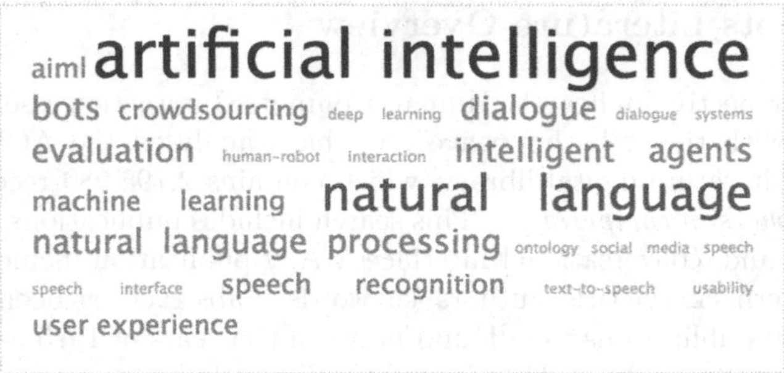

aiml **artificial intelligence**
bots crowdsourcing deep learning **dialogue** dialogue systems
evaluation human-robot interaction **intelligent agents**
machine learning **natural language**
natural language processing ontology social media speech
speech interface **speech recognition** text-to-speech usability
user experience

Fig. 2. Most common authors' keywords used in the papers addressing user studies

The fact that the authors' keywords not always properly represent the focus of the paper is acknowledged and can be considered a limitation of this analysis. But as a "thermometer" of the research domain, the word-cloud evidences the predominance of studies addressing aspects of Artificial Intelligence and Natural Language Processing when compared to more HCI-related topics like 'user experience' or 'usability'. Other terms suggesting more specific studies on users' perception, impact, adoption, etc., were not revealed.

This result suggests that technical challenges referring to advances in AI and NLP have been a research priority, and the efforts are not balanced when it refers to understanding the real impact of the technology to the users and to society. As already stressed by [6] and [31], although the engagement potentials of the chatbots have already been explored, how to design them to promote impact and a consequent "social good" is an emerging topic that deserves attention [7].

In line with that, in the next section, a field study that applied a Facebook chatbot in a humanitarian scenario is briefly summarised, illustrating why studies of this nature are essential for the success of the technology.

3   A Case Study Involving First-Time Users

As fully reported and analysed in [19], the authors of this paper piloted a study in the humanitarian context in Kenya. A Facebook Messenger chatbot was promoted for citizens to access Uchaguzi[5], a socio-technical initiative based on a crowdsourced platform to ensure peace and transparency during the presidential elections, which happened in October 2017.

The platform is based on Ushahidi[6], which collects and maps geo-tagged and validated reports from citizens that experienced any incident violating human rights or corruption. The reports can be generated directly on the platform website, via SMS, Twitter, phone, and in the context of this study, via the chatbot available on Uchaguzi's Facebook page.

---

[5] https://uchaguzi.or.ke/.
[6] www.ushahidi.com.

Advertised on Facebook, the chatbot attracted more than 3,000 visits. Despite of that, only 55 reports to the platform were completed via the chatbot. In around 50% of the visits, users just browsed and left the application. Reports were actually created in 38% of the visits (1,152), but the users either abandoned or got lost while interacting with the chatbot, and did not complete the interaction. The contents of these incomplete reports were manually extracted by technical volunteers that actually added 900 of them to the platform.

The interaction design and logged data were subsequently inspected by a specialist [19] and some design issues were identified. Nevertheless, the main barrier faced by the users that actually intended to create a report was the mismatch between the design and their expectation. Following Facebook best practices, the design mixed conversations and Graphical User Interface (GUI) elements [5]. The far majority of users, though, ignored (or did not make sense) of the GUI, which supposed to facilitate the interaction, and have tried (and failed) to engage in a pure conversation. A fully conversational interaction would not be the best solution while conversations are expected to breakdown due to technological limitations [5], therefore frustrating and disappointing inexperienced users.

The findings reported in [9] are in line with that. Also investigating the impact of Facebook Messenger chatbots from first-time users' perspective, the study involved 16 participants and evaluated 8 popular chatbots. Participants revealed that their expectations were not met and reported to be either disappointed or frustrated with the restricted natural language capabilities and the limited set of features offered by the chatbots.

As pointed out by Følstad and Brandtzæg [6], chatbots hold great potential as an inclusive technology, opening doors of digital services to people still unfamiliar with them. In the study in Kenya [19], it opened the doors of a crowd-sourced based platform to more than 1,500 people that tried to generate a report during the presidential elections. The impact, though, could be even bigger if more people could have made sense of the functioning of the chatbot, followed the navigation and fully engaged with the service. This could potentially be possible if the design had considered the first-time users need to understand the interaction style, eventually being more thoroughly guided throughout the service.

As [2] states, deploying a chatbot as a service interface is not only a matter of developing a new front-end, because users have new motivations and patterns of use in this case. Without understanding the people who use the chatbots, how do they use it, and their goals and expectations, it is hard to predict a sustainable adoption and impact of this technology.

4   Interaction and Design Questions

The empirical experience summarised above illustrates the need for further investigations on interaction and design towards fully exploring the potentials of chatbots for a positive social impact. Aiming at situating the state of the art in this domain, in this section, we look at publications addressing users' studies (as described in Sect. 2) to find answers to the three interaction and design questions raised in 2007 [4].

4.1 Appropriate Interaction Style

(1) What will be an appropriate style of interaction with clever computers?

The recent platforms for chatbots design are usually featured with powerful tools for creating conversational interfaces in the most popular languages, but they do not define the interaction style, which is a designer's choice [16]. As the examples below evidence, it does not exist only one interaction style that fits all chatbots and chatbots users.

In [20], the study focused on the interaction with a virtual home assistant in a domestic environment. The authors claim that in this scenario the interaction is not exactly 'conversational'. Instead of a dialogue, the interaction with the device tends to be an isolated action embedded in the householders' dynamic and conversations [20].

Considering also textual chatbots, [31] suggests taking the context into account when selecting the right interactive elements for mobile chatbots, such as displaying a menu of options or voice input to reduce errors, and typing when the task requires reflection or a confirmation.

Particularities of a specific group of users were evidenced in [19], situated in the humanitarian context, and [9], which analyses a variety of chatbots. In both cases, the authors shed lights on the specific needs and expectations of first-time users that may impact adoption and further appropriation of the technology.

As for any other interactive technology, in order to understand what is indeed the appropriate interaction style for a chatbot, it needs to be designed for (or with) groups of users, considering their specific needs and goals, and also be evaluated from the users' perspective. Different users' goals and platforms, such as Slack, Facebook Messenger, mobile conversational agents, or virtual home assistants, may lead to significant implications for the interaction style. Despite that, chatbots design usually follow a presumably one-size-fits-all approach, in which particular preferences, contexts, and needs are not considered [6].

As pointed out by [6], designing chatbots challenges some interaction and design foundations, since the traditional focus on graphical interfaces moves towards designing for services and a conversational flow, which is not fully predictable and very dependent on the input by the users.

For supporting designers/developers with possibilities, in [18], the authors propose a framework with six key dimensions along which chatbots may differ:

1. Type: performing informative, collaborative (with users) or automated tasks.
2. Direction: input only (monitoring conversations), output only (adding content to the conversation without considering the input), both.
3. Guidance: human-mediated or autonomous;
4. Predictability: deterministic or evolving (with learning components);

5. Interaction style: dull (using simple words and repetition), alternate vocabulary (adding alternative phrases to the dull), relationship builder (building a rapport, more spontaneous/funny behaviour, requiring planning conversational flows), human-like (learn from the history of conversations thus offer more meaningful interactions);
6. Communication channel: text, voice, or both.

Although displaying a range of possibilities with variable technical complexity, for example excluding or including AI components, this is a generic framework with no intention to provide design guidelines.

Considering the diversity of possibilities and expectations from users, as [2] states, it is crucial to inform potential users about the chatbots capabilities, what they are able (and not able) to deliver.

Evaluating: Assessing the success or adequacy of a chatbot interaction style also challenges traditional concepts as usability, as the humanised relation between user and chatbots brings to light a number of subjective aspects, some of them hard to be formalised and measured.

Radziwill and Benton [21] and Zamora [31] are some of the authors that have investigated quality attributes expected for chatbots. Some human-like attributes considered in these studies together includes *knowledgeable, likeable, politeness, sensitive to social concerns, reliable, enjoyable, personable, smooth, seamless, personality traits*, among others. In addition, [11] explores aspects of *playfulness* and [30] is pursuing *empathy*, both considering also automated detection methods to evaluate the chatbot. Another study [29] from a machine learning perspective explored as chatbots characteristics *self-consciousness, humour, purity, IQ* and *EQ (intelligence and emotional quotient), memory, self-learning* and *charisma*. As mentioned in [19], the adequacy of these characteristics may vary from context to context and according to the group of users. In the humanitarian context, for example, while humour can be inappropriate, empathy may play a role in building up trust.

Some of the attributes above mentioned have already been investigated in the context of HCI or user experience, like pursuing and enjoyable interaction [14], for example. Even in those cases, specific investigation is required to deal with the particularities of conversational interfaces. The complexity of humanised attributes such as *sensitiveness to social concerns, personality traits*, etc., requires a multidisciplinary approach for detection and evaluation considering users' perception and consequent impact.

4.2   Appropriate Tasks

(2) What kinds of tasks will be appropriate for computers and when should humans be in charge?

As the literature suggests, users' perception and expectations from chatbots may change dramatically from one platform to another, considering textual chatbots, virtual home assistants, Slack, etc. Studies addressing the real impact of chatbots for the users are still rare [12], and some authors actually question the reputation of chatbots with regard to their usefulness, arguing that their development is often pushed by marketing pressure, without taking into account users' real needs and motivations [6].

Looking more specifically at voice-based interfaces, both [20] and [12] highlight the need for more studies on social and interactive aspects of this technology in daily life. For [20], this literature gap is significant and little is known about the real impact of the technology and how interaction design should properly address it. The study reported in [31] had 54 participants in India and the United States using voice and text chatbot applications to report their perceptions on, among other things, what chatbots were good for. Beyond usual menial tasks, some people reported interest in chatbots for fulfilling emotional needs, such as someone to provide motivation or someone to listen without judging. Other participants found chatbots adequate for sensitive content that is too embarrassing to ask another human about. A preference for not engaging with potentially risky tasks, which could fail due to mishandling data, such as social media and finance-related data were also pointed out in this study. There is still a lack of trust in technology, as further discussed. Similarly, participants in [12] were reluctant to use conversational agents for complex or sensitive activities.

In another study [1], 146 chatbots users based in the US revealed that they are mainly looking for having some tasks related to assistance or information executed promptly and efficiently. Some users also reported entertainment, fun, or social and relational factors, such as reducing loneliness, as a motivation for using chatbots. In [13], though, the authors warn about potential risks of dealing with humans' emotions, such as leading to an excessive emotional attachment.

The experience in Kenya [19] suggested the potential of chatbots for crises situations where people with different levels of familiarity with technology could make use of a known user-interface to report issues. Otherwise, they would have to remember or install specific platforms for this end.

As discussed in [6], chatbots hold potential for positive social change, which can be related to well-being, welfare, supporting learning or connecting people. While the majority of applications are still dedicated to media access, marketing and customer service [6], applications like virtual therapists[7], virtual friend[8], or support to deal with distressful situations like harassment at workplace[9] are emerging. However, to consolidate the technology, systematic ways to measure the positive impact and drawbacks of these applications are necessary.

4.3 Towards Trustfulness

(3) How can clever computers be designed to be trustworthy, reliable and acting in the interests of their owners?

The experience reported in [19] illustrates the contrast between the users' expectations to engage in a proper conversation with the pre-set-answers based

---

[7] https://woebot.io.
[8] https://replika.ai/.
[9] https://talktospot.com/.

design. Other reports in the literature also focus on the mismatch between the users' expectations and system operation and the consequent resistance in assigning complex tasks to the conversational agents [9, 12, 31].

Dealing with the immaturity of the technology in keeping a natural conversation is the current main obstacle to gain users' trust and confidence. Moore et al. [16] have framed these design challenges of managing the dialogue and the conversational context as Conversational User Experience (UX).

Keeping the Conversation Flow: The openness of conversational interfaces and variations in the user input are the main challenges in chatbot design and evaluation [28]. In the current state of the technology, any chatbot design has to properly address conversations breakdowns [6]. Recognising that, as part of their design guidelines Facebook suggests that designers cannot expect perfection, because people behave in an unexpected way [5]. To properly perform their tasks, especially the AI-powered chatbots require substantial adaptation and maintenance [2]. For assisting the interaction design, in [26] the authors introduce a tool to support designers exploring and prioritising dialogue failure points with suggestions on how to fix them; and in [28], a qualitative method for inspecting the communicability of the chatbot is proposed.

Whether there is a boundary for that, a limit of tolerance from the users to deal with conversations breakdown is still an open question.

Keeping the Context: The human capacity to infer things and deal with ambiguities in a conversation is not yet mastered by the 'clever computers'. Managing the conversation context is probably one of the most challenging aspects of designing a chatbot [25]. Participants of the study in [8] felt that, finding it difficult to use chatbots for complex tasks as they are constantly unsure about the chatbots' contextual state. The mismatch between the chatbot's context in the conversation and the user's perception of the chatbot's understanding leads to confusion and consequent dialogue breaks [8]. Reflecting this feeling, participants of [3] wished their virtual assistant could clarify unclear requests or context and better handle errors before giving a random or generic answer like 'I don't know how to help with that'. The authors in [8] suggested a graphical tool added to the chatbot interface displaying the conversational context and providing interactions with the context values. The recent publication on Conversational UX [15] provides a framework that includes an interaction model for keeping a conversation flow, conversational patterns, a method for navigating conversational interfaces, and performance metrics.

Beyond the quality and naturalness of a conversation flow, building trust may also refer to human characteristics of the interlocutor, including the chatbot attitude. As an example, being trustworthy has been a target for a fashion-related chatbot [27]. To achieve that, specific features and vocabulary that would also work better to gain someone's trust in a purely human context have been considered in the chatbot design.

As previously mentioned in the Sect. 4.1, pursuing human characteristics has been considered a desirable aspect for a chatbot [21, 31]. However, there is a lack of experiences in the literature regarding the users' perception of trust and how human elements may impact that in terms of engagement and motivation. In [2], the authors refer to this dilemma mentioning Anna, a chatbot launched by a furniture retailer in 2006 that was considered unsuccessful for being too human, thus diverting the real purpose of the chatbot.

The discussion around trust can take a different level when shedding lights on ethical behaviours, such as bias. In [24], for instance, the authors investigate how to handle race-talks with a chatbot from a socio-technical perspective. AI-based applications require a wider and deeper discussion on ethical aspects, as initially addressed in [23].

5 Discussions and Research Directions

The literature review revealed several gaps in the user-centre research on how to properly design and evaluate chatbots considering a diversity of contexts, types of services and how to cope with the current limitations of technology without compromising trustworthy.

According to the Diffusion of Innovation model by [22], a technology in its infancy is usually in the hands of the innovators and early adopters, typically users with a higher tolerance for risk and complexity. However, the majority of people tend to have different expectations and thresholds when adopting it (or not). For this reason, we argue for the importance of boosting user-centred research towards filling these gaps.

By answering the interaction and design questions from [4], it was possible to build a panorama of the state of the art and find some directions for further research towards fully exploring the potential of chatbots, summarised as follows:

Interaction style should vary according to the platform, the chatbot capabilities, target audience, and context of use. Studies addressing how users are interacting with chatbots in specific platforms started to emerge mainly targeting the home assistants, but further research should consider also:

- Addressing other specific platforms (and users' motivations) like Facebook, Slack, Skype, etc.
- Experiences 'in the wild', in which variables like quality of connectivity, diversity of devices, multiple languages, etc., tend to emerge.
- Guidelines on defining the chatbots capabilities according to the context, such as when using or not AI, mixing graphical elements, etc.
- Pursuing systematic ways to design and evaluate human attributes, considering both the adequacy from the users' perspective and ethical boundaries.

Appropriate tasks for chatbots so far include improving productivity of menial and routine activities, and entertainment. There is a recognised potential for using chatbots for fulfilling emotional needs, addressing sensitive topics with privacy, and in humanitarian contexts.

- Further research is necessary for assessing the real value and impact of a diversity of applications to specific target audiences, especially those that touch emotional aspects of the users or aim to promote positive social changes.

Trustworthy is still an aspiration for most of the chatbots mainly due to the current limitations associated to conversational interfaces. Guidelines to keep an acceptable user experience in such scenario have just emerged, but additional research should include:

- Addressing limits of users' tolerance and impact of conversation breakdown on technology acceptance.
- Guidelines on how to communicate chatbots capabilities to (new) users.
- Systematic ways to assess trustworthy from the users' perspective.

6   Final Remarks

By analysing some computer science literature related to user studies on chatbot and conversational interfaces, this paper evidenced that despite the popularity of the technology in the market and the fast-growing number of users and applications, the users' perspective is a very recent subject of research. Yet, some reports of failure due to users' frustration or disappointment are emerging. The reasons are many, including not properly addressing limitations of the technology, excess of humanness, and also due to the mismatch between expectations and needs and the chatbot operation. We argue that the need for more user-centred research is significant and urgent in order to establish the technology within different contexts and for specific groups of user, therefore fully exploring the technology potential and ensuring its endurance.

References

1. Brandtzaeg, P.B., Følstad, A.: Why people use chatbots. In: Kompatsiaris, I., et al. (eds.) INSCI 2017. LNCS, vol. 10673, pp. 377–392. Springer, Cham (2017). https://doi.org/10.1007/978-3-319-70284-1_30
2. Brandtzæg, P.B., Følstad, A.: Chatbots: changing user needs and motivations. Interactions **25**(5), 38–43 (2018). https://doi.org/10.1145/3236669
3. Cho, J.: Mental models and home virtual assistants (HVAs). In: Extended Abstracts of CHI 2018, NY, USA. ACM (2018). https://doi.org/10.1145/3170427.3180286
4. Harper, R., Rodden, T., Rogers, Y., Sellen, A. (eds.): Being Human: Human-Computer Interaction in the Year 2020 (2008)
5. Facebook: Messenger platform design best practices (2018). https://developers.facebook.com/docs/messenger-platform/introduction/general-best-practices
6. Følstad, A., Brandtzæg, P.B.: Chatbots and the new world of HCI. Interactions **24**(4), 38–42 (2017). https://doi.org/10.1145/3085558
7. Følstad, A., et al.: SIG: chatbots for social good. In: Extended Abstracts of the CHI 2018, New York, USA. ACM (2018). https://doi.org/10.1145/3170427.3185372
8. Jain, M., et al.: Convey: exploring the use of a context view for chatbots. In: Proceedings of CHI 2018, New York, USA, pp. 468:1–468:6. ACM (2018)
9. Jain, M., et al.: Evaluating and informing the design of chatbots. In: Proceedings of the 2018 Designing Interactive Systems Conference. DIS 2018, New York, USA, pp. 895–906. ACM (2018). https://doi.org/10.1145/3196709.3196735

10. Johnson, K.: Facebook messenger passes 300,000 bots (2018). https://venturebeat.com/2018/05/01/facebook-messenger-passes-300000-bots/

11. Liao, Q.V., et al.: All work and no play? In: Proceedings of the 2018 CHI 2018, NY, USA, pp. 3:1–3:13. ACM (2018). https://doi.org/10.1145/3173574.3173577

12. Luger, E., Sellen, A.: "Like having a really bad PA": the gulf between user expectation and experience of conversational agents. In: Proceedings of CHI 2016, pp. 5286–5297 (2016). https://doi.org/10.1145/2858036.2858288

13. Mensio, M., Rizzo, G., Morisio, M.: The rise of emotion-aware conversational agents: threats in digital emotions. In: Companion Proceedings of the Web Conference 2018. WWW 2018, pp. 1541–1544 (2018)

14. Monk, A., et al.: Funology: designing enjoyment. SIGCHI Bull.: Suppl. Interact. **2002**, 11 (2002). https://doi.org/10.1145/568190.568208

15. Moore, R.J.: A natural conversation framework for conversational UX design. In: Moore, R.J., Szymanski, M.H., Arar, R., Ren, G.-J. (eds.) Studies in Conversational UX Design. HIS, pp. 181–204. Springer, Cham (2018). https://doi.org/10.1007/978-3-319-95579-7_9

16. Moore, R.J., Arar, R.: Conversational UX design: an introduction. In: Moore, R.J., Szymanski, M.H., Arar, R., Ren, G.-J. (eds.) Studies in Conversational UX Design. HIS, pp. 1–16. Springer, Cham (2018). https://doi.org/10.1007/978-3-319-95579-7_1

17. Oracle Corporation: Can virtual experiences replace reality? The future role for humans in delivering customer experience (2018)

18. Paikari, E., van der Hoek, A.: A framework for understanding chatbots and their future. In: Proceedings of the 11th International Workshop on Cooperative and Human Aspects of Software Engineering. CHASE 2018, pp. 13–16. ACM (2018)

19. Piccolo, L.S.G., Roberts, S., Iosif, A., Alani, H.: Designing chatbots for crises: a case study contrasting potential and reality. In: Proceedings of the British HCI Conference. ACM (2018). http://oro.open.ac.uk/55325/. (Early Access)

20. Porcheron, M., Fischer, J.E., Reeves, S., Sharples, S.: Voice interfaces in everyday life. In: Proceedings of CHI 2018. CHI 2018, pp. 640:1–640:12. ACM (2018)

21. Radziwill, N.M., Benton, M.C.: Evaluating quality of chatbots and intelligent conversational agents. CoRR **abs/1704.04579** (2017). http://arxiv.org/abs/1704.04579

22. Rogers, E.: Diffusion of Innovations, 5th edn. Simon and Schuster

23. Salge, C.A., Berente, N.: Is that social bot behaving unethically? Commun. ACM **60**(9), 29–31 (2017). https://doi.org/10.1145/3126492

24. Schlesinger, A., O'Hara, K.P., Taylor, A.S.: Let's talk about race: identity, chatbots, and AI. In: Proceedings of CHI 2018, pp. 315:1–315:14 (2018)

25. Shevat, A.: Designing Bots: Creating Conversational Experiences, 1 edn. O'Reilly

26. Shmueli-Scheuer, M., et al.: Exploring the universe of egregious conversations in chatbots. In: Proceedings of the 23rd International Conference on Intelligent User Interfaces Companion. IUI 2018 Companion, NY, USA, pp. 16:1–16:2. ACM (2018)

27. Vaccaro, K., et al.: Designing the future of personal fashion. In: Proceedings of CHI 2018, pp. 627:1–627:11. ACM (2018). https://doi.org/10.1145/3173574.3174201

28. Valério, F., et al.: Here's what I can do: chatbots' strategies to convey their features to users. In: Proc XVI Brazilian Symposium on Human Factors in Computing Systems. IHC 2017, pp. 28:1–28:10. ACM (2017). https://doi.org/10.1145/3160504.3160544

29. Wei, C., Yu, Z., Fong, S.: How to build a chatbot: chatbot framework and its capabilities. In: Proceedings of the 2018 10th International Conference on Machine Learning and Computing. ICMLC 2018, pp. 369–373. ACM (2018). https://doi.org/10.1145/3195106.3195169

30. Xu, A., et al.: A new chatbot for customer service on social media, NY, USA, pp. 3506–3510. ACM (2017). https://doi.org/10.1145/3025453.3025496

31. Zamora, J.: I'm sorry, Dave, I'm afraid I can't do that: chatbot perception and expectations. In: Proceedings of the 5th International Conference on Human Agent Interaction. HAI 2017, pp. 253–260. ACM (2017). https://doi.org/10.1145/3125739.3125766

Chatbot Personalities Matters
Improving the User Experience of Chatbot Interfaces

Tuva Lunde Smestad[✉] and Frode Volden

Norwegian University of Science and Technology, Gjovik, Norway
`tuva.smestad@gmail.com, frodev@ntnu.no`

Abstract. In this study, we investigated the impact of a match in personality between a chatbot and the user. Previous research have proposed that personality can offer a stable pattern to how chatbots are perceived, and add consistency to the user experience. The assumptions regarding the effects of personality was investigated by measuring the effects of two chatbot agents, with two levels of personality, on the user experience. This study found that personality has a significant positive effect on the user experience of chatbot interfaces, but this effect is dependent on context, the job it performs, and its user group.

Keywords: Chatbot personality · User experience ·
Conversational agents · Conversational interfaces ·
Personality framework · User-centred design

1 Introduction

Recent advances in machine learning have contributed to fast improvements in Artificial Intelligence (AI) and Natural Language Processing (NLP) of conversational user interfaces (CUI). Access to AI has become widespread, and through Application Programming Interfaces (API's), chatbots have access to vast amounts of information and knowledge through thousands of databases online. All this sounds promising, and explains in large part why chatbots have seen a rebirth recently, but all this does not matter if chatbots cannot live up to the expectations of users. Predictions find chatbots to be a big part of an AI powered future, but recent reviews have found them to be unintelligent and non-conversational [22,23]. We should therefore not be carried away by the positive outlook researchers presents in regards to the possibilities of advances in AI for chatbot technology, as the reality is that most chatbots are "falling flat" [23]. Despite cautions and recent negative reviews, 57% of companies have implemented or are planning to implement a chatbot in the near future [9] and chatbots are estimated to save companies $8 billion by 2022 [12]. Companies reap the benefits of chatbots, while users find them unintelligent and pointless; what effects might this have on the user experience and the future of chatbots?

In an effort to improve how chatbots are perceived and the value they can potentially provide, we propose that personality can be used to improve the user

© Springer Nature Switzerland AG 2019
S. S. Bodrunova et al. (Eds.): INSCI 2018 Workshops, LNCS 11551, pp. 170–181, 2019.
https://doi.org/10.1007/978-3-030-17705-8_15

experience of chatbots. Through this paper we will provide evidence to support that a match in personality between a chatbot and the user will have a positive effect on the user experience. We investigated this by designing and comparing two chatbot personalities: one agreeable and the other conscientious. The agreeable personality was designed through a user-centred design approach based on the personality framework presented in the author's Master's Thesis [27]. The conscientious personality was designed to be the opposite of the agreeable personality, and therefore assumed to not be appropriate for the user group. The user experience of both chatbot versions were measured by using the AttrakDiff measurement instrument created to assess the pragmatic and hedonic quality and attractiveness of interactive products. The experiment found that the agreeable chatbot personality had a significant positive effect on the user experience when compared to the other conscientious chatbot personality. The goal of this research is to contribute to the understanding of how we can improve the design of chatbots, and fill a gap in research related to the user experience of chatbots, by focusing on personality.

2   Background and Related Research

Emotional intelligence is an important part of how humans perceive themselves as intelligent beings. Psychologists describe emotional intelligence as the ability to tailor behaviour to environment through necessary emotional processing [4]. This ability is crucial to conversation, as conversation happen through dynamic relationships between the conversational actors. Human social interactions consists of much more than just language understanding, and if we want to improve how chatbots are perceived by users we have to understand how we can make them become convincing social actors. Emotional intelligence is important for humans to perceive conversational agents (CAs), such as chatbots, as thinking beings with a mind of their own [1,10,17]. Research on CAs and emotion have mainly focused on embodied conversational agents (ECA) [2,15,25,28] as the focus has been on "affective computing". Chatbots, however, are limited to a textual interface (including text-to-speech) where its ability to display physical gestures and read users physical expressions is limited. It is therefore necessary to understand how chatbots can be perceived as convincing social actors through written interactions.

In human interaction we make use of several social cues that dictates how we behave and how we are perceived by our conversational partners. Five primary social cues have been defined [8]:

1. **Physical:** face, eyes, body, movement
2. **Psychological:** preferences, humour, feelings, empathy
3. **Language:** interactive language use, spoken language, language recognition
4. **Social dynamics:** turn-taking, cooperation, praise, question answering, reciprocity
5. **Social Roles:** doctor, teammate, opponent, teacher, pet, guide

Our social interactions are dynamic, in which we mirror and change our behaviour to our conversational partners. Our social role influences how we behave in different situations; we act differently if we take on the role as a parent than we would as a friend. One of the driving forces behind how humans behave as social actors is personality. Our personality can be used to influence our environment, emotions and cognitions as well as our motivations. Personality has been believed to be the stable pattern that dictates the behaviour of a CA [4, 30]. Personality is defined as a "dynamic and organized set of characteristics possessed by a person that uniquely influences their environment, cognitions, emotions, motivations, and behaviors in various situations" [16]. Research have found that personality plays an important part in regards to how users perceive CAs, and can be the determining factor to whether users wish to interact with the agent again [4]. In addition personality has been found to offer consistency to the interaction [4, 21], in particular, for CAs a consistent personality helps users feel that they are talking to only one person throughout the conversation.

2.1   Anthropomorphism and Humanness

To understand how humans perceive CAs and why personality plays an important part to managing this, we must first understand the concept of anthropomorphism. Anthropomorphism is defined as "the attribution of human personality or characteristics to something non-human, as an animal, object, etc." [6]. Anthropomorphism is therefore human's ability to attribute human characteristics, motivations, beliefs, and feelings to non-human entities. Researchers have found that anthropomorphism is a normal occurrence in human-computer interaction [13, 25], and that personality can be used as a design variable to manage how users anthropomorphise computers [30]. The "humanlike mind" is an essential component of anthropomorphism, as humans needs to consider the machine as a thinking being to some extent in order for them to perceive the CA as having a mind of its own [26]. Which personality the individual users attribute to the inanimate object however can be very different based on how it behaves, how it looks, and the personality of the individual user.

While anthropomorphism is encouraged in order to build an emotional relationship between the human and the CA, humanness can be used to determine the extent to which we want humans to anthropomorphise the system. Humanness is defined as "the extent to which an agent is designed to act and appear human [...] encompassing the objectively established human capabilities (having eyes, a face or the ability to respond politely)" [18]. Researchers have found that levels of humanness affects how humans anthropomorphise a CA, as well as being an important factor for managing trust [5, 7, 14, 18, 24]. Researchers distinguish between anthropomorphism and humanness in that anthropomorphism relates to the psychological attribution of humanlike features on to something non-human, while humanness relates to the extent to which something looks or acts human [7, 19, 20]. This distinction is important, because while anthropomorphism is encouraged, different levels of humanness can have both negative and positive effects on how humans perceives the agent. The much cited term "the uncanny valley" [19] describes the effects high levels of humanness can have on human users. Robots that resembles humans to a very high degree are perceived as creepy, and humans interacting with them feel uncomfortable or fearful of it.

When users anthropomorphise a CA, the humanlike characteristics they attribute to the system is determined by how they perceive the system. Therefore, designers can control, through personality, how users attribute characteristics to the CA, and use humanness to manage user's expectations and trust. The level of humanness should support the given personality, and manage expectations users have regarding what it can do and how it behaves.

3 Design Methodology

The chatbot personalities built for this experiment were based on a personality framework defined and presented in the original publication [27] and summarised in this section. This framework follows a user-centred design (UCD) approach to gather the necessary insights and knowledge to build a suitable personality for the intended user group. As most chatbots implemented today acts as extensions of services provided by brands, this framework will focus on designing chatbot personalities that are suitable for users and the brand they represent. The four identified components are as follows:

1. The brand mission, goals and values
2. A deep understanding of the users and their needs
3. The role/job of the chatbot
4. An appropriate personality model

The first component must be met to ensure that the chatbot's personality and behaviour are consistent with the goals, values and tone of voice of the brand it represents, and supports the mission of the brand. The second component must be met to ensure that the personality supports the goals of the users, and to determine which personality traits that are appropriate for the user group. The third component is important as it dictates the social role of the chatbot, which again will help find appropriate traits that are compatible with its role. The final component, an appropriate personality model, is necessary to organise and map out the personality traits into a suitable framework. This project used the five-factor model.

3.1 Brand and User Group

The chatbot domain was based on a real brand, to apply the framework in a real life setting with real users and real needs. This will help inform suitable personality traits, the appropriate social role, and focus the research around a specific use case. The chosen brand and domain was chosen at random and only used to provide as an example to build the personality framework to inform the chatbot personality. The brand's mission is to increase consumption of fruit and vegetables, and the intended user group for the chatbot prototype are young couples living together, in the age group 25–40, preferably with small children.

3.2   Chatbot Personality Description

In order to test the chatbot's personality in relation to the user experience, two levels of personality were designed and tested. The first, Chatbot A, was given an agreeable personality that was the result of the user-centred design approach defined using the personality framework mentioned earlier. The other, Chatbot B, was designed to be the "opposite" of Chatbot A and was given a conscientious personality. Chatbot A's personality organised within the five factors are as follows:

Agreeableness: cheerful, trusting, amiable, humble, polite, helpful
Extroversion: affectionate, friendly, fun-loving, confident
Conscientiousness: reliable, consistent, perceptive
Openness: insightful, original, clever, daring
Neuroticism: no traits

Chatbot B on the other hand is low in agreeableness, extroversion and neuroticism, moderate in openness and high in conscientiousness. Both versions of the chatbot works as a dinner planner, helping young couples plan meals for the whole week. The appropriate social roles given to the chatbots were assistant and motivator, as their job is to assist with meal planning and motivate change. Both chatbots are equal in all regards expect their personalities; they offer the same services, performs the same tasks and creates the same value for users (at least in regards to achieving tasks). The differences in personality will be displayed through their choice of language and tone of voice (see Table 1).

Table 1. Difference in personality in responses between Chatbot A and Chatbot B

User expressions	Chatbot A	Chatbot B
I need your help with dinner tonight!	Cool cool;) What are you in the mood for?	Do you have a preference?
Something that's quick to make	In a hurry today huh? Here's a selection of 3 meals that takes less than 30 min to make:	Quick recipes:
Dinner tonight was delicious!	That's wonderful: D should I recommend this recipe again?	OK, recommend recipe in future?
My kids never eat enough vegetables! Can you help?	The struggle with children ey? They're tricky when it comes to healthy foods, but I have a few tricks up my sleeve:	Yes, three ways to help children eat more vegetables:

Fig. 1. Chatbot Bella's avatar

Both chatbots were given the same appearance in the form of a graphic representation of a human avatar (see Fig. 1). As mentioned earlier research have found that higher levels of humanness increases trust and are more familiar to users [18,20,29], but to keep the distinction clear that the chatbot is not in fact human, the chatbots were given a human avatar rather than an image of an actual human. Chatbot A and Chatbot B were given the name Bella, and a female gender despite research suggesting that female agents are more likely to be attributed negative stereotypes, and receive implicit and explicit sexual attention and swear words [3]. Investigating the effects of gender was outside of the scope of this research, and a female gender was found to be appropriate in regards to the intended user group. Both personalities were quantitatively assessed throughout the design process to ensure that they were perceived as intended by users, and that users were in agreement regarding how they perceived the two personalities.

3.3   The Chatbot Prototype

The chatbot prototypes were built using the Chatfuel bot builder platform, and the experiment was run through Facebook's Messenger platform. The chatbots interacts through written input and output, and did not support speech-to-text. The chatbot skills included, planning dinner for the whole week or evening, help using leftover ingredients, help eating healthier or increase consumption of vegetables, and add to and accessing grocery lists.

4   Experiment Methodology

The experiment was conducted to answer the research question: *Will chatbots with a defined personality improve the user experience of chatbot interfaces?* In the experiment the independent variable *personality* was manipulated into two levels (Chatbot A and B), to assess whether it has an effect on the dependent variable *User Experience*. The experiment uses the following hypotheses:

$H_1 1$: *Personality affects the user experience of chatbots*
$H_1 2$: *Chatbot A will have a positive effect over Chatbot B*

In addition to the hypotheses stated above, data was collected regarding participants preferred version and their reasoning for this.

4.1   Experiment Setup

Participants were recruited through convenience sampling, all within the age group of 25–40 years of age, 8 females and 8 males. The sample consisted of couples living together, either married or unmarried. 12 of the 16 participants had children in kindergarten or primary school. The participants were not aware of the goal of the experiment; they were invited to test two versions of a chatbot interface. Participants evaluated the two chatbots by completing a series of tasks using each chatbot. In order to compare the two chatbot versions, the participants will be their own control group as the experiment design will allow for a between & within-subjects design using a two by two factorial design, see Table 2. Half of the group will test Chatbot A first, while the second half will test Chatbot B first; to avoid a sequence/interaction effect. The participants will be presented with the same form for each chatbot.

Table 2. Experiment design of the two-by-two factorial design

Experiment design				
Group 1	Chatbot A	AttrakDiff evaluation	Chatbot B	AttrakDiff evaluation
Group 2	Chatbot B	AttrakDiff evaluation	Chatbot A	AttrakDiff evaluation

4.2   Data Collection: AttrakDiff

User experience is defined in ISO 9241-210 as "all the users' emotions beliefs, preferences, perceptions, physical and psychological responses, behaviours, and accomplishments that occur before, during and after use". Usability is the most widely known definition to determine whether a product is good or bad, and therefore an important part to determine a great user experience. Usability is defined in ISO 9241-210 as the "extent to which a system, product or service can be used by specified users to achieve specified goals with effectiveness, efficiency and satisfaction in a specified context of use". Hassenzahl believes that this definition is too task oriented, focusing on task completion and reaching goals, simplicity and efficiency, and forgetting about the "fun". AttrakDiff was built to assess the user experience by looking at usefulness and usability in the pragmatic quality, independently from the hedonic qualities of stimulation, challenge and motivation, and attractiveness [11]. The AttrakDiff form assesses personal user rating of a products usability and design.

Pragmatic Quality: Usefulness and usability of the system.
Hedonic Quality: Motivation, stimulation and challenge for the user.

The AttrakDiff measurement instrument consists of 28 seven-step items of opposing adjectives ordered into a scale of intensity. The middle values of an item group creates a scale value for pragmatic quality (PQ), hedonic quality (HQ - include HQ-I and HQ-S) and attractiveness (ATT). HQ-I and HQ-S are the sub-qualities of stimulation and identity of hedonic quality. The pragmatic quality will asses usability and usefulness of the chatbot, while both hedonic and attractiveness qualities will be used to assess the satisfaction with each version.

5   Results

The data collected through the AttrakDiff form was analysed by running a paired samples t-test. The statistics will be used to test $H_1 1$: *Personality affects the user experience of chatbots*, and $H_1 2$: *Chatbot A will have a positive effect over Chatbot B*. Descriptive statistics and the results of the paired samples t-test of the AttrakDiff data can be found in Table 3. Personality has two levels (Chatbot B = conscientious, Chatbot A = agreeable) and user experience has four factors (Pragmatic Quality, Hedonic Quality-Stimulation, Hedonic Quality-Identity, Attractiveness).

Table 3. Descriptive statistics & paired samples t-test AttrakDiff results, B = Chatbot B, A = Chatbot A

Descriptive statistics & paired samples t-test								
	N	Minimum	Maximum	Mean	Std. deviation	t	df	Sig.(2-tailed)
PQ_B	16	4	6,43	5,47	0,60	$-2,152$	15	,048
PQ_A	16	4,86	6,71	5,93	0,56			
$HQ\text{-}I_B$	16	3,57	5,43	4,77	0,57	3,239	15	,006
$HQ\text{-}I_A$	16	4	6,29	5,48	0,53			
$HQ\text{-}S_B$	16	2,57	6,57	4,78	1,19	2,934	15	,010
$HQ\text{-}S_A$	16	5,14	6,14	5,62	0,30			
ATT_B	16	3,9	6,3	5,34	0,78	$-4,069$	15	,001
ATT_A	16	5,14	7	6,35	0,45			

The paired samples t-test found that there is a significant difference in the scores between Chatbot B and Chatbot A, where all four factors of the user experience showed a significant positive effect between Chatbot B and A. These results suggests that personality has a positive effect on the user experience of chatbots, as all four factors of user experience was scored higher for Chatbot A than Chatbot B. As shown in Fig. 2, Chatbot A performed better in both hedonic and pragmatic qualities than Chatbot B and shows the mean score of each user experience factor and how the two personalities scored compared to each other. Figure 3 shows both personalities compared in the attractiveness rating.

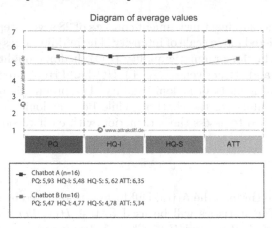

Fig. 2. Diagram of average values

In addition to the AttrakDiff evaluation, each participant was also asked at the end of the experiment to answer which of the two chatbots they preferred. Twelve of the sixteen participants preferred Chatbot A over Chatbot B, three males and one female preferred Chatbot B. Those who preferred Chatbot B also rated it higher in pragmatic qualities, but rated Chatbot A higher overall.

6   Discussion and Limitations

The agreeable personality of Chatbot A had a more positive effect on the user experience than the conscientious personality of Chatbot B. This does not mean that an agreeable personality is always better than a conscientious personality. Instead it shows that for this specific user group the agreeable personality was more suitable. In other situations where the chatbot represents another brand in another domain, towards a different user group, an agreeable personality might not be appropriate. The aim of our research was to support the assumption that a chatbot's personality should match its domain and user group.

The personality framework was built for chatbots that represents brands, where the chatbot acts as an extension of the services provided by the brand. Therefore the two personalities did not incorporate traits from the neuroticism factor, as traits found in this factor could represent the brand in a negative way. In addition to the lack of "negative" traits, users were only exposed to the two personalities in a short session. Longer exposure and interactions over longer periods could potentially have different results than those presented in this experiment. Another limitation in regards to the research methodology was

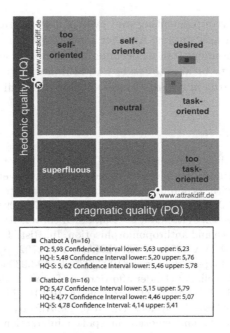

Fig. 3. Results Attrakdiff

the use of AttrakDiff, as it is not created for evaluating chatbots, but interactive products in general. AttrakDiff assesses interactive products through opposing adjectives, and participants noted that some of the adjectives included in the form was difficult to define when testing a chatbot. This is because some adjectives could be negative in a personality, but more positive when assessing a product. In addition, pilot tests found that minor errors made by the chatbot during interactions with users had a large impact on the overall perception, which made it necessary to limit user's freedom when interacting with the chatbot during the experiment. They were therefore not free to ask the chatbot whatever they wanted, but instead they were given tasks that the chatbots were trained to handle. Not allowing users to freely interact with the chatbots could have impacted the overall perception.

7   Conclusions and Future Work

The findings from the statistical analysis of the results found a significant difference between the pragmatic quality, hedonic quality and attractiveness of Chatbot A and Chatbot B. The results of the paired-samples t-test found that there was a significant positive effect on the user experience of Chatbot A compared to Chatbot B. Based on these results we can keep our research hypotheses $H_1 1$ and $H_1 2$, and we can conclude that personality does affect the user experience of chatbot interfaces.

For future research we want to investigate the long-term effects of chatbot personalities on the user experience. In addition to developing the personality framework further; by implementing and evaluating the framework in different domains and for other user groups. Another aspect for future research is to adapt the AttrakDiff measurement tool to become more suitable for CUIs. In addition to this, having a tool to be able to assess and evaluate the user experience when the CA grows and learns in regards to the specific user will become important.

References

1. Balzarotti, S., Piccini, L., Andreoni, G., Ciceri, R.: "I know that you know how i feel": behavioral and physiological signals demonstrate emotional attunement while interacting with a computer simulating emotional intelligence. J. Nonverbal Behav. **38**(3), 283–299 (2014). https://doi.org/10.1007/s10919-014-0180-6
2. Beun, R.-J., de Vos, E., Witteman, C.: Embodied conversational agents: effects on memory performance and anthropomorphisation. In: Rist, T., Aylett, R.S., Ballin, D., Rickel, J. (eds.) IVA 2003. LNCS (LNAI), vol. 2792, pp. 315–319. Springer, Heidelberg (2003). https://doi.org/10.1007/978-3-540-39396-2_52
3. Brahnam, S., De Angeli, A.: Gender affordances of conversational agents. Interact. Comput. **24**(3), 139–153 (2012). https://doi.org/10.1016/j.intcom.2012.05.001
4. Callejas, Z., López-Cózar, R., Ábalos, N., Griol, D.: Affective conversational agents: the role of personality and emotion in spoken interactions. In: Conversational Agents and Natural Language Interaction: Techniques and Effective Practices: Techniques and Effective Practices, pp. 203–223 (2011). https://doi.org/10.4018/978-1-60960-617-6.ch009
5. Dautenhahn, K., Ogden, B., Quick, T.: From embodied to socially embedded agents-implications for interaction-aware robots. Cogn. Syst. Res. **3**(3), 397–428 (2002). https://doi.org/10.1016/S1389-0417(02)00050-5
6. Oxford English Dictionary: Anthropomorphism. www.oed.com/view/Entry/8449?redirectedFrom=anthropomorphism&
7. Epley, N., Waytz, A., Cacioppo, J.T.: On seeing human: a three-factor theory of anthropomorphism. Psychol. Rev. **114**(4), 864 (2007). https://doi.org/10.1037/0033-295X.114.4.864
8. Fogg, B.J.: Persuasive technology: using computers to change what we think and do. Interactive Technologies, Elsevier Science (2002). https://doi.org/10.1145/764008.763957
9. Forrester: Chatbots are transforming marketing (2017). https://www.forrester.com/report/Chatbots+Are+Transforming+Marketing/-/E-RES136771
10. Griol, D., Molina, J.M., Callejas, Z.: Towards emotionally sensitive conversational interfaces for E-therapy. In: Ferrández Vicente, J.M., Álvarez-Sánchez, J.R., de la Paz López, F., Toledo-Moreo, F.J., Adeli, H. (eds.) IWINAC 2015. LNCS, vol. 9107, pp. 498–507. Springer, Cham (2015). https://doi.org/10.1007/978-3-319-18914-7_52
11. Hassenzahl, M., Platz, A., Burmester, M., Lehner, K.: Hedonic and ergonomic quality aspects determine a software's appeal. In: Proceedings of the SIGCHI Conference on Human Factors in Computing Systems, CHI 2000, pp. 201–208. ACM, New York (2000). https://doi.org/10.1145/332040.332432
12. JuniperResearch: Chatbot infographic key statistics (2017). https://www.juniperresearch.com/resources/infographics/chatbots-infographic-key-statistics-2017

13. Lee, E.J.: The more humanlike, the better? How speech type and users' cognitive style affect social responses to computers. Comput. Hum. Behav. **26**(4), 665–672 (2010). https://doi.org/10.1016/j.chb.2010.01.003

14. Lee, J.D., See, K.A.: Trust in automation: designing for appropriate reliance. Hum. Factors **46**(1), 50–80 (2004). https://doi.org/10.1518/hfes.46.1.50_30392

15. Lester, J., Converse, S., Kahler, S., Barlow, S., Stone, B., Bhogal, R.: The persona effect: affective impact of animated pedagogical agents, pp. 359–366 (1997). https://doi.org/10.1145/258549.258797

16. McTear, M., Callejas, Z., Griol, D.: Affective conversational interfaces. The Conversational Interface. LNCS, pp. 329–357. Springer, Cham (2016). https://doi.org/10.1007/978-3-319-32967-3_15

17. Mencia, B.L., Pardo, D.D., Trapote, A.H., Gómez, L.A.H.: Embodied conversational agents in interactive applications for children with special educational needs. In: Technologies for Inclusive Education: Beyond Traditional Integration Approaches: Beyond Traditional Integration Approaches, p. 59 (2012). https://doi.org/10.4018/978-1-4666-2530-3.ch004

18. Meyer, J., Miller, C., Hancock, P., de Visser, E.J., Dorneich, M.: Politeness in machine-human and human-human interaction. Proc. Hum. Factors Ergon. Soc. Annu. Meet. **60**(1), 279–283 (2016). https://doi.org/10.1177/1541931213601064

19. Mori, M.: The uncanny valley. Energy **7**(4), 33–35 (1970). https://doi.org/10.1109/MRA.2012.2192811

20. Nass, C., Moon, Y.: Machines and mindlessness: social responses to computers. J. Soc. Issues **56**(1), 81–103 (2000). https://doi.org/10.1111/0022-4537.00153

21. Norman, D.A.: Emotional Design: Why We Love (or Hate) Everyday Things. Basic Books, New York (2007)

22. Orf, D.: Facebook chatbots are frustrating and useless (2017). https://gizmodo.com/facebook-messenger-chatbots-are-more-frustrating-than-h-1770732045

23. Piltch, A.: Talk is cheap: why chatbots will always be a waste of time (2017). www.tomsguide.com/us/chatbots-waste-our-time,news-22562.html

24. Prada, R., Vala, M., Paiva, A., Hook, K., Bullock, A.: FantasyA – the duel of emotions. In: Rist, T., Aylett, R.S., Ballin, D., Rickel, J. (eds.) IVA 2003. LNCS (LNAI), vol. 2792, pp. 62–66. Springer, Heidelberg (2003). https://doi.org/10.1007/978-3-540-39396-2_11

25. Reeves, B., Nass, C.: The Media Equation: How People Treat Computers, Television and New Media Like Real People and Places. Cambridge University Press, New York (1996)

26. Schroeder, J., Epley, N.: Mistaking minds and machines: how speech affects dehumanization and anthropomorphism. J. Exp. Psychol.: Gen. (2016). https://doi.org/10.1037/xge0000214

27. Smestad, T.L.: Personality matters! Improving the user experience of chatbot interfaces (2018). http://hdl.handle.net/11250/2502575

28. Stern, A.: Creating emotional relationships with virtual characters; from: emotions in humans and artifacts. Trappl, R., Petta, P., Payr, S. (eds.) (2003)

29. Terada, K., Jing, L., Yamada, S.: Effects of agent appearance on customer buying motivations on online shopping sites. In: Proceedings of the 33rd Annual ACM Conference Extended Abstracts on Human Factors in Computing Systems, pp. 929–934. ACM, Seoul (2015). https://doi.org/10.1145/2702613.2732798

30. Xiao, H., Reid, D., Marriott, A., Gulland, E.K.: An adaptive personality model for ECAs. In: Tao, J., Tan, T., Picard, R.W. (eds.) ACII 2005. LNCS, vol. 3784, pp. 637–645. Springer, Heidelberg (2005). https://doi.org/10.1007/11573548_82

Part III
The Future of Decentralized Governance: An International Workshop

Preface for the Future of Decentralized Governance Workshop
Encryption, Blockchains, and Personal Data

Harry Halpin

Inria, 2 rue Simone Iff 75012 Paris, France

`harry.halpin@inria.fr`

Abstract. The governance of decentralized techno-social systems is one of the most important and inherently interdisciplinary questions facing the future of the Internet. The widespread use of encryption for security, as well as the explosion of blockchain technologies, shows vast potential but these technologies are heavily under-theorized currently. The proceedings volume includes the four full papers presented at the workshop.

Keywords: Decentralization · Governance · Standards · Blockchains

1 Introduction and Aims

Currently, there is a generalized crisis in governance as traditional governance is subsumed by the Internet. On the Internet, there has been revelations of US mass surveillance and massive abuse of personal data. The traditional governance bodies of the Internet from the ITU to W3C seem hard-pressed by Silicon Valley companies, which has lead to widespread disillusionment. At the same time, the European Union's General Data Protection Directive is attempting to enforce European rights, but purely through legal rather than technical means. Yet there have been new technologies based on encryption, such as blockchain technologies, that claim to be able to revolutionize governance. At the same time, there are numerous perils, such as the rise of opaque AI decision-making systems and the consolidation of power in the hands of a few technologists instead of a rapid democratization of technology.

Given these technical and political developments, new and improved models that take into account user involvement and improve meaningful participation need to be developed, along with fundamental Internet rights that can both be adopted by national governments, supra-national bodies, corporations, and cities as well as made into running code. These principles will likely have to do with the guarantee of privacy, data protection, and other fundamental rights that are especially impacted by the Internet. In particular, this workshop explored the understanding of the interface between technology, rights, and governance processes.

2   Workshop Summary

As the first pioneering workshop on interdisciplinary internet-based approaches to decentralization and governance, the workshop was a resounding success in clarifying the hard problems facing this emerging field. The workshop lasted for a half-day at St. Petersburg University and attracted attendance from Russian academics involved in internet studies, citizens involved in digital rights, and the rapidly growing Russian blockchain commercial sector.

2.1   Blockchains and Governance

The possible governance revolution of blockchains was the prime subject of debate. The workshop began with Alina Vladimirova (Russian Academy of Sciences) on "Blockchain Revolution in the Global Environmental Governance: Too Good to Be True?," where the policy aspects of blockchain technology in terms of environmental governance were brought to the forefront. For example, could blockchains be required to prevent companies from altering their carbon footprints? Alexandra Giannopoulou (University of Amsterdam) then discussed "Distributed Data Protection And Liability On Blockchains," noting that the traditional centralized model of data protection and privacy is incompatible with decentralized blockchains that make personal data public by default, and that work has to be done in order to make blockchains privacy-preserving and compliant with laws like the General Data Protection Regulation of the European Union. Jaya Brekke (University College London and Durham University) gave an invited talk on "The Decentralization 'Fix' and the Persistence of The Political" that reviewed how even what appeared to be algorithms to reach consensus were unable to solve political problems within the blockchain community, leading to blockchain forks. The topic of forking was considered one of the genuinely new governance phenomena in blockchains that merits further study.

2.2   Secure Messaging and Privacy

The next debate was over encryption and decentralization. Halpin (Inria and MIT) started with "Decentralizing the Social Web" where he gave a history of how a failure in governance at traditional Web standards bodies like the W3C led to the failure to decentralize the early Web, despite many engineers being keenly aware of the dangers of centralization and thus producing technologies like OAuth and the Semantic Web; these technologies ended up being re-cuperated as Facebook Connect and the Like Button. The urgent need for better secure messaging for social movements was brought forward by Iness Ben Guirat (Inria) in "Privacy for Social Movements." Moxie Marlinspike (Signal Foundation), inventor of the popular end-to-end encrypted messaging application Signal whose underlying protocol is used in WhatsApp and even Skype, gave the keynote on "The ecosystem is moving."[1] Moxie Marlinspike defended the use of centralization as a way to keep features, including security fixes and privacy

---

[1] https://signal.org/blog/the-ecosystem-is-moving/.

features, updated and so keep Signal usable and secure. He argued that criticism of Signal's use of phone numbers was misguided, as it was better to keep contacts on the phone rather than on a centralized server like Wire or as accessed via Facebook Connect. Interestingly enough, after discussion at the workshop, Signal released a new feature to keep the sender of a message anonymous from the Signal server itself,[2] a real step forward in terms of privacy for millions of users.

3   Outcomes and Reflections

The workshop led to a fruitful interdisciplinary and cross-cultural conversation between legal scholars, social scientists, and technologists from both academia and the non-profit sector. Despite their differences, these diverse participants were all united in evolving the Internet to be a decentralized space for collective empowerment, rather than a monopoly of platforms based on extracting value for isolated individual users. While the vision of Internet Science came before the surge of new blockchain technology and spread of privacy-enhanced technologies like Signal, the success of these technologies show that the Internet still may fulfill its potential for the common good. The results of this workshop will lead to further policy recommendations to the European Commission by the NEXTLEAP project[3] and future work on this topic at Internet Science and related conferences.

Acknowledgments. The workshop is funded in part by the European Commission H2020 NEXTLEAP Project (Grant No. 6882). We would like to acknowledge the reviewers: Moritz Bartl (Center for the Cultivation of Technology), Marios Issakides (University College London), Andrew Feenberg (Simon Fraser University), Z. Isadora Hellegren (Internet Foundation in Sweden), Bogdan Kulynych (EPFL), Francesca Musiani (CNRS) and Sarah Myers West (USC Annenberg).

---

[2] https://signal.org/blog/sealed-sender/.
[3] http://nextleap.eu/.

Decentralizing the Social Web

Can Blockchains Solve Ten Years of Standardization Failure of the Social Web?

Harry Halpin[✉]

Inria, 2 rue Simone Iff, 75012 Paris, France
harry.halpin@inria.fr

Abstract. For over a decade, standards bodies like the IETF and W3C have attempted to prevent the centralization of the Web via the use of open standards for 'permission-less innovation.' Yet today, these standards, from OAuth to RSS, seem to have failed to prevent the massive centralization of the Web at the hands of a few major corporations like Google and Facebook. We'll delve deep into the lessons of failed attempts to replace DNS like XRIs, identity systems like OpenID, and metadata formats like the Semantic Web, all of which were re-cuperated by centralized platforms like Facebook as Facebook Connect and the "Like" Button. Learning from the past, a new generation of blockchain standards and governance mechanisms may be our last, best chance to save the Web.

Keywords: Standards · Social web · Decentralization · Blockchain

1 Introduction

Far from being a mere technical concern, the promise and failures of decentralization via open standards in terms of Internet governance are a matter of pressing public concern. The fate of the Internet as a common socio-technical infrastructure for our personal data is one of the most intimate yet political questions of future generations. Due to controversies around the selling of personal data by companies like Cambridge Analytica and the passage of laws like the General Data Protection Regulation in the European Union, the general public is waking up to the world-historical danger posed by the system of control created by the rise of a few centralized platforms such as Google and Facebook.

Interestingly enough, ordinary software engineers were aware of the dangers of centralization at the very advent of social networking[1] and have long been attempting to build practical decentralized systems to counter these threats to

---

[1] Let us not forget that the first versions of Twitter actually offered the support of decentralized XMPP, and this decentralized Twitter was turned off not by the programmers, but by the management who could see no demand to support decentralization. At the time, users didn't understand decentralization, much less want it (personal communications with Blaine Cook, founding engineer at Twitter).

© Springer Nature Switzerland AG 2019
S. S. Bodrunova et al. (Eds.): INSCI 2018 Workshops, LNCS 11551, pp. 187–202, 2019.
https://doi.org/10.1007/978-3-030-17705-8_16

human freedom. Given that the original World Wide Web itself was created via open standards like TCP/IP, HTTP, and URIs, it should come as no surprise that the strategy deployed by these grassroots computer programmers to counter the control of Google, Facebook, and other centralized platforms was primarily based on creating new open standards for decentralizing social data and protecting personal data.

Social data is data about the relationships between people and their environment, and so can be considered a commons in terms of ownership and possibly governance [11]. Social data would clearly include data like maps and public government or scientific data. On the other hand, personal data is considered data that reveals information about an individual, and thus the ownership and governance of this data can be considered a matter of self-determination of the individual [12]. Personal data would include personal names, addresses, identity card numbers, and so on. Of course, this division relies on inscribing a number of ontological categories that ultimately may not actually hold true. *All data is social* as it is dependent on a complex web of social relationships that characterize a process of collective individuation (as put by Stiegler), where - at any given moment - the individual is considered a result of continual co-evolution with their socio-technical infrastructure [7]. However, what is clearly self-evident is that regardless of the dialectic between social collectivity and individual autonomy, data itself is not as simple as individual or even collective property rights: One does not "own" data in the same manner one owns a coat or a house. Data around "friends" is neither clearly social nor personal: To which "friend" does the link of friendship belong? However, this does not mean that individuals have no rights over their data and so social data should automatically belong to whichever platform, such as Facebook, harvests this data. Instead, data literally co-creates the individual and society, and so their digital data is part of their very self. This viewpoint towards personal data brings it into the realm of fundamental rights, where the harvesting of personal data is more akin to a new kind of cognitive slavery, and just as everyone has the right to both self-determination in terms of their body and thought, and via mutual association vis-á-vis larger society, social data should also be controlled ultimately by the people who co-create this data. In terms of *decentralization*, no trusted third party should be given control of data, but instead individuals and groups should maintain control over their own data [13].

Although there have been attempts to inscribe the autonomy of data via legal means such as the General Data Protection Regulation, it is an entirely another question whether there can be decentralization of our social data via technological means like open standards. The history of this engineer-based movement for decentralization is far older than the advent of "blockchain" technology, although the advent of blockchain-based systems offer something new: An approach of guaranteeing the integrity of global common knowledge, albeit at the cost of privacy. While there is a frenzy of activity around Ethereum, Ethereum has yet to prove itself as a working technical alternative to Silicon Valley's centralization of the Web, as Ethereum's initial design ignored many of the lessons learned from computer science research into distributed systems and programming language theory. More dangerously, technically the approach to simply decentralize existing social systems may inadvertently lead honest yet naïve programmers to create a new and even more dangerous form a control society masquerading as a liberatory future: For example, a version of the Chinese 'social credit' system could easily be built in a decentralized manner using blockchain-based smart contracts.[2] While it is possible Ethereum or another as yet unnamed technology will usurp the Web, at this point the issues of governance and standards for blockchain technologies are still in their early stages. Given that the future of human autonomy itself now is intertwined with technologies, we must revisit the tangled history of failed attempts to decentralize the Web 1.0 that was recuperated into the Web 2.0, so that those that creators of the next Web do not repeat the tragedy of the Web 2.0 as a farce.

2 Identity: The Foundation of the Social Web

In a simplistic abstract sense, identity is the capability to distinguish one object from another.[3] This capability typically results in socially embedding discrete names on the level of an individual, such as a personal names and uniquely identifying national identity numbers. The first article that imagined the potential political promise of decentralized identity standards was *The Augmented Social Network: Building Identity and Trust into the next-generation Internet* [8], which began with a statement that seemed to be naïve, but also prefigured many of the fundamentally political questions at the heart of social networks: "Might a 'next generation Internet' help to reinvigorate democracy by providing a platform that makes it easier for citizens to inform themselves about public policy debates, self-organize, and participate in the process of governance?" The primary claim was that the main missing technical component was "a form of persistent identity that serves civil society" for the Web that would "cross traditional borders," and so create an "augmented social network," doing for the social collectivity that which Engelbart's project to augment the human intellect had done for the individual with the invention of the personal digital computer [8]. The vision of persistent identity was that "each time we go from one social network to another we do not need to restate who we are, what our interests are, or who we know" so that people would be able to re-engineer a new kind of social network, as "the design of the technical infrastructure underlying online communication is increasingly determined by for-profit entities that seek to monetize every aspect of our discourse" rather than realize the global democratic potential of the Internet [8]. Note this article on the dangers of the possible commercial centralization of identity was written before Facebook was even founded. Ironically, the authors

---

[2] https://www.wired.co.uk/article/chinese-government-social-credit-score-privacy-invasion.

[3] For a detailed metaphysical and cognitive treatment of identity, Brian Cantwell Smith's *On the Origin of Objects* presents a metaphysics where objects are "carved" via registration from the underlying metaphysical flux [2].

proposing a persistent identity for decentralized social networking seemed to think the technical problems were trivial.

The Web does not include any notion of personal identity by design as the same web-page was meant to be displayed to every user in order to enable scalability via the REST architecture [4]. While web-sites were designed to have persistent identities such as *www.example.org* via the Domain Name System (DNS), users had no identifiers or personal data associated with them, although this led to the creation of invisible, ad-hoc techniques for associating personal data with offline identities via third-party "tracking" cookies. Instead of a single cross-Web identity, users had to create a new identity - a set of attributes containing personal data - across every website such as a new name, a new profile photo, and a new password. In contrast, DNS was invented at nearly the beginning of the Internet itself and pre-dated the Web, and has long been a centralized registry for the identity that mapped human-readable domain names for web-sites to IP addresses.[4] Originally this first internet identity infrastructure for names created and ran by a single IETF member, Jon Postel on a voluntary basis. When Postel managed to reconfigure eight of the twelve 'root' DNS servers via a simple email (against the wishes of the US government), there was a crisis of formal decision-making inside the IETF. In response, the US government approved the creation and transfer of DNS to a California non-profit called ICANN (Internet Corporation for Assigned Names and Numbers), given a limited duration license by the US Department of Commerce, and ICANN took over the running of DNS in 1998 (shortly after Jon Postel died).[5] ICANN was given a nominally democratic structure and eventually in 2014 the United States government handed over power over DNS indefinitely to ICANN. The sheer centralization of naming authority in the hands of ICANN was viewed by many advocates of decentralization with suspicion. There were also concerns of its financial monopoly on domain names, where in a form of "digital feudalism," ICANN enables domain registrars to charge web-site owners rent for simply having a name on the Web, and it handed over the selling of top-level domains like *.com* to registrars like Verisign or to nation-states such as *.fr* for France. Nevertheless, the system remained fairly functional for decades, but ICANN never assumed power of giving digital identities to end-users.

It struck a few enterprising individuals that one possible business model would be to create a new kind of centralized DNS for the personal identity of individuals and organizations, and ordinary people would have to buy their identity from their start-up. In other words, their startup could be a for-profit self-anointed ICANN for individual identity. Although replacing ICANN seems to be progressive, these start-ups would replace a nominally democratic non-profit with a startup that would have a for-profit governance structure. The first to try this business model was Drummond Reed, whose startup Cordance created

---

[4] https://datatracker.ietf.org/doc/rfc1591/.

[5] https://www.wired.com/2012/10/joe-postel/.

their own system of "eXtensible Resource Identifiers" (XRIs). With the new centralized XRI scheme, individuals would be given new names such as *+drummond*.[6] XRIs could be resolved by XDI (XRI Data Interchange), an equivalent to the DNS system for XRIs, which would in turn retrieve an XRDS (Extensible Resource Descriptor Sequence) that then describes the person's attributes such as age and photo. However, XDI was ran by a single organization called *XDI.org* that held a license to patents from Reed's Cordance company [9]. Perhaps XRIs were standardized at OASIS because, unlike W3C or IETF, OASIS allowed its standards to contain patents and for the license-holders to demand licensing fees. In fact, Reed's Intermind startup even brought up the patents to the W3C, forcing the W3C to create a royalty-free patent licensing scheme.[7] Although Reed claimed to give the patents to the non-profit XDI.org, others at OASIS such as Verisign, believed they had been re-licensed and the entire scheme was a get-rich-quick scheme by a patent troll. Regardless, while XRIs was under development, Reed tried to insert XRIs in as many other standards as possible. Their strategy for deployment of XRIs seemed to include getting adoption via new standards that companies would implement by default, including a newly minted OpenID standard. Eventually the W3C stepped in and OASIS closed the standardization process, effectively ending XRIs.[8] Attempting to force a get-rich-quick scheme business model into an "open standard" was rejected by the governance of the more authoritative standards bodies like the W3C, which although there is no formal governance relationship between W3C and OASIS.

The developer Brad Fitzpatrick, creator of LiveJournal, in 2005 wrote (with the help of David Recordon at SixApart) a blog post called "Thoughts on the Social Graph" where he stated "there doesn't exist a single social graph (or even multiple which interoperate) that's comprehensive and decentralized. Rather, there exists hundreds of disperse social graphs, most of dubious quality and many of them walled gardens."[9] In response, Fitzpatrick and Recordon created OpenID.[10] The vision of OpenID was originally that an OpenID would be a "Single Sign-On" client, allowing a user to login into many different web-sites. The main issue is that they envisioned that a user would become their persistent OpenID identifier across all digital services. This OpenID identifier could be an XRI, or perhaps something more mundane like a URL. If a website supported OpenID, a user could simply sign-in *once* into their "identity provider" and then other websites could import their identity and related personal data into a website without even using their password. Sadly, OpenID made a crucial mistake: People don't confuse their own personal identity with their credit card number, and so they are equally unlikely to confuse their personal identity with a text string like a URI or OpenID. By identifying users by things they didn't

---

[6] https://www.oasis-open.org/committees/download.php/15376/xri-syntax-V2.0-cs.html.

[7] https://www.w3.org/1999/04/P3P-PatentBackground.html.

[8] https://lists.w3.org/Archives/Public/www-tag/2008May/0078.html.

[9] http://bradfitz.com/social-graph-problem/.

[10] https://openid.net/specs/openid-authentication-2_0.html.

understand, such as XRIs and URIs, OpenID was expecting to create an entire new mode of social interaction. Rather than try to force new modes of social identity (where users created new identifiers or cut-and-paste URIs into forms to identify themselves), decentralized social systems should build on existing social patterns such as e-mail and telephone numbers that users already understand and use on a daily basis. The fundamental mistakes made around user experience and an overly-complicated standard led to virtually no uptake, so most major sites like Facebook and Google eventually gave up on OpenID 1.0 (and 1.1) by 2015. The real value of open standards comes from patent commitments and the building of an actual community of developers around these standards, yet this community assumes users actually want these standards to begin with and can use them in their everyday lives.

OAuth is currently the most successful standard for transferring personal data between sites, but OAuth does not specify a name for an identity like XRIs or OpenID. Before OAuth, if a web application wanted to retrieve a user's personal data from a website on a social networking platform like Facebook or a large platform like Google, the password for a user's Google or Facebook account had to be transmitted to the web application, which posed a security threat as it allowed third-party applications unrestricted access to personal data, like all of a user's email. Twitter engineer Blaine Cook didn't want to have the responsibility for the passwords of his users, and realized that the OpenID architecture had the aforementioned usability concerns. Therefore, in 2006 Blaine Cook started the OAuth standard to enable the secure authorization of the transfer of information from one site to another.[11] In essence, OAuth creates a time and scope delimited token, and allows one website to request user information, and then redirects the user back to the site to authorize this access. If the user agrees, the user is redirected back to their originating website, which then gains the ability to get a scoped and permissioned access to the user's personal data via a shared secret the user has explicitly authorized. The protocol did not specify the kinds of data that could be transferred or the user experience. OAuth went through standardization at IETF (Internet Engineering Task Force), the oldest and largest multi-stakeholder standards bodies on the Internet. The IETF fixed a number of security holes, although it increased in complexity through different versions. Regardless, OAuth was by far the most successful of all the standards to decentralize social data, as Google, Facebook, and other large identity providers took up OAuth and many smaller sites enabled OAuth-backed login protocols. There are today perhaps more OAuth transactions than Visa transactions. However, OAuth identity providers became centralized due to the "NASCAR problem," namely that users could not either run their own identity provider or cognitively manage to chose from a large list of identity providers, leading personal identity to be recentralized in Google and Facebook Connect. Ironically, Google, Facebook, and Twitter all deploy a profile of OAuth called OpenID Connect.[12]

---

[11] https://tools.ietf.org/html/rfc6749.
[12] https://openid.net/connect/.

3   Metadata: The Semantic Web Revisited

Metadata can be thought of as how to categorize everything that we may want to identify, including the attributes of the identified objects. These attributes may include data such as the favorite color and city of birth of an individual, but may also include links to other objects (such as a list of friends) or categories (such as nationality and profession). Therefore, it seems that either a tightly defined list of categories and data needs to be defined (as done by OpenID Connect or an open-ended standard way of describing all possible metadata could be used, as put forward by Tim Berners-Lee's Semantic Web standards [1], a set of standards for metadata developed by the W3C. At the time in 1999, the most widely used standard for data formats was W3C's XML (eXtensible Markup Language),[13] a generalization and simplification of SGML (Standard Generalized Markup Language).[14] This was not accidental, as SGML was a structured language for books that was the inspiration for HTML (HyperText Markup Language). However, while XML was suitable for hierarchical data, and although HTML did manage to add links (as did XML with the confusing W3C XLink standard[15]), such a language was not suitable for graph-based data. The social media revolution was conceived when the link in HTML was generalized to be more than a link that took a user between web-pages, but a link that represents friendship. In this way, the concept of a network of friends became transformed into a social graph.

As there was at the time no standard for graph-based data, the W3C decided to invent RDF (Resource Description Framework) in 1999.[16] RDF was an attempt to create a standard for decentralized information sharing, which Tim Berners-Lee assumed would more naturally fit on top of the link-based Web than the tree-based XML standard. Just as Bitcoin came into prominence as a technique to get around the financial blockade of Wikileaks, the Semantic Web's utility for describing social relationships had a real use-case due to repression and censorship on the Internet. The earliest known decentralized social network, the Friend-of-a-Friend (FOAF) network, came into being as an attempt to build a social network that could not be censored by the Iranian government, who at the time in 2005 had cut Iranian users off from the Internet.[17] FOAF was not only the first vocabulary for a decentralized social network, but came to be in 2000 before centralized social networks such as Facebook (2004) and Myspace (2003) and even Friendster (2002) were even founded.[18]

---

[13] https://www.w3.org/TR/xml/.

[14] https://www.iso.org/committee/45374.html.

[15] https://www.w3.org/TR/xlink/.

[16] https://www.w3.org/TR/1999/REC-rdf-syntax-19990222/.

[17] http://xmlns.com/foaf/spec/. Also see the article *Open Social Networks: Bring Back Iran* by Dan Brickley, inventor of FOAF: http://danbri.org/words/2008/01/07/249.

[18] It should be noted that the first social networking sites can be considered AOL Messenger and SixDegrees, which were founded in 1996, before FOAF but also before well-known social networking sites like Myspace and Facebook.

The W3C Semantic Web arrived stillborn as RDF made a number of design errors. First, although a more user-friendly syntax called N3[19] that appeared similar to JSON was proposed by Tim Berners-Lee, instead the W3C standardized a very difficult syntax, RDF/XML, that attempted to squeeze the RDF graph model into an XML tree-based serialization (as explained in Sect. 4).[20] The W3C justified the impossible-to-read syntax of RDF/XML by asserting that only machines would read RDF via parsers and programmers would use some more advanced visualization tools, but twenty years later these tools have not appeared. The second mistake made by RDF was its believe that simplistic logic-based inference was necessary to build into the syntax so that RDF could detect, for example, that a "friend" was a type of "social connection" and the inverse of "enemy." The lead semanticist of knowledge representation-based artificial intelligence, Patrick Hayes, did manage to make a fairly straightforward formal semantics to enable these kinds of inferences.[21] Still, the very term "semantics" caused much confusion but very little in the way of working applications. Indeed, academics took over the W3C's standardization of the Semantic Web. With a plethora of Semantic Web standards ranging from the RDF query language SPARQL, to more than half-a-dozen mostly incompatible versions of the Web Ontology Language OWL, and even attempts to interoperate with XML via GRDDL, chaos reigned. The entire Semantic Web stack of technologies to this day are difficult to use and inefficient for real-world deployment compared to traditional databases, and attempts to add "Web Services" to the Semantic Web failed.[22] Attempting to force adoption of a technology via premature standardization is a recipe for failure.

Another attempt to maintain the spirit of the decentralized Web was microformats, an initiative founded by a group of developers around Tantek Çelik.[23] Microformats was created purposefully outside of the W3C as it was felt that the W3C would both bureaucratically slow down development and also attempt to force the use of RDF. The idea was quite simple, that interoperable "microformats" would be embedded in HTML that would allow the uniform sharing of data across web-sites. Technically, if the right semantic tags (i.e. tags with a meaning, not for presentation) were embedded into HTML markup using the span and div tags, then automated web-scrapers could extract metadata from the website's HTML itself. Microformats was a design argument against RDF and RSS, which wanted websites to host their metadata in separate files from the HTML itself. The argument used by microformat supporters was that websites were incentivized to keep their HTML up-to-date, but not serve separate files for metadata. As it was easy to add microformats to existing HTML, microformats

---

[19] https://www.w3.org/DesignIssues/Notation3.html.

[20] https://www.w3.org/TR/rdf-syntax-grammar/.

[21] https://www.w3.org/TR/rdf-mt/.

[22] While there were entire books published and billions of euros spent in European Commission project grants, there is to date no working Semantic Web Services. For the details of perhaps the largest failed research attempt of the Web, see Dieter Fensel et al. [3].

[23] http://microformats.org/.

did indeed spread like wildfire across the Web in 2007, with adoption by Web 2.0 sites such as Flickr. However, ironically as search engines such as Yahoo! Search-Monkey and Google's RichSnippets started consuming large amount of microformats, it became increasingly obvious that web-developers were very error-prone when adding microformats to their websites [10].

Despite the large amount of developer interest in microformats and academic interest in the Semantic Web, ultimately both of these initiatives were recuperated by the Facebook and Google platforms. While the W3C tried to catch up to make microformats compatible with the Semantic Web via the awkwardly-named GRDDL standard to convert microformats to RDF[24] and the RDFa standard[25] to allow RDF to be embedded directly into web-pages, Facebook had its own plan to embed metadata into the Web for its own purposes. David Recordon, known for being the co-editor of "Thoughts on the Social Graph" and designer of OpenID Connect, joined Facebook. At Facebook, Recordon made a new specification, the *Open Graph Protocol*, to embed a limited number of vocabulary items in web-pages.[26] This Open Graph Protocol could describe strictly delimited types of books, movies, food, and other items of interest, so the Open Graph Protocol was neither "open" nor a RDF "graph" nor even a "protocol." In a self-serving clever twist by Facebook, it also came with cut-and-paste Javascript that would allow any web-page to embed a "Like" Button that would harvest this metadata and send it back to Facebook. This effort took off, and as of 2017 over 6% of the top 10,000 sites on the Web features a "Like" Button.[27] Ironically, the Semantic Web's largest deployment to date is Facebook's "Like" button [10], allowing Facebook to collect metadata on user likes across the entire Web in a privacy-invasive manner.

Google was not to be left out of the proprietary metadata game. While the W3C believed that RDF would enable the creation of hand-crafted decentralized ontologies describing domain-specific metadata formats, in reality Google ended up centralizing the creation of metadata.[28] An evolution from the parsing of microformats by Google Search and Google's own competitor to RDF, microdata, that they put into HTML,[29] *schema.org* systematized the kinds of domains that Google users were trying to discover, ranging from shopping to recipes. Google refused to work with the W3C, instead opting to standardize schemas with other browser vendors such as Microsoft and Yandex, and eventually letting the community provide input via a non-binding W3C Schema.org Community Group. In the end, Google incorporated metadata from Wikipedia's Wikidata effort [14], creating the Google Knowledge Graph. The Google Knowledge Graph is a closed and proprietary version of the Semantic Web that serves as the backbone of Google's massive data collection efforts and powers their

---

[24] https://www.w3.org/TR/2007/REC-grddl-20070911/.
[25] https://www.w3.org/TR/2015/REC-rdfa-core-20150317/.
[26] http://opengraphprotocol.org/.
[27] https://trends.builtwith.com/cdn/Facebook-CDN.
[28] https://schema.org.
[29] https://www.w3.org/TR/microdata/.

machine-learning algorithms. Rather than open standards for the decentralized social data, each Silicon Valley company has their own knowledge graph, a closed proprietary metadata collection. RDF currently is used for open public data and some other fields like library science, today we still do not have the ability to specify in a standardized way social metadata. The problem may ultimately itself may not be technical: The ability to describe and represent the objects in our world in a digital space without falling into the trap of pre-inscribing all possible categories remains one of the greatest unsolved problems in the terms of metaphysics itself.

4   Transport: The Bits on the Wire

Transport is the application-level format used to actually transfer data (and metadata) from one identity to another over a network protocol (such as TCP/IP). Traditionally on the Web the transport mechanism was given by HTTP. In terms of decentralization, RSS was one of the most successful open standards that nearly - but ultimately failed - to decentralize the Web. RSS originally was an abbreviation for RDF Site Summary in 1999, created by R.V. Guha, co-designer of the RDF standard and AI expert. However, the original version of RSS was difficult for developers to understand and even parse, due to the use of the syntax of RDF in XML, although the RSS-dev Working Group continued to evolve the design into RSS 1.0, but RSS 1.0 remained virtually unusable (which was the version of RSS championed by Aaron Swartz).[30] Therefore, a new version of RSS was created by David Winer, which succeeded insofar as he removed any traces of RDF, and stuck to a simple XML-based syntax. This version of RSS was rebranded "Really Simple Syndication" in RSS .91 and .92 to prevent confusion with the RDF version of RSS.[31] The RDF version of RSS was a failure despite the informal Working Group continuing to work till 2008. The simplified XML version of RSS allowed blog rolls, audio files, and other data to be syndicated across web-sites, exploding in usage from 2002 onwards. Winer's RSS played a crucial, if mostly hidden, role in the infrastructure of what was called "the Web 2.0." The spread of RSS was eventually stopped by the splintering of the standard itself, as developers and users were stymied by incompatible versions. The W3C kept attempting to press adoption an RDF-based version of RSS 1.0 due to Tim Berners-Lee's desire to keep pushing the adoption of the Semantic Web via open standards. Likewise, David Winer placed the stewardship of his competing XML version of RSS, now re-branded RSS 2.0 (in order to leap-frog across RSS 1.0) in the Berkman Center at Harvard rather than W3C/MIT, as Harvard did not push for the support of RDF like the W3C.[32] Therefore, developers could not sensibly determine how to support the RSS-based decentralized web with multiple versions of distinct incompatible standards with competing

---

[30] RSS-dev Working Group RDF Site Summary (RSS) 1.0 2000. http://web.resource.org/rss/1.0/spec.

[31] RSS 0.2 (2002) http://backend.userland.com/rss092.

[32] RSS 2.0 (2003) https://cyber.harvard.edu/rss/rss.html.

version numbering schemes. Due to this ego-driven standardization failure, the decentralized RSS-based Web 2.0 was cripplied at birth. The IETF finally managed to fix the wreckage of the three different incompatible versions of RSS by creating the XML-based Atom, but by then it was too little, too late.[33] In the wild, RSS usage was split between the different incompatible formats.[34] Facebook and Twitter dropped RSS support, and eventually in 2013 Google canceled support of their popular RSS reader. The hope of decentralizing the Web 2.0 via decentralized status feeds was dead.

The Extensible Messaging and Presence Protocol (XMPP) was a standard meant to enable real-time XML-based messaging.[35] Unlike the HTTP-based Web that required users to "pull" web-pages to their browsers, XMPP was built on a "push" model that let new content be sent to users. In addition to its core architecture, XMPP also had its own persistent and federated identity system for users, and so was a complete system for instant messaging. Therefore, XMPP had a moment of surprising success, with many chat clients adopting XMPP as a foundation of decentralized interoperability, including Google Talk. However, XMPP failed to evolve into a decentralized real-time alternative to the Web. At first this may be surprising, as new functionality, such as that needed to replicate the features of Facebook, could be added to XMPP as it was an extensible standard. Extensibility was both a blessing and a curse, as it also led to overwhelming complexity: XMPP spawned its own mini-standards body, the XMPP Foundation, wherein hundreds of extra features were added. The XMPP core became more and more unwieldy itself, eventually reaching over 200 pages; the ability of developers to implement these standards, much less make them interoperate, became non-existent. As it became more and more difficult to gain interoperability, the XMPP standards became more of an hindrance than a boon for the creation of a decentralized social web, with the lack of interoperability holding back development. One by one, client support for XMPP dwindled. In 2015, Google Chat finally completely dropped XMPP, and chat clients such as Signal and WhatsApp came about that didn't support XMPP. Indeed, attempting to replicate the organic functionality of centralized silos using a single standards-based framework led to complexity, which created a lack of interoperable implementations, causing the decline of the XMPP eco-system. What appeared to be one foundation of a decentralized Web's transport layer ended up being abandoned in 2018,[36] although it maintains some usage amongst

---

[33] https://tools.ietf.org/html/rfc5023.

[34] The vast majority using RSS 2.0, followed by Atom, and then previous RSS versions in 2018.

[35] https://xmpp.org/rfcs/rfc3920.html.

[36] XMPP also was the backbone for the ill-fated and confusing Google Wave, which was dropped by Google in 2010 although idealistic software developers such as Kune and SwellRT are working on trying to build a decentralized social web on top of XMPP.

developers and activists due to support of the OTR[37] and OMEMO encrypted chat applications.[38]

Pubsubhubbub was an invention of decentralized web pioneer Brad Fitzpatrick, who left Livejournal to work at Google and who had authored earlier the "Thoughts on the Social Graph." Pubsubhubbub standardized the "publish-subscribe" push model over HTTP, so that HTTP replace XMPP.[39] Pubsubhubbub allowed RSS-based sites to be pushed dynamic real-time content, and so could have - at least in theory - enabled the real-time updates needed for a decentralized Facebook and Twitter without relying on a clunky XMPP-based architecture. The various parts were knitted together into OStatus,[40] including a new Atom-based ActivityStreams format[41] that was meant to provide social updates such as "friend requests" adds in a decentralized manner, using Pubsubhubbub to communicate. OStatus was incarnated as a federated free software alternative to Twitter, *status.net*, eventually being given over to the Free Software Foundation as GNU Social. Yet by the time the federated social web was ready to be used, it was too late: Facebook and Twitter were entrenched, and Google had given up on attempting to produce an open social web, instead centralizing in Google Plus and shutting down their RSS reader.

5   Lessons Learned

Far from naïvely programming a dystopia of centralized personal collection, ordinary programmers were the first to take seriously the threats posed by Facebook, Google, and the like to our digital social lives. Before even the advent of Facebook and competing platforms like Google Plus and Twitter, programmers started building protocols to help citizens re-seize control over their personal data in order to build a decentralized and democratic social web. Yet this task ended in failure, and as of 2018 the consolidation of power and control over the social web by a few large corporations seems unparalleled. The difference is today that ordinary people are now aware of the dangers of a centralized social web due to increasing hacking attacks on these irresistible honey-pots and the abuse of personal data for political purposes. Yet given programmers had over ten years to address the centralization of social data, why did these efforts fail? To a large extent, the key failing is that the programmers tried to solve the problem of centralization via the purely technical means of standards rather than taking into account the larger social, economic, and political world into which their code was embedded.

Given a technical standards-based approach, a mundane reason for the failure of the decentralization of the Web was a failure of a unified strategy pushed

---

[37] https://xmpp.org/extensions/xep-0364.html.

[38] https://xmpp.org/extensions/xep-0384.html.

[39] http://pubsubhubbub.github.io/PubSubHubbub/pubsubhubbub-core-0.3.html.

[40] https://www.w3.org/community/ostatus/wiki/images/9/93/OStatus_1.0_Draft_2. pdf.

[41] http://activitystrea.ms/specs/atom/1.0/.

by responsible standards body, due to a lack of intellectual clarity over the necessary minimal components to standardize and a simple way for programmers to implement them. This would normally be the job of a standards body such as W3C or IETF to plan, but it seemed that these standards bodies developed a strategy far too late. Up until W3C formulated a (failed) plan in 2013,[42] decentralized social standards were often ran by a small group or even a lone coder, such as David Winer's version of RSS hosted at Harvard Berkman (apparently put there to spite W3C at MIT, who would have attempted to force the usage of RDF in RSS). There were even worse iterations of this, such as the attempt to create "standards" such as XRIs by rather questionable entrepreneurs or via "one shot" standards bodies such as the OpenID Foundation. Early on, large projects such as Project Higgins of the Berkman Harvard Center and XRI-based startups like Cordance also all ended in failure, defeated by their own needlessly complex architectures. Of the plethora of standards for a decentralized social web, in terms of real-world deployment what happened (again and again) is that a few of the larger companies such as Google or IBM would adopt components as suited their business strategy (and killed, like RSS or XMPP by Google, as soon as convenient), while the rest of the components were relegated to small open source projects.

Rather than blame Silicon Valley entirely for the failure of a decentralized web, history shows that hackers are their own worst enemy. Rather than traditional multi-stakeholder standards bodies taking responsibility for developing a single suite of decentralized standards that would serve the needs of stakeholders like the general public and entrepreneurs, standards bodies transformed into strange religions around data formats. The example par excellance is the Semantic Web effort of Tim Berners-Lee and the W3C. For example, the use of RDF needlessly fractured the RSS standard and for years forced development of social standards outside the W3C. When the Social Web community decided to develop a W3C Social Web Working Group in 2014, the group failed to produce a unified standard.[43] Under the incompetent leadership of chair Arnaud LeHors of IBM,[44] the W3C Social Web Working Group produced *three* incompatible versions of the same standards for transport and metadata: The Semantic Web-centric Linked Data Notifications,[45] the microformat-enabled (rebranded "IndieWeb") WebMention,[46] and a JSON-format for ActivityStreams 2.0.[47] The reason for this train wreck of a standards Working Group was because a small fanatical cult around Berners-Lee and his Social Linked Data[48] project pushed the use of RDF,

---

[42] The W3C Social Activity's scope is https://www.w3.org/Social/. Note that I organized the strategy and wrote the W3C Social Web Working Group charter.

[43] As founder of the W3C Working Group, I stepped down when it became clear the W3C started to force RDF on the Working Group against the will of developers.

[44] IBM seemed interested primarily in placing any patents related to the OpenSocial into W3C's Royalty-Free patent policy.

[45] https://www.w3.org/TR/ldn/.

[46] https://www.w3.org/TR/webmention/.

[47] https://www.w3.org/TR/activitystreams-core/.

[48] Called "Solid," see https://solid.mit.edu/.

although Berners-Lee himself did not directly interact with the standards process. Afraid of offending RDF developers, the W3C pushed through RDF and IBM sent ActivityStreams 2.0 off the rails via starting the absurd task of creating a meta-model for all possible social actions, (see footnote 47) Çelik's group of microformat developers created Micropub,[49] and the entire situation became so confused that the W3C had to publish a guide to their non-interoperable protocols.[50] Although a next-generation Pubsubhubbub simplified as WebSub[51] and ActivityPub[52] show promise (being used on decentralized Twitter clone Mastodon), in retrospect rather than co-operate in order to bring decentralization forward, engineers preferred to engage in ideological debates over data formats whose only real-world impact was preventing a decentralized Social Web from ever being launched.

6   Next Steps: Blockchain Technology

Could blockchain technologies create a decentralized web? When Bitcoin emerged in 2008, it seemed only useful in transferring money. Yet the underlying technology, a blockchain, seemed to offer a new technology for decentralization. While previous attempts to decentralize social data focused on incremental fixes to the Web, blockchain technologies presented a radical alternative that hearkened back to the golden days of peer-to-peer systems in 2001, but combined peer-to-peer technology with strong cryptography: Blockchain technology provides a publicly transparent and decentralized ledger that is configured to track and store digital transactions in a publicly verifiable, secure, and hardened manner to prevent tampering or revision. It is both pedagogical and necessary to take into context the failures of the original attempt to decentralize the original Web in the context of the rise of blockchain technologies. Protocols based on distributed ledgers are branded "Web 3.0" to contrast this wave with the centralized social media platforms of "Web 2.0."

As Bitcoin appeared *deux ex machina*, one crucial advantage Bitcoin had over other technical efforts is their lack of a cult-like leader, as the identity of Nakamoto has never been revealed. This is not the case with Vitalik Buterin and Ethereum, where Buterin's influence has been decisively important in issues like the crisis caused by the DAO hack.[53] Yet his influence and the influence of the Ethereum Foundation in general seems to be tempered over time by other developers. An informal governance body, often consisting of coders that have commit access to the production version of the code, has informally developed in both Bitcoin and Ethereum; a meritocracy that mirrors the early stages of the development of the IETF. Attempts to create more structured organizations such as the Bitcoin Foundation have failed, and instead a process more akin to the IETF

---

[49] https://www.w3.org/TR/micropub.
[50] https://www.w3.org/TR/social-web-protocols/.
[51] https://www.w3.org/TR/websub/.
[52] https://www.w3.org/TR/activitypub/.
[53] https://www.wired.com/2016/06/50-million-hack-just-showed-dao-human/.

RFC process was started by the Bitcoin Improvement Proposal (BIP) process[54] started by Amir Taaki, and then in the Ethereum Improvement Proposals (EIP) process.[55] The phenomena of "forking" is another genuine innovation that can measure popular support of a standard. Popular support for these proposals can be judged simply by the amount of miners that take up the new proposal, and the more diverse eco-system of exchanges and third-party applications that follow a particular "hard fork" can empirically measure its success.

The key contribution of blockchain technologies is their trail-blazing built-in economic model based on decentralized payments. It is precisely the lack of a funding model that led many open-source and free software projects to either fail or be controlled by large platforms that are funded via surveillance-based advertising; a prime example is the sponsorship of Google of various open-source projects that are then placed behind the cloud. Yet with a new funding model and venture-capital putting billions of dollars into startups working on decentralized protocols, it appears the initial funding boom that built the "Web 1.0" in the 1990s has returned. Although this amount of funding has attracted a large amount of disreputable "get rich quick" start-ups, nonetheless a large amount of talented engineers would rather work on blockchain technologies than for Silicon Valley.

In terms of open standards, all the traditional multi-stakeholder open standards bodies were also dependent on the support and funding of a few Silicon Valley companies, as shown by the standardization of DRM led by Google, Microsoft, and Netflix at the W3C [5]. In effect, the decentralized standards of Web 2.0 failed in part due to being reliant on the noblesse oblige of a few large companies. As attempts to standardize blockchain technologies at the W3C and IETF have either so far failed or produced standards of dubious technical value, there is now the chance to re-start standardization with a fresh slate. It may be too late to save the W3C, as the Verifiable Claims work at W3C[56] is a confused mixture of Semantic Web technology and blockchain technology that ignores the fundamental fact that the Semantic Web is dependent on a centralized domain name system [6]. Blockchain advocates should beware working with the dubious characters of failed decentralization efforts in the past, as the W3C Verifiable Claims work is now backed by Drummond Reed, whose new Evernym and Sovrin Foundation seem to simply be repeating XRIs with blockchain technology. This new decentralized "identity" blockchain solution is aiming to work with IBM's centralized "blockchain solution" Hyperledger, which is also led by the same person, Arnaud LeHors, that attempted to force the use of RDF and so failed as chair of the W3C Social Web effort.

Although political and social forces have been arrayed against the hackers working on creating a decentralized social web, it is the hackers that have defeated themselves so far. Therefore, ironically the attempts to create a decentralized Social Web have almost entirely been recuperated. The Semantic Web

---

[54] https://github.com/bitcoin/bips.
[55] https://eips.ethereum.org/.
[56] https://www.w3.org/TR/verifiable-claims-data-model/.

fueled proprietary knowledge graphs, and Berners-Lee's vision of the web as a database of open knowledge based on RDF failed to materialize. By the time OpenID had matured into OAuth 2.0, it was extensively deployed by both Google and Facebook as identity providers - as well as most web-sites and mobile apps as relying parties - to centralize control of the authentication and authorization process in the hands of a few Silicon Valley companies. The largest user of RDF and metadata ended up being the Facebook "Like" Button. Will the blockchain revolution bring a new decentralized web into existence, or simply become the technical infrastructure of further control and centralization? Only time will tell, but the future of decentralization is at stake, and so human freedom in an increasingly digital world depends on the new ways of governance - or perhaps better phrased, *ungovernance* - that are being developed by the next generation of "digital native" blockchain hackers.

References

1. Berners-Lee, T., Hendler, J., Lassila, O.: The semantic web. Sci. Am. **284**(5), 34–43 (2001)
2. Smith, B.C.: On the Origin of Objects. The MIT Press, Cambridge (1996)
3. Fensel, D., Facca, F.M., Simperl, E., Toma, I.: Semantic Web Services. Springer, Heidelberg (2011). https://doi.org/10.1007/978-3-642-19193-0
4. Fielding, R.T., Taylor, R.N.: Principled design of the modern web architecture. ACM Trans. Internet Technol. (TOIT) **2**(2), 115–150 (2002)
5. Halpin, H.: The crisis of standardizing DRM: the case of W3C encrypted media extensions. In: Ali, S.S., Danger, J.-L., Eisenbarth, T. (eds.) SPACE 2017. LNCS, vol. 10662, pp. 10–29. Springer, Cham (2017). https://doi.org/10.1007/978-3-319-71501-8_2
6. Halpin, H.: Semantic insecurity: security and the semantic web. In: Society, Privacy and the Semantic Web-Policy and Technology (PrivOn 2017) (2017)
7. Hui, Y., Halpin, H.: Collective individuation: the future of the social web. The Unlike Us Reader, pp. 103–116 (2013)
8. Jordan, K., Hauser, J., Foster, S.: The augmented social network: building identity and trust into the next-generation internet. First Monday **8**(8) (2003). https://firstmonday.org/ojs/index.php/fm/article/view/1068/988
9. Lim, D.: Patent Misuse and Antitrust Law: Empirical, Doctrinal and Policy Perspectives. Edward Elgar Publishing, Cheltenham (2013)
10. Mühleisen, H., Bizer, C.: Web data commons-extracting structured data from two large web corpora. LDOW **937**, 133–145 (2012)
11. Ostrom, E.: Governing the Commons. Cambridge University Press, Cambridge (2015)
12. Schwartz, P.M.: Property, privacy, and personal data. Harv. L. Rev. **117**, 2056 (2003)
13. Troncoso, C., Isaakidis, M., Danezis, G., Halpin, H.: Systematizing decentralization and privacy: lessons from 15 years of research and deployments. Proc. Priv. Enhancing Technol. **2017**(4), 404–426 (2017)
14. Vrandečić, D., Krötzsch, M.: Wikidata: a free collaborative knowledgebase. Commun. ACM **57**(10), 78–85 (2014)

Distributed Data Protection and Liability on Blockchains

Alexandra Giannopoulou$^{(\boxtimes)}$ and Valeria Ferrari

Blockchain and Society Policy Lab, IViR, University of Amsterdam,
1018 WV Amsterdam, The Netherlands
{a.giannopoulou,v.ferrari}@uva.nl

Abstract. Blockchains and the GDPR pursue similar objectives where they seek to grant users greater control over their personal data. While the latter pursues this goal by imposing duties of care to centralized controllers and collectors of data, blockchains go a step beyond by trying to eliminate these stakeholders and the need to trust them. Nevertheless, the rules set out by the GDPR apply whenever personal data are at stake, and various actors of the blockchain ecosystem risk liability for controlling of processing data in violation of privacy requirements. A possible solution is to re-contextualize the concepts of data controlling and responsibility, as framed by the GDPR, in light of blockchains' enhanced individual autonomy. In this paper, we set the framework for a further inquiry on the role of users as both data subjects and data controllers of distributed ledgers.

Keywords: Blockchain · Decentralization · Data protection

1 Introduction

The development of decentralized technologies at scale is the holy grail for the reorganization of social structures. The variant degrees of decentralization as well as the different structures that are created around it, aim to reinforce individuals and achieve collective social empowerment [10, 11]. Blockchain technology represents the latest technological solution to decentralize the problem of trust in key societal and economic interactions. The growing interest in blockchains reflects a renovated call for reorganization of power and for the elimination of unnecessary and untrustworthy intermediaries.

Blockchain is a combination of pre-existing technologies [6, 7] which results in a digital medium with disruptive potential. It is an append-only distributed database that connects a decentralized network of nodes using a range of cryptographic methods. The participants of the network coordinate with each other based on algorithmic consensus rules encoded in the blockchain protocol and they continuously update the database. The applications of the technology promise to eliminate the need of trust, of trusted intermediaries and of trusted institutions from a number of human activities.[1] The protocol ensures full transparency; the mathematical verifiability of the transactions managed through the digital infrastructure offers an alternative to centrally organized institutions and intermediaries [3]. Blockchain technology provides thus a mechanism

S. S. Bodrunova et al. (Eds.): INSCI 2018 Workshops, LNCS 11551, pp. 203–211, 2019.
https://doi.org/10.1007/978-3-030-17705-8_17

to guarantee security in the recorded transactions among parties that do not know or trust each other.

The distributed technological architecture of the blockchain requires also the articulation of governance principles because the continuously growing involvement of new actors creates a need for more organised decision-making processes. The extent to which these new actors control and process data is partially defined by their activity in the governance of the project, but mainly it is defined by the architecture of the blockchain technical infrastructure at the various layers of its stack. The combination of these qualities will also determine the legal qualification of their role as well as their legal liability.

In light of these considerations, it becomes apparent that technological and governance choices of decentralized systems have an impact on legal compliance [5]. If blockchain technology presents itself as an alternative to centralized models of information and value management, it is nonetheless subject to traditional law enforcement within the respective legal frameworks. In that regard, territoriality, privacy, data protection and liability pose a legal challenge when applied in blockchain technological applications.

The recent reforms of data protection rules in the European Union dictate that the technological design of web services and applications must take into account data controlling and processing rights and obligations dictated by the legal framework. The General Data Protection Regulation,[2] which came into effect on May 25, 2018 - requires the restructuring of most of the systems and processes that handle data collection and processing services in order to implement user rights and actor obligations. Decentralization is a priori not incompatible with data protection rules. However, the centralized model of data processing and control that the GDPR implies - which presupposes traditional single providers of computing processes - makes these rules hard to satisfy in the context of decentralized blockchains. In principle, both blockchain technology and the GDPR aspire to increase transparency, user agency, and trust. The GDPR, on the one hand, does so by identifying central actors who have increased control of the data processing and by assigning responsibilities to specific parties. On the other hand, the distributed and decentralized architecture of the blockchain ensures trust and transparency not by relying on few central actors but by incentivizing the use of the processing power of its distributed user base. Thus, if the goals of blockchains and the GDPR are similar, their approaches diverge on a fundamental level.

Nevertheless, as a distributed database running worldwide, blockchains are required to comply with data protection laws. Compliance with the GDPR will be necessary for all blockchain applications whose activities include *"processing of personal data in the context of the activities of an establishment of a controller or processor in the European Union, regardless of whether the processing takes place in*

---

[1] According to the creator of Bitcoin, Satoshi Nakamoto, 'what is needed is an electronic payment system based on cryptographic proof instead of trust, allowing any two willing parties to transact directly with each other without the need for a trusted third party.'

[2] Regulation (EU) 2016/679 of the European Parliament and of the Council of 27 April 2016 on the protection of natural persons with regard to the processing of personal data and on the free movement of such data, and repealing Directive 95/46/EC. Hereinafter GDPR.

the Union or not". What is worth investigating is which data will fall under the scope of application of the GDPR obligations and whether legal compliance can be imposed on or ensured by actors that emerge in various blockchain applications. If the GDPR introduces the concept of privacy by design, it is interesting to examine how blockchain's technological design can be crafted as to accommodate data protection rules.

2 Defining Personal Data on the Blockchain

Data storage and processing is at the core of any blockchain. The data protection principles of the GDPR will only be applied to data that are qualified as personal[3] according to the definitions introduced in the Regulation. Additionally, the analysis issued by the Article 29 Working Party on the concept of personal data [2] serves as interpretation guidelines for the Courts. The obligation to ensure compliance will firstly depend on the qualification of the data stored and processed in the blockchain. While storage and processing of personal data fall into the material scope of data protection regulations, data that are not qualified as personal are not subject to the same regime. If the qualification of personal data applies, the data protection rules established by the GPPR generally require the consent of the data subject for the collection, storing and processing of that data. Moreover, such qualification implies mandatory duties of care for personal data protection and creates accountability for the actors involved in the personal data processing.

At the current state of its technological development - and according to the CJEU's case law interpreting the concept of personal data, blockchains operating as databases that process data worldwide are likely to fall under the scope of application of the GDPR. The determination of the data stored on the blockchain as personal data or not is, however, one of the core issues that need to be addressed in order to identify the regulatory requirements the technology must be compliant with. The fluid, ever-expanding, and contextual approach to qualifying data as personal, coupled with rapid technological progress in data aggregation and analytics, is progressively transforming the GDPR into "the law of everything". For example, it is not uncommon for data to be "anonymous at the time of collection, but turn into personal later, just sitting there, simply by virtue of technological progress" [8].

Data stored and processed on the blockchain could potentially qualify as personal data if they refer to identifiable natural persons. For example, there are the data which identify or which are associated with transactions occurring between the users. These can include fragments of plain data, but most of the data in question are stored in encrypted and hashed form on the blockchain. Because of the type of the information that they usually convey, these data are called transactional data. Also, the public keys of the users that participated in the transactions, which serve to refer to the sums of funds each account owns and can spend over the network could be qualified as personal

---

[3] According to article 4(1) GDPR, personal data are defined as 'any information relating to an identified or identifiable natural person'.

data. The qualification of these data as anonymous[4] would make them fall outside of the scope of application of the GDPR.

Besides the plain data - which are only very rarely stored on the blockchain for efficiency purposes, transactional data in encrypted and hashed form, as well as public keys, are considered pseudonymous data in the context of data protection regulation. Namely, encrypted data are vulnerable to decryption techniques that revert the data to its original state and thus revealing information related to an identified or identifiable person. Similarly, hashes can be linked to the data they have been derived from and can lead to the identification of the data subject. Hence, while widely used to ensure security in transactions, these techniques do not guarantee anonymity but merely pseudonymity.

According to article 4(5) of the GDPR, pseudonymisation is defined as "the processing of personal data in such a manner that the personal data can no longer be attributed to a specific data subject without the use of additional information, provided that such additional information is kept separately and is subject to technical and organizational measures to ensure that the personal data are not attributed to an identified or identifiable person". Techniques of pseudonymisation do not prevent personal data from being attributed to the data subject [9] and from falling under the scope of the GDPR. Therefore, in absence of other legitimate purposes for processing as provided by the GDPR, the storage and processing of these kinds of data requires the consent of the data subjects, in compliance with obligations and rights that the regulation ascribes to users and actors. This consent is hardly proved or expressed in blockchain transactions.

Both hashing and encryption techniques have already been identified by the Article 29 Working Party [1] as pseudonymization (hence, not as anonymization) techniques, since the re-identification of the data subject may be considered difficult but it is not irreversibly prevented. However, even if the re-identification of pseudonymous data on the blockchain can be successful, the effort required to achieve it remains dependent on the methods used for encrypting or hashing the data and on the prerogatives of data storage on the blockchain. Thus, the difficulty in re-identification depends on various variables that can be more or less related to the technology used. In general, pseudonymous data qualify as such every time re-identification can be achieved within a reasonable amount of time and effort.

Even if qualified a priori pseudonymous, public keys could, in certain circumstances that relate to the technical and architectural choices on the blockchain, not lead to the identification of a natural person applying re-identification technical efforts within the constraints of reasonable means as described in the GDPR. In general, practice has shown that public keys can be linked to a natural person in a variety of ways, but there can be instances where such identification becomes less easy.[5] At the

---

[4] According to the Article 29 Working Party's Opinion on Anonymisation Techniques, data are considered anonymous only when their processing irreversibly prevents identification.

[5] For instance, some end-users applications allow the generation of a new public key for each transaction, so that it becomes harder to link a set of transactions to an identifiable user. Moreover, cryptocurrencies like Monero deploy sophisticated techniques such as ring signature and Ring Confidential Transactions that prevent to link transactions and funds to public keys.

same time, data that is at a given point considered anonymous are susceptible to lead to identification because of the availability of technological advancements at an environment where data are destined to be stored for an undetermined amount of time. In fact, the qualification of anonymous data is tied to the absence of re-identification processes. However, the qualification of unequivocal anonymity becomes more difficult for data stored on blockchains, because - given the lack of time restrictions that storage on blockchains implies - the technological evaluation of anonymity becomes more fluid. Thus, anonymous data approach the qualification of pseudonymous every time the probability of de-anonymization is increased in light of new technological breakthroughs. The legal significance of such shift in qualification from anonymous to pseudonymous data is that the data in question falls again into the scope of application of the GDPR.

Stretching the meaning of adequacy and necessity in the GDPR's principle of minimisation of personal data processing has been put forward as a possible work-around for the pseudonymous data that are stored on and off-chain [4]. According to Article 25(1) GDPR, the implementation of *"appropriate technical and organizational measures, such as pseudonymisation, which are designed to implement data-protection principles, such as data minimization, in an effective manner"* is necessary. The prerogatives of the compliance with such requirements for blockchain systems' architects remain uncertain, because the application of the GDPR to the technology is unclear. Respecting the obligation of data minimization through the architectural design choices of the blockchains could quickly demonstrate the limits of the proposed solution. For example, it is unclear which of the various applications of encryption methods would better respond to the data minimization obligation since the technological progress on this domain is in constant flux.

As the GDPR hints, the technological design can be set-up as to achieve legal compliance and provide to users the tools they need to invoke their data protection rights; thus, users could exercise their rights by being involved in the technological design choice process by selecting technology that are more compliant with privacy rules. The limits of user empowerment are challenged when determining if 'appropriate technical and organizational measures' were adopted by the blockchain architecture, such as for example pseudonymization using designated secure technologies or personal data storing technological choices.

The interplay between qualifications of personal and non-personal data and the consequent legal requirements that apply to blockchain-based projects will, therefore, be a determining factor in the technological decisions during the life of the project in question. Finally, the immutability of blockchains poses a particular challenge in front of the user control over their personal data introduced by the GDPR. The use of technological solutions when facing legal challenges could end up reconciling these two characteristics representing transparency on the one hand and privacy on the other. According to the state of the accepted technological standards at the time regarding encryption or data storage and processing, the redeployment of a blockchain by the application of forking of the integrality of the chain could be perceived as a tool that ensures more appropriate data protection systems. However, the unforeseeable consequences of these technological choices could end up harming the core structure and ideology that justified the creation of blockchain technology.

3 Architecture-Based Liability of Actors

Architectural choices in the design of blockchain technology are determined by the objectives of ensuring transparency, enhancing security as well as privacy and, finally, empowering users while ensuring scalability. More specifically, the interplay between decentralization and privacy aims at enhancing user control. The choices that define the interactions between the technology and the actors involved proceed to demonstrate the prioritization between the diverse goals and interests that finally produce what is an optimal balance between them. The final design reflects these choices, as the degree of decentralization of each system will define the degree of control attributed to different actors. The compliance of blockchains with the rules of the GDPR looks, as of today, improbable, as some fundamental technical features of decentralised technologies are in direct conflict with the latter. However, the malleability of the technical design, the variety of possible governance schemes and the interests vested in the development of the technology open possibilities to the construction of GDPR-compliant blockchains [4]. Which choices such a construction would require is yet to be understood.

In building decentralised ledger technologies, the conflicting objectives of transparency and data protection impose a balancing process that depends on, and ultimately influences, the roles and responsibilities of various actors involved in the creation and maintenance of the network. The legal obligations and responsibilities enshrined in the GDPR, apply - in presence of data qualified as personal - to those actors that perform controlling and processing functions over personal data, as defined by the legal instrument itself. The liability of actors for storing or processing data through a blockchain network depends, firstly, on the qualification of the data stored on blockchains as personal data. Then, the question that needs to be tackled is: which actors are, in the context of blockchains, susceptible to be qualified as data controllers and data processors as referred to by the European Regulation?

In centralised data storage infrastructures, a single legal entity is generally responsible for a given server or cloud. In blockchains, instead, the data storage and processing is sparse among a network of uneasily identifiable computers, and the design of the technology tells us very little about the actual use of data from the actors involved.

According to the GDPR, *"'controller' means the natural or legal person, public authority, agency or other body which, alone or jointly with others, determines the purposes and means of the processing of personal data"*. In a blockchain scenario, this definition could, at first sight, be best attributed to developers, as they "set[s]-up the code design and (the facto) govern[s] the distributed ledgers" [12]. Developers have, in public blockchains, the technical capability to determine how data are validated, stored and processed by the nodes of the networks. However, they are - at least in theory - bound to the network consensus considering that, for them to successfully upgrade or modify the protocol, the network of validating nodes must demonstrate their agreement with the stated choice by upgrading their functioning accordingly. Therefore, as long as developers are merely executing what the majority of the consensus group agrees on, they cannot be considered actual stakeholders in the blockchain's governance system nor can they be considered a source of independent determination over the processing of data [4].

The GDPR gives individuals control over their personal data; but it also assumes that clearly identified (or identifiable) actors have control over storing and processing of such data and are therefore accountable for such control. Potential liability under the GDPR could, therefore, apply to those parties that emerge as centralised sources of power within the blockchain ecosystem, as they mediate the interactions between users, and between users and the digital ledger. These comprehend a varied range of entities such as platforms (e.g. Ethereum, Filecoin, Dash etc.), service providers (cryptocurrencies exchanges; wallet providers), and companies that build all sorts of applications on top the blockchain protocol.

Consider, for example, a company crowdfunding itself by issuing a token on the Ethereum platform. Upon the receival of the funds, the company will collect and eventually analyse all the public keys - and associated data - of the users (eventually pseudonymised) which participated to the token sale; these pseudonymous data, however, will also be publicly accessible on the Ethereum blockchain, sacrificing the privacy of the company's clients in favor of the necessary transparency of the ledger. Can, therefore, the company be held liable with regards to the users' data protection rights? Or should, instead, the Ethereum platform - which builds the technical infrastructure and defines the modalities of data processing - be considered the data controller?

This question certainly does not have a clear-cut answer. The use of the data and the ability to determine the means of data processing vary significantly based on the governance and technological design of each blockchain protocol and platforms built on top of it. The roles of actors of the blockchain space do not directly correspond to the definitions as provided in the GDPR. Moreover, the hierarchy of the blockchain stack adds complexity to the identification of roles and responsibilities with regard to the processing of data.

The technical design of blockchains imposes that the entire networks share and validate the ledger of information. Hence, no single data processor which, according to the GDPR definition, is "*a natural or legal person, public authority, agency or other body which processes personal data on behalf of the controller*" - can be identified. Rather, such qualification could apply to all the nodes running the blockchain in order to validate transactions such as for example miners or qualified nodes.[6] However, in these examples the GDPR fails again to apply in a sound and clearcut manner. Each individual node, or miner, is in fact unable to determine the validation process, as its functioning is dependent upon the rules embedded in the protocol and on the

---

[6] Note that the present paper refers generally to so called "public", "permissionless" blockchains, in which any user can access the data, enter the network as validator or record transactions with no attribute-based or geographical restriction. As recognised by the CNIL opinion in the issue, "private" blockchains to do not pose specific problems concerning the attribution of liability for GDPR compliance. In fact, as private blockchains are developed and maintained by one or more identified actors, they perform as traditional databases whose storage is distributed but centrally controlled.

cooperation of the consensus group.[7] Moreover, only certain kinds of nodes (i.e. "full nodes", "super nodes") download the entire blockchain and contribute to validate and support the shared ledger, and the level of involvement of nodes in the processing of data varies depending on the consensus algorithm and on the level of openness of the blockchain setup.

As long as the data stored on the ledger is considered personal data, blockchain's technical design is highly problematic for GDPR compliance. Distributed storage of information, transparency and immutability are, in fact, fundamental conditions of blockchain technologies, as they are functional to the purpose of creating a trusted, tamperproof repository of information for a network of users that do not necessarily trust each other. Such design, therefore, can be seen as something more than the product of interests or choices of few controlling parties. It represents, ideally, the solution to a collective problem: that of cooperation in geographically sparse peer-to-peer networks of anonymous users.

Users adhering to a blockchain network do not commit to a unilateral transfer of their own data to a controlling party. Rather, they store information in a system in which they are both subjects and controllers, given that all users - as well as companies, platforms and other potential key-players - share the same information and are subject to common, consensus-based, processing rules.

Each individual is, in permissionless blockchains, entitled to become not only a user but also an active participant in the storage and processing mechanism set out by the blockchain protocol. This is where the GDPR mismatches the blockchain technological setting: a clear distinction between data controllers and data subjects, as spelled by the legal instruments, cannot be identified in DLTs. Further inquiry on the re-contextualisation of the concepts of data controlling and responsibility, as framed by the GDPR, in light of blockchain's enhanced individual autonomy is awaited, and it could solve compliance issues in decentralized technologies.

4 Conclusions

The greatest involvement of users in data processing that occurs in blockchain networks reflects, somehow, the GDPR attempt to grant users a higher degree of control over their own data. However, as long as the processed data qualifies as personal data as defined by the GDPR, the dictatum of the European legal instrument does not stop to exert its effects because of the ideological purposes underlying distributed technologies. The present work has addressed possible interpretative ways of fitting GDPR notions – namely, the definition of personal data, of data controllers and data processors – to distributed ledgers technological contexts. In this regard, the paper points out that – while they can certainly be reconciled at a conceptual level – data protection requirements and the organisation of information through blockchains present several points of conflicts. The highlighted problems are not exhaustive, and further issues,

---

[7] Miners are, for instance, unable to individually influence changes in the protocol. They cannot alter or modify the data. They don't get to choose which data are stored on the blockchain nor the criteria based on which data get stored.

such as the enforceability of the right to erasure and the right to rectification in blockchain technical scenarios, deserve focus as well. This work, therefore, calls for broader researches into viable solutions to make GDPR and blockchains a sound match.

References

1. Article 29 Working Party, Opinion 04/2014 on Anonymisation Techniques, 0829/14/EN
2. Article 29 Working Party, Opinion 4/2007 on the Concept of Personal Data, 01248/07/EN WP136
3. Dingle, S.: In Math We Trust: Bitcoin, Cryptocurrency and the Journey to Being Your Own Bank. Tracey McDonald Publishers, Bryanston (2018)
4. Finck, M.: Blockchains and data protection in the European Union. EDPL 4(1), 17–35 (2018). https://doi.org/10.21552/edpl/2018/1/6
5. Ibanez, L.D., O'Hara, K., Simperl, E.: On Blockchains and the General Data Protection Regulation (2018). https://eprints.soton.ac.uk/id/eprint/422879
6. Nakamoto, S.: Bitcoin: A Peer-to-Peer Electronic Cash System (2009). https://bitcoin.org/bitcoin.pdf
7. Narayanan, A., Clark, J.: Bitcoin's academic pedigree. Commun. ACM 60(12), 36–45 (2017). https://doi.org/10.1145/3132259
8. Purtova, N.: The law of everything. Broad concept of personal data and future of EU data protection law. Law, Innov. Technol. 10(1), 40–81 (2018). https://doi.org/10.1080/17579961.2018.1452176
9. Schmelz, D., Fischer, G., Niemeier, P., Zhu, L., Grechenig, T.: Towards using public blockchain in information-centric networks: challenges imposed by the European Union's general data protection regulation. In: Proceedings of 2018 1st IEEE International Conference on Hot Information-Centric Networking (HotICN 2018), pp. 223–228 (2018)
10. Wright, A., De Filippi, P.: Decentralized Blockchain Technology and the Rise of Lex Cryptographia (2015). https://doi.org/10.2139/ssrn.2580664
11. Wright, A., De Filippi, P.: Blockchain and the Law: The Rule of Code. Harvard University Press, Cambridge (2018)
12. Zetzsche, D.A., Buckley, R.P., Arner, D.W.: The distributed liability of distributed ledgers: legal risks of blockchain, University of New South Wales Law Research Series. Law Working Paper Series, Number 2017-007 (2017). http://doi.org/10.2139/ssrn.3018214

Blockchain Revolution in Global Environmental Governance: Too Good to Be True?

Alina V. Vladimirova(✉) 📵

Institute of Oriental Studies of the Russian Academy of Sciences,
Moscow, Russia
alina.v.vladimirova@gmail.com

Abstract. Is a blockchain revolution happening now or has its hype been seriously overstated? In the data-driven world, blockchain technology can potentially bring many benefits to people and organisations that suffer from a lack of information infrastructure or access to reliable integrated data. So, there is no surprise that leading actors of global environmental governance, including the United Nations and the World Bank, have started to support initiatives to develop blockchain platforms. However, the successful implementation of this technology and its ability to contribute to effective environmental policies depend on a range of factors that are often difficult to manage. In this paper, we aim to systematise theoretical and practical approaches to blockchain platforms in environmental management as well as to analyse existing barriers to this adoption. Based on our study, we concluded that the main obstacles preventing a blockchain revolution in global environmental governance are not connected to technological development, but rather to modern information cultures and worldviews.

Keywords: Blockchain · Global environmental governance ·
Sustainable development · Open data

1 Introduction

The blockchain technology is relatively new; it was introduced in 2008 in a whitepaper by an anonymous programmer (or a cohort) working under the name of Nakamoto [1]. During the following decade, the original cryptocurrency 'Bitcoin', which started off at 0.0001 USD in 2009 [2], has enormously risen in price and reached a peak of 19,783 USD in December 2017 [3]. Even though in September 2018, the Bitcoin price was around 6,300 USD [4], this currency is indeed a success story that has made people pay great attention to the software and the idea behind it. It had led to numerous attempts to apply this technology to other fields and issues, including natural sciences.

Many specialists argue that there is a so-called 'blockchain hype' and that this technology has been hailed as the 'solution for everything' [5]. Nevertheless, many prominent scholars are very optimistic about this topic and publish papers in the most distinguished journals, including *Nature*, presenting a range of rosy perspectives on environmental 'cryptogovernance'; they claim that it can generate trust through stable

S. S. Bodrunova et al. (Eds.): INSCI 2018 Workshops, LNCS 11551, pp. 212–223, 2019.
https://doi.org/10.1007/978-3-030-17705-8_18

and transparent records, help with environmental monitoring, guarantee that a planned event will happen independently of the changing human will, empower citizens, especially local communities, and even bypass central authorities [6]. A publication like this one can leave readers with a strong impression that all possible obstacles could be and should be overcome by a collaboration of scientists, developers, psychologists and lawyers because, in the end, we all need blockchain for sustainability.

It seems that global public agrees with these arguments for the most part. Advocates of blockchain are welcomed by leading actors of global environmental governance, such as the United Nations [7] and the World Bank [8], and blockchain projects connected to effective resource management are supported not only by business, but also by national authorities and nongovernmental organisations and expert communities. Probably, this blockchain hype was influenced by the understanding that humanity needs completely new models of development and environmental monitoring technics. Although 'green growth' became a buzzword and a core proposal of the U.N.'s Sustainable Development Goals (SDG), recent studies show that, even with the best practices available now, decoupling economic growth from resource use will remain elusive and our environmental problems will continue to worsen [9].

Thus, in this paper, we aim to systematise emerging theoretical and practical approaches to projects that some people hope can potentially lead to a blockchain revolution in global environmental governance. We also analyse possible barriers to this technological adoption by focusing on the exploration of specific pitfalls for the natural science. For this research, we mainly use a cross-case study methodology and data available from open sources; however, we intentionally pay special attention to cases of blockchain's use in Russia.

2 Blockchain Technologies in Environmental Governance: The Current State-of-Affairs

In May 2016, the Russian Carbon Fund, with IT-support from Airalab, officially unveiled a public and programmable Ethereum-based independent system called the Integrated Program for Climate Initiatives (DAO IPCI) [10]. This project received positive feedback from Russian [11] and global media [12], which claimed that this group had started the blockchain revolution in the environmental field. The fund itself was not aiming to start a revolution, but rather to allow participants in greenhouse gas credit-based or quota-based emissions trading schemes to use smart contracts to minimise transaction costs and to make the issuance and transfer of mitigation units highly reliable, transparent and protected from manipulations [13]. Despite the media buzz, this project was neither the first, nor the only one in environmental management, but it serves as a very interesting case for our research for two reasons.

First, the foundation of the DAO IPCI is connected to a nongovernmental Carbon Registry, which, according to its developers, was created because of major dissatisfaction with the functionality of the governmental registry [14]. In many ways, this story resembles the invention of Bitcoin, which many people believe was an outcome of the Financial crisis of 2007–2008 [15] and the widespread blame placed upon central banks and other regulators [16]. The decision to make the DAO IPCI platform is indeed in tune with blockchain advocates, who point to the advantages of the technology for various governmental demands.

Second, programs conducted with the support of the Russian Carbon Fund have a clear orientation toward global environmental governance. We can find it in documents presenting the ideology of the projects; the stated motivation of two out of four elements in the list of the Carbon Registry is the direct inclusion of environmental values in the business processes of the Eurasian Economic Union (EAEU) and the rise of the international climate regime based on the Paris Agreement [17]. As an example of practical implementation, in March 2017, the DAO IPCI together with the Aera Group, which is the largest supplier of carbon credits in Africa, pioneered the very first worldwide carbon credit transaction using blockchain technology [18].

It is important to mention that collaboration on an international level is not a unique property of the DAO IPCI; it has become quite common for the whole 'blockchain in government' field. If we look at the dataset "Blockchain in Government Tracker" [19] published by Morris, we easily capture this trend. In Fig. 1, we have visualised the relationship structure of the actors included in Morris' dataset using a bimodal network model. Circles represent government entities, or their nongovernmental partners, and

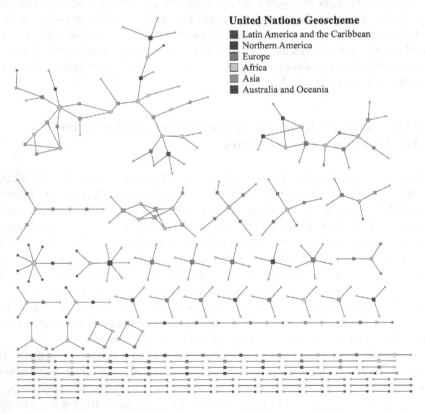

Fig. 1. Network structure of 'blockchain in government' projects (circles represent organisations, squares represent projects). Data source: Blockchain in Government Tracker.

squares are projects. We have coded regions where the projects were started according to the United Nations Geoscheme [20] and then used colour to show this attribute. Organisations that are successfully developing blockchains tend to offer their solutions not only to other countries, but also to entities in other regions. It makes us curious about the further evolution of the field and its leaders, especially because of the known effects of network structure formation on an innovation's diffusion and performance [21]. However, among the possible ways to explore these data, examining the diversity of projects types marked as 'blockchain' is the most important for the current paper.

There is no precise definition of a blockchain; some authors note that the term is being used to describe everything from a system for inter-bank transactions to a supply chain database for Walmart, and so they conclude that it has become too widespread and is quickly losing its meaning [22]. The International Standards Organisation (ISO) is trying to fill the gap [23], but the development of a blockchain terminology standard requires time and significant effort. Nevertheless, without understanding what blockchain is and what its properties are, we cannot assess the usefulness of the technology for governance or recommend specific solutions for environmental problems. First, we need to know the typology.

Luckily, the fast evolution of blockchain has already forced specialists to introduce various typologies and classifications for it. For the purposes of our analysis, it is probably better to start systematising projects connected to different aspects of environmental governance by categorising blockchain-like database applications into three groups: public blockchains, federated (or consortium) blockchains and private (or fully private) blockchains [24]. Often, but not always, this classification is supplemented with a permissioned and permissionless dichotomy [25]; a permissioned blockchain is not necessarily a private system and Bitcoin is both public and permissionless. Another typology needed when we talk about the implementation of technology. It is useful to distinguish between 'IT services', 'blockchain first', 'development platforms', 'vertical solutions' and 'APIs and overlays' [26]. These variations are presented in the "Blockchain in Government Tracker" dataset. For example, Deloitte and IBM are in the 'IT services' set, Bitcoin and Ethereum are typical cases of the 'blockchain first' set, while R3 prefers to work with vertical, industry-specific, solutions.

The type of a particular blockchain project depends on the needs and problems that it is supposed to address; another aspect of our analysis is to figure out the purposes of an existing project that we are interested in. We have identified several ones. First, there are special eco cryptocurrencies inspired by Bitcoin's success. DAO IPCI is an example of a system with tokens, while SolarCoin [27] is an altcoin that can be sent to a Bitcoin wallet and converted into hard cash. SolarCoin was launched in 2014 and is now used by projects working with solar energy in different parts of the world, such as SolarChange [28], Solcrypto [29] and ElectriCChain [30]. Here, in a special subtype, we also suggest putting environmental activism start-ups that offer a reward (both in coins and services) for plastic and aluminium waste, including Plastic Bank for SocialPlastic [31] and RecycleToCoin [32].

Blockchain-powered marketplaces for renewable energy are increasing, which is an important step for global environmental governance. Solar energy is considered one of the best available solutions to reduce emissions, so its use is supported and promoted by numerous initiatives. Propagators of blockchains have placed themselves within the discourse on environmental activism as they dedicate such platforms both for commercial solar electricity producers and individuals living in homes with solar energy panels on roofs. They clearly link blockchains to the SDG. As developers of one of the recent projects has stated, their platform for renewable energy certificates (REC) aims to help big and small organisations with green targets and to strengthen cross-border sustainability efforts, even though at the moment it mainly contributes to Singapore's transition to a low carbon economy as part of its Paris COP-21 agreement [33]. Of course, there are other blockchains in the energy sector that can be adopted just to increase an organisation's effectiveness. These digital ledgers naturally have a strong connection to the environmental impact of an organisation even though their prime goal is not so much about the improvement of environmental monitoring instruments as about reducing the costs. Nevertheless, there are a number of blockchains in the energy sector that are interesting cases including UK-based Electron [34], the first energy blockchain platform scaled to a national level.

Another type of project consists of those which are not purely environmental, but can be used as elements in global programs to solve environmental problems or help to manage international organisations in the field. The first subtype includes those platforms that operate in the emerging shared economy, which needs blockchains such as Provenance [35] to effectively trace resources or products. The second subtype is connected to fundraising issues. For example, BitHope [36] and BitGive [37] try to improve the environment worldwide by increasing the transparency of donations spending and by fighting charity frauds. The third subtype is for blockchain-based decentralised management tools, such as Backfeed [38], that can be used to set equity-sharing schemes, as crowdsourcing mechanisms and as instruments of indirect coordination for large groups of individuals.

As we can see, there is already a range of blockchains that can serve the aims of environmental management and this typology will continue to broaden. We could start to think about new actors of global environmental governance and their possible impact on the field. However, before being inspired by these examples, we have to analyse the barriers and drawbacks of blockchain technology within the natural capital framework.

3   Barriers to Blockchain Adoption in Global Environmental Governance

As there are different types of blockchains, there are different types and levels of barriers to adopting this technology. Some of them are general for the diffusion of any new technology, some of them are linked to blockchain applications in any field and some of them are quite specific to blockchains in global environmental governance. While talking about perspectives of blockchains, it is good to remember that even the use of websites as a tool for environmental data management could be quite problematic and face barriers that are of a technical, structural, managerial, cultural or conceptual nature [39]. Different parties set different priorities, so developers usually pay more attention to the challenges and limitations of scalability, security, privacy and compliance. They are worried that these issues are still insufficiently explored and addressed, since this emerging technology is still in its infancy [40].

Meanwhile, environmentalists are focusing on such questions as the "insane energy consumption of Bitcoin", which alone requires 73.12 TWh annually [41]. It is indeed an important issue for green activists, because its electricity network is mostly fuelled by coal-fired power plants in China; even with a conservative emission factor, this results in an extreme carbon footprint for each unique Bitcoin transaction [42]. No surprise that Bitcoin was marked as "unsustainable" [43] and the impression that all blockchains have the same negative ecological impact has spread.

How it is possible, then, that projects like "ClimateCoop – The Climate Consortium Blockchain" [44] can win in a competition such as the "Exploring Synergistic Solutions for Sustainable Development 2018"? The answer is the type of blockchain. ClimateCoop is an example of a platform designed for global environmental governance, since its authors want to fully decentralise climate actions based on a matrix governance approach [45], however, it is a consortium type of blockchain. So, it will not use Proof-of-Work (PoW), but probably one of the modern voting or multi-party consensus algorithms that are characterised by low energy consumption and a short transaction approval frequency (100x msec) [46].

The question concerning the energy consumption of blockchains is not the only issue connected to insufficient knowledge that can create problems for this technology adoption. Specialists have already started to warn against myths, misperceptions and wrong or misleading facts about blockchains that can harm the development of this technology and its diffusion a lot. One of these misconceptions is that blockchain records are highly reliable because they are immutable, transparent, free from time delays and human errors. Generally speaking, many people think that blockchain implementations result in the availability of data, which are of a better quality and can be shared effectively.

Indeed, there is an urgent need among global environmental governance actors. As Annan stated about the SDG in *Nature*, "Data gaps undermine our ability to target resources, develop policies and track accountability. Without good data, we're flying blind. If you can't see it, you can't solve it" [47]. Dissatisfaction with the availability of reliable and consistent environmental data has been around for ages; the digital revolution has not caused it, but has given hope that the situation can be changed. In 2018, it is already the 20th anniversary of the Aarhus Convention, which empowers people with the right to access environmental information [48] but, as scholars argue, it remains elusive [49] and there are still serious problems in environmental governance that are significantly influenced by the existing practices of generation, collection, sharing and analysis of data.

Availability of information is the fundamental prerequisite for dialogue in the green public sphere that should happen between a number of parties [50]; blockchains can transform not only ways of collecting and storing information, but also ways of sharing it. However, blockchain adoption alone cannot guarantee the veracity of data or documents registered, even though it definitely can increase the transparency and stability of records. We also need to accept the fact such technologies for effective data management are almost useless when there are no data. Unfortunately, it is too often the case for the environmental field.

So, where are environmental data generated and who is in charge of its disclosure through the use of blockchains or other modern technologies? Usually, green activists and scholars blame governmental entities and corporations for the absence of open data. From such a point of view, the situation looks like a struggle: environmental organisations, academics and other civil society representatives unsuccessfully promote better provisions for access to environmental information while authorities argue that in this case, their efficiency would be reduced and that disclosure of these data should be the exception and confidentiality should be the rule [51]. Another root of the problem is that old administrative habits are hard to break [52]. It is a reasonable claim, partially because natural resources are one of the prime traditional sources of political and economic power, so existing practices are important for the stability of systems and authorities will do their best to limit blockchains destructive effects.

Indeed, even though some authors explain that new technologies let us witnesses a qualitatively new phase in the relationship between information processing and environmental governance [53], it is difficult to change relational systems with a set of established roles and self-induced practices. Meanwhile, the ability of academics and civil society representatives to influence a transition to new institutional structures and processes is limited not only by external forces, but also by endogenous factors. In the research literature, we have found a range of them, but here we would like to pay attention to the fact that "just as governance systems effectively create exclusive boundaries, so do knowledge systems" [54] and that in many ways scholars can prevent their desirable inclusion in environmental governance themselves. In 2014, there was very important research published on the enablers and barriers for using publications by the Gulf of Maine Council, which gave recommendations on how to effectively organise the communication of marine environmental information [55]. While there are numerous publications on science policy that debate effective coastal and ocean management, including special papers collections [56], we have decided to use this particular study and its methodology to analyse endogenous factors further.

We have started to explore possible barriers to blockchain adoption connected to the issue of environmental data access by interviewing scholars engaged in the "Gray Whale Monitoring Programme," jointly funded by projects Sakhalin-1 and Sakhalin-2. We have selected this Programme as our case because of two the most important for us characteristics; the value of the data and organisation of communications. We know that this more than the 20-year-old program is considered to be very successful and has produced multiple types of valuable data for the photo-identification, distribution, and behaviour of whales, their food resources, acoustic environment, etc. [57] That is notable results taking into account this grey whale subpopulation is included in the Red List of the International Union for Conservation of Nature (IUCN) [58]. We also know that facilitation of communication with academia and the public are present in this case as well and in many ways made it unique. It is the first time when NGOs successfully used the power of the global media to put pressure on public banks around the world, so they included the special condition of the loan agreement; to take advice from a group of independently convened whale scientists for the duration of the Project [59]. It seems, the operators are also proud of the dialogue which they call "open and transparent and proved constructive" [60] and mention that among participants are "the first and only oil and gas company to date to initiate this kind of cooperation between companies and the scientific and environmental communities" [60].

As we found out, both projects promised to provide open access to those data, which was allowed by their agreement with the Russian government, and to support scientific publications [61]; however, these goals were faced with barriers. We have found numerous evidence that 15 years later, these data are still not accessible and they have been insufficiently used by external experts and even by experts engaged in the Programme. For example, there are no studies of this population structure done with such modern methods as network analysis even though this approach to marine mammals studies is valuable enough to be introduced by a paper in *Science* [62]. It is also obvious that these data can have a strong impact not only on environmental issues, but also on computer science; the photo-identification database, for instance, can be used to develop techniques of image classification in machine learning.

Here, we suggest to discuss a few barriers connected to the knowledge system. For example, two data cultures exist within the scholarly community that is engaged in this gray whale population study. While some scholars share the values of open science and follow guides developed by the international community to fight the current replication crisis, some crucial experts in the "Gray Whale Monitoring Programme" see the disclosure of data as a violation of their intellectual property rights and against the norms of scientific ethics. Notably, the first group is ready to assess their professional success using the Hirsh index and modern scientometrics practices, while the second group does not value citations much and thinks that publications by other authors with their data are unacceptable even if references are given. The case is extremely interesting, considering that these projects employ researchers as contractors, so the companies are the data owners; however, they let their contractors decide if they want to open the data. As results, there are already precedents when some contractors ignored or refused requests to share data even when the requests were from other scholars working within the Programme.

The existing data management practices should be changed to overcome the barriers and effectively support scientific collaboration. For example, a blockchain platform can be used to trace grey whales during migrations, and these data can be accessible by environmentalists worldwide. Of course, such distributed ledgers are not the only possible solution, but they could be interesting for the Projects because they increase the transparency and accountability of the Programme. Thus, this technology adoption can build more trust in their reputations of responsible operators. Moreover, national governments also can use these information systems to present strong evidence that they are meeting their international commitments to protecting biodiversity.

4 Conclusion

Blockchains offer numerous opportunities to solve some of the most crucial needs of global environmental governance, which has to become more efficient to meet the challenges of sustainable development. Modern institutions (cultural rules, societal norms and legal frameworks), technical infrastructure and actor networks that shape human-environment relations exhibit strong path-dependence and inertia, stabilising the prevailing system configurations and impeding major processes of change [63]; yet many activists and media embrace the idea of the blockchain revolution, which can disrupt these structures and support transition from centralised regulation to inclusive forms of governance and a participatory agenda.

Professional environmentalists remain much calmer and try to explore what this technology can offer to particular practical issues, such as the problem of insufficient evidence for effective policies or the deep science-policy divide, which are significantly influenced by existing practices of generation, collection and sharing of data. We also see that environmentalists express a desire to introduce more sophisticated information systems that will know how to identify (and reward) the ability of companies to create sustainable value [64]. Based on the cases we analysed for this study, we conclude that existing blockchains have already started to work in this direction and we can see diverse implementations based on different types of blockchains. There has also been a diffusion of blockchains and, even though at the recent UN World Data Forum there was no panel on the topic, the technology was mentioned in a statement by the UN Deputy Secretary-General [65].

As with any new technology, blockchains face barriers to their diffusion; some of them are general and some of them very specific. Unfortunately, technology development issues can be less problematic than those concerning cognitive and knowledge background. Blockchain is not a panacea, and it alone cannot change the access to important environmental data. There are numerous possibilities to adopt blockchains to preserve existing power structures and, as studies have already shown, it is an illusion that an increase in transparency inevitably leads to a higher level of accountability [66]. Shifts in global environmental governance, the transition to open science and the spread of new data cultures are what we need to implement blockchains efficiently—not the blockchain revolution, but rather the evolution of people in the digital age.

References

1. Nakamoto, S.: Bitcoin: A Peer-to-Peer Electronic Cash System. https://bitcoin.org/bitcoin.pdf. Accessed 05 Apr 2017
2. Baghla, S.: Origin of Bitcoin: A Brief History from 2008 Crisis to Present Times. https://www.analyticsindiamag.com/origin-bitcoin-brief-history/. Accessed 01 Oct 2018
3. Bitcoin Hits a New Record High, But Stops Short of $20,000. http://fortune.com/2017/12/17/bitcoin-record-high-short-of-20000/. Accessed 03 Oct 2018
4. Bitcoin Price Index - Real-Time Bitcoin Price Charts. https://www.coindesk.com/price/. Accessed 01 Oct 2018
5. Russo, A.: Busting the Blockchain Hype: How to Tell if Distributed Ledger Technology Is Right for You. https://www.weforum.org/press/2018/04/busting-the-blockchain-hype-how-to-tell-if-distributed-ledger-technology-is-right-for-you/. Accessed 19 Sept 2018
6. Chapron, G.: The environment needs cryptogovernance. Nature **545**, 403–405 (2017)
7. Douglass, K.: The Flipside of the Bitcoin: How Blockchain Could Underpin Sustainable Energy. http://www.newsroom.uts.edu.au/news/2018/09/flipside-bitcoin-how-blockchain-could-underpin-sustainable-energy. Accessed 05 Oct 2018
8. Blockchain and Emerging Digital Technologies for Enhancing Post-2020 Climate Markets. World Bank, Washington, DC (2018)
9. Hickel, J.: Why Growth Can't Be Green. https://foreignpolicy.com/2018/09/12/why-growth-cant-be-green/. Accessed 18 Sept 2018

10. DAO "Integral Platform for Climate Initiatives". https://ipci.io/. Accessed 04 Oct 2018
11. Блокчейн-революция в экологии. http://climaterussia.ru/chistye-tehnologii/blockchaine-revolution. Accessed 1 Oct 2018
12. The Russian Blockchain Revolution. http://www.sustaineurope.com/the-russian-blockchain-revolution-04042917.html. Accessed 04 Oct 2018
13. Decentralized Autonomous Organization "Integral Platform for Climate Initiatives". White Paper 5.0. DAO IPCI, Moscow (2018)
14. Давыдова, А.: Параллельные климатические вселенные. https://www.kommersant.ru/doc/2994855. Accessed 18 Sept 2018
15. Akolkar, B.: 10 Years Post the Global Financial Crisis of 2008, Here's a Look where Bitcoin Stands Today. https://www.coinspeaker.com/2018/09/16/10-years-post-the-global-financial-crisis-of-2008-heres-a-look-where-bitcoin-stands-today/. Accessed 18 Sept 2018
16. Minford, P.: Who Was Really Responsible for the Financial Crisis? https://www.weforum.org/agenda/2015/05/who-was-really-responsible-for-the-financial-crisis/. Accessed 18 Sept 2018
17. Программа интеграции климатических инициатив. https://www.carbonregistry.ru/program. Accessed 28 Sept 2018
18. Russian Carbon Fund and Aera Group Pioneer the First Worldwide Carbon Credit Transaction. http://www.greenbusinessnewsafrica.com/russian-carbon-fund-and-aera-group-pioneer-the-first-worldwide-carbon-credit-transaction/. Accessed 01 Oct 2018
19. Morris, C.: Blockchain in Government Tracker. https://airtable.com/universe/expsQEGKoZ-O2lExKK/blockchain-in-government-tracker. Accessed 09 June 2018
20. UNSD - Methodology: M49 Standard. https://unstats.un.org/unsd/methodology/m49/. Accessed 06 Mar 2017
21. Muller, E., Peres, R.: The effect of social networks structure on innovation performance: a review and directions for research. http://www.sciencedirect.com/science/article/pii/S016781 1618300284. Accessed 10 Oct 2018
22. Jeffries, A.: 'Blockchain' Is Meaningless. https://www.theverge.com/2018/3/7/17091766/blockchain-bitcoin-ethereum-cryptocurrency-meaning. Accessed 07 Aug 2018
23. ISO/TC 307 - Blockchain and Distributed Ledger Technologies. https://www.iso.org/committee/6266604.html. Accessed 28 Sept 2018
24. Buterin, V.: On Public and Private Blockchains. https://blog.ethereum.org/2015/08/07/on-public-and-private-blockchains/. Accessed 19 Sept 2018
25. Glt, F.: Distributed Ledgers and Blockchains: A Semantic and Ideological Dichotomy. https://medium.com/coinmonks/distributed-ledgers-and-blockchains-a-semantic-and-ideolo-gical-dichotomy-e6149d2d619. Accessed 19 Sept 2018
26. Mougayar, W.: Implementing Blockchain: Who Are You Going to Call? https://www.coindesk.com/which-blockchain-implementations/. Accessed 19 Sept 2018
27. SolarCoin. https://solarcoin.org/. Accessed 07 Sept 2018
28. SolarChange Reward for Solar Owners. Accessed 02 May 2018
29. Digital Assets for a Future Earth. https://www.solcrypto.com/. Accessed 21 Sept 2018
30. ElectriCChain|The Solar Energy Blockchain Project Site for Climate Change & Beyond. http://www.electricchain.org/. Accessed 21 Sept 2018
31. Plastic Bank: Stop Ocean Plastic. https://www.plasticbank.org/. Accessed 04 Sept 2018
32. RecycleToCoin. https://www.bcdc.online/recycletocoin. Accessed 21 Sept 2018
33. SP Group Launches One of the World's First Blockchain-Powered Trading of Renewable Energy Certificates. https://www.spgroup.com.sg/wcm/connect/spgrp/e3854238-5db1-4f4-2-8e3d-3f7fcfa74e32/%5B20181029%5D+Media+Release+-SP+Group+launches+one+of+the+world%27s+first+blockchain-powered+trading+of+renewable+energy+certificates.pdf?MOD=AJPERES&CVID=. Accessed 31 Oct 2018

34. Electron|Blockchain Systems for The Energy Sector. http://www.electron.org.uk/. Accessed 07 Sept 2018
35. Every Product Has a Story. https://www.provenance.org/. Accessed 07 Sept 2018
36. Bitcoin Crowdfunding for Charity. https://bithope.org. Accessed 21 Sept 2018
37. Bitgive - Vastly Improving Philanthropic Impact with Blockchain Technology. https://www.bitgivefoundation.org/. Accessed 21 Sept 2018
38. Backfeed|Spreading Consensus. http://backfeed.cc/. Accessed 07 Sept 2018
39. Arts, K., et al.: Environmental communication in the information age: institutional barriers and opportunities in the provision of river data to the general public. Environ. Sci. Policy **55**, 47–53 (2016)
40. Mosakheil, J.H.: Security Threats Classification in Blockchains. https://repository.stcloudstate.edu/msia_etds/48. Accessed 29 Sept 2018
41. Busnel, J.-C.: Bitcoin as an Environmental Subsidy to Alternative Energy. https://medium.com/@the_unbanked_banker/bitcoin-as-an-environmental-subsidy-to-alternative-energy-1e91c427ab9e. Accessed 28 Oct 2018
42. Bitcoin Energy Consumption Index. https://digiconomist.net/bitcoin-energy-consumption. Accessed 21 Sept 2018
43. Malmo, C.: Bitcoin Is Unsustainable. https://motherboard.vice.com/en_us/article/ae3p7e/bitcoin-is-unsustainable. Accessed 23 Aug 2018
44. Exploring Synergistic Solutions for Sustainable Development 2018. https://www.climatecolab.org/contests/2017/exploring-synergistic-solutions-for-sustainable-development . Accessed 03 Oct 2018
45. Simplaceanu, S., Vecsei, B.: ClimateCoop – The Climate Consortium Blockchain - Exploring Synergistic Solutions for Sustainable Development 2018. https://www.climatecolab.org/contests/2017/exploring-synergistic-solutions-for-sustainable-development/c/proposal/1334-268. Accessed 03 Oct 2018
46. Tamayo, D.A.: Making Blockchain Real for Business. https://www.slideshare.net/DiegoDiaz49/1-ibm-blockchain-explained. Accessed 27 Sept 2018
47. Annan, K.: Data Can Help to End Malnutrition Across Africa. http://www.nature.com/articles/d41586-018-02386-3. Accessed 02 Mar 2018
48. Public Participation – Home. http://www.unece.org/env/pp/welcome.html. Accessed 10 Sept 2018
49. Weaver, D.: The Aarhus convention and process cosmopolitanism. Int. Environ. Agreements **18**, 199–213 (2018)
50. Weaver, D.: The Aarhus Convention: Towards a Cosmopolitan International Environmental Politics (2015). http://eprints.keele.ac.uk/2310/1/Weaverphd2015.pdf
51. Krämer, L.: Transnational access to environmental information. Transnatl. Environ. Law **1**, 95–104 (2012)
52. Sand, P.H.: The right to know: freedom of environmental information in comparative and international law. Tul. J. Int. Comp. Law **20**, 203–232 (2011)
53. Mol, A.P.J.: Environmental Reform in the Information Age: The Contours of Informational Governance. Cambridge University Press, Cambridge (2008)
54. Stocker, L., Burke, G.: A new methodological framework for improving sustainability and climate change governance. In: Hartz-Karp, J., Marinova, D. (eds.) Methods for Sustainability Research, pp. 95–112. Edward Elgar Publishing, Cheltenham (2017)
55. Cossarini, D.M., MacDonald, B.H., Wells, P.G.: Communicating marine environmental information to decision makers: enablers and barriers to use of publications (grey literature) of the Gulf of Maine Council on the Marine Environment. Ocean Coast. Manag. **96**, 163–172 (2014)

56. MacDonald, B.H., Soomai, S.S., Santo, E.M.D., Wells, P.G.: Science, Information, and Policy Interface for Effective Coastal and Ocean Management. CRC Press, Boca Raton (2016)
57. Байбарза, И.: Эксперты: популяция серых китов на шельфе Сахалина ежегодно увеличивается на 3–4%. https://tass.ru/nauka/4036033. Accessed 03 Feb 2018
58. The IUCN Red List of Threatened Species. https://www.iucnredlist.org/en. Accessed 10 Sept 2018
59. Martin-Mehers, G.: Western Gray Whales Advisory Panel: Stories of Influence. IUCN, WWF, IFAW (2016)
60. Владимиров, А.В., Ильяшенко, В.Ю., Олейникова, Е.А., Черняховский, И.О.: Серые киты. Сахалинская история/Gray Whales. The Sakhalin Story. ИП Волкова М.А., Москва (2012)
61. Требования общественных экологических организаций в отношении нефтегазовых проектов "Сахалин-1" и "Сахалин-2". Ответ оператора проекта "Сахалин-2" компании "Сахалин Энерджи Инвестмент Компани Лтд.". https://www.ecosakh.ru/index.php/neft-gaz/sa2/item/985-требования-общественных-экологических-организаций-в-отношении-нефтегазовых-проектов-сахалин-1-и-сахалин-2-ответ-оператора-проекта-сахалин-2. Accessed 23 Sept 2018
62. Allen, J., Weinrich, M., Hoppitt, W., Rendell, L.: Network-based diffusion analysis reveals cultural transmission of lobtail feeding in humpback whales. Science **340**, 485–488 (2013)
63. Pahl-Wostl, C., Nilsson, C., Gupta, J., Tockner, K.: Societal learning needed to face the water challenge. Ambio **40**, 549 (2011)
64. Baldarelli, M.-G., Baldo, M.D., Nesheva-Kiosseva, N.: Environmental Accounting and Reporting: Theory and Practice. Springer, New York (2017). https://doi.org/10.1007/978-3-319-50918-1
65. Statement by UN Deputy Secretary-General Amina J. Mohammed at the opening of the UN World Data Forum. https://undataforum.org/WorldDataForum/wp-content/uploads/2018/10/dsg-worlddataforum-speech.pdf. Accessed 30 Oct 2018
66. Fox, J.: The uncertain relationship between transparency and accountability. Dev. Pract. **17**, 663–671 (2007)

Privacy and Social Movements

Iness Ben Guirat[✉]

Inria, 2 rue Simone Iff, 75012 Paris, France
iness.ben-guirat@inria.fr

Abstract. Privacy is an often controversial, misunderstood, and underestimated concept, including on purpose by actors like governments
or the Silicon Valley giants of Google, Apple, Facebook, and Amazon (GAFA). Unfortunately, due to today's technologies, the potential
for intrusions into personal privacy have increased exponentially. Even
though there are different laws that protect privacy (i.e. GDPR) what is
considered to be private by individuals and what is legally protected as
private can differ. Different apps have different privacy policies, which
leads to the protection of usually limited types of information, but not
others. This situation is dangerous for social movements. Hackers and
academics have been developing tools like Tor and Signal to encrypt our
messages, and protect the right to privacy and anonymity. However, so
much more needs to be done, both from a technical perspective, and
through advocacy. Individuals, NGOs, activists: Everyone is a potential
target of surveillance. In this paper we discuss the impact of privacy
violations on social movements and the tools for encrypted messaging
currently used by social movements. We show that the misunderstand-
ings around privacy by users and the causes that prevent the developing
of better tools for social movements.

Keywords: Privacy · Social movements · Metadata

1 Introduction

Privacy is power. When violated, governments and all those who have access to
our personal data have power over us. Personal data is used to make very important decisions in our lives. It can be used to influence our decisions and shape our
behavior, and so is a great tool to exercise control over us. We lose control when
our privacy is being violated. Cambridge Analytica is one recent example that
shows how personal data has been used in an experiment to determine whether
can personal information be used to control humans.[1] When surveillance technologies are aimed at social movements, the dangers are very real, as numerous
examples demonstrate.

Recent examples show that surveillance on the Black Lives Matter movement
is widespread across the U.S. The FBI and the U.S. Department of Homeland

---

[1] https://www.theguardian.com/news/series/cambridge-analytica-files.

© Springer Nature Switzerland AG 2019
S. S. Bodrunova et al. (Eds.): INSCI 2018 Workshops, LNCS 11551, pp. 224–232, 2019.
https://doi.org/10.1007/978-3-030-17705-8_19

Security were met with a lawsuit by a group of human rights lawyers after authorities failed to release information regarding their surveillance of Black Lives Matter members. Police were also accused of using phone surveillance on activists, who they identified as "threats" [1]. The documents, which include FBI emails and intelligence reports from November 2014, suggest that federal surveillance of Black Lives Matter protests went far beyond normal intelligence-gathering. Intelligence-gathering by the federal government had employed open-source information, such as social media, to profile and keep track of activists [2].

In countries like Saudi Arabia, United Arab Emirates, Qatar, and Morocco the link between privacy violations and oppression is not hard to see. Especially after the Arab Spring, a spontaneous movement that gained power from social media, violations of privacy are being used aggressively to prevent the power of social movements. Various countries have been shopping for sophisticated cyber-surveillance systems and zero-day hacks aimed at social movements. For example, BAE systems is a Danish company known for selling these tools to these countries: *"Youd be able to intercept any internet traffic. You could pinpoint people's location based on cellular data. You could follow people around, you put in an opponent's name and you will see all the sites and blogs, and the social graph related to that user"* said a former employee of BAE.[2] In Tunisia, especially before the revolution, the entire internet and all phones were monitored by the government controlled telecommunications system. Even those who relied on tools more secure than SMS and made sure that their traffic was sent over TLS when using sites like Facebook eventually got caught and their devices were seized.

Cyber-surveillance is a means to silence, censor, and repress social movements, and so social movements are becoming aware of the issue. In Oaxaca, Mexico, during the uprising of the teacher's union (APPO), which faced severe and deadly repression by federal police, the sheer availability of mobile telecommunications was perceived by some to be a possible threat to social movements. During protests, governments choose sometimes to monitor their devices rather then shutdown the internet. As put by "Blax" in Oaxaca, Mexico: *"The mobile phone network was absolutely working during the 2006/2007 protests. That is really strange"* [3].

One particular issue that has been underestimated with regard to privacy is metadata. It is important for social movements to be educated and understand what metadata is and how gathering metadata can violate our privacy on the internet, even when the data is protected by encryption. Metadata means "data about data". It is defined as the data that gives information about the actual communication rather than the content of the communication itself. Some apps use it to summarize basic information about data; for example the time and date of file creation, the author of the data, the location in a computer network where the data was created. One example that is dangerous to social movements is how digital pictures store the time, location, and camera type that took the photo in the image file, so when this photo is uploaded it reveals information.

---

[2] https://www.bbc.com/news/world-middle-east-40276568.

Even more dangerous to social movements is that when a user sends an (even possibly encrypted) message or email, she is likely to reveal metadata that is at least revealing who is messaging whom, which helps to build a social graph. A social graph is a representation of interconnections of relationships in a social network. One of the greatest threats of "metadata" is that one does not need the content to reveal the full extent of what sort of communication is taking place. An experiment from Stanford University that examined the phone metadata of about 500 volunteers show that telephone metadata can alone reveal a surprising amount of personal detail via the social graph [4]. The N.S.A. correlates 164 "relationship types" in social graphs using queries like "travelsWith, hasFather, sentForumMessage, employs" [5]. Various private companies or other national governments are using the same techniques to map social movements, and this social graph puts activists in danger. Unfortunately, some secure messaging apps still upload the contact list of the users to a centralized server and therefore provides the social graph of the user [6].

In dangerous places like Syria, Iraq, and Egypt activists often use encrypted emails or secure messaging apps, yet they are still under the threat of their governments because of metadata. Several cases have been witnessed when activists don't message each other for an extended period of time and then they start sending emails between each other, governments may speculate that they are organizing a protest or some other kind of activity which can result in retaliation, imprisonment or even torture. Some activists think that they can simply turn off their cell phones and then they are protected. However if a large group turns off their cell phones, in the same place at the same time, this can be considered as metadata and can be perceived as incriminating evidence by metadata analysis.[3] Also, just the fact of encrypting can put someone under the threat. In Egypt users of PGP have been questioned and put under the attention of the government even if they didn't do anything. Under Article 22 of the Cybercrime Law, it is illegal - and punishable with additional jail time - to use encryption to carry out one of the crimes listed in the law (e.g. threatening public safety, inciting violence or discrimination, etc.) or to hide evidence related to those crimes. Because the law does not define these crimes clearly, law enforcement can use it to target a broad range of legitimate activity, like journalism or community organizing, and to impose even harsher punishments if they find encryption tools on those targets devices [7].

First, we do a brief meta-analysis of usability studies in secure messaging. Then we will propose in the next section a categorization of the most used messaging applications, where we evaluate several properties and explain the importance of these properties for both users and developers, and lastly we will demonstrate the gap in privacy protection as needed by social movements.

---

[3] https://ssd.eff.org/en/module/problem-mobile-phones.

2 User Needs

After the Snowden revelations, the need to protect our privacy is even more urgent among activists in dangerous places. According to a series of interviews done by Halpin et al. [8] 93% of high risk users from social movements wanted better privacy compared to 60% of low risk users. Several new implementations of end-to-end encrypted messaging protocols have appeared, and commonly used chat applications have been updated with these implementations as well. Even large companies like Google and Facebook have joined this effort and tried to implement algorithms for better privacy in their products like Whatsapp and Allo [6].

However the gap between what users want and what developers give is huge. One of the causes to this gap is the lack of communication between these two groups. Even though the developers of these apps aim to enhance security and privacy for the high risk users there is no real contact with them. Conferences and events aimed at informing social movements about encryption for social movements like RightsCon and the Internet Governance Forum (IGF) almost never happen in countries where there is a real need for internet for the social movements. Studies like those of Abu-Salma et al. [9], which does have a large sample of interviewees, also lack a more mixed cultural background that can make a difference in the results. For example, Viber is no longer popular in the Middle East because it is based in a company in Israel. The choice of users is not based on security nor usability features but more on the perceived trustworthiness of the creator of the messaging app and where the server is hosted.

There is also a gap between the academia and the users. When the latter try to analyze the tools they are using to see if they can trust them, they almost never read academic papers. Formal verification has never been mentioned among all users interviewed during the interviews of the NEXTLEAP project [8]. One of the causes is that academic papers have impenetrable jargon. They are written by experts for experts: *"I frequently find myself baffled by the writing in journals in my own specialty"* [10]. We notice that most of the participants of Abu-Salma et al. study [9] think that service providers can read encrypted messages, and 51 out of 60 participants do not trust open-source messaging apps, as they believe that security requires obscurity. In the Halpin et al. study on social movements, low-risk users do not see open-source as important [8], but 46% of high-risk users understood that open-source was necessary for trust. We argue that High-risk users have a more urgent need to verify the tools they are using either by themselves or by someone they trust. As one user put it, *"All security experts whom I trust all use Signal, I think they looked at the source code, I did not but I have to trust them"* [8]. Academic papers and reviews are indeed unreadable and not easily understood, but low-risk users do not have the urgent need to over search for the kind of information in these papers, but high-risk activists would want to understand these papers and code audits if possible to make the right choice in using their tools.

One last gap we think it represents an obstacle to secure message is usability. Unfortunately, there is little research in this field that has led to concrete improvements in the applications. The messaging app Signal is known by the majority of users for being the most reliable application when it comes to security and privacy. However, users of Signal still rely on other messaging apps because of the low usability of Signal, especially for non-technical users. For example, there are no good instructions for recommended actions such as key verification which leads the users to confusion. A study has showed that users without knowledge of asymmetric encryption failed to avoid risky behavior because they were not able to understand the verification process, and most users failed to reach the verification features on Signal at all. A shortcut would be useful for first time users of Signal [11]. Also, some properties that have no impact on security are seen to be very important and even impact the opinions of users on the security properties. For example, the quality of service (QoS) of the calls of each messaging application is important as 40 out of 60 participants in the Abu-Salma et al. study [9] said that a tool that offers high-quality services can also be assumed to be more secure. The perceived competence developers of tools demonstrate by delivering high QoS makes participants assume that they will also do a good job on security.

3   Tools for Better Privacy

Despite these gaps and problems, there are several messaging apps that exist today that emphasize privacy and security. We present in Table 1 a short and simple summary of properties of the most popular secure messaging applications. Unlike previous work, we assume that these properties are the easiest to understand by those who do not have substantial formal knowledge of the security and privacy properties, and these requirements are the most essential ones for the majority of users in social movements. We understand that different users have different threat models therefore different desired properties, but our goal in this paper is to reach the majority of users of social movements.

Most activist users in interviews are more concerned about privacy and security than usability [8], and these users would like to use the messaging applications that most of their friends are using. Therefore we propose a strategy for users to choose the messaging application according to the privacy properties first, and then focus on usability. Our argument is we consider privacy as more important as for social movements, a lack of privacy puts more people in danger. However, usability is also important because there is no reason to use a messaging application if the social group of the user is not using it.

Privacy Properties:

- **Metadata.** Does the messaging application upload the social graph to a server?
- **Install Authentication.** Is there a second passphrase or code needed to use the application that only the specific end-user knows when re-installing the app?
- **Open Source.** Is the messaging application open source?

- **Verify by phone call.** When installing the app, does the user verify themselves with a phone call?

For Usability:

- **Notification about E2E:** Most users have a little knowledge about end-to-end encryption (E2E), therefore does the app notify the users that their messages are end-To-end encrypted and what that means?
- **E2E by default:** All the apps in the analysis have end-to-end encryption, but is E2E set as the default?

Table 1. Important properties of messaging applications.

Messaging apps	Signal	Whatsapp	Telegram	Wire	Viber
Metadata	✗	✗	✗	✗	✗
Install Authentication	✓	✓	✓	✗	✗
Open Source	✓	✗	✓ ✗	✓	✗
Verify by phone call	✓	✓	✗	✓	✓
Notification about E2E	✗	✓	✓	✗	✗
E2E by default	✓	✓	✗	✓	✓

Unfortunately none of the messaging apps that exist today are able to hide metadata as all collect phone numbers in order to access the social graph, except for Wire that has the possibility to register via email. Even though that most developers believe that hiding metadata is the second most important feature after end-to-end encryption, developers still use phone numbers to register accounts which can identify the user or reveal the social graph of the user, particularly if the local telephone company is a hostile adversary (as is the case in many countries with large social movements where the telecommunications infrastructure is controlled by the government). Some developers think that the collection of phone numbers is important for other features like the push of notification of arriving messages [8]. Most users are aware of the danger of exposing their social graph, and for this reason Signal is mostly criticized about obliging users to register with phone numbers. However each messaging application for usability reasons has to have a social graph so that a new user knows how to contact their friends and colleagues using this messaging application. Signal is aware of this situation and has been working on finding a solution to not upload the social graph into their server, as even storing the hash of a user identifier still maps out the social graph, although new designs to use a SGX enclave to safely use phone numbers for contact discover are still under development.[4] In contrast, Wire seems to be more privacy-preserving as it allows a user to use

---

[4] https://signal.org/blog/private-contact-discovery/.

their e-mail to register, but Wire still uploads the social graph to its server and even data-mines this graph to recommend new connections.

One future area for work is ways of hiding metadata beyond the social graph, such as the IP address and geolocation of the app. Tools like Tor are used by an increasing number of activists to ensure their anonymity and can help hide metadata. All social movement users interviewed by Halpin et al. were interested in anonymization to resist metadata collection [8]. One solution is Tor, a circuit-based low-latency anonymous communication service [12]. The Onion Routing (Tor) system ensures perfect forward secrecy, integrity checking, configurable exit policies, and location-hidden services. Tor provides a reasonable trade off between anonymity, usability, and efficiency. Onion Routing is designed to anonymize TCP-based applications like web browsing, secure shell, and instant messaging. Clients choose a path through the network and build a circuit, in which each node in the path knows its predecessor and successor, but no other nodes in the circuit [12]. Yet secure messengers do not integrate with Tor, and it appears only Signal integrated with "domain fronting" and now possibly with VPN via its "censorship resistance" feature.[5]

Two-factor authentication for installation is very important in the case of device seizure. According to NEXTLEAP interviews 60% of high-risk users are concerned about device seizure more then any other security property. In the case of no two-factor authentication, anyone who have access to the phone SIM card can reinstall the application and have access to all new messages without anyone else knowing. This is very dangerous because a government-owned telephone company or even the server of the messaging app itself can also impersonate users. However the second factor allows the use of password only (no cryptographic keys) which leads sometimes to problems since the majority of users forget the passwords and eventually give up on the use of the second factor authentication in general (59% of people forget their passwords between 1 to 5 times a year).[6] Wire and Viber do not allow users to have a second factor authentication for new installations.

For some properties, we notice that there is a misunderstanding of these properties by the majority of users which leads to a lack of use of a messaging application. As discussed in the previous section, open-source has conflicting opinions. While most activists believe that they can only trust an open source messaging app, normal users think that security must require obscurity, and so therefore the code should be hidden. The same holds with verification with phone calls. According to most participants in the study of Abu-Salma [9] (53 out of 60), there is no mass surveillance of phone calls. They believe that any communication through the GSM network is more secure since any sensitive information (like bank information) is sent via GSM. This is of course wrong for several reasons: First in most countries governments are legally allowed to acquire information from telecom companies about users, and also the GSM net-

---

[5] https://www.wired.com/2016/12/encryption-app-signal-fights-censorship-clever-workaround/.

[6] http://www.passwordresearch.com/stats/statistic409.html.

work relies on the protocol SS7 which from a cryptographically perspective is not a secure protocol. As for notification about E2E, we believe that this property is important because the majority of users (57 participants out of 60 in the study of Abu-Salma) do not differentiate between point-to-point encryption between client to server (as is the default on Telegram) and E2E encryption (like What-sapp and Signal). These users think that when they use a messaging app where the messages are E2E encrypted, the server can still read their messages so they do not trust the messaging application. E2E by default can be very mislead-ing. Only Telegram does not have E2E (called "Secret Chat" in Telegram) by default, and all participants interviewed in Abu-Salma study who use Telegram do not use Secret Chat when communicating with individuals either because the overhead of switching between the two modes is high, or because they just forget to use E2E, especially for participants who frequently use the default mode to send group messages (and E2E can not be turned on for group messages in Tele-gram). Whatsapp and Telegram (when the optional "Secret Chat" is turned on) have a notification when a user first start communicating with another user that explain E2E and tell the users that the app is not able to read the messages. For future work, we propose for developers and academia to present documentations and explain for users what each of these properties mean in terms of possible concrete harms.

4 Conclusion

This work has summarized the important relationship between privacy and secure messaging apps for use in social movements. The internet has the poten-tial to be a great tool for social movements, but also has the power to destroy democratic ideals, and so Internet privacy is a battle that has to be won. We also showed some of the problems and gaps in secure messaging tools that prevent privacy and security from reaching users, including activists. A major problem is the lack of research on the usability and privacy which we believe is the result of the gap between the academia, developers and users. At the end, we pre-sented secure messaging tools, and all these tools need better features either from a usability perspective or to enhance their security and privacy features. Depending on the threat model, different messaging apps may be more suitable for activists than users who are less at risk. For example we discussed that high-risk users are more concerned about device seizure therefore a messaging app that ensure two-factor authentication for new installs like Signal, Telegram or Whatsapp may be more useful. However, Telegram fails to ensure end-to-end encryption by default which leads to confusion and in some cases serious prob-lems. As for Wire vs Signal, Signal is more effective when it comes to not storing the social graph, which is very important especially in the case of social move-ments where activist do not want to reveal their contacts. Wire does not require a phone number for registration, but at the cost of uploading the sensitive social graph to their server and doing data-mining. These messaging application are very important for organizing and communicating but also for surveillance by oppressive regimes, and integration with other metadata-hiding software like Tor should be a high priority. Future work should be focused more on usability as we discussed that the gap between the security and the usability, if reduced, would result in more usage of a encrypted messaging applications like Signal with better security, which are currently not used in favor of less secure apps that have better usability features like Telegram.

Acknowledgments. We would like to thank the reviewers for their helpful comments and suggestions, and to Moxie Marlinspike for clarifying the situation with regards to Wire and phone number collection. The author is funded in part by the European Commission H2020 NEXTLEAP Project (Grant No. 6882).

References

1. McDermott, M.: State surveillance of black social movements lives on in 2017. Telesur (2017)
2. Joseph, G., Hussain, M.: FBI tracked an activist involved with black lives matter as they travelled across the U.S., documents show. The intercept (2018)
3. Leistert, O.: Resistance against cyber-surveillance within social movements and how surveillance adapts. Surveill. Soc. 9(4), 441 (2012)
4. Mayer, J., Mutchler, P., Mitchell, J.C.: Evaluating the privacy properties of telephone metadata. Proc. Nat. Acad. Sci. **113**(20), 5536–5541 (2016)
5. Risen, J., Poitras, L.: N.S.A. gathers data on social connections of U.S. citizens. The Guardian (2013)
6. Johansen, C., Mujaj, A., Arshad, H., Noll, J.: The Snowden phone: a comparative survey of secure instant messaging mobile applications (authors' version). arXiv preprint arXiv:1807.07952 (2018)
7. Sayadi, E.: Would your internet activity put you at risk of going to jail in Egypt? Accessnow (2018)
8. Halpin, H., Ermoshina, K., Musiani, F.: Co-ordinating developers and high-risk users of privacy-enhanced secure messaging protocols. In: Cremers, C., Lehmann, A. (eds.) SSR 2018. LNCS, vol. 11322, pp. 56–75. Springer, Cham (2018). https://doi.org/10.1007/978-3-030-04762-7_4
9. Abu-Salma, R., Sasse, M.A., Bonneau, J., Danilova, A., Naiakshina, A., Smith, M.: Obstacles to the adoption of secure communication tools. In: 2017 IEEE Symposium on Security and Privacy (SP), pp. 137–153. IEEE (2017)
10. Wyke, T.: Is science becoming too hard even for scientists? Experts worry academic papers are now so unintelligible that no one can read them. MailOnline (2015)
11. Schröder, S., Huber, M., Wind, D., Rottermanner, C.: When signal hits the fan: on the usability and security of state-of-the-art secure mobile messaging. In: European Workshop on Usable Security. IEEE (2016)
12. Syverson, P., Dingledine, R., Mathewson, N.: Tor: the second generation onion router. In: Usenix Security (2004)

Part IV
Internet as an Issue: An International Workshop on Government and Media Narratives

Internet as an Issue: An International Workshop on Government and Media Narratives

Polina Kolozaridi

Institute of Education — National Research University Higher School of Economics, Club for Internet and Society Enthusiasts, Moscow

Internet is often regarded as an issue for discussion or as an object to be developed and restricted. Any of these approaches supposes some preliminary understanding, imaginary or special knowledge about what is the internet and how one can deal with it. When talking about the state policies we should take into consideration this multiplicity of meanings and forms of the internet.

The aim of the workshop was to reveal the elements which constitute the internet as an issue. We have tried to explore the variety of approaches, systematize and clarify how Internet becomes an issue for regulation and discussion, who and how is constructing it. Despite different backgrounds of scholars participating we share common basis here. It includes historically-sensitive analysis, more analytical, than activist approach as well as mild social constructivism, as we do not consider internet to be a predetermined entity, but an evolving issue.

Building on several approaches, we will try to analyze both structures and content of policies and discourses connected with them. Using social imaginaries studies we are analyzing how policies, media and knowledge about the internet have been changing depending on actors' configuration and time. We also consider the structure and boundaries of policy-makers and stakeholders as actors involved in constituting the internet as an issue.

The article by Inkyu Kang and Alexander Marchenko suggests a historical approach towards understanding the internet on a national level. In their work they consider South Korea and Russia to figure out their peculiarities in comparison with each other and opposing them to a more global understanding of the internet.

There are two historical papers, both of which undermine the understanding of state as an entity inevitably restrictive towards the internet. Ilia Bykov and his co-authors work on the "bloggers law" illustrates how government might control the content in the online services and how it fails. Bykov et al. analyze how the bloggers law was implemented and what followed from its implementation in the courts across Russia. The way law was implemented was different from its descriptions in media and blogosphere. Probably this was one of the reasons why the law was cancelled.

The second historical paper is an article by Polina Kolozaridi which critically analyzes the NGOs and boundaries of organizations dealing with the internet. The key claim of the text is that the limitation of multistakeholder approach can be overcome by suggesting performance framework and imaginaries as viable theoretical alternatives to understanding agency in Internet governance and Internet history. The author traces back NGOs roots in Russia and distinguishes, rather widely, the "stages" of non-governmental organizations development. Some of them were established by state and business. However, it does not define them deterministically, as we need to take into account historical context: post-Soviet state and late Putin government both participated in establishing NGOs, but the latter now is completely different in its political motivations and actions. Finally, Kolozaridi suggests to switch from the rough understanding of an organization as a unity with strict boundaries and to consider it instead as collective entities with imaginaries concerning the internet.

The next two papers share this interest towards using sociotechnical imaginaries theory and STS in internet policy research. The article by Dmitry Muravyov proposes a theoretical investigation of why and how imaginaries might be used in policy research. The key idea here is critique towards "the state" as a unitary actor with a single and linear vision of how internet should be developed and argues against understanding internet policy-making that directly follows from this vision. Drawing on Sheila Jasanoff approach, Muravyov undermines such vision and suggests a term "imaginary coalitions" which "is introduced here to provide an explanatory framework that would capture relationships between actors based on imaginaries they share".

Finally, Alexandra Keidiia suggests an operationalization of the imaginaries approach studying the documents produced by the Ministry of Digital Development and Communication of the Russian Federation. In this analysis different visions of what is the aim of technological development and "information society" are explicated and analyzed as sites of sociotechnical imaginaries. The key result is that this development is not an aim *per se*, but an instrument for making egalitarian society in future. The paper also sets a number of questions for the further research agenda as, for example, adding new data from other ministries, taking other actors into consideration and finally, she suggests to approach the multiplicity of actors. These questions might bring new challenges for understanding internet as an issue.

Governing Through Imagination: Approaching Internet Governance in Authoritarian Contexts

Dmitry Muravyov(✉)

Higher School of Economics, Myasnitskaya 20, Moscow, Russia
dvmuravyov@gmail.com

Abstract. Despite the fact that working with imaginaries is already widely acknowledged in Internet studies their use in Internet policy studies still remains limited. In this paper I approach studying Internet governance from the perspective of "sociotechnical imaginaries". I argue that this concept can prove to be especially useful in studying authoritarian policy-settings and elucidate relationship between stakeholders in the field of Internet governance.

Keywords: Sociotechnical imaginaries · Internet governance ·
Russian internet policy

1 Introduction

Internet regulation in contemporary Russia has become an issue for a lot of debates in recent years. State initiatives like Yarovaya law and Telegram block have sparked a scholarly interest in understanding Internet governance as well as political concerns about the current condition of digital rights in Russia both within the country and abroad. However, neither journalism nor academia have managed to provide an explanation that would take into consideration political complexities of authoritarian policy-making as well as nuances that come into the equation when we speak about the Internet governance.

What appears to be troubling in narratives on the Russian Internet is how easily a complex process of political struggles between different stakeholders, visions, and hopes is reduced to a long-standing state-society conflict. In this conflict the civil society represents all progress that occurs and the state becomes demonized and totally dismissed. While such a perspective is certainly not completely devoid of its academic and political value, it seems that it disguises nuances by withholding the strong opposition between, say, "surveillance" and "freedom" [14]. For instance, it seems problematic to take the state as a unitary entity that always acts like one. Rather, as vast literature suggests, we should approach it thinking of multiplicity of actors that drive Internet development in a certain political context [2,9]. The degree to which such multiplicity of stakeholders yet remains unknown but it is still too hastily to rush and take the state for granted.

© Springer Nature Switzerland AG 2019
S. S. Bodrunova et al. (Eds.): INSCI 2018 Workshops, LNCS 11551, pp. 237–243, 2019.
https://doi.org/10.1007/978-3-030-17705-8_20

So rather than shut down the discussion on how Internet is governed in contemporary Russia, we need ways to reopen it. In this paper I suggest that one of the ways to do that is to approach the concept of "sociotechnical imaginaries" [7] that can shed light on the relationship between actors' imagination, i.e. their visions of what Internet's political future should be and its development. Imaginaries framework allows to disassemble a state into smaller entities and to question the relationships among these entities as well as their allegiance to the state itself. That is, it can provide another way to analytically capture multistakeholderism by treating stakeholders as actors who posses certain imaginaries concerning the Internet. Governmental agencies, business actors, IT companies and civic activists can have partly shared, common or completely different visions of what the Internet's political future should be like. Discovering these visions can be an interesting goal in itself, but it can also serve as an entry point for the further research. For example, if we observe that a government and some civic activists surprisingly have a similar vision of Internet what prevents them from cooperating? In the following parts, I will try to develop this argument by considering the concept of sociotechnical imaginaries as well as its implications for studying Internet governance and multistakeholderism.

2   From Imagination to Governance and Back

In contemporary research on Internet governance, there has been a turn towards combining Internet policy studies and STS [12]. One of the key features of this turn is to comprehend "seemingly stable arrangements of IG arise from the chaos of taken for granted, mundane, and often apparently unrelated activities of internet design, regulation, and use" [4]. The reason for such a turn was wide criticism aimed at mainstream IG scholars who focused on formal and legal aspects of governance missing what constitutes governance in a networked environment [15]. In a lot of ways STS informs scholarship in Internet governance by turning its scholars' attention to mundane practices, the role of technology in maintaining everyday governance, the agency of all actors involved as well as inform existing researches on controversies in IG (e.g. net neutrality) and theories of multistakeholderism.

However, I suggest that at least one more way to bring STS to IG can be proposed. The concept of "imaginary" has gained a lot of interest from STS scholars for a really long time especially in subfields like anthropology of science. Not until recently though that this concept started to be used by scholars interested in politics of science & technology. I state that by exploring Internet imaginaries from the STS-perspective we can be more attentive to the processes of "emergence", "stabilization", "moments of resistance" and "extension" [7] that connect both political and technological aspects of Internet governance. Specifically, I suggest that studying imaginaries can contribute to existing scholarship on multistakeholder models in Internet governance.

To elaborate that argument, I will turn to examining Jasanoff's argument on imaginaries in detail, as well as its possible contributions to multistakeholder models.

Jasanoff's basic argument concerning the relationship between society and science & technology is that social imagination concerning technology and technological development are produced simultaneously [8]. Thus, imagining the Internet as well as the Internet as a technology "both embeds and is embedded in social practices, identities, norms, conventions, discourses, instruments and institutions – in short, in all the building blocks of what we term the social" [8, p. 3]. In other words, they are co-produced.

Consequently, Jasanoff's idiom of co-production is closely linked to her work on imaginaries. The latter is to be understood as "collectively held, institutionally stabilized, and publicly performed visions of desirable futures, animated by shared understandings of forms of social life and social order attainable through, and supportive of, advances in science and technology" [7, p. 4], making it possible to reconnect both imagination and politics of technology. How does it become possible? Imagination as a social practice "combines some of the subjective and psychological dimensions of the agency with the structured hardness of technological systems, policy styles, organizational behaviors, and political cultures" [7, p. 24]. The idiom of co-production addresses the complexity of the ways in which social world and technology are interconnected and how each of them contributes to the development of the other. The concept of sociotechnical imaginaries pinpoints to the role imagination concerning science and technology can have direct political repercussions by enabling and disabling certain policy decisions, social connections, technological infrastructures.

Multistakeholder models consider Internet governance and regulation as "the development and application by governments, the private sector and civil society, in their respective roles, of shared principles, norms, rules, decision-making procedures, and programmes that shape the evolution and use of the Internet" (WSIS 2005). In other words, multistakeholder models presume that in such political setting all stakeholders involved have a say about how Internet should be regulated, however the nuances may vary. For instance, Doria suggests at least two definitions of possible power distribution assumed in multistakeholder models:

> (1) those that uphold the belief in a structure with equivalent stakeholders who participate on an equal footing; and (2) those that uphold the belief that one stakeholder is more equal than the other stakeholders and that the primary stakeholder discharges their duty by consulting the other stakeholders before making decisions [3, p. 116]

Multistakeholderism is usually used in scholarship on global Internet governance when speaking about institutions such as Internet Governance Forum (IGF), Internet Corporation for Assigned Names and Numbers (ICANN) and Internet Engineering Task Force (IETF). However, multistakeholderism can also be understood as taking into account the multiplicity of actors who have stakes in governing and regulating the Internet on a national level. As I mentioned before, even in authoritarian policy-settings taking the state as a unitary entity can present a problem for an analyst and lead to oversimplification of real practices that happen behind the facade of the "state".

This is the moment when exploring imaginaries can help us to disassemble the state into more actors. By approaching policy documents, public speeches, conducting interviews and interrogating other types of data, we can realize that several governmental agencies within the state can have their own stakes and diverging interests. What follows from such analysis is the "temporary disappearance" of the state as an analytical category. Indeed, state still acts, and its effects are quite visible, but such analytical move allows us to engage with other types of agency that can exist within it. Studying imaginaries can also demonstrate subtle transformations of a single actor that could not be seen by more traditional IG scholarship with its focus on formal institutions and regulations. For example, Milan and ten Oever in their research on ICANN demonstrate that its history actually experienced three generations of civil society advocates who had contrasting imaginaries about how human rights should be understood and protected [11]. Implying the presence of multistakeholderism apriori is, however, as ambiguous as implying that state acts as a unitary entity. This problem will be discussed later in the article.

3   Prospects and Challenges of Applying Imaginaries Framework to Studying Internet Governance

Exploring imaginaries in Internet studies is not a new topic. There are numerous prominent works in Internet studies that involve working with imaginaries [1,5, 10], however, in all of these studies this concept is used to trace historical roots of becoming of the Internet, rather than to explore current political struggles that surround its contemporary governance. The argument lying behind this paper is that exploring imaginaries can be a fruitful line of inquiry when we think about Internet governance.

It is of special importance in authoritarian policy-settings where work on imaginaries also allows to make up for existing drawbacks of IG research. As it was already mentioned, a common critique of mainstream IG scholarship aims at its narrow focus on legal and formal institutions. In policy contexts where the influence of such factors is not so widespread finding other ways to academically approach IG can be very helpful. If one applies such framework it becomes possible to discover new practices, actors and aspects of Internet ordering that have been previously unseen due to the country's public standing as an authoritarian regime.

To capture how Internet governance is organized from imaginaries perspective one can start with asking the following questions. What is the meaning-making process behind construction of IG on a national and local level? Why certain actors make alliances and others engage into a conflict? How global ideas of Internet politics are connected with such ones on a national level? Why certain policies are more persuasive in a public domain than others? What are the underlying rationale that actually drives Internet policies in authoritarian regimes if one is to presume that their goals cannot be limited exclusively to the securitization and suppression of freedom of speech?

There are also some questions and challenges that can be worth considering when one is approaching imaginaries in studying IG. Is it possible to elucidate certain "moments of resistance" [7] that happen contrary to dominant national imaginary of IG? Is it possible to distinguish between several imaginaries within a stakeholder that would classically be labeled as a "state" or a "civil society"? To put it in other words, are existing institutional demarcations aligned with certain imaginaries? I propose that it might be useful to turn attention to ways in which these demarcations can blur, intertwine, and make possible new alliances that are socially and politically significant? If that is so, can we speak about "imaginary coalitions" that transcend institutionally established political boundaries? On what common grounds can such coalitions exist? To quote Jasanoff, "...multiple imaginaries can coexist within a society in tension or in a productive dialectical relationship" [7, p. 4].

I suppose that such coalitions would be able to communicate successfully and pursue a policy outcome that would be beneficial to all parties involved due to the shared process of meaning-making. Such process is established when parties share a common imaginary of how Internet governance should be organized, i.e. what Internet is, what key stakeholders should be involved and which political goals Internet's existence is aimed at. This concept may be useful in analyzing complex politics of IG especially when we speak about political contexts where multistakeholderism is explicitly present. However, it is not purely a theoretical question so far as there are other conditions that may prevent actors from cooperating even if they share a common imaginary. This question is the one that should be addressed empirically. It is, however, of crucial importance since exploring such demarcations can bring to light existing limitations of formal institutional analysis and highlight stakeholders that were previously unseen.

4   Conclusion

As I have already mentioned, it is problematic to a priori assume that the political setting of IG in question presents a site where multiplicity of actors and plurality of interests is to be found. Rather, multistakeholderism is not only a set of research assumptions but also a normative and political ideal. As Hoffman demonstrates by studying ICANN and IGF, such ideal holds within itself certain promises, or imaginaries: "the promise of global representation, the promise of democratising the transnational sphere and the promise of superior policy outcomes" [6]. Consequently, multistakeholderism itself is a performative concept that is assembled of these promises and should be used cautiously. However, imaginaries are not limited to visions exclusively, they are also embodied in social practices:

> The fictional quality of the concept does not imply that the tale is out of touch with the real world, or that organisations are just pretending to follow the multi-stakeholder approach [6, p. 44].

The point to make here is that a researcher must be careful with its analytical assumptions that concern the essence of actors and boundaries between them. Exploring imaginaries of different social actors can help to establish these troubling categories and distinctions that constitute the field of IG.

Understanding IG from the perspective sheds light on a topic that has been on a radar of some scholars for a long time. Governing and regulating Internet is not only about social arrangements, but as DeNardis writes:

> Whether one likes it or not, there actually is matter: buildings, power supplies, switches, fiber optic equipment, routers, and undersea cables. Many scholarly approaches from law, economics, and communication inherently focus on content, applications, or usage and do not reach into many of the material and virtual technological functions of Internet governance. Many coordinating tasks are not visible to general Internet users and many of the organizations that carry out these tasks are also not visible [2, p. 6].

In its turn, Jasanoff's work on sociotechnical imaginaries pays special attention to ways in which visions of (un)desirable are entangled with science and technology in their making and stabilization of the social order. Exploring imaginaries can assist researchers in studying complex infrastructures that are involved in mundane IG by turning their attention to the normative dimensions of these infrastructures [13].

Considering it all, I state that research agenda that would bring together an exploration of imaginaries and IG can be a fruitful way of researching not only well-studied polities but also gives the possibility of understanding Internet governance in authoritarian policy-settings. I state that in studying authoritarian policy-settings one should be extremely cautious about the analytical assumptions of actors' essence and boundaries implied in the research. As it was demonstrated in the paper, a priori assuming both state's unity and the presence of multistakeholderism can have significant drawbacks. I suggest that one of the ways to map actors, who are, at the same time, are stakeholders, is to employ imaginaries framework that would help to establish the relationship between institutional and informal demarcations that constitute the field of Internet governance. The concept of "imaginary coalitions" is introduced here to provide an explanatory framework that would capture relationships between actors based on imaginaries they share.

References

1. Barbrook, R.: Imaginary Futures: From Thinking Machines to the Global Village. Pluto Press, London (2007)
2. DeNardis, L., Raymond, M.: Thinking clearly about multistakeholder internet governance. GigaNet: Global Internet Governance Academic Network (2013)
3. Doria, A.: Use [and abuse] of multistakeholderism in the internet. In: Radu, R., Chenou, J.-M., Weber, R.H. (eds.) The Evolution of Global Internet Governance, pp. 115–138. Springer, Heidelberg (2014). https://doi.org/10.1007/978-3-642-45299-4_7

4. Epstein, D., Katzenbach, C., Musiani, F.: Doing internet governance: practices, controversies, infrastructures, and institutions. Internet Policy Rev. **5**(3), 3–14 (2016)
5. Flichy, P.: The Internet Imaginaire. MIT Press, Cambridge (2007)
6. Hofmann, J.: Multi-stakeholderism in internet governance: putting a fiction into practice. J. Cyber Policy **1**(1), 29–49 (2016)
7. Jasanoff, S., Kim, S.H.: Dreamscapes of Modernity: Sociotechnical Imaginaries and the Fabrication of Power. University of Chicago Press, Chicago (2015)
8. Jasanoff, S., et al.: States of Knowledge: The Co-production of Science and the Social order. Routledge, Abingdon (2004)
9. Malcolm, J.: Multi-stakeholder Governance and the Internet Governance Forum. Terminus Press, London (2008)
10. Mansell, R.: Imagining the Internet: Communication, Innovation, and Governance. Oxford University Press, Oxford (2012)
11. Milan, S., ten Oever, N.: Coding and encoding rights in internet infrastructure. Internet Policy Rev. **6**(1), 1–17 (2017)
12. Musiani, F.: Practice, plurality, performativity, and plumbing: internet governance research meets science and technology studies. Sci. Technol. Hum. Values **40**(2), 272–286 (2015)
13. Musiani, F., Cogburn, D.L., DeNardis, L., Levinson, N.S.: The Turn to Infrastructure in Internet Governance. Springer, Heidelberg (2016). https://doi.org/10. 1057/9781137483591
14. Soldatov, A., Borogan, I.: The Red Web: The Struggle Between Russia's Digital Dictators and the New Online Revolutionaries. Hachette UK, London (2015)
15. Ziewitz, M., Pentzold, C.: In search of internet governance: performing order in digitally networked environments. New Media Soc. **16**(2), 306–322 (2014)

Imagining Internet in Contemporary Russia: An Attempt in Operationalization of Sociotechnical Imaginaries

Alexandra Keidiia[1,2]([envelope])

[1] Saint Petersburg State University,
University Embankment 79, Saint Petersburg, Russia
alexandrakeydiya@gmail.com
[2] Club for Internet and Society Enthusiasts, Moscow, Russia

Abstract. This paper is an attempt of operationalization of sociotechnical imaginaries using government documents of Ministry communication and digital development. We offer our methodological framework for working with this concept and highlight features of government imaginaries.

Keywords: Sociotechnical imaginaries · Information society · Russian Internet · Document analyze

1 Introduction

Jasanoff's definition of sociotechnical imaginaries as an analytic tool allows to capture complex interconnectedness between sociality (as well as politics) and technology. However, such definition's drawback can also be seen as too broad and even all-encompassing. That makes it problematic to provide an operationalization that would be analytically clear. In our work we try to deal with this problem by deriving certain questions from Jasanoff's theoretical work on imaginaries and co-production that can be directly used to analyze our data. Also in the work we will be raised the question of the features of the government imaginaries.

The central object of our research is one of executive agencies - the Ministry of Digital Development and Communication of the Russian Federation, whose agenda includes the development of digital communication technologies in general and in particular the development Internets technologies. The ministry was founded in 2008 was firstly established under the name Ministry of Mass Communications. After the May's decrees of Putin in 2018 digital development has been added the ministry's work agenda and made separate project group for working on this issue.

© Springer Nature Switzerland AG 2019
S. S. Bodrunova et al. (Eds.): INSCI 2018 Workshops, LNCS 11551, pp. 244–251, 2019.
https://doi.org/10.1007/978-3-030-17705-8_21

2   Data

Why do we choose for our research this ministry from all the plurality of departments that have the Internet-issue in their agendas? Firstly, we can trace the more obvious operationalization of the imaginary in the strategic and project documents of the ministry of communications. Jazanoff defines imaginary in this way:

> ...we redefine sociotechnical imaginaries in this book as collectively held, institutionally stabilized, and publicly performed visions of desirable futures, animated by shared understandings of forms of social life and social order attainable through, and supportive of, advances in science and technology [3].

Working with documents gives us a picture how imaginaries can be reproduced by the state actor. In the document we do not see the conflicts and disputes that could accompany its adoption, the preparatory working on the substantive content of the document. I assume that most likely documents can not convey the dynamics of the expansion of the imaginary. In this case, we can consider the texts of strategies and concepts - the collective work of the whole world and the places where there are stabilized imaginary, shared not only by one ministry, but also by the whole government.

Secondly, the ministry is the executive agency and we have an assumption that the struggle and the change of different imaginaries are located not only in the ministry's documents but also in public rhetoric about the policy pursued by the ministry.

In the course of our analysis, we have worked with strategies that were created and implemented by the ministry: "The concept of the development of the information society in the Russian Federation" (2008) [8], "The Strategy for the development of the information technology industry in the Russian Federation for 2014–2020 and the perspective of 2025" (2013) [10], "The concept of developing mechanisms for providing public municipal services in electronic form" (2013) [9]. Strategies reflect the main areas of work of the ministry: interaction with citizens and business, scientific and educational state projects, projects to improve the efficiency of public administration.

We also turn to the public speeches of senior officials of the ministry on forums, conferences and other events since 2016. Information about these events is posted in free access on the official website of the ministry [7]. Appeal to public speeches is not accidental because all corpus of them are a "control group" for checking imaginaries which were found in documents. We assume that speeches are a form of reporting about existence and achieving imaginaries from documents. Moreover, we can check rhetorical figures in public speeches that represented like a tool for attracting allies to a certain imaginary.

3   Methodology

We offer our methodological framework for solving this issue with using interpretative qualitative analysis method. Based on the works of Jasanoff about the sociotechnical imaginary [3,4], we have prepared a list of questions for data:

1. Do the texts include representations of the desired undesirable future?
2. Whether the representation of the future is structured around any value category?
3. Is it possible to analytically capture the processes of stabilization and expansion of the imaginary? What resistance do these processes meet?
4. What technical and material tools can be used to implement the representation of the future?

In response to these questions, we have the opportunity to highlight in the texts several types of categories for further analysis: representation of the future; using instrument which makes the future category possible; a category of values around which the imaginary exists; contradictions/controversies in which the imaginary is included. The questions are arranged accordingly: the first and the second questions are the directly formed "core" of the imaginary; the following questions help to understand how the existence of the imaginary is possible in the context of the ministry's work.

4   Dealing with Main Categories

While we were analyzing the ministry's strategies, we had found such categories of desirable/undesirable future as *the information society*:

> this Strategy is the basis for preparing and clarifying <...> documents defining the goals and directions of activities of public authorities, as well as the principles and mechanisms of their communication with organizations and citizens in the field of information society development [7].

In the document, the information society is defined as the development of information and telecommunication technologies, as well as increasing the intensity of usage of these technologies by citizens (in other words, a user appears as one of the actors).

Two more categories of the future that had been discovered are *e-government*...:

> The solution is provided through the measures specified in the Concept (of the development of the information society) to improve the efficiency of interdepartmental and inter-level information exchange, to integrate the state information systems and resources, to improve regulatory support of the standardization and administration of public services, to improve the system of provision of services to the citizens and organizations by state and local governments [7].

...and *the development of the information technology industry*:

the implementation of the Strategy will establish the basis for the further activities of the state that are directed on the integrated development of the industry through the interaction of its participants as well [8].

The document defines the industry as the creation of background for the emergence of digital platform-based business projects, also for the wide usage of technology in trading operations and reporting and for the development of fundamental research technologies that can accelerate the economic processes in the country.

Why are we considering this data as categories of the future? Firstly, these strategies present projects that are only scheduled for a specific period. Furthermore, we can point out the words that indicate the connection to the category of the future - "shaping" and "development" (these words as well emphasize a linear movement to a new condition or the creation of something new).

What is the purpose and objectives of the implementation of the described categories of the future? Answers to this question will help the next step of operationalization-connecting the category of the future with the value category. Let us turn to the direct quotes from the documents:

- *The information society*

    The purpose of the shaping and development of the information society in the Russian Federation is improving the quality of citizens' life, ensuring Russia's competitiveness, developing the economic, socio-political, cultural spheres of society and improving the system of government by using of information and telecommunication technologies [6].

Also interesting at this step are those areas that are the priorities in the formation of the information society. They are: equality of access to the Internet infrastructure and content in the network, improvement of the quality of medical and educational services and preserving the multinational culture of the state by using information technologies, creating a scientific agenda in the field of information technologies, and last but not least-fight with using information technologies to threaten national security. However, this is the only one place of the imaginary, where the prevailing assertion of government controls for security. Some researchers argue that imaginary of total state control is the dominant one. But our data does not match this. I will try to reveal this thesis by referring to the intellectual tradition of the concept of the information society. This step will help to understand why the state's features in ministry's imaginary recede into the background.

In this case, it would be interesting to refer to the works of scholars who worked with the concept of the information society and look at how the ministry of communication adopted it.

Understanding the information society to which belong such characteristics as focus on the importance of knowledge, modification of management systems for processing and transmitting large amounts of information, application of technologies for the mobilization of social and economic processes spread in the 60s [1]. Mansell assumes that the dominant visions of the information society of period and sum up its specifications:

> Notwithstanding the strong association between social transformation and technological innovation in much of this early scholarship, the main orientation of what would become the pervasive dominant vision of 'The Information Society' is strongly informed by the idea that if better versions of the underlying technologies could be built, they should be developed in order to drive economic growth and to augment military strength [6].

There is also an alternative critical view on this concept. The authors with this point of view argue that the representation of the information society as a better future is not without drawbacks. The issue of the unequal mediated world environment will also be acute in the informational society future although power relations as such are called into question. In the case of the ministry of communication, I see a hybrid understanding of the information society with the inclusion of both a dominant and an alternative point of view on the concept.

– *E-government*
> The measures described in an actual concept aim at increasing the effectiveness of the development of e-government in the Russian Federation and suppose raising the percentage of citizens using the mechanism for obtaining state and municipal services in digital form [9].

The main areas that are touched on in this project are: building e-government infrastructure, simplifying and legislatively approving e-government services.

– *The development of the information technology industry*
> The objectives of the Strategy are increasing the transparency of decision making in the public sphere, the transparency of business operations, increasing the investment attractiveness of the Russian economy and reducing the level of corruption. Solving these tasks in the framework of the Strategy is impossible without the development of the information technology industry like an instrument [10].

The main directions of the strategy are the formation of a scientific and technological agenda for research, simplification and acceleration of business processes by using information technologies. The value of participation and exchange is one of the key parts of the development of the country in the field of business and trade.

5   Operationalization of the Social Imaginaries Theory

The information society as an imaginary is the most widely documented and includes e-government and the development of the information technology industry. But how does it include it? Summarizing, we can provide for each category of the future its own value shared principle. In the case of e-government, we are talking about improving the efficiency of public services and public administration; development of it-industry - about market competitiveness. In our opinion, the industry and the government are a kind of the achievement of the information society as a project of an egalitarian Russian society with support for spreading it-technologies both in the infrastructure section and in for users' actions. What, in turn, are the instruments to achieve the future of e-government and the information technology industry?

The instruments for the industry development include the growth of human capital and education quality in the field of information technology, support for priority IT studies, development of export of IT products and services [10]. E-government primarily imply the restructuring of the authorities of the departments that work with direct applications of citizens (for example, receiving documents) and their transfer to multifunctional centers of public services, as well as the creation of such soft and hardware infrastructure would allow to take on a large flow of complaints. Certainly the inclusion into the imaginary information society other imaginary does not occur without interpretative work on the explanation of the existing imaginary's. In this case, imaginary e-government and the development of the IT industry are not an end in themselves. They act as an instrumental support for the information society including at a stage of a choice of instruments for realization imaginary.

Let us turn to the question of the stabilization and expansion of the imaginary between sociality and technology. The imaginary that is enclosed in a state document is already relatively stable since the document has been adopted and binding. Of course, these judgments do not apply to all government documents about the Internet. There are cases when public discussion organized by coalitions of non-state stakeholders resist the adoption of lows that has a certain value-colored image of the future Internet in the country (for example, Yarovaya law).

Why do imaginary of the ministry of communication not meet with public resistance from other stakeholders? I assume that the main reason lies in the generalizing imaginary of the information society that appeal to shared and generally understood values (in fact, technologies are integrate into this frame). The conflict of the imaginaries does not occur because other stakeholders think that they are talking about the same understanding of future with using informational technologies.

6   Conclusion

Working with the concept of sociotechnical imaginary can be a tool for moving to the analysis of internet policies. During the analysis, we were able to fix a generalizing ministry's imaginary in which the existence is possible only with the help of other imaginaries. The generalizing imaginary of the information society included electronic government and development of information technologies as instrument The imaginary is not a development project for separate spheres of the government control or scientific research. Information society (with supporting e-governance and development of it-industry) is a tool for an attempt to build an egalitarian information society through technologies, based on the state as a technological platform and highly developed IT-sphere, corresponding to the main scientific and business standards.

The analysis of imaginaries' content in state documents sets another string of questions. Firstly, can we determine institutionally divided state departments and ministries as actors which create their unique imaginaries? In the case of the ministry this thesis is unclear because the creation of strategies was only ministry's communication working but implementation of strategies was accomplished not only by the ministry of communications, but by a set of other departments. Secondly, can documents indicate an important process of existence imaginary such as an expansion? As the analysis showed, it is not possible to fix this process in documents and public speeches. Moreover, it is impossible to observe in the documents the processes of disputes and conflicts of several imaginary ones.

However, some of the specifics government imaginary become more explicit after documents analyze. For example, the state imaginary has clear-cut time boundaries because the term of its implementation is written down in the normative documents. Are any projects in the framework of the particular government imaginary actually being implemented in the time specified in the document? The solution for this issue is an appealing to policy analysis. Also, sometimes in the state imaginary there will be future expressed through the statistical data, for example, number of internet users for particular year.

In my opinion, the search for answers for these questions is a possibility to improve scholarship of researching the peculiarities of state sociotechnical imaginaries in particular. The best way to solve these problems is the comparison of the imaginaries of the whole pool of state actors, whose area of authority includes the Internet.

References

1. Bell, D.: The Social Framework of the Information Society. MIT Press, Cambridge (1979)
2. Common information about ministry. https://minsvyaz.ru/ru/ministry/common/
3. Jasanoff, S., Kim, S.H.: Dreamscapes of Modernity: Sociotechnical Imaginaries and the Fabrication of Power. University of Chicago Press, Chicago (2015)
4. Jasanoff, S., et al.: States of Knowledge: The Co-production of Science and the Social Order. Routledge, Abingdon (2004)
5. Mansell, R.: Imagining the Internet: Communication, Innovation, and Governance. Oxford University Press, Oxford (2012)
6. Mansell, R.: The life and times of the information society. Prometheus **28**(2), 165–186 (2010)
7. Public speeches. http://minsvyaz.ru/ru/activity/
8. The concept of the development of the information society in the Russian Federation. https://minsvyaz.ru/ru/documents/3004/

9. The concept of developing mechanisms for providing state and public municipal services in electronic form. https://minsvyaz.ru/ru/documents/4087/
10. The Strategy for the development of the information technology industry in the Russian Federation for 2014–2020 and the perspective of 2025. http://minsvyaz.ru/ru/documents/4084/

Actors to Be Distinguished: The Case of NGOs as Stakeholders of Russian Internet

Polina Kolozaridi[1,2(✉)]

[1] Higher School of Economics, Moscow, Russia
poli.kolozaridi@gmail.com
[2] Club for Internet and Society Enthusiasts, Moscow, Russia

Abstract. Internet governance is supposed to include a number of stakeholders with their own agenda. However, the mapping of stakeholders on the national level demonstrates that there can be different imaginaries of the internet held by one actor. The research is aimed at analyzing this diversity in historical context. We focus on one stakeholder which is the civic society or, in organizational terms, NGO. I correlate the change of the boundaries of this stakeholder with different performance of visions. I suggest to understand this stakeholder as the one which is performed by different organizations depending on the historical context. Russian context specifics also include the state as an actor that enables existence of other actors, including NGO.

Keywords: Internet governance · Stakeholder analysis · Internet in Russia

1 Introduction

Internet as an infrastructure, bunch of services and a communication space is important for different groups as well as individual actors. Both on a country-level and a global level they contribute to the internet development and therefore are interested in its regulation. This interest is a basis for the multistakeholderism approach to internet governance.

The very idea of multistakeholderism arises from the organizational studies and used to be primarily applied to corporations where stakeholders have been both economical and political actors who "can affect or [are] affected by the achievement of the organization's objectives" [1]. Internet stakeholders can be described more precisely: "the stakeholders generally include governments acting in behalf of their citizens, civil society and non-governmental organizations that are self-selected advocates of the interests of the global public good as they understand it, the private sector commercial organizations that reflect the businesses that affect and are affected by the Internet, the Internet technical community that is responsible for the development and maintenance of the network itself, and academics" [2]. This is not a utopian view, but an everyday agenda for practice of multinational organizations like ICANN or IGF who aim

© Springer Nature Switzerland AG 2019
S. S. Bodrunova et al. (Eds.): INSCI 2018 Workshops, LNCS 11551, pp. 252–260, 2019.
https://doi.org/10.1007/978-3-030-17705-8_22

to include a plenty of people from different regions into the governance process [3]. The limitation is that it is a definition of the global stakeholders, not the national ones.

Who are the actors included in such process but not the organizations? I consider that this is an important limitation of this top-down approach: speaking about organizations as if they have been the only type of collective entity. Organization's structure becomes here an ideal, however their boundaries might not be as clear. I suggest that stakeholder model therefore becomes an ideal one, while the borders of the real organizations are not as clear. So groups perform as organizations with different visions of desirable futures in order to participate in governance process. This connection of vision, group and performance is similar to what Jasanoff suggests in her concept of co-production of sociotechnical imaginaries [4]. But how visions or imaginaries, as Jasanoff suggests, are embedded in groups actions and performed in governance process? Whether such questions correspond with stakeholders' theorising?

Conflicts and controversies which help to ensure internet development are based on the group interests, e.g. service and domain providers, media and governments. This framework of multiple stakeholders' negotiations of global associations like UN, UNESCO etc. Hofmann states that one of the key problems of this is, as she calls it, that "multi-stakeholder narrative clearly represents the romantic 'mode of emplotment' (White 1978, 66). The various political and academic origins of the multi-stakeholder concept described above all share a sense of change for the better" [5]. The idea of the shared sense puts a question of boundaries between actors based on whether they have this sense or not. Of course, these boundaries might not be the same as the institutional ones. Organizations might have their own imaginaries which partly correspond with the institutions' roots as well as the role in governing process [6]. This preliminary study does not include the detailed analysis of the imaginaries, but provides a frame for understanding of the structure and changes of where is the boundary between government and non-governmental sector.

Such research is rather new, as stakeholders on a national level might not act as well as the global ones. One of the reasons is that they are not included into specific governing practices like those which exist on the global level. Here might be a lag between theory and practice. If we try to indicate controversies, e.g. between commercial and non-commercial stakeholders, you firstly need to make a clear distinction between them. It is particularly important when we are dealing with countries which are not typical Western ones (it is a big question if there is any really typical one, however). Working with the Russian case of Internet governance we realized that the pure types of actors are difficult to separate from each other. The borderline between the state and business seems to be blurred and it is difficult to understand how society might participate in such a configuration. Therefore, we decided to historicize at least a part of the field in order to understand how the stakeholders might be distinguished.

This study is aimed at problematizing the boundaries which might constitute the social or NGO sector of internet governance in Russia. The research is mostly based on historical open data and it is more about posing the problem, then solving it. Taking into consideration post-Soviet context, it is important to make this research historically-structured and context-sensitive. Therefore we provide a linear narrative of how the actors came into being, who organized them, what is their key role and finally, how they are connected with social and public sphere, state and business. Finally we shall analyze their boundaries and return to the problematization of the multistakeholder framework. The fieldwork included the key organizations observation based on their participation in any group discussions and political events featured in media and public political discussions. So first stage of the study was to figure out associations and events and then to distinguish particular organizations. We have used open resources and Web Archive to find them as well as information of their actions.

There was a problem with the definition, as non-governmental organizations are not the same as Civic society (as this group is named, e.g. in ICANN classifications). Therefore we use a more official name NGO which includes non-governmental and non-commercial organizations which might have a claim of being socially oriented/perform as civic actor. This is rather weak definition, and we return to its problematization in the conclusion.

2   1990-th: The Melting Pot

Here we'll list several organizations established in these years. There organizations were chosen as cases from the variety of organizations which started in 1990-th due to the reasons of diversity in their roots and their scale: we have chosen the most prominent basing on the documents we have read about the history of that period.

One of the first NGO in the Russian internet was established in 1992 by Kurchatovsky Institute and RSFSR government. Its name is Russian Institute for Public Networks (RIPN, ROSNIIROS in Russian) and it was responsible for domain registration until 2001. Kurchatovsky Institute was the first organization where internet connection with other countries took place in USSR in 1991. If we try to categorize RIPN, we should be context-sensitive to what particular government it was back then and what was the role of the institute. The state in 1992 was quite different from what it is in 2018 as well as the internet (for example there was no WWW at that period). The next nine years RIPN had been registering domains therefore it also became a business structure. It was not strongly connected with international organizations of the same type, e.g. ICANN.

Later another educational initiative was organized, it was called RELARN (Russian Educational Academic Research Network). In 1994–1998 there were several grant programs for universities from Russian Scientific Foundation and George Soros foundation which helped universities to buy computers and start using internet. In the next decade universities and scientific organizations became less engaged in internet development both in means of infrastructure and content. In 1993 the Coordination Center for TLD RU (CC for TLD RU) was established in order to coordinate RIPN by Internet Service Provider companies of that time: Demos Plus, Techno, GlasNet, SovAm Teleport, EUnet/Relcom, X-Atom, FREEnet. It later became the key administrator of domains in Russia: .ru, ·рф and also works with new domains which appeared in 2010-th, like .MOSCOW or ·ДЕТИ. Probably, CC structure had representatives from almost all the possible stakeholders and it was almost possible during all the 1990-th when state was not very interested in internet, IT-business was not developed and the percentage of internet users in Russia was rather low (below 3%) [7].

ROCIT (Regional Social Center for Internet Technologies) is now also a hub where social, business and state structures work together. It started in 1996 and organized a first Russian Internet Forum (RIF) in 1997. At that period it was mostly a space and event for informal communication of internet pioneers. There were also several complete grassroot organizations, which were established by online activists and key persons of RuNet. Probably the most comprising was EZHE which called themselves "a professional association, self-regulatory organ, in fact a guild of Russian Internet actors". There were "journalists, designers, advertisement producers, programmers, ideologists, analysts who contributed to internet development" [8]. It was established in 1997 by Alexander Malyukov and Leonid Delitsyn. EZHE activity started at the same year with several initiatives like mailing list, newspaper EZHE-Pravda, FRI-gallery (Fizionomii Russkogo Interneta, Faces of Russian Internet), network competition ROTOR etc. EZHE is very close to that group which is described in "Our Runet" as a densely connected group [9].

Different groups which were both NGOs, but with quite different background and ways of operating, acted in 1990-th and almost never met all together. Probably if we tell them today that they were one type of actor/stakeholder they would be very surprised. The government made the first attempt to bring them all together in 1999, and the meeting was not successful in terms of unifying the two groups. We see the evidences of those who had been there and also journalists' book "The Red Web" which described these events many years ago after conversations with those who had been there [10]. Despite their commercial interests, they had very little in common as organizations, meaning structure, resources and ideology. 1990-th was a period when civic and social sector was forming on the basis of post-soviet, early business structures and groups of enthusiasts. The most well-documented imaginary was connected with the latter, as these enthusiasts also participated in media and public events.

3   2000-th: Business Becomes the Issue

The borderline between 1990-th and 2000-th is rather evident because there were big political changes in Russia of that period. Firstly, the former president Boris Eltsin left his presidency and Vladimir Putin came to his place. It was not a change with no alternatives, as conservative parties as well as different oligarchy-based political interests were very strong at that period. The internet resources were firstly included in Putin's campaign. In this period the first e-resources constructed by Putin's political campaign leader, Gleb Pavlovsky, were initiated. There were hired may people who worked in the first internet journalistic projects and became famous in EZHE etc., like Anton Nossik or Artemii Lebedev. Partly the same people became the pioneers in blogosphere, they had very famous accounts on Livejournal. Therefore even despite big changes in political situation I cannot say that the internet actors changed immediately. Business structures became more and more important in the 2000th. If the first RIFs were almost amatuer, later they developed into business meetings. Their structures changed accordingly. RIPN was no later the registration organ, it was replaced by a distributed network of business registrators controlled bby CC as a root registrator. To the end of 2000-th RAEC appeared and becomes more important structure than ROCIT and both worked more with business actors than with enthusiasts.

Enthusiasm moved to blogosphere which was amateur, politicised and at the same time more open and easy to enter than the web. Livejournal, Liveinternet and Diary.ru became very popular. Livejournal was also a politically saturated platform in Russia, sometimes serving as a public space. There were several attempts to make a bloggers association. One was Alexander Morozov's Kant club (Moscow), also Livejournal ambassadors organized groups of people in different regions and sometimes these communities survived until nowadays. The word "blogger" became synonymous to "civic" and "contemporary". Almost at this time a president became a blogger [11,12].

In 2008 Dmitry Medvedev was elected as a president of Russian Federation and he started a number of reforms called "modernisation". In fact it was partly digitalization, e.g. one of the initiatives was e-government, e-democracy, open government, open data etc [13]. All these initiatives started top-down, there were not much open data initiatives on the national level until the state became interested in it. Pirate Party of Russia was also established in 2009 and it was not as oppositional to government at the first period, but mostly anti-copyright. Until 2011 the relations between social and state organizations were supposed to be established as quite positive. 2000-th was also a period of more close connection of social and business actors. At the same time infrastructure providers (like Internet Service providers) and content providers (services and web resources, online diaries etc.) became further from each other as the IT-sector grew and became more diverse. From 2009 to 2011 internet regular users percentage almost doubled and became more than a half-Russia. Despite being a very unsaturated period in terms of a new organizations and public events this decade became a basis for associations. It also set up an imaginary of the internet as a part of IT-industry, rather than a sphere of enthusiasts' interest (which was before) or government control which followed. Of course, this periodization is rather vague and not comprehensive, however it might be useful for highlighting different roots of what is distinguished as non-governmental especially when the actor which is usually constructed as "government" is not active.

4   2010-th: Here Comes the State

2011 was a year of probably most important political and social momentum when the internet became an issue for the state. It is rather difficult to articulate the exact reason. In some way is was due to Bolotnaya protests or electoral falsifications discussed online. In my previous research with Shubenkova we have studied internet as a social good or threat and in analysis of government documents we have seen the turn to the idea that there are two types of technologies: "ours" and potentially dangerous "foreign/global" [14].

Government became a more significant actor in providing infrastructure and laws, both encouraging the industry, censoring content and creating new barriers like Yarovaya law. It also established organizations like ASI (Agency for Strategic Initiatives) and FEED (Foundation for Internet Initiatives Development, FRII in Russian) both aimed at developing startup culture and increasing the usage of technologies for civic purposes.

One more aspect was growth of censorship and restrictive initiatives which came not only from the government, but also from non-governmental organizations. One is Liga of Secure Internet organized in 2011 by an orthodox businessman Konstantin Malofeev who worked with kazaks and cyber-patrols ("kiberdruzhina") to protect people and especially children from "unsecure content". They were not the only one, e.g. in Tyumen cyber-patrol started as a grassroot movement which became more and more popular in the middle 2010-th. Cyber-patrol means that people who seek for the inappropriate content, inform their providers and ask to place int to a blacklist.

Contrary to that some of the Pirate party members and other internet activists established RosKomSvoboda in 2012. It was organized after a government law of making a list of prohibited websites and rapidly became a prominent organization opposing governmental laws about the internet. They use a radical manner, organize online and offline protest initiatives and make an index of Internet freedom which indicates Russia's low standing in it. After Yarovaya law and Telegram blockings RosKomSvoboda each time acted as a social organization connected to technology specialists (mostly Internet Service Providers in different regions) and lawyers. In contrast with RAEC who participate in government discussions and lobbying process, they are mostly activists with all the activist repertoire and resources which excludes direct participation in policy-making.

To sum up this period, it is a turn to internet development which included government as well as new activists with radically different positions of how they imagine the internet: as a space of threats (cyberpatrol) or a space of freedom (RosKomSvoboda). Following the 2000th state went on understanding the internet as an entity to develop and control and became and important actor.

It would be quite naive to say that the government came to an empty field, where there is lack of collective actors, but it changed the field consequently and for different reasons. The NGO as an actor has been always more or less connected with government, but of course it depends on what is government at each period precisely.

5   Analysis and Conclusion

The understanding of stakeholder in Russian case seems to be problematic. Taking into consideration the broader sense of the word, we find that stakeholders change through different periods as well as the political context. If we try to connect the actors and their roles, according to the more precise definition, we'll need another theoretical approach towards what is governmental and what is civic.

Following the very brief historical research above we see that the boundaries of "social" were constructed as a response to the external challenge or initiative. The initiatives had come from educational, worldwide and Russian government and business in 1990-th and in that period what can be called "nongovernmental" actor was in fact a mixture of quite different organizations. A decade later most of them became parts of business or disappeared and for almost ten years there were no new actors on this stage, but instead what happened was the rebuilding of the stage itself: the IT-industry came into being, the language and imaginary changed. Finally, in 2010th the government, which previously initiated new structures and actors, became also a trigger for new movement: turning RAEC as a critical structure, RosKomSvoboda and finally, Liga for the safe internet, all of them acted out as stakeholders of the internet from the partaker also known as society.

The framework of this research was focused on finding exclusively the actors who are displayed in some public events and/or associations. Themselves they are, like the global institutions, a frame for acting out a performance of being a stakeholder.

Developing this metaphor, we can describe the whole process of internet governance debates as the performance process, taking more seriously Goffman approach with stages of the perfomance [15]. It might therefore include the material conditions, division to frontstage and backstage, the public which changed in different periods as well as the participants of the performance. At the global level multistakeholder approach is analysed as the one being constructed or debated [16], but rarely performed. Even working with imaginaries, like Robin Mansell or "fiction" like Hofmann cited above, researchers miss the performance, moving towards documentation. Of course, this theoretical frame is more difficult to apply to historical data, however it can be fruitful at least to set the problem and question conditions of each actor.

Applying it to this data we figure out, that the process of internet governance in Russia can be described as a play in several acts with different stages. The division into decades is not the ideal one, however even using it, we see that the first did not include such actors as the state or even business as a leading actor. So the actor performing "social" acted out with educational and business ones, being at the same time close to them and not defining itself as an opposition to any. The second act was conducted in a different situation: all the participants became more business-oriented than before and the internet became an issue for those who own money and power. However the performance of how "social" might act started in 2010-th with the resistance to state initiatives or their co-development (like Liga for the Safe Internet). When the state appeared on this stage, the NGO changed their role and started acting out reacting to its action.

This analysis demonstrates a high degree of context dependence in understanding of what we can call a stakeholder of the internet and what "society" means. There is no core ideology like "users rights" or "privacy" or anything similar to what we can see in the global scene. However, it does not mean that there are no stakeholders, but probably it can be a reason to revise the frameworks of understanding which could include this variety as well. As far as "stakeholder" is a term which refers to organization theory, we can rethink it in a more universal way, talking about collective beings, but not organizations. The latter might have less strict borders and more diverse repertoire of performances. The stakeholders of the internet in non-Western countries might not be organized as the global ones, their own borders as well as interrelations might be different and they co-develop according more to the other actors and historical conditions than to some global institutional roles.

The limitation of this research is that I do not take into consideration the materiality of the internet and itself it does not become an actor here, only being a matter of discussion and other actors' visions and performance.

References

1. Freeman, R.E.: Strategic Management: A Stakeholder Perspective, p. 13. Pitman, Boston (1984)
2. Liddicoat, J., Doria, A.: Human rights and Internet protocols: comparing processes and principles (2012). Accessed 13 July 2015
3. Hofmann, J.: Multi-stakeholderism in Internet governance: putting a fiction into practice. J. Cyber Policy $1(1)$, 29–49 (2016)
4. Ibid
5. Jasanoff, S.: Future imperfect: science, technology, and the imaginations of modernity. In: Dreamscapes of Modernity: Sociotechnical Imaginaries and the Fabrication of Power, pp. 1–47 (2015)
6. Mansell, R.: Imagining the Internet: Communication, Innovation, and Governance. Oxford University Press, Oxford (2012)
7. Public Opinion Foundation. Internet in Russia polls results. https://fom.ru/SMI-i-internet/13585
8. EZHE.ru website. http://ezhe.ru/
9. Konradova, N., Schmidt, H., Teubener, K.: Control + Shift: Public and Private Usages of the Russian Internet. BoD-Books on Demand (2006)
10. Soldatov, A., Borogan, I.: The Red Web. Public Affairs, New York (2015)
11. Etling, B., Alexanyan, K., Kelly, J., Faris, R., Palfrey, J.G., Gasser, U.: Public discourse in the Russian blogosphere: mapping RuNet politics and mobilization (2010)
12. Koltsova, O., Koltcov, S.: Mapping the public agenda with topic modeling: the case of the Russian livejournal. Policy Internet $5(2)$, 207–227 (2013)
13. The Federal Law of the Russian Federation #8-FL: On the access to information on the activity of the state and local authorities, 9 February 2009

14. Shubenkova, A., Kolozaridi, P.: The Internet as a subject of social policy in the official discourse of Russia: a benefit or a threat? J. Res. Soc. Policy **14**(1), 39–54 (2016)
15. Goffman, E.: The Presenting of Self in Everyday Life (1956)
16. DeNardis, L., Raymond, M.: Thinking clearly about multistakeholder internet governance (2013)

Trying to Keep Bloggers Under Control: The Birth and Death of the "Bloggers Law" in Russia (2014–2017)

Il'ia A. Bykov[iD], Andrei Y. Dorskii[iD],
and Irina A. Gladchenko[(✉)][iD]

Saint Petersburg State University, 199034 Saint Petersburg, Russia
i.bykov@spbu.ru, dorski@yandex.ru, irinaglad94@mail.ru

Abstract. The article analysis paradoxes of governmental regulation of blogging in Russia based on the case of legislation for bloggers, which was adopted as law in 2014 and is known as the "Bloggers Law". From the beginning, the law has been criticized by Western media and liberal opposition in Russia as restrictive towards the freedom of speech in the Russian Internet. The case has been analyzed with public policy analysis approach, including precise examination of policy aims, implementation, and results. The authors analyze all fourteen trials in Russian courts which tried to enforce the law. Due to complete inapplicability of the law, it has been quietly repealed by authorities in 2017. The authors argue that this case indicates complicity and in-linearity of media system development in Russia, reflecting national problems with controlling the global digital communication.

Keywords: Bloggers · Censorship in Russia · Internet censorship · Political communication · Russian studies

1 Introduction

This article aims to evaluate the government policy toward bloggers in Russia. The study focuses mainly on the case of the "Bloggers Law" which has been adopted in the 2014 and has been aborted in 2017. It seeks to answer the following research questions: (1) why the "Bloggers Law" has been adopted? (2) how did the law actually regulate blogging in Russia? (3) why the "Bloggers Law" has been repealed? (4) what are the results of its existence for the freedom of expression on the Russian Internet? These questions are extremely important as the Russian media landscape is rapidly transforming, and blogging has become a significant part of the national mass communication system. The "Bloggers Law" attempted to treat blogs as mass media outlets making bloggers equal to journalists with all related rights and duties. It means that Russian authorities considered bloggers as an important part of the media landscape.

In this article, the authors synthesize existing research on Russia's domestic Internet policy toward blogging. Methodologically, the article relies mainly on secondary sources, including translations of Russian documents as well as written in English. The article begins by tracing the concept of information control on the RuNet

© Springer Nature Switzerland AG 2019
S. S. Bodrunova et al. (Eds.): INSCI 2018 Workshops, LNCS 11551, pp. 261–271, 2019.
https://doi.org/10.1007/978-3-030-17705-8_23

(as the Russian-language internet is called), further discussing the policy analysis method applied in this study. Next, we examine the case of the "Bloggers Law" and theorize about governmental Internet regulation limits in Russia, concluding with a call to find a realistic approach in these studies.

2 Literature Review

Recent studies in the field of mass communication policy in Russia point out the tendency for greater regulatory pressure from the government [7, 14, 17, 30, 32]. It looks like the authorities start a regulation tightening of the online sphere after a series of demonstrations in Moscow and other big cities in 2010–2011 [39]. In 2012, a set of legislation has been enacted. It allowed the government to block an access to any website in Russia without acquiring a court order. A blacklist of Internet sites containing illegal content was introduced. The blacklist includes sites and pages that (1) are deemed extremist; (2) contain child pornography or promote suicide and drugs; (3) violate copyright laws in the online environment; and (4) call for non-sanctioned protests [29, p. 263]. Since 2012, Russian Internet service providers have to block users' access to the websites and pages from this blacklist. The blacklist is maintained by a department of the Ministry of Communications and Mass Media, the Federal Service for Communications, Information Technology, and Mass Media Supervision, better known as the Roskomnadzor.

Until 2011–2012, Russian media landscape was considered as fragmented with a considerable level of freedom of speech in different parts of media outlets and on Internet. Dunn argues that it consisted of two parts: the first, which includes most of the national television, was kept under strict control, and the second, including most of the Internet, has been permitted a significant degree of freedom [8]. Bodrunova and Litvinenko underline that Russia being fundamentally fragmented society also has fundamentally fragmented media system, counting four segments relevant with post-industrial, industrial, rural and migrant/Caucasian communities [3]. Toepfl distinguishes five spheres in Russian media landscape: "(1) a sphere of official media that transmits the ideology of the hybrid regime (consisting of state-controlled TV channels, radio channels, newspapers, Internet news sites and politicians' blogs); (2) a sphere of mainstream commercial media where reports are slightly critical of, but largely loyal to, the regime (including, for instance, leading yellow press newspapers and news sites controlled by business persons with close ties to the Kremlin); (3) a sphere of liberal-democratic media (consisting of oppositional Internet TV channels, radio channels, news sites and blogs of political activists); and two spheres of (4) communist and (5) nationalist media, consisting of smaller clusters of online news sites, newspapers and blogs" [36]. Apparently, the exponential growth of the Internet use in Russia changed media landscape dramatically and attracted attention from authorities.

Several authors insist that the new Internet policy aims at "gradually isolating the Russian Internet from the global infrastructure" [17]. The blacklist of websites and pages can be treated as a first step toward firm Internet control as in China, where all major Western online social media sites, including Facebook, Twitter, YouTube, and Google are banned [6]. Usually, authoritarian regimes establish infrastructures to control the message domestically. However, Maréchal argues that "compared to China, Russia rarely uses obstacles to access (which include infrastructural and economic barriers as well as shutdowns and application-level blocking), relying instead on censorship and intimidation" [14].

Also, international software and communication companies are a very significant problem to deal with [13]. They work as Internet intermediaries having opportunities to limit regulatory pressure from the government. Hence, no surprise that issue of data localization has emerged. According to Sargsyan, data localization is "one of the series of attempts by state actors to configure intermediaries' private infrastructure for their political goals, such as a provision of privacy and security or easy access to data for legitimate and illegitimate reasons" [30]. The issue of the Internet intermediaries is highly complicated. On the one hand, the Internet intermediaries are able to balance the power of governments all around the world. On the other hand, they challenge democratic norms by producing a monopolistic and largely uncontested new expression of power [42].

The politics of online sphere greater regulation seems predictable to deal with the Internet intermediaries and the uncontrollable Internet audience. However, Morozov argues that Internet censorship is not necessarily the only condition for authoritarian regimes to survive [15]. For example, during Medvedev's presidency, the authorities used a very open and proactive communication strategy [35, 40]. Russian officials started actively promoting their own online presence by having a blog and use Twitter and by investing in electronic government platforms, including online access to public data [29, p. 254]. Theoretically, the combination of both approaches still looks possible.

3 Research Design and Methodology

The study applies the methodological policy analysis framework toward the regulation of blogging in Russia. The authors believe that policy analysis is the practically oriented approach which is very useful in terms of differentiating objective studies from ideologically biased opinions [1, 20, 34]. Policy analysis is closely associated with the legislative analysis. The policy analysis usually starts with the process of legislation adoption, then it continues with collecting the data on the law implementation and analyzing cases and finishes with the results of the policy. The legal framework works as an objective fact given in written norms, laws and court decisions.

Our study consists of three consecutive parts: (1) analysis of the law's adoption, (2) analysis of the law's implementation, and (3) analysis of the statements about the law by the Roskomnadzor' officials. The "Bloggers Law" adoption went through all necessary steps in the Russian parliament and was signed by the President. The law is a public document and still is available by the automated system for legislation process of the State "Duma" [41]. Control over the legislation on the bloggers has been entrusted to the Roskomnadzor. The public statement made by the official is a reliable source which helps to understand the evolution of the government's attitude to the problem researched in the article. The study examines the officials' interviews in the periods of adoption, implementation and immediately after the abolition of the law. The qualitative approach has been used.

As well in the present law we can find a number of positions which seems to be quite specific and demand explanations – for example, a definition of a blogger. Thus, a discourse analysis attempt took place. For the discuss tracing purpose media monitoring was undertaken. The sample was formed according two periods: from 2014, which is the year of law's adoption, to 2017, which is a year of law's abortion, and from 2014 and back without restrictions as we supposed to find the beginning of the discussion. The resources for the analysis were "Rossijskaya gazeta" as an official government outlet; "RIA Novosti" as one of the most quoted news agency in Russian media and Russian social media segment [37]; "gazeta.ru", "rbc.ru" and "RBC Daily" as a part of rbc.ru outlet, "Kommersant", "Vedomosti" websites. The last five outlets were randomly chosen from the media rating of Integrum analytical company [23].

The policy results study based on the open data analysis of legislation and court decisions in Russia. Due to Russian legislation, all court judgments' information is public and indexed in special resources. For this reason, data for the study were collected using special court decisions' databases: "Electronic justice. Bank of arbitration courts decisions", "Adjudication decisions. RF", "Gcourts.ru", and "RosPravosudie".

4   Research Results

Introduced at the beginning of 2014, the new law requires from the bloggers with more than 3.000 daily readers to register with the mass media regulator, the Roskomnadzor, as a mass media agent, and be ready to provide authorities with users' information [41]. The background note of the law states that "the bill is designed to protect the rights of citizens and to organize the dissemination of information and exchange of data between users on Internet" [41]. It makes sense to notice that the idea of censorship is highly popular in Russia. Thus, "49% of all Russians believe that information on the Internet needs to be censored, while 42% of Russians believe foreign countries are using the Internet against Russia and its interests, and 24% think the Internet threatens political stability" [16].

We found out that it is difficult to trace the discussion about the bill, both in the mass media and in the Parliament. The bill was adopted as a part a so-called set of anti-terrorist sanctions, in the context of prohibitive measures regarding personal data and foreign participation in the Russian media, so there was hardly any discussion neither in Parliament before 2014 nor with the community which is supposed to regulate. Though an attempt of making some kind of homogeneous blogger community took place in 2017 [4], it ultimately failed as the so-called the Council meeting did not gain a quorum. It is quite interesting that in this case parts supposed to reach a compromise, but one side got a different idea of the Council's organization purpose, i.e. bloggers expressed caution about legislators' intentions. Nevertheless, it was interesting to find a media material from 2008, dated February 12, concerning proposed amendments to the communication law. It was supposed to to adopt the mandatory registration of Internet sites, the number of visits per day exceeds 1000 [29]. We can easily explain the given number. This provision corresponds to article 12 of the current version of the communication law, where the printed media with a circulation of 1000 copies and above are subject to mandatory registration. However, it still doesn't clarify the number 3000 visitors per day, as well as government interest to forming legislative frames for users' activities.

However, the very first draft of the law didn't have any mentioning of the bloggers. The law was initiated by the group of the members of State "Duma" headed by Yarovaya. It was submitted on January 15, 2014. The mentioning of "bloggers" appeared at the second reading of the bill. Finally, the "Bloggers Law" (The Federal Law 97-FZ) was signed by President V. Putin on May 5, 2014. Basically, the "Bloggers Law" added to and changed several articles in the Federal Law "On information, information technologies, and information protection", enriching Russian jurisprudence with a new concept, such as "blogger". According to the law, the blogger is "the owner of the site and (or) pages of a site in Internet, where public information is located and a daily access to it is more than three thousand users" [39]. As well the article states a list of rules regulating dissemination of information by the bloggers. Also, the law states that the bloggers who attract more than 3.000 daily visitors must register at the Roskomnadzor as a mass media. So, the Roskomnadzor started a new list of bloggers. Popular bloggers were obligated to store their electronic communications with Internet users for six months and submit this information to the authorized state bodies upon request. The Roskomnadzor assigns the blogger status according to its own statistics. The law did not protect bloggers from any manipulation with online statistics by fake accounts or spam bots.

The Russian "Bloggers law" was criticized by international media as "draconian" (Russia, 2014) and "restrictive" [12] because it is limiting "space of freedom of expression on Internet" [2]. The most popular bloggers criticized the law pointing out its practical inapplicability. For example, Anton Nossik, who is considered to be "Internet guru" in Russia, wrote in his blog that he is not going to be registered as a blogger as there is no real punishment in legal terms for not doing it, however, considering the blocking of popular social networks like Facebook, Twitter, LiveJournal and Google in Russia as a highly possible scenario [18]. Several researchers have analyzed the normative content of this law, publishing several articles on the subject [9, 10, 19, 28]. They concluded that the adoption of this law was politically motivated. Forced application of the term "blogger" in the document leaves many open issues for the law's applicability in judicial proceedings.

To our surprise, there were only 14 cases of judicial decisions concerning law regulation. Moreover, about 2208 bloggers have been registered by the Roskomnadzor in 3 years of its existence which is not a significant number for RuNet [21]. The subjects were selected on the basis of a search query specified as "Spreading public information by blogger". Nine cases are devoted to the issues related to business reputation, honor and dignity protection. Three cases contain issues concerning prosecutor's lawsuit on information access restriction. Other cases concern the claims for intellectual property protection.

According to the documents, in two cases it was not possible to reveal that the defendant is the owner of the blog. In six cases the law was admitted as inapplicable, as the court did not identify the defendants as bloggers. For these cases, the decision reasons were the next:

- the respondent's page attendance is not enough to determine the page as "a blog" in terms of the law (Supreme Court of the Chuvash Republic Definition, the case № 33-5045/2014);
- the defendant is not registered by the Roskomnadzor as a blogger (Ivanovo Regional Court Definition, the case № 33-685/2015);
- the qualification of the defendant as an organizer of information flow on the Internet raise doubts (Saint-Petersburg City Court Appeal Definition, the case № 33-12852/2016).

In accordance with one of the given cases, the court concluded that only an individual person can be treated as a blogger. By making this decision the court appeals to the requirement that blogger is to post on the website his name and initials. This requirement contained in article 10.2, part 5 of the law. Nevertheless, examination of five randomly selected blogs showed that none of them contained the required information [5]. However, the court qualified as a blogger LLC "Mail.Ru" and the social network "Moj Mir" ("My world") as a blog (Moscow City Court Resolution, the case № 4A-5816/2015, January 28, 2016). Remarkably, in Saint-Petersburg the LLC "Mail. Ru" was qualified as a blogger, whereas a social network "Moj Mir" was not considered as a blog (Saint-Petersburg City Court Appeal Definition, the case № 33-12852/2016, July 14, 2016). An understanding the social network as a single blog by Moscow City Court contradicts the judgment decision in Tomsk. The similar issue caused a different decision: "a registered user created an online diary using the LiveJournal service, so he is the owner of the relevant page on the site and is able to post its text messages or other information (content)" (Seventh Arbitration Court of Appeal Decision, the case № A45-2536/2015, August 10, 2015). This statement suggests as a blogger a single user, whose page is visited by more than 3.000 users per day. So, the networking social service cannot be considered as a blogger. These contradictions indicate certain problems in defining terms "blog" and "bloggers". Vadim Ampelonskiy, the press-secretary of the Roskomnadzor, has noted in the interview: "If you run a website with quotes from an individual, then this resource can be called a blog" [11]. However, the Roskomnadzor used to register the communities and organizations as bloggers as well. In this way, the Roskomnadzor registered "Community № 1 about Apple" at the social network "Vkontakte" and the page "Feed your brain" at the social network "Moi Mir" as bloggers [22]. Based on the analysis of all given cases, we can draw the most important conclusion that all court decisions were determined not by the applicability of the law, but by other legislation which are the rules introduced before and outside the context of the "Bloggers Law".

At the very beginning, the head of the Roskomnadzor Alexander Zharov warmly welcomed the adoption of the new law. "The owner of the site and blogger … certainly should be responsible for the content he disseminated", said A. Zharov [27]. The requirement to specify the blogger's name on the Internet page as well as in the list of the bloggers were perceived by officials as a way to combat anonymity. From this point of view, anonymity is the thing that provokes a person to violate "moral, ethical and legal boundaries" [33].

However, very soon it became clear that in the practice there are many problems with unobvious solutions. Representatives of the Roskomnadzor have been talking about it in a week before the law came into force at a meeting with the Internet community. First, should a social network service, or a group in a social network, or an organization be considered as a blogger? On July 23, 2014, deputy head of the Roskomnadzor Maxim Ksenzov assured that only individuals would be considered as bloggers [23]. Nevertheless, a week later the Roskomnadzor started to treat the law in a different way, registering as bloggers the group in "Vkontakte" and a page in "Moi Mir", as well as many others non-individuals. It looks like having no volunteers to register as bloggers the Roskomnadzor decided to register all who would like to register.

Second, how the daily audience of the site should be counted? It turned out that different measurement applications gave different results. In addition, it is unclear whether a person who has spent a few seconds on the given Internet page should be considered. The law makes no distinction between the casual visitor and the attentive reader. The Roskomnadzor announced that they are going to use the information only about users who have fully downloaded the page to the browser or browsing it for at least 15 s. Thus, in search of practical solutions the agency turned up in a conflict with the requirements of the law. As well, in contradiction with the law, officials announced plans to provide bloggers with QR-code, which bloggers would place instead of their real names. Thus, at the stage of the implementation of the law, the Roskomnadzor was confused and was ready even to violate certain norms of the legislation in order to be able to handle with others.

The Roskomnadzor confusion only has grown over time. The initial understanding of the law and the projects to implement it turned into trash. It also turned out that all agency activities for bloggers' supervision are not in demand nor by society neither by the public authorities. On March 4, 2015, the Roskomnadzor published the "Bloggers law" violations first statistics. It reveals that 60% of the violations are in the use of obscene language, 24% is in promoting drug use, followed by an insult of religious feelings, extremism and propaganda of Nazi attributes [24]. However, neither the police nor the Federal service for drug control nor the Prosecutor's office did not take any action to prosecute the identified offenders. Considering this information, no blogs were blocked by a court or by the Roskomnadzor.

At the same time, the bloggers' list register pace began to fall. It became increasingly clear that the law is not working in the way it has been designed. A number of initiative groups from Yekaterinburg and from Saint-Petersburg prepared amendment proposals to the law. Federal Antimonopoly Service representatives officially worked within Saint-Petersburg group. Nonetheless, the Roskomnadzor has objected categorically. It was stated, that the law works less than a year and any amendments are premature: "the opportunities it provides for interaction with the blogosphere have not been exhausted yet" [38]. A similar position was expressed by one of the authors of this work at the Federation Council for the information society development Temporary Commission. The experience of the law showed not only its complete inactivity but also the regulation complicity in general. The new rules introduction could only confuse the further situation.

Finally, in summer, 2017, the Roskomnadzor decisively surrendered. Alexander Zharov said: "the fact is that the Internet is rapidly evolving, and the laws do not always remain as effective as they were at the time of their adoption, and the law enforcement proves that the laws require correction. This applies to one part of the bill under discussion, and we fully support an abolition of a position in the legislation on a register of bloggers" [26]. So, from the Russian legislation has withdrawn the term the "blogger" and the other requirements for bloggers.

5 Conclusions and Discussions

Based on the above, we can say that the "Bloggers Law" was aimed to increase the responsibility of the bloggers by adding new functions to the government. But the analysis shows a complete confusion at all stages of the law's exiting, from the moment of a very crumpled discussion to the abortion moment passed unnoticed by the community that was supposed to be regulated. The attempt to make the blogger community more homogeneous took place but failed as parts had different views of the main purpose. It was difficult to follow the discussion towards the taken law because traces are very light, so we cannot clearly submit neither the discussion in Parliament nor in or with the blogger community. One of the possible explanations for creating the law deal with the idea of Internet self-censorship.

The introduction of the law got certain public attention in Russia and abroad, but not its abortion. However, the law had been widely ignored due to the lack of liability for its violation. Only fourteen cases in courts for all Russia looks extremely ridiculous as well as 2208 bloggers who have been registered by the Roskomnadzor for three years. As the Blogger Council case shows, these results may undermine the government's reputation, its ability to provide effective policy toward Internet. Thus, three years after its adoption the "Bloggers Law" was quietly repealed by authorities due to the problems connected to its implementation. The law has been declared as ineffective. Presumably, the act had been associated with the uncertainty and ambiguity of its normative content, the legal insecurity of its application and the lack of social conditions for using it.

It is also worth noting the officials' position expressed at the very beginning of the law's adoption and at the very end, when the ineffectiveness of the law was recognized. No wonder, that it had radically chanced from positive to relatively negative. It is quite entertaining that in the gathered sample there are two materials with almost the same titles: "Roskomnadzor supports the "Bloggers Law" published in 2014", and "Roskomnadzor supports the abolition of the "Bloggers Law" published in 2017".

It seems that the law has marked the limits of politically motivated governmental regulation and pointed out real constraint for government to restrict Internet freedom. Within the limits it is worth highlighting, first of all, technical limitation. We can see the problem on the definition level already, as well as on the technical control level, for example, in creating bloggers list or the sites closure by Roskomnadzor. Secondly, there are legal restrictions expressed in the impossibility of finding clear frames for regulation function. Finally, there are social-political restrictions looking back at which we can see the reaction of society to such attempts including professional and bloggers communities, Internet Russian users, journalists. And we can suppose that the reaction was mostly negative rather than positive, otherwise the law would have been valid to the present time. At the same time public reaction can also damage the foreign policy image of the Russian government as there were plenty of materials about the adoption of the law in mass media, but not to its abolition which went practically unnoticed. Thus, we can see that the fragmentation of media landscape remains in Russia while media segments are constantly shifting due to the dynamic nature of the networked communication.

References

1. Bardach, E., Patashnik, E.M.: A Practical Guide for Policy Analysis: The Eightfold Path to More Effective Problem Solving. CQ Press College, Washington, DC (2015)
2. Birnbaum, M.: Russian blogger law puts new restrictions on Internet freedoms. Washington Post, July 31 2014. https://www.washingtonpost.com/world/russian-blogger-law-puts-new-restrictions-on-internet-freedoms/2014/07/31/42a05924-a931-459f-acd2-6d08598c375b_story.html?utm_term=.0f894fec4812
3. Bodrunova, S., Litvinenko, A.: Four Russias in communication: fragmentation of the Russian public sphere in the 2010s. In: Democracy and Media in Central and Eastern Europe 25 Years On. Peter Lang, Berlin (2015)
4. Bol'shinstvo populyarnyh blogerov proignorirovalo Sovet blogerov v Gosdume. [Most popular bloggers ignored the Bloggers Council in the State Duma]. Rbc.ru (2017). (in Russian). https://www.rbc.ru/politics/19/06/2017/5947e6469a794764344b7a27
5. Deibert, R., Palfrey, J., Rohozinski, R., Zittrain, J. (eds.): Access Controlled: The Shaping of Power, Rights, and Rule in Cyberspace. MIT Press, Cambridge (2010)
6. Dorskii, A.: "Zakon o blogerah": pravoprimenitel'naja praktika [The "Bloggers Law": law enforcement practice]. Interactivnaya nauka 7, 56–58 (2016). (in Russian)
7. Duffy, N.: Internet Freedom in Vladimir Putin's Russia: The Noose Tightens. American Enterprise Institute, Washington, DC (2015)
8. Dunn, J.A.: Lottizzazione Russian style: Russia's two-tier media system. Europe-Asia Stud. 66(9), 1425–1451 (2014)
9. Haliullina, L.: Prava, objazannosti i otvetstvennost' blogera kak subjekta virtual'noj kommunikacii [Rights, duties and responsibilities of a blogger as a subject of virtual communication]. Biznes v zakone. Jekonomiko-juridicheskij zhurnal 3, 168–170 (2015). (in Russian)
10. Kapustina, A.: Pravovoj status subektov informacionno-kommunikativnoj dejatel'nosti v Internete [The legal status of the subjects of information and communication activities on the Internet]. Aktual'nye problemy gumanitarnyh i estestvennyh nauk 11(7), 43–46 (2015). (in Russian)
11. Luganskaja, D.: Kak budet s 1 avgusta rabotat' zakon o blogerah. [How will the "Bloggers Law" work after August 1?]. Roskomnadzor (2014). (in Russian). http://rkn.gov.ru/press/publications/news26537.htm
12. MacFarquhar, N.: Russia quietly tightens reins on web with the 'Bloggers Law'. The New York Times (2014). https://www.nytimes.com/2014/05/07/world/europe/russia-quietly-tightens-reins-on-web-with-bloggers-law.html
13. MacKinnon, R., Hickock, E., Bar, A., Lim, H.: Fostering Freedom Online: The Role of Internet Intermediaries. UNESCO, Paris (2014)

14. Maréchal, N.: Networked authoritarianism and the geopolitics of information: understanding russian internet policy. Media Commun. **5**(1), 29–41 (2017)
15. Morozov, E.: The Net Delusion: The Dark Side of Internet Freedom. Public Affairs, New York (2011)
16. Nisbet, E.: Benchmarking Public Demand: Russia's Appetite for Information Control. Center for Global Communication Studies, Philadelphia (2015)
17. Nocetti, J.: Russia's 'dictatorship-of-the-law' approach to internet policy. Internet Policy Rev. **4**(4) (2015)
18. Nossik, A.: Est' li zhizn posle 1 avgusta? [Is there a life after August 1?] (2014). (in Russian) https://dolboeb.livejournal.com/2673975.html
19. Palehova, E.: Pravovoj status blogera i osobennosti ego otvetstvennosti [The legal status of the blogger and the features of his responsibility]. Predprinimatel'skoe pravo **2**, 60–65 (2015). (in Russian)
20. Patton, C., Sawicki, D.: Basic Methods of Policy Analysis and Planning. Routladge, London (2012)
21. Raibman, N.: Roskomnadzor prekratil vesti reestr blogerov. [Roskomnadzor stops to run the bloggers list]. Vedomosti (2017). (in Russian). https://www.vedomosti.ru/politics/articles/2017/08/01/727388-roskomnadzor-reestr-blogerov
22. Reestr sajtov i(ili) stranic sajtov v seti Internet, na kotoryh razmeshhaetsja obshhedostupnaja informacija i dostup k kotorym v techenie sutok sostavljaet bolee treh tysjach pol'zovatelej seti Internet. [The register of sites and(or) pages of sites on the Internet on which public information is located and access to which during the day is more than three thousand Internet users]. Roskomnadzor (2017). (in Russian). https://rkn.gov.ru/opendata/7705846236-Bloger/data-20170323T0000-structure-20140822T0000.xml
23. Rejting rossijskih SMI – iyul' 2018. [The rating of Russian media – July 2018]. Integrum (2018). (in Russian). https://integrum.ru/ratings/smi/media/jan18
24. Roskomnadzor dal razjasnenija i rekomendacii po zakonu o blogerah. [Roskomnadzor gave explanations and recommendations on the "Bloggers Law"]. RBC Daily (2014). (in Russian). https://rkn.gov.ru/press/publications/news26408.htm
25. Roskomnadzor opublikoval pervuju statistiku narushenija zakona o blogerah. [Roskomnadzor published the first statistics on violations of the "Bloggers Law"]. Roskomnadzor (2015). (in Russian). https://rkn.gov.ru/press/publications/news30852.htm
26. Roskomnadzor podderzhal otmenu zakona o bloggerah. [Roskomnadzor supports the abolition of the "Bloggers Law"]. Roskomnadzor (2017). (in Russian). https://rkn.gov.ru/press/publications/news46672.htm
27. Roskomnadzor podderzhal zakon o blogerah: za svoi slova nado otvechat'. [Roskomnadzor supports the "Bloggers Law": one must answer for one's words]. RIA Novosti (2014). (in Russian). https://rkn.gov.ru/press/publications/news25062.htm
28. Rybina, T.: Problemy pravovogo statusa blogera [Problems of the legal status of the blogger]. Nauka i sovremennost' **40**, 40–44 (2015). (in Russian)
29. Samoilenko, S., Erzikova, E.: Media, political advertising and election campaigning in Russia. In: Holtz-Bacha, C., Just, M. (eds.) Handbook of Political Advertising, pp. 253–268. Routledge, London (2017)
30. Sargsyan, T.: Data localization and the role of infrastructure for surveillance, privacy, and security. Int. J. Commun. **10**, 2221–2237 (2016)
31. SF nameren rezko uzhestochit' kontrol' za blogosferoj. [SF intends to dramatically tighten control over the blogosphere]. Rbc.ru (2008). (in Russian). https://www.rbc.ru/society/12/02/2008/5703cb1d9a79470eaf769293
32. Soldatov, A., Borogan, I.: The Red Web: The Struggle Between Russia's Digital Dictators and the New Orange Revolution. Public Affairs, New York (2015)

33. Sovsem bez interneta Rossija ne ostanetsja. [Russia will not remain without the Internet]: Kommersant (2014). (in Russian). https://rkn.gov.ru/press/publications/news28368.htm
34. Stone, D.: Policy Paradox: The Art of Political Decision Making. W. W. Norton, New York (2011)
35. Toepfl, F.: Blogging for the sake of the president: the online diaries of Russian governors. Europe-Asia Stud. **64**(8), 1435–1459 (2012)
36. Toepfl, F.: Four facets of critical news literacy in a non-democratic regime: how young Russians navigate their news. Eur. J. Commun. **29**(1), 68–82 (2014)
37. Top-3 samyh citiruemyh informacionnyh agentstv v SMI – yanvar' 2018. [Top 3 most cited media news agencies – January 2018]. Medialogiya (2018). (in Russian). http://www.mlg.ru/ratings/media/federal/5830/
38. V Roskomnadzore schitajut prezhdevremennymi popravki k zakonu o blogerah 12 maja 2015 goda [Roskomnadzor considers premature amendments to the "Bloggers Law"]. RIA Novosti (2015). (in Russian). https://rkn.gov.ru/press/publications/news32326.htm
39. White, S., McAllister, I.: Did Russia (nearly) have a Facebook revolution in 2011? Soc. Media's Challenge Authoritarianism Polit. **34**(1), 72–84 (2014). https://doi.org/10.1111/1467-9256.12037
40. Yagodin, D.: Blog Medvedev: aiming for public consent. Europe-Asia Stud. **64**(8), 1415–1434 (2012)
41. Zakonoproekt № 428884-6: v arhive. [The Law 428884-6: archived]. Automated system for the legislation process of the State "Duma" (2014). (in Russian). http://asozd2.duma.gov.ru/main.nsf/(Spravka)?OpenAgent&RN=428884-6
42. Zuboff, S.: Big other: surveillance capitalism and the prospects of an information civilization. J. Inf. Technol. **30**(1), 75–89 (2015). https://doi.org/10.1057/jit.2015.5

The Internet is Plural: The Sociopolitical Shaping of the Russian and Korean "Internets"

Inkyu Kang[1] and Alexander N. Marchenko[2]

[1] Pennsylvania State University, Erie, PA 16563-1501, USA
iuk14@psu.edu
[2] Saint Petersburg State University, 199034 Saint Petersburg, Russia
a.marchenko@spbu.ru

Abstract. This study investigates the evolution of the Internet in Russia and South Korea. Focusing on two of the most wired nations, this study explores how sociopolitical forces have transformed the Internet. Although very different "internets" have developed in the two countries, both countries' constitute signs revolving around the "West." While Korea passionately embraced the Internet as an attempt to join the "advanced world," Russia has been wary of the interconnected computer networks spearheaded by the United States and its allies including the UK, Germany and France. This paper investigates the Internet in terms of a sign system that bears specific meanings within society, shaping its adoption, use and development.

Keywords: Russia · South Korea · Internets

1 Introduction

The Internet is not a mere tool. It also constitutes a sign system. Consumption always involves cultural meanings and values, as Baudrillard (1998) suggests, and technology is no exception. The Internet has to be made meaningful to be adopted and made use of by members of society. A tool is a material entity that can exist by itself, but a sign always refers to something other than itself. Anything can be a sign as far as it stands for something else, and "all meaningful phenomena are signs" (Chandler 2017, p. 2).

The Internet as a semiotic system provokes meanings in relation to other signs or discourses such as "democracy," "progress," "privacy," "freedom of speech" and "national security." What meanings are assigned to the Internet and how they are articulated to specific social practices are influenced heavily by cultural, economic and historical factors within society.

Do both Russia and South Korea have the Internet? One is obliged to say "yes." Do they have the same Internet? The answer can hardly be the same. The Internet has not only meant different things in the two nations, but it has also been adopted and used differently, evolving into different media. This fact reminds us of a very important point: The Internet is not one, but many.

Many discussions of the Internet have maintained two basic premises. First, the adoption of the Internet is determined predominantly by the income level of a society (Norris 2001; Chinn and Fairlie 2010; Zhang 2013). Second, it is assumed to be a

© Springer Nature Switzerland AG 2019
S. S. Bodrunova et al. (Eds.): INSCI 2018 Workshops, LNCS 11551, pp. 272–281, 2019.
https://doi.org/10.1007/978-3-030-17705-8_24

single, homogenous entity, as the singular proper noun, "the Internet," suggests. The Internet is also often claimed to be endowed with certain inherent characteristics: "anonymity," "decentralization" and "lack (or difficulty) of regulation" (Connery 1997, p. 170; Jazwinski 2001, p. 185; Wolfe 2001, pp. 12–13).

This paper critically evaluates these popular beliefs by analyzing two different cases: Russia and South Korea ("Korea" hereafter). They have made remarkable achievements in terms of Internet penetration and broadband adoption. Russia started making its presence felt in cyberspace during the early 2010s, dethroning Germany as the European country with the highest number of unique visitors online (comScore 2011). In 2013, Russian emerged as one of the most commonly used languages on the Web, second only to English, in terms of the number of websites (Moscow Times 2013). Korea has been one of the most wired nations on earth since the early 2000s and a key innovator in the information and communication technology (ICT) industry.

For some reason, however, these two major players have not been taken seriously in Internet studies, which is certainly a huge omission. Russia is not only the world's largest country by landmass, but it is also one of the fastest growing economies—both online and offline. Korea may be a relatively small country compared to Russia, but it has been referred to as the "time machine" or "world's best laboratory" to predict the future of broadband services and "to look to for answers on how the Internet business may evolve" (Forsberg 2005, p. B1; Taylor 2006).

Russia is gradually gaining popularity among Internet researchers, but the scope is limited to the political aspects of the Web including governance, censorship and regulation, especially in the West (e.g. Frederiksen 2014; Nocetti 2015; Denisova 2017; Toepfl 2018). Korea is not very different. Although the country has been a popular topic in terms of its dynamic cybercultures or government ICT policies, the socioeconomic factors that have driven Korea's Internet dissemination have rarely been investigated in academia.

In spite of Russia's unmistakable significance, its Internet environment has long been under the radar of Western European and North American researchers due mainly to ideological and geopolitical reasons even after the dissolution of the Union of Soviet Socialist Republics (USSR). Korea has been ignored for a different reason: The country simply does not follow the "general pattern" (Norris 2001, p. 56).

Interestingly enough, Korea started embracing the Internet en masse while the nation was deep in economic depression in 1998. It gave a headache to many scholars looking for a neat economic framework. They had to scratch their heads to make sense of why Koreans, whose country was plunging into recession, suddenly became passionate about going online (Kang 2014).

2 Russia and Korea: How They Became Wired

Russia and Korea are vastly different countries. It would be easier to find differences than similarities in terms of size, population, economic structure, major industries and education system. While Korea became an early adopter of the PC-based Internet in the late 1990s and the early 2000s, the Internet boom arrived relatively late in Russia during the early 2010s. As of 2016, 76.4% of the Russian population was using the

Internet. In 2010, however, the rate was merely 37.1%, which soared to 70.4% in 2015, nearly doubling the penetration rate in five years.

This dramatic change was thanks mainly to hand-held devices such as mobile phones and tablet PCs, aided by the popularity of social media like VKontakte (VK), Odnoklassniki (OK.ru), Facebook, Twitter and Instagram (GFK 2015). What took Russia so long to catch up? Because the country stretches from Eastern Europe to Asia, it is costly and time-consuming to roll out the fiber-optic backbone across the nation to provide reliable Internet access. Since Russia is almost double the size of the United States, its geographical vastness provides a unique challenge. As a result, broadband connection costs varied significantly from region to region. According to a 2010 report, "in major cities such as Moscow, St. Petersburg, and Yekaterinburg, unlimited-traffic broadband costs about $10 to $15 per month—compared with Murmansk, where it can cost as much as $120 a month" (Aguiar et al. 2010, p. 9).

Russia shows the importance of regional differences within a country, which many researchers have failed to address, focusing instead on differences among countries. A study suggests that Russia faces two major obstacles in morphing into an information society: size and state control (Daveluy 2012). The geographical barriers, however, have disappeared rather quickly. For example, Moscow constituted over 70% of all Internet users in 1998, which dropped to 11% by 2013 (Nagirnaya 2015, p. 129).

Predicting the diffusion of the Internet based on physical factors can be misleading. It would also be simplistic to explain Russia's dramatic change solely in terms of technological innovation; technology is never an autonomous entity that exists in a vacuum. The rapid development of the ICT sector in Russia is inseparable from its human factors, especially well-educated people. Russia has consistently been ranked as one of the best-educated countries for decades thanks to its strong public education that took root during the Soviet period. As a result, almost 95% of Russian adults attain upper secondary education, which is significantly higher than the OECD average of 74% (OECD 2015).

Even after the collapse of the USSR, the traditional emphasis on sciences and technology has remained strong, giving Russia a competitive edge in ICTs. It was no coincidence that Yandex launched one of the earliest search engines in 1997. Rambler, a lesser-known Russian search engine, was launched in 1996, two years earlier than Google started its business.

Russia and Korea are two of the few places where Google has failed to take the lion's share. As of May 2018, for example, Yandex's search engine market share (desktop) was 54.96%, while that of Google was 40.24% (Statscounter 2018). The dominant position of a single portal in numerous online services tends to turn Internet use into a highly centralized experience, even though "decentralization" is often talked about as part of the nature of the Internet.

Similarly, Korea's most popular search engine is not Google, but its domestic counterpart Naver. It took a whopping 75.2% of the PC-based search market in 2018, followed at a distant second by Google (11.8%) and third by Daum (10.2%), according to a survey (Kim 2018). Like Yandex, the Korean portal is more than a search engine; it provides news, email, social media, and shopping services.

One of the most notable aspects of the Russian Internet is the strong role of the government. Government intervention is discussed mainly in terms of authoritarianism, particularly in the case of Russia. It would be unfair, however, to talk about the leadership of the state solely in connection with regulation or oppression. For example, Russia's profound scientific discoveries and inventions have been indebted largely to the active role of the government, such as sending the first artificial satellite into space, pioneering laser technologies, and building the first electronic digital computer in Europe. Russia's high education level and impressive technology literacy are no exception. In 2007, then-Deputy Prime Minister Dmitry Medvedev announced a national plan to computerize all schools in Russia to provide every student with access to the Internet.

Although the Korean government has not been blamed as harshly as its Russian counterpart, it has taken a highly paternalistic approach in every possible area. The Kim Dae Jung administration (1998–2003), for instance, systematically promoted the ICT sector under the slogans of "New Economy" and "Knowledge Superpower" when the country was sinking into an economic morass in the late 1990s. The government saw the Internet as an opportunity to transform the country into a knowledge-based economy by launching subsidized college programs in game development, enacting policies to evaluate buildings based on quality of data lines, and privatizing Korea Telecom in an attempt to boost competition in the industry.

In 2007, Korea became the first country to implement the real-name system, which required every user to submit extensive personal information, including their full name, resident registration number, date of birth, address and phone number, before leaving comments on popular websites. The government claimed that the policy was aimed at promoting public good by minimizing malicious comments. In 2011, it again caught the world by surprise by passing the "Juvenile Protection Act." Dubbed the "Cinderella Law," this act forbids young Koreans aged 16 and below from accessing online games from midnight to 6:00 in the morning.

The real-name system was abolished in 2012 as the Constitutional Court ruled unanimously that the law was unconstitutional for violating the freedom of speech. The Shutdown Law is still effective as of 2018, and quite a few lawmakers support the law, which they believe can help prevent video game addiction. Both the extremely successful ICT policies and the highly controversial laws are two sides of the same coin of the Korean government's paternalistic leadership.

3   The PC as a "Study Tool"

Before embracing the Internet, Koreans welcomed the personal computer (PC) far more passionately than the Japanese. This fact effectively refutes economic determinism; Japan obviously had an upper hand because they had a considerably higher average income during the 1980s through the 1990s. The Japanese customers were lukewarm about the PC until the late 1990s, losing the opportunity to adopt the landline Internet.

The different results in the two neighboring countries were caused by different associations assigned to the same machine. Like many people in different countries, the Japanese saw the PC as a "business machine," which would not be surprising, considering that IBM stands for "International Business Machines." The situation was similar in the USSR, where the PC was perceived predominantly as a business tool.

In Korea, on the other hand, the PC was widely marked as an "educational device" from the beginning. Parents did not think twice about getting the expensive machine for their children, expecting that such efforts would enhance their children's chances in school. Earlier PC manufacturers, such as Daewoo, GoldStar (now LG) and Sambo, marketed their products as "electronic tutors" during the mid 1980s through the early 1990s.

In 1985, for example, Samsung ran a print ad featuring two dolls in traditional costumes enacting a classroom situation. "A teacher who knows more teaches better," says the teacher appearing on the computer monitor. The copy goes, "Our family tutor: Samsung SPC-1500." In the same year, Daewoo published a magazine ad for its MSX computer "IQ 1000." A beaming bespectacled boy is sitting at a computer, and his classmates watch in awe and astonishment: "IQ 1000, the choice of the best student in our class!"

In other countries, the PC was commonly placed in the living room so that it could be shared easily among family members. In Korea, however, it was typically installed in a child's own room that is called a "study room." It would be logical for a "study tool" to be put in a "study room," but the results were somewhat unexpected. Children started played games on their "study machines" behind closed doors, making PCs the dominant gaming platform in Korea. Most game consoles, including Game Boy, PlayStation, Xbox and Wii, have failed in the Korean market, because they were not appealing to parents for being obvious "gaming devices" (Kang 2017). The popularity of PC games soon opened doors for online gaming.

All of a sudden, Korea was hit hard by the Asian financial crisis in 1997. Not surprisingly, people did not have added disposable income at that time, but there were a guaranteed number of people looking for inexpensive entertainment, leading to the explosive growth of the PC bang. This place may look like an Internet cafe, but it is uniquely Korean; it is a 24-h video game arcade for online gamers and online chatters, which sells drinks and instant cup noodles. Some patrons take a nap in a recliner, waiting for the first bus in the morning. The number of PC bangs grew rapidly, blanketing the whole country. It increased from about 100 in 1998 to almost 25,000 by 2001.

It is often believed that online gaming is an asocial activity, but it does not have to be in Korea. Many Koreans go to a PC bang together, playing MMORPGs (massively multiplayer role-playing games) in the same physical space. It is not uncommon to discuss tactics with fellow gamers across the room. Even online chatting in Korea readily turns into face-to-face interactions in a matter of hours—or minutes. Many PC bangs are equipped with sofa benches called "love seats" for couples or potential couples (Herz 2002):

> If you really watch the love seats, though, it becomes apparent that they're not so much a porch swing as an Internet-mediated bar stool. Every so often a girl will saunter by one of the stations, eye the occupant, and then sit down – or not. As it turns out, singles are video-chatting in game rooms all over town. If they hit it off, the guy says something like, "I'm sitting at love seat number 47 at this particular PC baang [sic], if you'd care to join me." If the girl is sufficiently intrigued, she hops on the subway or walks – nothing is more than 20 min away in central Seoul. She cruises by, checks him out, and if she likes the look of him in person she sits down, hoping the lighting and shading algorithms she uses to enhance her features in the video chat don't make her seems unglamorous in person.

The Internet in Korea is not a mere online experience but is often blended inter-actions, which Robert Putnam called "alloys of silicon and flesh" (Potier 2004). The PC bang played the role of a test bed for broadband, while working as the "third place" for children between school and home to get away from their parents' watchful eyes. Many of those who had tried the high-speed Internet at a PC bang wanted to get one at home. Since both the government and hardware manufacturers had disseminated utopian discourses of the Internet, it was not difficult to convince their parents to subscribe to high-speed broadband.

4 The Internet as a Sign System

The familiar "study tool" association was assigned to the Internet in the mid 1990s. The common metaphor of the "sea of information" was used in Korea, but it had an added meaning: the sea of information in English. Korea had desired to join "the advanced world," and the Internet was considered the shortcut to the most up-to-date information from the West. Since there were few Korean websites until the late 1990s, going online meant being able to understand English, the global language, assigning extra meanings to the Internet: "progressive," "advanced" and "cool."

> Korean youngsters use the Internet not because they need information, but because they want to be seen as advanced. Most of the students [Yoon] interviewed have a positive attitude towards the Internet. Yet most of the interviewees confess that they do not need the information found on the Internet (Yoon 2001, p. 254).

It was the symbolic meanings of the Internet that attracted users in its initial stage in Korea. The Internet is a sign system that bears specific meanings within society, and in Korea it signifies the "West," the model for the country's modernization. The Internet symbolizes the "West" in Russia, too, but its implications are strikingly different. To many Russians, the Internet signifies a "threat from the West." Manuel Castells argues for a strong connection between the development of the Internet and capitalism:

> The information technology revolution was instrumental in allowing the implementation of a fundamental process of restructuring of the capitalist system from the 1980s onwards. In the process, this technological revolution was itself shaped, in its development and manifestations, by the logic and interests of advanced capitalism (Castells 2010, p. 13).

The Internet was initially spearheaded by the United States along with its ideo-logical and economic allies such as the UK, Canada, Germany and France. Now the global network is under the influence of technology giants, such as Google, Facebook and Twitter, headquartered in California. It would be no surprise, then, Russia is wary of the Internet as a country that has challenged the U.S.-led world order. As a matter of fact, Edward Snowden exposed in 2013 that the United States National Security Agency (NSA) had operated extensive surveillance programs, including PRISM, that can access a vast quantity of emails, phone calls and other data from the servers of Google, Facebook, Microsoft, Yahoo and Apple.

"It is not a secret that the U.S. controls the Internet," said Victor Levanov, a renowned Russian blogger (Kremlin 2014). He was asking a question to President Vladimir Putin at a 2014 media forum in St. Petersburg. Levanov suggested that a large number of Russian websites of news media and government organizations were attacked during the Crimean crisis. It is a sentiment shared by many Russians. According to a 2015 study, for example, 42% of the whole population believes that "foreign countries are using the Internet against Russia and its interests" (Nisbet 2015). The same survey shows that 49% of Russians think that information on the Internet needs to be censored. As a result, the Russian government is reportedly considering creating a "sovereign Internet" or "parallel Internet" (Sputnik 2018).

Understanding the Internet as a sign system is very important, because the meanings assigned to the Internet shape its use and the future evolution of the technology. In other words, different meanings lead to different "internets." For example, the rapid adoption of the Internet in Korea cannot be separated from its educational overlap or its symbolic meaning of "progress." Likewise, the government's heavy investment in ICTs cannot be explained without utopian discourses of the Internet, such as "new growth engine" or "knowledge superpower" when Korea was faced with a grim economic backdrop (Kang 2017).

In spite of their striking differences, a number of similarities can also be found between Russia and Korea. In Korea, the state has played an essential role in key areas like in Russia, including economy, education and culture. Its well-known state-led industrialization was heavily influenced by the Soviet "Five-Year Plans" adopted during the 1960s by the military junta of Park Chung-hee (1962–1979). The government has also played an essential role in adopting both the computer and the Internet by incorporating them into regular school curricula in the late 1980s and the late 1990s, respectively.

Government control of the Internet is often discussed in terms of authoritarianism, but the relationship is not always that simple. The Internet in Korea, for example, has been tightly controlled by the state, but the country is still known for its one of the most vibrant civil societies in the world. In particular, Korea used to have the controversial "real-name system," which required all users to provide their names and registration numbers in order to post comments on popular websites with more than 100,000 visitors a day. Although many countries have concerns over online abuse, the measure introduced was seen as "heavy-handed as a first step" (Lewis 2007).

Until the real-name system was repealed in 2012, "anonymity" virtually did not exist in Korea, proving the irrelevance of discussing anonymity as one of the inherent characteristics of the Internet (Kang 2011). Even today, Korean Web services have strict regulatory policies. Almost every popular site is equipped with an automatic censorship system, and when somebody wants to leave comments on a portal site, the user is supposed to avoid particular words generally considered "inappropriate" or "indecent." If they are included, the whole posting will be rejected. Of course, these regulatory measures are not always successful. Many users skillfully get around the barrier and make the original points by slightly modifying the taboo words.

5 Toward the De-Westernizing Study of *Internets*

This paper starts from the belief that "outliers" like Russia and Korea can offer a powerful counter-argument against conventional approaches. When the Internet is viewed as a universal entity, the heterogeneity and diversity of the technology can be easily missed or ignored. Along with this totalizing effect, there is another issue with the mainstream approaches: West-centrism. Media and communication studies have often been criticized for their Euro/West-centric ideologies (Curran and Park 2000; Gunaratne 2005).

> It has become routine for universalistic observations about the media to be advanced in English books on the basis of evidence derived from a tiny handful of countries. Whether it be middle-range generalization about, for example, the influence of news sources on reporting, or grand theory about the media's relationship to postmodernity, the same few countries keep recurring as if they are a stand-in for the rest of the world. These are nearly always rich Western societies, and the occasional honorary "Western" countries like Australia (Curran and Park 2000, p. 3).

It is not very surprising to observe similar biases reproduced in Internet studies. Making an issue of how some of the most significant cases have been put aside as deviant is not just a normative criticism to gain them deserving positions; it is also a pragmatic effort to draw attention to ill-attended phenomena that could help present a more elaborate and nuanced picture of the relationship between society and the Internet. The existence of the "deviations" proves that Internet usage cannot be fully grasped through statistical data.

This case study explores the cultural shaping of the Internet in Russia and Korea. Unlike traditional approaches focusing on what impacts the Internet has on society, it considers how broader sociocultural forces influence the adoption, use, and evolution of the Internet. Although called by the same name, "Internet," the technology has been reinvented as many different versions. Unfortunately, many discussions of the Internet have ignored the fact that much diversity can be found within the Internet.

As Storey (1996, pp. 5–6) rightly stated, "To deny the passivity of consumption is not to deny that sometimes consumption is passive." The power of consumers comes from their complexity and multifariously that make it impossible to predict what they will buy and how they will use it (Fiske 1987; Storey 2006, p. 158). The reason the relationships between technology and users, between technology and society, and between society and users cannot be neatly modeled for generalization is that they are not homogenous entities. Users are not identical and societies are not homogenous.

The Internet is inseparable from its perception and use within society; it is not a disparate entity but a local, social practice. The term "Internet" is unable to account for such variety and complexity. The singular proper noun may diffuse the misleading notion that the whole world shares the same medium. So a more appropriate terminology would be "internets"—in a different context George W. Bush mistakenly used the term—considering its diversity in content and form.

This paper seeks to challenge such common-place assumptions, offering a context-specific analysis of the "internets" in Russia and Korea through a comparative and media historical perspective. It is basically an attempt to look at power dynamics both on and around the Internet, considering it not only as a technology but also as a cultural form that constitutes part of a larger complex of media technologies, industries, policy, and other social factors influencing and influenced by specific user practices.

Although this paper has analyzed trajectories of the shaping of the internets in Russia and Korea, the levels of analysis taken here—Russia and Korea—are still too broad, not to mention the "cross-national analysis" that many scholars rely on. Since Russia and Korea are not homogenous, ethnographical approaches are needed to properly see and understand how people deal with the "internets" in their daily lives.

References

Aguiar, M., Boutenko, V., Michael, D., Rastogi, V., Subramanian, A., Zhou, Y.: The Internet's New Billion: Digital Consumers in Brazil, Russia, India, China, and Indonesia. The Boston Consulting Group, Boston (2010)

Baudrillard, J.: The Consumer Society: Myths and Structures. Sage, London (1998 [1970])

Castells, M.: The Rise of the Network Society. Wiley, West Sussex (2010)

Chandler, D.: Semiotics: The Basics. Routledge, New York (2017)

Chinn, M.D., Fairlie, R.W.: ICT use in the developing world: an analysis of differences in computer and Internet penetration. Rev. Int. Econ. **18**(1), 153–167 (2010)

ComScore: comScore releases overview of European Internet usage in September 2011 (2011). https://www.comscore.com/Insights/Press-Releases/2011/11/comScore-Releases-Overview-of-European-Internet-Usage-in-September-2011?cs_edgescape_cc=RU. Accessed 15 June 2018

Connery, B.A.: IMHO: authority and egalitarian rhetoric in the virtual coffeehouse. In: Porter, D. (ed.) Internet Culture, pp. 161–179. Routledge, London (1997)

Curran, J., Park, M.: Beyond globalization theory. In: Curran, J., Park, M. (eds.) De-Westernizing Media Studies, pp. 3–18. Routledge, New York (2000)

Daveluy, D.: The landscape of digital technologies in Russia (2012). https://www.inaglobal.fr/en/digital-tech/article/landscape-digital-technologies-russia. Accessed 14 June 2018

Denisova, A.: Democracy, protest and public sphere in Russia after the 2011–2012 anti-government protests: digital media at stake. Media Cult. Soc. **39**(7), 976–994 (2017)

Fiske, J.: Television Culture. Routledge, London (1987)

Forsberg, B.: The future is South Korea. San Francisco Chronicle, p. B1, 13 March 2005

Frederiksen, M.D.: To Russia with love: hope, confinement, and virtuality among youth on the Georgian Black Sea coast. Focaal **2014**(70), 26–36 (2014)

GFK: Проникновение Интернета в России: Итоги 2015 года (2015). https://www.gfk.com/fileadmin/user_upload/dyna_content/RU/Documents/Press_Releases/2016/Internet_Usage_Russia_2015.pdf. Accessed 15 June 2018

Gunaratne, S.A.: The Dao of the Press: A Humanocentric Theory. Hampton Press, Cresskill (2005)

Herz, J.C.: The bandwidth capital of the world. Wired, August 2002. http://www.wired.com/wired/archive/10.08/korea.html. Accessed 9 Nov 2018

Jazwinski, C.H.: Gender identities on the World Wide Web. In: Wolfe, C.R. (ed.) Learning and Teaching on the World Wide Web, pp. 171–189. Academic Press, San Diego (2001)

Kang, I.: Going online in the PC graveyard: the sociocultural evolution of Japan's mobile internet. In: Jin, D. (ed.) Global Media Convergence and cultural Transformation: Emerging Social Patterns and Characteristics. IGI Global, Hershey (2011)

Kang, I.: It all started with a bang: the role of PC bangs in South Korea's cybercultures. In: Kim, K., Choe, Y. (eds.) The Korean Popular Culture Reader, pp. 56–75. Duke University Press, Durham (2014)

Kang, I.: Technology, culture, and meanings: how the discourses of progress and modernity have shaped South Korea's internet diffusion. Media Cult. Soc. **39**(5), 727–739 (2017)

Kim, K.: Which portals do you use? JoongangIlbo (2018). http://news.joins.com/article/22435278. Accessed 15 June 2018

Kremlin: Медиафорум независимых региональных и местных СМИ (2014). http://www.kremlin.ru/events/president/news/20858. Accessed 19 July 2018

Lewis, L.: Chat room bullies face end to their internet anonymity. Times (2007). http://www.timesonline.co.uk/tol/news/world/asia/article2005592.ece. Accessed 1 Jan 2011

Moscow Times: Russian Language Second Most Popular on the Internet (2013). https://themoscowtimes.com/articles/russian-language-second-most-popular-on-the-internet-22602

Nagirnaya, A.V.: Development of the internet in Russian regions. Reg. Res. Russia **5**(2), 128–136 (2015)

Nisbet, E.: Benchmarking Public Demand: Russia's Appetite for Internet Control. Center for Global Communication Studies, Philadelphia (2015)

Nocetti, J.: Contest and conquest: Russia and global internet governance. Int. Aff. **91**(1), 111–130 (2015). https://doi.org/10.1111/1468-2346.12189

Norris, P.: Digital Divide: Civic Engagement, Information Poverty and the Internet in Democratic Societies. Cambridge University Press, New York (2001)

OECD: OECD Better Life Index: Russian Federation (2015). http://www.oecdbetterlifeindex.org/countries/russian-federation/. Accessed 28 April 2019

Potier, B.: How did internet affect election? Harvard Gazette (2004). https://news.harvard.edu/gazette/story/2004/12/how-did-internet-affect-election/. Accessed 17 July 2018

Sputnik: Russia has the means to create its own version of the internet as a worst-case scenario contingency, according to a high-ranking Foreign Ministry official (2018). https://sputniknews.com/science/201807031065998910-internet-analogue-development-contingency/. Accessed 19 July 2018

Statscounter: Desktop search engine market share in Russian Federation - May 2018 (2018). http://gs.statcounter.com/search-engine-market-share/desktop/russian-federation. Accessed 15 June 2018

Storey, J.: Cultural studies: an introduction. In: Storey, J. (ed.) What is Cultural Studies?: A Reader, pp. 1–13. Arnold, London (1996)

Storey, J.: Cultural Theory and Popular Culture: An Introduction. University of Georgia Press, Athens (2006)

Taylor, C.: The future is in South Korea. Business 2.0, 14 June 2006. http://money.cnn.com/2006/06/08/technology/business2_futureboy0608/index.htm. Accessed 15 June 2018

Toepfl, F.: Innovating consultative authoritarianism: internet votes as a novel digital tool to stabilize non-democratic rule in Russia. New Media Soc. **20**(3), 956–972 (2018). https://doi.org/10.1177/1461444816675444

Wolfe, C.R.: Learning and teaching on the World Wide Web. In: Wolfe, C.R. (ed.) Learning and Teaching on the World Wide Web, pp. 11–22. Academic Press, San Diego (2001)

Yoon, S.: Internet discourse and the *habitus* of Korea's new generation. In: Ess, C. (ed.) Culture, Technology, Communication: Towards an Intercultural Global Village, pp. 241–260. State University of New York Press, Albany (2001)

Zhang, X.: Income disparity and digital divide: the internet consumption model and cross-country empirical research. Telecommun. Policy **37**(6–7), 515–529 (2013)

Author Index

Printed in the United States
By Bookmasters